A Time for Reflection

A Time for Reflection

The Parallel Legacies of Baseball Icons Willie McCovey and Billy Williams

Jason Cannon

ROWMAN & LITTLEFIELD
Lanham • Boulder • New York • London

Published by Rowman & Littlefield
An imprint of The Rowman & Littlefield Publishing Group, Inc.
4501 Forbes Boulevard, Suite 200, Lanham, Maryland 20706
www.rowman.com

86-90 Paul Street, London EC2A 4NE, United Kingdom

British Library Cataloguing in Publication Information Available

Library of Congress Cataloging-in-Publication Data

Names: Cannon, Jason, author.
Title: A time for reflection: the parallel legacies of baseball icons Willie McCovey and
   Billy Williams / Jason Cannon.
Description: Lanham, Maryland: Rowman & Littlefield, 2025. | Includes bibliographical
   references and index. | Summary: "A Time for Reflection brings to light the
   captivating stories of African American Hall of Famers Willie McCovey and Billy
   Williams. Often overshadowed by their teams' superstars, these Alabamans would
   become two of baseball's best through hard work and strength of character"—
   Provided by publisher.
Identifiers: LCCN 2024025545 (print) | LCCN 2024025546 (ebook) |
   ISBN 9781538184578 (cloth) | ISBN 9781538184585 (epub)
Subjects: LCSH: McCovey, Willie, 1938–2018. | Williams, Billy, 1938– |
   African American baseball players—Biography.
Classification: LCC GV865.M2934 C36 2025 (print) | LCC GV865.M2934 (ebook) |
   DDC 796.357092/273—dc23/eng/20240816
LC record available at https://lccn.loc.gov/2024025545
LC ebook record available at https://lccn.loc.gov/2024025546

For my parents

Contents

Preface   ix

PART I: MOBILE   **1**

1   The Cradle   3

2   "Stretch" and "Young Blood"   15

PART II: SUPERSTARS   **37**

3   "Smooth as Velvet"   39

4   Charlie's Lament   57

5   "See You Down the Road"   75

6   1969   95

7   "An Unwilling Constituency of Pitchers"   113

PART III: THERE AND BACK AGAIN   **135**

8   "He Isn't Dealing with Hamburger People"   137

9   Oakland, or "The Sun and Billy Williams"   153

10   The Birth of History   167

PART IV: ENSHRINEMENT   **189**

11   "A Time for Reflection"   191

12   Narratives   215

Epilogue: Bobby Richardson Calls	231
Acknowledgments	235
Notes	239
Bibliography	263
Index	265
About the Author	279

Preface

I was taking a short break from working on a project about former Chicago Cubs owner Charlie Murphy when I read a headline announcing the sad news that Willie McCovey, who busted out like a house afire for the San Francisco Giants in 1959 en route to a Hall of Fame career, had passed away at the age of 80. It was October 31, 2018. Halloween. Orange and black. The Giants released a statement that read, in part, McCovey had passed away "peacefully." Giants president and CEO Larry Baer remarked, "San Francisco and the entire baseball community lost a true gentleman and legend, and our collective hearts are broken." The release detailed his wonderful major league debut when he went 4-for-4 against Hall of Famer Robin Roberts followed by other gaudy statistics that McCovey compiled during his 22 seasons in the big leagues. The article included captured tweets from Barry Bonds and Orlando Cepeda, a statement from commissioner Rob Manfred, a recap of McCovey's 1962 World Series line drive that Yankees second baseman Bobby Richardson snared, a few other quotes, and the names of several family members, who must now carry on without him.[1]

Even though I grew up following the Giants as a kid in Central California during the 1980s, it struck me how little I knew about McCovey. His smashing debut sounded familiar, but I had no idea he was one of only seven players in the history of the game to win three notable awards: Rookie of the Year, MVP, and All-Star Game MVP. I pivoted my chair, and my eyes canvased the bookshelf to locate his biography. I would set that text aside and read it as soon as time allowed. I scanned repeatedly to find McCovey's story, but it wasn't there. Mays, Marichal, Alou, Cepeda, Murakami, yes, but no text about Mac. I returned my attention to the laptop and used Google to search for one. Again, nothing. I quickly reached for a pen and a Post-it note out of a desk drawer and scrawled "STRETCH" on the sticky, square pink paper. I underlined it once. When the project before me concluded, I wanted to explore Willie McCovey's story.

That Post-it note sat on my desk for two years. It rested there through Brexit and COVID-19. The vigor of the note's stickiness weakened with time, and it peeled away from the wood. I wound up unceremoniously throwing it away as my wife and I boxed up our things when we moved to another state, but McCovey's story remained firmly affixed to my mind. In the early spring of 2022, I returned to Stretch in earnest. Where to start? I left a message for Clauzell McCovey, Willie's younger brother, who lives in Mobile, Alabama. I had no idea if he would be willing to speak with me or not. This idea could be short-lived.

Everything changed when I received a voicemail from Allison McCovey, Willie's daughter. I called her back and explained my interest in writing about her father, hoping she would ignore the slightly inconvenient fact that I was a complete stranger to her. We wound up chatting for about 20 minutes, and she expressed her openness to pursuing the project.

Not long after my conversation with Allison, I received a text message from someone in the Cubs organization asking if I might be interested in helping to compile the stories of their beloved Hall of Famer, Billy Williams. I agreed without hesitation. I would love to, I replied. Several weeks later, with spring training in full swing, I traveled down to Mobile to interview Clauzell, whom I had since spoken with, about his brother, Willie, and explore the holdings of its Local History and Genealogy Library. I was sitting in front of a computer combing through microfilm when a Chicago number lit up my (on silent) phone. I got up and went outside to take the call. Awe overwhelmed me when I answered—it was my friend on the line, along with a special guest, Williams himself. They were calling me from the Cubs' Spring Training facility in Mesa, Arizona. "You're down in Mobile right now?" Williams asked me.

"Yes, sir," I replied.

"I used to go fishing in Eight Mile Creek all the time," Williams said.

"I'll check it out before I leave," I promised.

It turns out that McCovey and Williams were born just a handful of miles away from each other in 1938. Their similar paths from Alabama to Cooperstown created a wonderful pairing.

I have encountered no shortage of incredible stories involving McCovey and Williams on and off the field over the past several years. McCovey launched home runs further than a lot of players and fans had ever seen them go. "Over the scoreboard" is not an uncommon description of where those homers landed. Williams once went 8-for-8 in a doubleheader against Houston, and an Astros pitcher finally settled on having his catcher tell him what pitch was coming next as their only strategy of getting him out. Off the field, Williams and McCovey were both humble and kind. "They came out of the same mold," notes Joe Amalfitano, who spent time with both of them in the Cubs and Giants organizations. Amalfitano's perspective was echoed to me by many people.

A special blend of class and fierce competitiveness, Billy Williams and Willie McCovey fashioned incredible baseball careers and, in doing so, established themselves as superstars in two of America's most consequential cities: Chicago and San Francisco. Their breathtaking feats on the field, along with their extensive work for the Cubs and Giants franchises after their playing days and the personal relationships they built with people in their communities as citizens, make them enduring icons in our collective public memory. Friends since their teenage years, the lives and careers of Williams and McCovey are essential to baseball history, and their impact will endure for generations to come.

Part I

MOBILE

"IN THE NEWS"

State Herd Averages 547 Pounds of Milk. . . . Farmers Who Plan to Make Application for a Crop Loan Should Arrange to See Their Banker or Loan Agency Immediately. . . . Baseball Holdouts Promise Squawking Season. . . . Germany Building One of the Greatest Navies in World. . . . The Crazy Current Styles in Women's Hats Designed by. . . . Alabama: Fair, Warmer in North Portion Wednesday. . . . Frankenstein: It Makes You Shiver! . . . Mel Ott, with His Thirteenth Home Run and Single, Twice Drove in the Tying Runs Today as the Giants. . . . The Chicago Cubs Kept Chipping Away at Lou Fette's Offerings. . . . The Dad-Line Forms at Sears. . . . For Savings. . . . Federal Barge Line Departs Mobile: Westbound to New Orleans—Every Wednesday. . . . Cincinnati Pitcher Hurls His Second Consecutive No-Hit, No-Run Game. . . . International Brigade Head Quits with Praise for American Fighters. . . . Antilynching Bill Insult to South, Harrison Shouts

Chapter 1

The Cradle

Sylvania Jones cradled the baby boy firmly in her typical manner. Despite her body's weakened condition stemming from a terminal illness, Sylvania willed her arms strong as she held and tended to him lovingly as only her undying devotion allowed. This child, her maternal grandson, had spent hours in her arms during the course of his young life, relentlessly crying, without sparing her a moment of tranquility, but this day proved to be different. His usual expressions of distress lay dormant. He rested quietly in her arms for the first time in his young life. Jones read tea leaves, and, after she died later that day, her daughter, Ester, perceived a unique quality in her baby. His calm demeanor held an innate understanding that his time with Sylvania had reached its end, his expressive emotions tucked away beneath a placid surface stilled by the sadness of loss. Although grieved by Sylvania's passing, the family nonetheless intuitively sensed that the youngest among them carried a spiritual connection that had quieted him as he shared his grandmother's final hours snuggled in her warm embrace. That bond of understanding indicated to them that he was destined for greatness.

That young child, Willie Lee, was born to Ester and Frank McCovey in the "Down the Bay" neighborhood of Mobile, Alabama, on January 10, 1938. Their snug A-frame house nearly burst at the seams with activity. The oldest son, Frank, had already moved out, but that still left six siblings to share a single bedroom and its pair of beds.[1] Ester, affectionately known as "Sugar," needed help running the full household, so Frances, 12 years Willie's senior, kept a close eye on her little brother from an early age. The McCoveys lived in a segregated neighborhood situated a 15-minute walk outside of Mobile's central district. The family had not always lived in Alabama, although its patriarch, Frank, had been born in the state.

Originally, Frank McCovey, with the second syllable of his last name pronounced with a long "O" as in "cove," was born in Alabama, where his family
knew all too well the burdens of the brutal life forced on African Americans
in the Deep South. Frank's parents, Frank Sr. and Adeline McCovey, earnestly worked the ground as sharecroppers on a plot of farmland that they
had retained in the aftermath of the South's slavery and Reconstruction eras.
Frank, 44, was nearly two decades older than Adeline, who was 26 when
Frank Jr. entered the world on Christmas Day 1890 in Monroeville, Alabama.
The baby's birth spurred his father to seek a line of employment beyond the
limiting parcel of earth. Frank Sr. heard of a new opportunity: the construction of a fresh road artery that would link western Alabama to eastern Mississippi, and, despite (or perhaps due to) his age, he traded in his farming
implements for construction tools in order to work on this significant project.
Leaving Adeline and their children, including young Frank Jr., behind for
the time being, McCovey joined the team of workers building the thoroughfare. He "followed the new road" to Shipman, a small Mississippi town six
miles west of the Alabama border that featured a train depot stop, enabling
the goods entering ports in Mobile Bay to be more efficiently distributed
throughout the South.

Constructing the new route proved to be backbreaking work. Countless
pine trees needed to be felled before the clay earth could be graded. The
resourceful McCovey recognized a unique opportunity that combined these
forests with the growing rubber, soap, and varnish industries. He tapped pine
trees, extracted their jelly-looking sap substance into tin boxes, and shipped
them off to a local factory. It was called "dipping turpentine," and this side
gig generated additional income he sent back to Adeline in Mobile. Months
later, after the road's completion, Frank Sr. brought his family to Shipman,
where they put down roots.

Over the ensuing two decades, the McCoveys established themselves as
effective farmers during the week and involved churchgoers on Sundays. As
he grew older, Frank Jr. helped his father extensively before taking over the
helm of the land. The McCovey's Shipman property was located in the same
neighborhood that also counted the Jones family as residents. Frank Jr. met a
young Ester Jones, who family historians believe did some work on the farm,
but their 19-year age gap did not initially portend a future of marital bliss,
and, in fact, he first wed another woman; however, the childless marriage did
not last for reasons unknown.

The breakup of McCovey's initial marriage did not deter the teenage Ester,
who fell in love with the disciplined and introverted man who went about his
business earnestly and quietly. Their neighborhood romance blossomed, and
the two wed. Their age difference raised some eyebrows in Shipman, but it
bothered neither Frank nor Ester. Frank's parents were themselves separated

by close to 20 years. For her part, Ester did not bat an eye at the perception that she was too young to marry McCovey, whom she referred to as "Mr. Frank." She exuded a formidable confidence in her ability to handle being an excellent partner. At one point, she turned to her nearly silent husband and declared, "You don't say much, Mr. Frank. I may have to talk for you."[2]

Locals throughout the rural town of Shipman knew Frank McCovey Jr. as a young deacon at Mount Olive Baptist Church. That small building sat amidst a seemingly endless stretch of flat land kept green by the drenching rains and humidity particular to southeastern Mississippi. Inhabitants of this surrounding area attended Sunday services and became familiar with this quiet and stoic church leader, even if they didn't quite get to know him well. Frank said little, but when he did speak, he meant what he said. He was very direct about communicating right from wrong if he thought someone needed to hear it. His son, Willie, would intentionally pattern himself after his father in the years ahead. Underneath Frank's tough exterior beat a heart that cared for the people of his adopted community, and McCovey showed it through his actions, dedication to the church's flock, and devotion to Ester.

Frank's work at the church infused his life with meaning and a higher purpose, but the deteriorating economic state of the country during the 1930s forced him to look elsewhere to meet the financial needs of his growing household. The Great Depression catastrophically impacted employment in the region, but McCovey snagged a valuable railroad job even though it meant commuting to Mobile, where the conditions weren't much better than those in Shipman. As one historian poignantly notes, "Paradoxically many of Alabama's poor people hardly knew that a depression had swept across the land."[3]

One saving grace was the transportation industry. It's likely that Frank knew of the Gulf, Mobile & Northern (GM&N) Railroad from his father's stories about the "new road" that reached west from Alabama into Mississippi. Throughout the 1920s, Mississippi's sawmills generated approximately 60 percent of the tonnage that was carried by the GM&N.[4] Now this transportation network was exploding thanks to the effective consolidation strategy deployed by company executives. McCovey joined it during a period of rapid growth. During this time period, the GM&N, which began in 1917, merged with the more well known but financially struggling Mobile and Ohio in 1940.[5] The result was the newly fashioned Gulf, Mobile & Ohio (GM&O) Railroad, which boasted a more extensive reach north. What followed next spurred further growth. America's entrance into World War II was a catalyst for substantially increased railroad activity. German U-boats began patrolling the Gulf of Mexico in May 1942 and terrorized shipping lanes between the Southern states and ports along the Eastern Seaboard.[6] Forced to transport oil by other means, companies in the South tapped the railroad system to move their product. It appears that McCovey performed several roles for the GM&O, and he made a solid living doing it. His sons, Willie and Clauzell, recall that their father worked as both a "wheelman," an individual who replaced the wheels on trains, as well as on the tracks themselves.[7]

Ester strongly preferred that Frank eschew traveling to Alabama and reunite with the family on a full-time basis. He agreed, and they soon moved back to Mobile and into a home at 906 Hamilton Street. Young Willie sprouted with the help of Ester's masterful work in the kitchen. She fed her family as "an incredible, understanding cook," Willie remembered. She prepared wonderful meals for him without okra, a food he despised. His parents called on all of their children to help around the house, and the responsibility of minding the chickens fell to Willie.[8] The years picked up steam, and he befriended local kids in his neighborhood. Unlike his brothers at home, Willie's new pals liked playing sports. Interestingly, sports were not of much interest to his siblings.

Multiple disturbing racial incidents occurred inside the McCovey home that impacted the household and deeply shaped Willie. He rarely (if ever) recounted them for the rest of his life. The story of the first troubling occurrence was shared within the family years ago. One night, they heard a loud knock on the door. "Open up! It's the law!" Thinking it could be a setup for a robbery, Frank exited the back door of the house with the intent of circling around to view the individuals. "Don't go out with a gun," Ester pleaded with her husband. "They're going to kill you." The lack of a phone magnified the helplessness of the moment.

The officers barged into the house and began searching it room by room, pulling out drawers and overturning things. They claimed to be looking for a fugitive and pointed out that the car in front of the house had Mississippi plates. At the time, Frances was sick. She had a painful ear infection and was wearing a sweet oil wrap around her head. "Take that off her," one of the officers demanded.[9] That was humiliation personified. Of course, they left without finding any such "fugitive" but impressed on the McCovey family a sense of vulnerability and distress. It's possible that Willie was very young when this happened and had little to no memory of it. This raid of intimidation may have even occurred before he was born in 1938, but it became a story of warning and speaks to the lifelong loathing that he felt toward Mobile.

The brevity of Willie's description of another event says a lot while saying little: "I remember a white fellow in his 20s coming to our house and addressing my father as 'boy.' That was hard to take," McCovey told a writer for the *Wall Street Journal* in 2017. The exact specifics surrounding this disturbing exchange remain unclear. A few years later, a young Willie worked at a whites-only eatery. "All the things that make you cringe was normal talk then," he said. "You took it or you walked away." He quit after seven days. At one point, the family relocated to 450 Maryland Street, but their house was relocated as part of the I-10 thoroughfare development project that ousted the family from that space. The hatred and prejudice directed at McCovey shaped the vulnerable youth in profound ways. His quiet nature concealed the sensitive countenance that resided underneath layers of stoicism. He was deeply hurt and angered by the racism that he experienced in Mobile. Did he compartmentalize his pain? Did he replay these moments in his mind like the rewatching of a film? Did he ever heal in some way? His family and closest friends aren't exactly sure. He never spoke about it.[10]

* * *

Whether through employment, monikers, or local legends, trains undoubtedly made Whistler, Alabama, a notable place to work and raise a family beginning in the mid-nineteenth century. In the decades prior to the Civil War, local lore has it that a certain Mr. McGee owned a large swath of land around Mobile Bay before he sold it to the Mobile & Ohio Railroad Company in 1853. McGee remained connected with Whistler, however, through its name, a moniker he bestowed on the town in honor of a locomotive driver who frequented the area. "It is said that when this engineer's train would approach the workmen building the original tracks for the M. & O. shops, he would salute them with an exceptionally loud blast from his whistle and they would exclaim 'It's Whistler! It's Whistler!' The town, therefore, seems to have gotten its name jointly from the engineer and his whistle," relayed one report.[11] Establishing that railroad catapulted local industries, and the town had drawn 1,509 residents by 1860.[12]

Although it may seem a bit counterintuitive for a Southern town, local historians argue that Whistler experienced its prime after the Civil War ended in 1865. Several influential businesses opened that same year around Eight Mile, a community located at Whistler's edge. Gustavus Adolphus Wirth, a German immigrant who owned and operated a whiskey distillery, started a turpentine still. Peter Peterson, an immigrant from Sweden, opened a store after spending years as a ship carpenter. Meanwhile, business for William Shelton's plantation continued to hum along at a good clip. His operation featured a distillery and sawmill among other ventures.

Simultaneously, cultural life in Whistler grew alongside its economic expansion, albeit along racially segregated lines. By decade's end, white inhabitants could choose from four different denominational churches.[13] Meanwhile, Whistler's Black residents assembled a pair of congregations: New Light Baptist Church in 1866 and Mount Sinai Baptist Church in 1868.[14] Seventy years later, churches continued to play a fundamental role in the municipality. The town's two Black neighborhoods, called Baptist Town and Methodist Town, coalesced around a local sanctuary.

Married in 1929, Frank and Jessie Mary Williams rented a house in Baptist Town located next to Whistler Elementary School. They had three boys and a girl prior to celebrating the birth of their fifth child, Billy Leo, on June 15, 1938. The couple established a warm, welcoming home that included a significant garden, featuring Frank's tomatoes and cucumbers alongside a cadre of ducks raised by Jessie Mary, on the outside and tightknit bonds on the inside.

Little Billy's childhood was full of family, friends, and outdoor adventures. Whistler was a close community. Neighbors brought over fresh fruit. Ethel Ayler, who was eight years older than Billy and went on to have a prolific career on the stage and screen, lived across the street. Along with his four older siblings—brothers Clyde, Adolph, and Franklin and sister Vera—Billy grew up attending Pilgrim Rest A.M.E. Zion Church and enjoying family fish fries at his maternal grandfather's house on Saturday nights surrounded by the warm atmosphere created by their aunts, uncles, and cousins. Tuesdays typically meant gatherings with Frank's side of the family on Mon Louis Island featuring cookouts, swimming, and dancing. The older Williams brothers were already into baseball, no doubt spurred on by the loving instruction of their father, who himself had played semipro ball. When not at home with the family, Frank was often at work, having been called down to the docks at all kinds of hours to unload arriving ships.

For decades, cotton lit the economic engine for the Mobile region, and its vast water network established a unique transportation hub, but other industries emerged. A paper mill located near Mobile County Training School provided jobs in addition to secreting a pungent smell that gave locals pause. Frank Williams worked for Murray Stevedoring on the docks unloading the cargo of arriving banana boats. He reported to the foreman, Louis Williams, whose light skin enabled him to oversee the operation as the foreman without being questioned by white employees. Louis, Frank's father, urged his son not to call him dad while at work so as not to reveal the truth about his racial identity. On weekdays, Frank returned to the house in his Ford Model A to find his kids on the porch waiting for him to come back before they walked to the bus for school. He brought bananas up to the house and flipped them one of the silver dollars he had earned during his shift.[15] Louis and Frank also handled carpentry jobs with aplomb. In the years ahead, Billy occasionally worked building gigs alongside them.

Meanwhile, Jessie Mary frequently scooped up her youngest child and brought him to work. "She would go in and out of white folks' homes to iron, clean, and stuff like that, so we didn't have nobody at the house. My father was working, and she would take me with her everywhere she went. So I would be with her up until I went to grade school," Billy explains.[16] When she had free time, especially during the summer months, Jessie loved to take all of her kids places. One of her favorite spots featured a stretch of beautiful, clear water where they all enjoyed a packed lunch.

While Mobile Bay stands as the most prominent water feature in the region, the vast tentacles of rivers and creeks that stretch into the fertile lands beyond the shoreline offered young Billy the opportunity to explore. No place beckoned him more intensely than Eight Mile Creek, a fishing haven where he spent countless hours of his youth. Billy also spent considerable time fishing with his grandfather, Louis. After finishing up for the day, they would visit a restaurant, and his grandfather would ask Billy what he wanted to eat. Breezing past any posted signs regarding race, he walked into the eatery and returned with whatever food they chose because nobody dared to question him.[17]

Although many youngsters enjoyed spending time by the water, Mobile and its satellite towns, such as Whistler, saw a unique generation of baseball players born in the region during the first decade of the twentieth century, establishing one of the game's true cradles. Frank Williams primarily stayed local while playing but nonetheless competed with and against some of the most talented ballplayers of that era, including Leroy "Satchel" Paige and Ted "Double Duty" Radcliffe. Paige started calling Frank Williams, a notable defensive first baseman, "Susie" because his dexterity around the base defined elegance and artistry. That's how Satchel saw things anyway, so the nickname stuck. "Susie" Williams befriended a fellow slick fielder from Whistler around his same age, third baseman Bill Robinson, who went on to play in the Negro Leagues for more than a decade, including the Chicago American Giants. Years later, Robinson kept a close eye on his friend's son, a newly promoted Billy Williams, and helped him adapt to life in Chicago, where he had settled following his playing career.

Baseball meant a great deal to this generation of Mobilians, and they passed on their love of the game. If not for the segregation policy instituted by professional baseball, more notable players from Mobile would be known today. Instead, they were forced to find other lines of work to care for their families. Many joined the service. Some, like Frank, remained at home to raise families. However, following in Jackie Robinson's footsteps, the subsequent generation of baseball players from Mobile, born in the 1930s, took the sport—and the nation—by storm.

In 1947, the year Willie McCovey and Billy Williams turned nine, Robinson debuted for the Brooklyn Dodgers, opening up the door for African Americans to play Major League Baseball. The dreams of young minority ballplayers who filled Mobile's fields now had someone whom they could point to and say, "That could be me." The connection to the Dodgers was particularly poignant around town because the Mobile Bears of the Southern Association was Brooklyn's Double A affiliate from 1945 to 1955 when the generation of McCovey and Williams grew up. Willie, due to his closer proximity, watched the Bears play at every opportunity.

Billy treasured times when his family would gather around to watch big-league baseball on television during Saturday afternoons. The conversations about strategy intensified as he dissected the happenings of the ballgame with his dad and brothers. He recalls one particular contest that featured the Milwaukee Braves and their notable right-handed pitcher, Lew Burdette, who won more than 200 games during his 18-year career. Frank pointed out to Billy that Burdette's aggressive approach presented the hitter with a notable opportunity to swing for success. "When you face a guy like Lew Burdette he's going to throw the ball right down the middle, so you be ready to hit the first pitch," he advised. Years later, after he reached the majors, Billy Williams found himself in the batter's box against Burdette. Sure enough, Frank proved prophetic. "Lew Burdette threw me a pitch right down the plate, and I took it. I was so excited the ball was right there, and I said, 'You should have listened to your father,'" Billy recalls chuckling. Did your dad give you a hard time about that? Another laugh. "He did, yeah, he did."[18]

* * *

For more than a century now, shrouded awe and mystery has enveloped Mobile's ability to produce Hall of Fame baseball players. Many in and around the game like to joke that there's something in the water. After all, something must be happening there to produce the highest number of enshrinees per capita of any city in America. A number of plausible theories have been discussed over the years: quality of competition, coaching passed down from older players to younger generations, or some combination of the two. However, one commonality links many of their stories together. It stresses the value of the game "tops" to their development as hitters. With baseballs in short supply (the kids occasionally procured one and beat it into mush over the course of two months, but it wasn't a solution to playing every day), youngsters in and around Mobile creatively used the resources available to them. "Double Duty" Radcliffe and his friends used to dip their baseball into kerosene. Sun set? No problem. Light it up and keep playing. Children throughout America played a variety of games that mirrored baseball. They played stickball throughout the streets of New York City, for example, but in the South, they played tops, a batting game that substituted bottle caps for baseballs. A thin stick, usually a broom handle, became a bat, and the game required only two players per side. The concentration and reflexes required to solidly strike a bottle cap with a broomstick helped all the kids around Mobile, including Williams and McCovey, cultivate their sublime hand-eye coordination and quick wrists.

Henry Aaron was a little older than our protagonists. Born on February 5, 1934, Aaron, who grew up in Toulminville, now a Mobile suburb, established himself during his teenage years as a tremendous (if unorthodox) hitter who batted cross-handed. His left hand gripped the bat handle above his right even though he was a right-handed hitter (a technique he later adjusted), but it was the unique weight transfer of his lower half that tops influenced the most. Aaron described that early development in his autobiography, *I Had a Hammer*. "I believe that my style of hitting was developed as a result of batting against bottle caps," he observed. "Even in the big leagues, I never swung the bat like other power hitters. Most great home run hitters—guys like Mickey Mantle and Harmon Killebrew and Reggie Jackson—hit with their weight way back on their back foot. But I was the opposite. I had my weight on my front foot—especially early in my career—and I got my power from lashing out at the last second with my hands. If you've ever tried to hit a bottle cap, you know that you can't sit back on your haunches. The way one of those things will dip and float, you've got to jump out and get it, and that's the way I always hit a baseball."[19]

Tops was as popular in Whistler as it was in Mobile. Baseballs were difficult to come by, and even if kids were fortunate enough to get their hands on one, it didn't last too long. Bottle caps, on the other hand, were in more ample supply, and that's how the sweet swing first initiated, a production of long hours of intense concentration and relentless practice. "We would go around early that morning and as you get a soda pop you get the top off, and the top falls off into the little pouch," Williams explains. "We would go around and collect all those tops, and then we'll play tops during the day with a little old stick, and you could make that damn top do everything. It would feed your eyesight the way you follow the ball with your hands and eyes and good hand eye coordination. That's what you got to have in baseball. I think because of the tops that kind of help you along the way."[20]

Like Aaron and Williams, McCovey and his friends had a system of acquiring bottle caps in their "Down the Bay" neighborhood. They worked for Miss Savannah, who owned a small corner store that sold, among other items, bottled soda. They stocked shelves, swept the floor, and pulled weeds from the garden behind the building. In exchange for their labor, she gave the kids a pile of bottle caps left behind by her customers. "There was a lady who had a corner store, and we would go down there. We would have to work for her, and she would put us on the books. Never did see no money, but we ate good. We would make sandwiches and all that kind of thing," remembers Clauzell McCovey, Willie's younger brother. "After we got off, there were tops that were in the machine, and she gave them to us. We would go out, and Willie would go out there and play with a broomstick or a handle, and they would hit tops. The guys that were throwing them they be throwing them all kinds of ways, and they would hit them tops until it got so dark you couldn't see."[21]

Mobile at dusk was abuzz with fireflies and whizzing tops until the sun sank behind the western horizon. Then it was time to go home. All the players would be ready to pick up where they left off tomorrow, especially when school was out for summer. There would be ample opportunity for them to take advantage of the adults trying to stay cool in the sweltering heat. A drink meant the chance to be refreshed, with the by-product of helping the enthused schoolkids hone their talents. "There weren't that many stores there but when you go to one or two or three stores a lot of people drink soda pops because the weather down there is so hot, you know, and people—there wasn't an iced tea—people would go in the store and get a Coca Cola or Seven Up, and they just opened the damn thing up right at the top," Williams says. "The owners of the stores would collect them for us. They wouldn't throw them away. They would collect them for us because they knew that this was how we played. I tell you people down there wanted to see you perform."[22]

Before entering high school, a unique circumstance gave Billy, 13, the opportunity to appear in his first semipro game in 1951. His older brother, Clyde, was scheduled to pitch for the Mobile Black Bears, a team featuring local talent, including the aforementioned Aaron. On this particular day, Clyde fell ill and couldn't pitch. The manager could shift his third baseman to the mound, but that still left him with a considerable problem; the hot corner was now unmanned. Billy, who often traveled to watch his brothers play for the Black Bears, stood nearby with his brother's uniform close at hand. "Put it on," the manager instructed. Williams acquitted himself well in the ballgame, and afterward, the skipper advised Billy that it would be best if he focused on cultivating his left-handed swing. Adding a little weight would also help his cause.[23]

* * *

Billy Williams spent his high school years at the Mobile County Training School (MCTS) from 1952 to 1956. The bus he caught every morning before seven spun its wheels past Vigor High, a school closer to his home but one that enrolled only white students. On arriving at MCTS, heavy rain occasionally forced the students to work their way around pooled water on exiting the bus. The buildings opened in 1918, several years after a fire tore through Plateau, a small enclave east of Whistler, and consumed the school. Isaiah Whitley, a teacher who first arrived in the area in 1910, left Alabama in order to raise money in the northern states to rebuild it at the same time that Booker T. Washington and Sears president Julius Rosenwald sought to invest money in rural Southern areas for Black students.[24] Their efforts resulted in the construction of MCTS. For his part, Billy enjoyed his science and woodshop classes but preferred to be in physical education, where he could play sports.

MCTS did not have a baseball team due to a lack of funds, but Williams played a lot of softball with his classmates. There was a field on the school grounds the students all referred to as the "bowl." Williams's only chance to play any type of organized baseball at this time occurred through the city of Mobile. He rode his bike several miles to participate in a city league, but that setup quickly took a backseat to the opportunity he received to play semipro ball. Williams did join the football team during his senior year. He spent the season at defensive end albeit at only 160 pounds. Williams never did put on a lot of weight. His playing weight during his 16 seasons in the major leagues hovered just below 175. On the gridiron, he showed his tremendous athletic ability and earned notice as a defensive standout. Grambling offered him an opportunity to continue with football in college, but he wanted to play baseball.

* * *

A skeptical Valena McCants couldn't help it. One of the most vital pillars of the Whistler community, the longtime teacher thought this high school junior might be just a little too old for the eighth-grade young lady with whom he was clearly smitten. She was looking out for everyone involved, but it soon became clear that it would be easier to rid the town of tops than to pry these two apart. The year was 1955 when Billy and Shirley Williams spoke as they walked to board a bus one day after practice. Their shared last name made them a perfect couple before they even met. Shirley and Billy got to talking as young people are wont to do, and the beginning of a lifelong partnership was born. There was a bit of a breakup in there early on and a "Dear, John" letter, too, but by the time they married on February 25, 1960, the firm foundation of a wonderful life together was set. They were married for 61 years.

Just five miles south of Billy's high school in Whistler, McCovey dreamed of one day playing professional baseball. As he entered Central High, Mac started playing more competitively. He linked up with local outfits who traveled around the region to find games. He was largely on his own, though. Central only offered softball. Playing sports developed into something more important to Willie than others in his family. His father, Frank, didn't find any value in it. His siblings may have dabbled in them, but they didn't prioritize it in the same way that he did. Willie, however, was obsessed. By the time he was 14 years old, a growth spurt had him standing tall and swinging a bat with sock. He briefly suited up for the Mobile Black Bears, but it was the Pascagoula Giants, a semipro team out of Mississippi consisting of young men old enough to drink, who caught wind of this intriguing prospect seven years their junior and asked McCovey to join their cause. Sugar wasn't having it, at least initially. The ballclub traveled throughout the South for games, and it gravely concerned her. "The guys had to plead with my mother to let me go," McCovey remembers. "She had every reason to be worried, too. All the guys were above the drinking age, so they'd stop off for beers after the games and I'd have to sit out in the car."[25] Ester relented. She wanted her son to be happy—and responsible—even if she didn't exactly see quite how her son could make a career out of baseball.

Soon thereafter, the Dodgers, presumably through their Mobile affiliate, established a three-day tryout camp to see if they could uncover any hidden gems in Mobile, but there was a catch. Black players could participate for only a sliver of time on the final day of the workout. Henry Aaron had been to one of these auditions and hadn't been signed. Despite the discouraging circumstances, McCovey gave it a shot. He showed up and went through the paces, but the Dodgers declined to follow up with him. "The black kids didn't really get much of a look and I guess I wasn't good enough during that hour because I'm here now," reflected McCovey years later while wearing his Giants uniform.[26]

Chapter 2

"Stretch" and "Young Blood"

The station wagon accelerated a little too quickly, spraying gravel from beneath its tires. The long car—packed full of bats and baseballs stuffed into the trunk by Willie McCovey's younger brother, Clauzell, for a quarter—sped away from view.[1] It was headed somewhere in Alabama, Louisiana, or maybe Biloxi, Mississippi, any place where an opponent waited. Willie's book bag lay underneath the porch as quiet descended on the yard. On occasion, neither student nor supplies made the trek to Central High; the enticement of playing baseball was too strong. The teenage McCovey, who towered above his peers thanks to that early growth spurt, had to duck a little to get into the car. "A lot of us think he got the name Stretch because he stretched for the ball. They called him Stretch because he was taller than everybody," said Cleon Jones, a New York Mets World Series hero in 1969.[2] Jones would know. He was and remains as knowledgeable a member of the local community as anyone. Born in 1942, he grew up in Plateau, Alabama, just down the street from Shirley Williams, Billy's future wife.

In addition to baseball, McCovey enjoyed football a great deal. He played a prominent role as the signal caller of a men's team after school, a venture that resulted in a very visible injury. One particular quarterback sneak produced a noticeably chipped front tooth after he unexpectedly broke into the open field before suddenly burying his face into an opponent's helmet. *Thwap!*

Academic study didn't intrigue a teenage McCovey, and he left school following his junior year in 1954. He preferred working at Malbis Bakery alongside his sister, Ethel, and hitting baseballs. There isn't any evidence to suggest that college was a goal for him; he wanted to become a professional ballplayer, but he needed an opportunity. McCovey's older brother, Wyatt, moved to Los Angeles to find employment, which he did, as a merchant. Willie visited him for Christmas in 1954, riding on the train across the country

15

free of charge courtesy of Frank McCovey's job, and decided that the City of Angels was for him: "I fell in love with Los Angeles. It was the first time I'd been away from home. I'd been to such places as Biloxi, Mississippi, to play sandlot ball, but this was my first big trip," McCovey told Arnold Hano.[3]

Just before the calendar flipped to 1955, Willie's life changed forever. Jesse Thomas had known McCovey for a number of years as a park director for the city, and Willie often played ball at the field that he ran. Thomas was well respected throughout Mobile, with a keen eye for talented players, and he helped them make connections in professional baseball. "He is active in the affairs of the Moulders Union, he is a scout for major league Ball Clubs, and he can be found promoting and furthering THE LEGITIMATE ASPIRATIONS OF HIS PEOPLE, without arousing the suspicions and ill will of the white people with whom he works most cooperatively," declared the *Mobile Journal*.[4] Thomas reached out to Alex Pompez, the former owner of the New York Cubans and now a scout for the New York Giants, for whom his brother, "Showboat" Thomas, had played first base.[5] At the vehement encouragement of Thomas, Pompez and the Giants sent representatives to Mobile with an invitation for McCovey to try out for the team in January, but he was still 2,000 miles away in California. Willie's father rejected the idea out of hand. No matter how persuasive the presentation appeared, Frank scorned the idea of his son trying to make a living by playing a game, and he wasn't shy about expressing his displeasure. Clauzell McCovey explained why. "My father didn't believe in that," he remembered. "He wouldn't have anything to do with any kind of sports like that because he equated that to gambling, and my father was a deacon and a minister. A lot of people don't believe me, but it's the truth: my mother wanted him to play, but my father didn't. When the recruitment guys came they was talking to my father, and my father got up and walked out. My mother stood there, and she talked to them."[6] Ester quickly wrote a letter explaining the matter to Willie and mailed it to Wyatt's place out in Los Angeles.

The Giants' interest stunned him. New York wanted him to try out for the chance to earn a professional contract? Impossible. "No, it is absolutely the truth," Thomas told Mac over the phone after he heard that the teenager doubted the reliability of the Giants' interest. "Alex Pompez, the great scout himself, who ran the Florida facility where the tryout would take place, wants you there personally," Thomas explained. The Giants offered McCovey a bus ticket and a chance. They provided round-trip travel from Mobile to Melbourne, Florida, the site of the complex.

The 65-year-old Pompez, a veteran owner in the Negro Leagues, had been in baseball for almost his entire adult life beginning with the Cuban Stars in 1916. He bought the New York Cubans in 1935 and forged a business relationship with Giants owner Horace Stoneham when the two reached a lease agreement for the Cubans to play home games at the Polo Grounds in 1944. Five years later, with the cloud of shaky finances looming over his team due in no small part to the beginnings of integration in the major leagues, Pompez agreed to refashion the Cubans as a de facto farm team for the Giants. The following year, Pompez withdrew his club from the Negro National League, and Stoneham promptly hired him to scout for the organization. In 1955, Giants farm director Carl Hubbell and director of player development Jack Schwarz tabbed Pompez to run the organization's Melbourne facility.[7]

McCovey turned 17 on January 10, and all he wanted for his birthday was antacids. The laborious bus rides that took him east from Los Angeles to Melbourne, located 70 miles southeast of Orlando, gave him too much time to think. He arrived at the facility and found the line of players checking into the camp. McCovey literally stood out—and not just because of the blue fedora he wore. The lean lefty already scraped nearly 6-foot-4, and he was skinny (call him 165 pounds), and he had never been in a situation like this before in his life. "I was scared to death," he confessed.[8] As Willie waited his turn to sign in, another nervous teenager stood near him, a dynamic young ballplayer from Puerto Rico. They acknowledged one another with a smile. "We checked in at the same time," reflects Orlando Cepeda. "Willie was ahead of me. It was all new to me. I didn't know anything about nothing. And I said to myself, how do we do this? I don't know. I walked in there and followed the rules. Willie's ahead of me, and we want to room together. I remember Willie had a small old glove. So we go on the field—a huge field with (four) diamonds—and I see McCovey hitting line drives, man. *Pow. Pow.* We had breakfast every single day. Willie's the same age . . . I was impressed with him and the way he could swing the bat. And he could run. Right after that we became friends."[9]

McCovey and Cepeda's meeting at registration proved remarkable. While the competition waged by the two young ballplayers to become the Giants' first baseman helped define that era of the franchise's history, their friendship off the field deepened substantially over the next decade. The inability of the organization to effectively play them alongside each other prevented the team from reaching its fullest potential. That competition, however, never flustered their bond. Over six decades after their inaugural meeting, Cepeda, who became McCovey's neighbor during the early 1960s, looked skyward after recalling memories of his friend and sighed. "I miss Willie," he says quietly. "I really miss Willie."[10]

The multiday camp began with coaches assigning players to a particular group and directing them to one of the facility's four fields. Then the evaluations commenced. The hopefuls took batting practice and worked in the field under the watchful eye of Giants' coaches, scouts, and Pompez himself. They saw that McCovey possessed a unique blend of raw talent. Everyone took one look at his height, reach, and the extension in his swing and echoed the nickname that his friends back home had bestowed upon him: "Stretch." He had to perform well because the competition for contracts was intense. Cepeda and José Pagán were just two of the many players competing for an offer.

McCovey immediately ran into a significant problem. He struggled mightily on the opening day of the camp, especially during the games portion of the tryout. Giants personnel met nightly to decide which kids to send home without offers. Salty Parker, who was set to manage the Giants' affiliate in El Dorado, recalled the coaches' bewilderment about Willie's scuffling to translate his skills into the game portion of the day. He seemed distracted. "There were four diamonds at Melbourne, and he's playing on one and watching the games on the other three. So there's a meeting one night, and all we talk about is Stretch. What are we going to do to get him interested? So finally one fellow said, 'Let's not worry about Stretch. All this is new to him. He'll come around eventually.' So we let him alone, and he did."[11] McCovey had some strong supporters in the room, including Parker. To their credit, the coaches worked through their own misinterpretation of McCovey. The kid was overwhelmed, not disengaged, and he knew better than anybody that the opportunity to receive a contract offer was quickly disappearing.

Alex Pompez sought out a dispirited McCovey and asked him why he was struggling so much. McCovey replied that he was nervous. Pompez then delivered the news that McCovey desperately needed to hear. The Giants suspected that underneath the scared teenager lay a special talent. "They are going to take a chance on you," the scout told the teenager as adrenaline coursed through his body. The news proved to be the anecdote to Willie's anxiety. The following morning, McCovey ripped line drives all over Melbourne. *Pow. Pow.*

Giants executive Jack Schwarz clearly saw the talent in front of him. "When this tall, broad-shouldered, slow-talking youngster began hitting long, high drives over the Australian pine trees along the outer outfield border, every scout and manager in camp began raving about him," he recalled.[12]

The initial contract offer from the Giants may have thrilled Willie, but his mother wasn't impressed. Rather than accept it as presented, Ester asked Schwarz for a $500 bonus. He quickly acquiesced. "He always had a soft spot for my mother," McCovey remembered.[13] The Giants assigned McCovey to Class D Sandersville of the Georgia State League for the 1955 season.

Located in central Georgia, some Sandersville citizens had expressed dismay at the possibility of integrating a local baseball team in Dublin, 30 miles to the south, just one year prior. However, the Giants nonetheless decided to send both McCovey and Ralph Crosby, an African American infielder from New York, to Sandersville. McCovey made himself a recognizable person in town as he slugged 19 homers and drove in a league-leading 113 runs.

His sensational baseball talent impressed everyone immediately. Regardless, Willie and Ralph could not room with their white teammates, so they lived in the Black section of town.

Most newspaper articles stuck to informing readers about McCovey's baseball performances, especially in short game recaps, but one article written during a rain delay in May provides some insight into the public's perception of Willie. He was an incredible talent. Everyone who witnessed his unique ability understood that they were watching the start of a great baseball career. However, even when writers praised McCovey, it appeared to be couched in stereotypes. Furman Bisher, the 36-year-old sports editor of the *Atlanta Constitution*, observed McCovey and Crosby playing catch as he talked to Sandersville manager Pete Pavlick in the stands. Their conversation focused on McCovey. "Willie is the best prospect in the league, if he isn't too lazy," Pavlick remarked. "He's got all the tools," he went on to add, *"if he isn't too lazy."* Perhaps Pavlick wanted to squash any possibility of a runaway ego in his young slugger. Nevertheless, this specific suggestion became an altogether too familiar refrain heard by the Black professional ballplayers who hailed from Mobile. Bill Adair, Henry Aaron's minor league manager in Eau Claire, pointed out that young Hammerin' Hank was quiet and may appear lazy to the untrained eye, but he wasn't. Aaron, who called Adair "a fair and good manager," addressed the notion of white people's perceptions in his autobiography *I Had a Hammer*. "I didn't have anything to say, and I didn't sprint around the field like Pete Rose. That wasn't my way; and it wasn't, or isn't, the way that a lot of black players do things. A lot of white people don't seem to understand—maybe Adair was an exception—that it's just human nature for some black people to do things deliberately. Maybe that comes from pulling a mule twelve hours a day and not getting paid: Why hurry?" Aaron wrote.[14] McCovey, too, did not socialize much, although he interacted with his teammates at the ballpark. In fairness to Pavlick, his comments clearly demonstrate that he recognized McCovey's abilities in addition to the evaluation of Willie's hustle. Stretch's actions suggest that Pavlick had more in common with Adair than not. McCovey accepted multiple invitations from Pavlick and his wife to share postgame meals with them at their home, and he expressed his gratitude to them during his Hall of Fame speech 31 years later.

In the same article, Bisher, who went on to have a legendary career in journalism, pointed out that McCovey's amazing feats had made him a local celebrity. Sandersville embraced the teenage sensation, and perhaps its citizens had learned a little something about social change along the way. Yet, in the same sentence in which he described Willie's athleticism throwing the baseball as "graceful," Bisher described him physically as having a "lean, soda-straw body" with long arms and "hands like a baby banana stalk.

His face was angular, the forehead sloping and his hair curled up in tight little knots." He concluded his column by noting that Pavlick had been sent to the Georgia State League by the Giants, "And so he came into a thin slip of a 17-year-old Negro boy named Willie McCovey, who may never be great to anybody else, but at least he's great in Sandersville."[15] Such were the societal dynamics that McCovey contended with during his first season in professional baseball.

On the field, McCovey proved right those in the Giants organization who took a chance on him in spite of his initial struggles at the Melbourne camp. The numbers are impressive. He batted .305 and socked 19 homers in 410 at-bats for Sandersville. Add 24 doubles along with 15 stolen bases and it's easy to see how this teenager caught everyone's attention. The league began the season with six teams but finished with only five. The campaign was reduced to 110 games, and four teams reached the playoffs. The Giants ousted the Hazlehurst-Baxley Cardinals in the semifinals to reach the championship series against the Douglas Trojans. Sandersville and Douglas split the first six games to force a deciding game seven. With the score tied, 5–5, in the ninth inning, a heavy rainstorm burst from the sky and forced league president A. O. Hadden, along with officials from the two teams, to call the game due to weather with both teams named cochampions.[16]

Among the teams in the Georgia State League was the Dublin Irish, the ballclub situated in the middle of the state that had integrated the previous season. Eleven years earlier, Dublin's First African Baptist Church hosted a public speaking competition that was won by 15-year-old Martin Luther King, Jr. He titled his talk "The Negro and the Constitution." The Irish were a Pittsburgh Pirates affiliate, and their roster included a 19-year-old infielder by the name of Franklin Williams. Imagine the joy when McCovey met Williams and the two teenagers realized they had grown up just a few miles from each other. Billy's older brother was two years McCovey's senior. After the season, McCovey made the very short drive from his Mobile neighborhood to Whistler in less time than it took him to trot around the bases after a homer. Willie, Franklin, and Billy spent increasingly more time hanging out together. They relaxed on the Williamses' front porch and talked extensively about baseball. When he wasn't working at his offseason job at a local recreation center, McCovey hopped in his car to visit a local girl whom he had begun dating. She attended college at Alabama State, and it wasn't uncommon for the Williams brothers to accompany him. Playing basketball together also made for an enjoyable afternoon. It was pretty difficult to slow down McCovey in the paint.

Around this time, one of the McCovey family's most famous stories occurred. It involved Willie, who had returned to Mobile from Georgia just a few weeks prior. One day in October, Ethel Campbell, his pregnant older sister, sensed that her baby was on the verge of being born, so she took immediate action. There wasn't going to be any waiting. She got up and left—walked right out the door of their latest house on Maryland Street and headed straight to the hospital on foot. Ester turned to Willie and sent him after her. He scrambled out of the house and jumped into his car. He picked up Ethel and drove her there quickly. Soon, she gave birth to a beautiful baby girl named Carolyn. The family celebrated, as mother and daughter were doing well.[17]

* * *

The venerable Ed Tucker loomed large in Mobile's baseball world. He owned the Mobile Black Bears as well as a restaurant and bar that provided a stage for a plethora of young musical entertainers who went on to superstardom, including Ray Charles and Stevie Wonder. "Every kid in the area who wanted to play baseball he would give him a chance. He saw a lot of players come through," Billy Williams said.[18] One of those players was the teenage Henry Aaron, who smoked line drives all over the field. Aaron played shortstop for Tucker's ballclub in 1951 when he was 17 years old, but he suited up for the team only when they played home games at Mitchell Field on St. Stephens Road. His mother would not allow him to go on road trips.

Ed Scott, another legendary baseball man in Mobile, had braved the pessimism of Estella Aaron and convinced her to allow Henry to play. Scott managed the Black Bears and scouted for the Indianapolis Clowns. Scott and Tucker made Aaron as comfortable as possible. In turn, he peppered Mitchell Field with frozen ropes. Lela Tucker remembered that she and her husband were sure to take care of young Henry financially. "In fact, he paid him double. It was a secret. All the other players were pa[i]d on Sunday, but Henry came around our house on Monday for his pay. If the other players had known about it, we would really have a problem," she admitted.[19] Aaron never forgot the opportunity that Tucker gave him or the additional money. "The owner of the team, a man named Ed Tucker, paid the players ten dollars after every game," Aaron wrote in his autobiography *I Had a Hammer*. "But he never paid me on Sunday. He would tell me to come by the house on Monday to get my money, and he or Mrs. Tucker would always stick a couple extra dollars in my hand."[20] Aaron returned the love after he made the big leagues. "Hank sends me a ticket to the All-Star game every year. He's never failed," Tucker said in 1970.[21] The tradition continued for 17 consecutive years beginning in 1955 before Tucker tragically died in a car accident in May 1972. Listed among Tucker's survivors in his death announcement that appeared in the *Mobile Register* were his wife, two sons, daughter, a host of relatives, and "very devoted friends, Mr. Hank Aaron of the Atlanta Braves and Mr. Billy Williams of the Chicago Cubs."[22]

Aaron had played for the Mobile Black Bears with Franklin Williams, whose younger brother Billy watched—no, studied—their games with incredible concentration. "I used to go down to watch my brother play, and Henry Aaron was on the team. I watched those guys play, and you just look and learn. Pick out a guy that's playing the outfield or second base, everywhere, you know, and look at that guy and just think about it," Billy recalled.[23]

Semipro baseball soon provided young Billy the opportunity to play the sport he loved since his high school did not have a team. He incorporated into his own game all of the good habits he picked up by closely watching the Black Bears. Now a few years older and stronger since he replaced Clyde in Mobile's lineup, Billy joined the team before his sixteenth birthday. Williams's new teammates, including Tommie Aaron, Henry's younger brother, took an immediate interest in helping the talented youngster improve but made it clear to him that mistakes needed to be corrected immediately. They coached Billy hard, especially on the importance of defensive fundamentals and base-running techniques, because they wanted him to be successful. "I was like 15 playing with guys 25, 26 years old. When you made a mistake they would grab you and say, 'If you want to be a baseball player you can't do that. You can't play like that if you want to play,' so you were taught at an early age how to play the game of baseball. It was good growing up down there because you knew they cared."[24]

Williams's abilities garnered attention quickly. Of particular note, Billy put a charge into the ball whenever he stepped into the batter's box. He had an innate ability to make contact with the baseball that stood out even when the teenager played among men a decade older. "I always had the quickness of the bat, you know, and I guess that's one of the things that made me a good hitter. It allowed me to wait and see the ball a little longer because I had the confidence I could get the bat to the ball. They say I hit balls out of the catcher's mitt way back here."[25] The team traveled to play games in various towns in Mississippi and, occasionally, New Orleans. He soon found himself linked up with one of his father's former teammates to barnstorm in the state of Florida for a little extra cash: Satchel Paige.

Paige emerged as a pitching phenomenon in the 1920s. Born in Mobile, likely in 1906 (it depends on whom you ask), Paige grew up in a town deeply divided along racial lines. The U.S. Supreme Court allowed this social, cultural, and political environment to flourish when it made its separate but equal ruling to conclude the *Plessy v. Ferguson* case in 1896. Satchel developed his pitching prowess at Mount Meigs, an all-Black reform school for youngsters who ran afoul of the law. Paige was assigned to the institution following a hearing during which he was charged and convicted of offenses ranging from truancy to stealing. He entered Mount Meigs midway through 1918.

Young Satchel Paige's indiscretions may have cost him his freedom during his teenage years, but the experience of learning baseball from coach Edward Byrd gave him a valuable gift he used for the rest of his life. Paige reflected on the impact of Mount Meigs and Byrd as an adult. "Those five and a half years there did something for me—they made a man out of me. If I'd been left on the streets of Mobile to wander with those kids I'd been running with, I'd of ended up as a big bum, a crook. You might say I traded five years of freedom to learn how to pitch," he said.[26]

Pitching soon became Paige's life, and he played alongside hundreds of ballplayers from Mobile to Chattanooga and back again over the next few years. At first, Satchel threw hard but wildly; he didn't always know where the ball was going. That dramatically changed after he joined the Birmingham Black Barons in 1927. Three mentors—Harry Salmon, Sam Streeter, and Bill Gatewood—worked with Paige on honing his craft. They constantly practiced, and, soon enough, the young flamethrower developed the ability to locate his fastball. Streeter coached Satchel to look at the plate before releasing the ball. "He got to the point where he had *good* control," Streeter said.[27]

Fast-forward to the mid-1950s, and the opportunity arose for teenagers Franklin and Billy Williams to barnstorm in Florida alongside Paige, whose life now hovered at the half-century mark. They jumped at the opportunity.

They pinged around the Sunshine State while Paige often arrived during the game's later stages in his white Cadillac. Says Williams, "Satchel came about the seventh inning and walked down to the bench, 'Come on big catch. Walk down here with me, and see if I can throw a couple across home plate.' He would take out a piece of gum, this is a true story, take the gum out of the wrapper, start chewing it, throw the wrapper down there and say, 'Sit right there behind that. Let me see how many I can throw over there.'" Paige utilized his pinpoint control to retire the side in order and then take a seat on the bench.

Pitching wasn't Satchel's only enjoyment. He also liked to swing the bat—at least that's what he told young Billy Williams. "He always called me, 'Young Blood.' 'Come on, Young Blood, I'm going to show you how to hit.' 'Yes, sir.' Long legs and wide like this standing up there. Called me 'Young Blood.'"[28] On one particular afternoon, the barnstorming game failed to commence due to a lack of equipment, so they waited for Paige to arrive. Sure enough, his white Cadillac emerged into view and was parked next to the field. Billy and Franklin explained the problem. "I got some balls and bats in the back of the car," he told them.

As they went around to the back of his car, they said hello to Lahoma, Satchel's wife. She kindly handed Billy and Franklin, who were getting low on money, five dollars each. "Here. You take five dollars, and you take this five dollars," she told them. "The old guys can take care of themselves." As she spoke, Paige popped the trunk. *Ugggghhhhh*, Billy remembers. The stench of dead fish enveloped the Williams brothers. Satchel had stashed all of his catch next to the baseball stuff in the Florida heat. The teenagers grabbed the equipment and quickly made their way back to the field. When Billy's cash flow whittled below $20, he decided to head home, content to have played baseball with memories that lasted a lifetime. "It was a great thrill moving around with him and now to hear a lot of people talk about Satchel Paige after the experience I had with him. It was something to be around him," he said.[29]

Three and a half decades after that barnstorming tour, Williams partici-pated in the annual induction ceremony held by the Mobile Hall of Fame. Satchel Paige had passed away eight years earlier, but he had been elected posthumously to be enshrined in the local institution. Billy honored Satchel by introducing him to the gathered dignitaries and presenting the awarded plaque to Paige's sister, Palestine Caldwell. She looked heavenward and poignantly declared, "You're gone Satchel, but you're not forgotten."[30] Afterward, she told Billy something stunning that still makes him laugh years later. "Satchel was a good baseball player, but I had another brother who was a better baseball player than Satchel Paige," she said. "But he liked *girls*."[31]

* * *

As his senior year at MCTS began to wind down in 1956, Billy wondered about what he would do next. His brother, Franklin, was playing in the Pitts-burgh Pirates minor league system. A number of his friends decided that they would join the military, but Billy wanted nothing more than to follow in his brother's footsteps and play professional baseball.

Williams's opportunity arrived in the form of Ivy Griffin, a scout for the Chicago Cubs, who had been watching the Mobile Black Bears for some time. Billy learned that Griffin was following the team from a policeman who was working security at Mitchell Field for one of Mobile's ballgames. Jackie Robinson and the local affiliate gave Williams a strong sense for the Brook-lyn Dodgers, but he was less familiar with the Chicago Cubs. He listened as the officer's words washed over him. Initially, Billy suspected that the scout wanted to sign Tommie Aaron, but he changed his mind on one of the Black Bears' next road trips to Moss Point, Mississippi. "Tommie couldn't make the trip, but he was still there," Williams recalled of seeing Griffin sitting in the stands. "So I got kind of itchy then, and said he might be looking at me to play the game of baseball."[32]

One late afternoon in the late spring of 1956, Ivy Griffin drove into Whistler and pulled up to a local store. He went inside and asked if anyone knew where the Williams family resided. Although initially reluctant to provide an unknown white man with that information, Griffin learned of the address after revealing that he was a major league scout and wanted to sign Billy to a contract. He thanked the proprietor and headed out.

Franklin Williams had been advising his younger brother to negotiate with any organization that came around to sign him up. He had learned all about bonuses paid to other players in the Pirates organization of which he was now a part. Billy listened intently, but when Griffin knocked on that front door, all that steely determination abandoned him. He listened in as Griffin explained the Cubs' offer to Frank, who fully supported Billy's ambition of being a ballplayer. The bonus was virtually nonexistent. A bus ticket. A chance. That's about it. The Cubs were thrifty spenders, but surely there was room for a few more dollars. However, they were so eager to sign the deal that it was accepted. Griffin handed Frank a cigar, and the contract was signed. In addition to a $200 monthly salary, Billy received an earful from his brother for accepting that first offer.

Shortly thereafter, a scary situation pressed the Cubs to assign the 17-year-old Williams to Class D Ponca City of the Sooner State League in late June. On May 31, outfielder Lou Johnson suffered a serious injury in a car accident that required surgery. Billy arrived in Oklahoma, on June 24. "When I went to Ponca City they would travel around in station wagons. It was raining, and Lou Johnson ran into a bank, and I think he cut half his ear off. He had been in the hospital and when I got signed I went down to make up the 25 man roster. I never did play that much," says Williams.[33]

A one Mr. Reed, who, along with his wife, hosted African American ballplayers in their home, including Johnson, met Billy at the bus station and informed Williams that he would be staying with his family. The segregation stunned him. "I was really surprised. Being from around Mobile, you'd figure that Oklahoma would be integrated, that you could go practically anyplace you wanted. I never thought I'd have to stay in a private home. I thought I'd move into a hotel where the other players were living, and keep in contact with the ball club," Williams recalled.[34]

Two days later, manager Don Biebel, with his team trailing, 10–3, in the opening game of a doubleheader, inserted Williams into right field. His first at-bat happened in the bottom of the sixth inning with the bases loaded. Williams delivered a two-run single up the middle. The Cubs lost the game, but Williams had his first professional hit. His dream had become a reality. However, the remainder of the season proved to be discordant. He appeared in only 12 more games. When Billy played, two things quickly became apparent: he had a habit of getting on base—he reached nine

times in 22 plate appearances—and he needed to continue working on his
outfield defense.

* * *

"Get up! Shake those sheets! Let's go play some baseball!" exhorted Cubs
scout Buck O'Neil. The prospects stirred in their beds, including 18-year-old
Billy Williams, who had been notified by the organization over the winter that
he was to report to camp for spring training in 1957. The Arizona sun just
peaked above the horizon and shone its warm light on the baseball diamonds
of the Chicago Cubs spring training complex in Mesa.

"In spring training, we lived in the barracks. Buck had the job of waking
up everybody in the morning. It would be about 5:30 or 6:00 in the morning,
Buck would take his shower. You could kind of hear the water running," Williams recalls. "And all of a sudden you hear the water cut off and Buck, you
know, getting all dressed and one of his favorite words in the morning, 'Get
up, shake those sheets, let's go play some baseball.' That's what he would say
all the time. Every morning he did that."[35]

After a particularly noteworthy round of batting practice, Williams began
to exit the batting cage when a gruff 60-year-old Rogers Hornsby—he of
the seven-time National League batting champion Hornsbys—instructed the
young lefty to stay put and keep swinging. Hornsby, who worked with Cubs
minor leaguers, sarcastically claimed that shaking the trees around Wrigley
Field would cause a decent number of fielders to tumble out without many
good hitters. However, he now stood absolutely still. Billy proceeded to take
cut after cut under Hornsby's watchful gaze. Eventually, after what seemed
like a lot longer than the actual 10 minutes of time, Hornsby signaled that
Billy could stop. "You've got a good swing," the 1942 Hall of Fame inductee
said monotonously. Although the words' intent hung mysteriously in the air
like a fly ball lost in the sun, this praise represented Hornsby's ultimate stamp
of approval. Billy would now be a protégé of the "Rajah," and the kid soaked
in everything Hornsby shared with him about hitting philosophy and knowing
the strike zone.[36]

Williams's spring training performance, buoyed by the unconditional support of the hypercritical Hornsby, earned him a starting role in Ponca City's
outfield for the 1957 season. Billy played very well for a team that did not
win a lot of games. The Cubs finished the season near the bottom of the standings: seventh out of eight teams with a record of 52–74. Nobody could blame
Williams, however. He rewarded manager Don Biebel by hitting all summer.
Slight of build, Williams sprayed the ball all over the field. "I was like six
o'clock straight up weighing about a 165 pounds, and I hit 17 home runs to
left field and center field. I couldn't pull the ball then," he says.[37] Billy led

the ballclub with a .319 average and .426 on-base percentage while appearing in a team-high 126 games. He turned 19 years old in June. He also drove in 95 runs. Williams's impressive performance earned the attention of league-wide observers. He garnered the first All-Star recognition of his career following the season.

For all of the memorable moments Williams had on the baseball diamond in 1957, his most indelible "on-field" memory from that season included neither bat nor ball but rather a firearm. On August 7, the Cubs welcomed the Ardmore Cardinals to Conoco Field for a three-game set. The Cardinals were led by J. C. Dunn, a former star at Southeastern State and known throughout Oklahoma as one of the state's top minor leaguers. He was Ardmore's player/manager. Dunn, already 31, was too old to be considered a player prospect to the St. Louis Cardinals, but perhaps he could reach the big leagues as a coach. Ardmore entered the game atop the Sooner State League with a record of 61–35. Dunn had compiled a robust .323 batting average with 36 doubles and 23 steals to go along with his other gaudy statistics.

In the series opener, the Cardinals and Cubs battled back and forth throughout the hot, steamy night and were tied at six heading into the bottom of the ninth inning. Back-to-back singles placed Cub runners at the corners with one out and brought up young Williams, who came through with a sharp grounder wide of shortstop that brought Gary Smith home with the winning run as lowly Ponca City knocked off the front-running Cardinals, 7–6. Several white Ardmore players chafed at being beaten on a hit by Billy Williams, the only African American in the stadium.

Early the next morning, several members of the Cardinals, including Jim Bradley, Jerry Keeler, and Coy Smith, returned to the Jens-Marie Hotel around 2:15 A.M. after a late night that included drinking, playing cards, and a meal following their 7–6 loss. When they came back to the hotel, the elevator was unattended, prompting the players to complain to the night manager, who subsequently called the porter, James Johnson, with a request to take the ballplayers back to their floor. Johnson, who later claimed in court that he had been in the bathroom and was therefore away from his post, returned to the elevator. As it ascended, the white Coy Smith teased Johnson, who was Black, by claiming that he had been "catnapping" instead of doing his job. According to one report, based on courtroom testimony, "As the conversation progressed remarks became more heated and as the men left the elevator the 24-year-old Smith insulted the 32-year-old Johnson."[38] Keeler testified that Smith chirped, "Kiss my behind."[39] An argument ensued, and Smith punched Johnson in the face. A local journalist covering the trial reported that Johnson told the jury that Smith hurled a vile racial epithet at him before the two ballplayers punched him and kicked him in the legs, including "up near my groin."[40] According to a report of the court testimony, Smith and Bradley had been out drinking.

Ignorant of Johnson's history as a military veteran and boxer, he probably surprised them when he broke free from their grasps and made it back to the elevator, which he deployed back to the hotel's main floor. Management summoned the police, and captain Joe Balcer and patrolman Jess Lee arrived at the hotel. The officers entered a scene that featured an upset J. C. Dunn, who had been summoned from his room, ridiculously proposing to fight Johnson in the hotel lobby. They immediately shut that down. Lee went out to the parking lot to stop Johnson, who had just left the building and gotten into his car, from leaving the premises. "Where are you going?" Lee asked him. "Going down home and get a gun," Johnson allegedly responded in part.[41]

Johnson downed a number of tranquilizer pills—by all accounts more than his prescribed daily allotment—and filled his .38 with slugs.[42] In what order no one ever learned. Fueled by rage caused by the insults and stinging punch to the jaw hurled at him by Smith, Johnson, covered with fresh bruises, prepared to reengage these same Cardinals at Conoco Field later that night.[43]

The series between Ardmore and Ponca City continued that evening. Fresh off his game-winning hit, Billy Williams was back in his customary left-field spot. In the top of the second inning, just as the Cardinals started a run-scoring rally, James Johnson walked up to the entrance, bought a ticket, and crossed into the stadium. Williams immediately noticed him. "I see that there's one Black guy walking in the ballpark. It was kind of strange at the time because no Black people came to the ballpark. So, I see this guy, he's sitting in the stands for about two or three minutes, and then he walked down by the dugout," he vividly remembers.

The crude visiting dugout sat along the east side of the ballpark. Johnson's eyes locked on the back of Coy Smith, who was leaning against the chicken wire fence behind the bench railing. Johnson approached him as the Cardinals rally continued. "You the one I had it out with last night?" Johnson asked Smith when he got close enough to speak to him without raising his voice. Smith wheeled around and immediately recognized the porter from the hotel. "Yeah," he said.

Johnson drew Smith closer, "I want to apologize."

Just as he spoke, J. C. Dunn, who had been standing on third base, broke for home on a batted ball. Simultaneously, Johnson pulled a handgun out of his right pocket. Billy watched the entire sequence play out in front of him. "Coy Smith knew who he was, and they took off, and this guy pulled out a .38, and he just *pow*, *pow*, *pow*. You could see the dust flying up like this where the shots hitting and the manager, Dunn, got hit in the side. They took off. So, I'm playing left field. The second baseman tried to hide behind second base.

The centerfielder jumped over the fence, and I'm in left field. I said, 'This guy's not shooting at me!' and I just stood there," Williams recalls.

Johnson unleashed five shots in total, two of which struck Dunn, who had just crossed home plate. One bullet entered Dunn's back and deflected off of his rib cage, while the other slug buried itself into the thigh of the manager's right leg. Coy Smith, who had sprinted across the diamond, avoided being hit. Johnson wanted to shoot him in the leg, but he missed. Just like that, he had emptied the chamber.

Security officials sprinted out to left field to protect Billy, although he alone recognized that the gunman had no interest in firing at him. Harold Goodman, the game's official scorekeeper and an off duty cop, immediately grabbed a nearby phone and called the police station. One eyewitness later claimed that as Johnson walked away from the field and back through the stands, he said aloud, "They beat up on me and they won't get away with it."[44] Officer George Andrews worked security at the game that night, and he quickly darted toward Johnson. "I had my gun out and was ready. I didn't know whether he had any more cartridges in that gun or not. But when he came out under the stands, he didn't have the gun in his hand," said Andrews.[45]

Johnson informed the officer that the gun was in his front pocket. Andrews arrested him and took him to the ticket office until backup officers arrived. Meanwhile, medical personnel hurried onto the field and rushed Dunn to the hospital for surgery. Doctors later downplayed the severity of his wounds, as neither was life threatening. Cops hauled Johnson, who possessed 10 additional cartridges in his pocket, to jail, and he soon faced a charge of assault with intent to murder. Williams recounts what happened next. "They had a little thing called Teen Town that you know the young kids go dancing and stuff like that. And after they called the game I went over to Teen Town and his daughter was there. So this one friend of mine that I knew from Ponca City, Oklahoma, his father—his brother had a car. His brother had just gotten out of the service and he said, That's his daughter right there. Talking about the girl. So, he told her what happened, and we had to take her down to the police station."[46]

The brief trial of James Johnson in district court lasted less than two days the following February. Deeply remorseful, he lamented going out to Conoco Field at all. That said, he frankly admitted that Coy Smith was the intended target. "I tried to shoot him in the legs. I didn't even know I had hit Mr. Dunn," he said. Even with Smith in mind, Johnson testified that he had no desire to kill the man. Otherwise, he would have simply pulled the trigger when he was standing a hair's breadth behind him in the dugout. The trial brought two other issues to light: the vulgar epithet Johnson testified that Smith hurled at him during their heated exchange at the hotel as well as the porter's consumption of more tablets than had been prescribed to him.

Ultimately, Johnson's attorney argued that his client was a "fall guy." For whom? Well, on the evening prior to the shooting, the Ardmore Cardinals had been beaten by Ponca City, 7–6, thanks to a game-winning plate appearance produced by Billy Williams. Johnson and Williams shared one thing in common: skin color. "Some Ardmore team members wanted to 'whip someone' since they couldn't win the ball game," the defense counselor maintained during final arguments. After deliberating for two hours and 15 minutes, the jury agreed with Johnson and declared the defendant not guilty. "I intend to do everything I can to be a good citizen," Johnson told reporters after the close of the trial proceeding.[47]

Billy Williams finished the 1957 season with a flourish. On August 31, he belted three home runs in a 9–2 rout of the Muskogee Giants to cap off an outstanding season, his first full campaign as a professional. He finished the season with a team-leading .426 on-base percentage to go along with 17 homers and 95 RBIs. He walked more than he struck out and showed what he could do in the running game by stealing 13 bases. His outstanding production earned him a promotion in 1958. Many years passed until Billy saw Ponca City again. He wanted to see where his career began and was officially introduced to Johnson, who was working on the exterior of the church. Billy remembers,

This is about four years later, five or six years later—I'm in the minor league, and I go to Ponca City, Oklahoma. I was in Wichita, and I go to Ponca City, Oklahoma, and, I'm riding around to see where I started and everything. I say, "Do you remember when I was down here that this one guy came out to the ballpark and shot up the ballpark? Where is this guy now?" He said, "Get in the car I'll show you." So, he took me around, and I came up to this church, alright, and he was out there. He was out nailing nails on the church. And he said, "Hey, there he is right there. He's a preacher now."[48]

J. C. Dunn recovered from the surgery in relatively short order. He allowed reporters and photographers into his hospital room the following day. With a little bit of time to process the events of the previous 48 hours, Dunn struck a notably conciliatory tone toward James Johnson. "I wasn't the man he was after," he noted. Dunn returned to the Cardinals lineup late in the season and helped the team capture the Sooner State League championship. He hit .330 the following season for the Dothan Cardinals in 1958, but, after playing ball for a few more minor league seasons, he retired from the game in 1961.

* * *

While Billy Williams was spending his inaugural professional season in Ponca City, Willie McCovey smashed his way through the Carolina League in 1956. Assigned to the Danville Leafs, Mac immediately caught everyone's attention in spring training when he hit a ball over a 30-foot fence that stood 420 feet from the batter's box.[49] Under the guidance of manager Salty Parker, who became an influential figure in his life, McCovey homered 29 times and smacked a league-leading 38 doubles even though he was more than five years younger than the league-average player. The superstar on the ballclub was Leon Wagner, a 22-year-old outfielder who hit .330 and crushed 51 homers. Wagner and McCovey became friends, and the former would find himself wearing a San Francisco Giants uniform the following season. McCovey also counted future big-leaguers José Pagán and Tony Taylor among his teammates in Danville. They combined to create a lethal offense that bashed baseballs throughout the Southeast and propelled the Leafs into the championship series against Fayetteville, although they lost in six games. Wagner, Pagan, and McCovey were among five Leafs selected to play in the East-West Carolina League All-Star game.

Following his sterling campaign, McCovey earned a promotion to the Dallas Eagles for the 1957 campaign. He was one of just two 19-year-olds in the Texas League, and again he more than held his own against much older competition. His peers took immediate notice in spring training. "He's a prospect if I ever saw one," declared Ray Murray, a 37-year-old catcher who had spent parts of six seasons in the major leagues.[50] Murray encouraged his young teammate not to get discouraged if the ball didn't fly out of the ballpark in Dallas. The deep right-field fence stood guard against the offensive assault of every player.

The Eagles rolled through the first half of the season. McCovey blasted his way throughout the league everywhere except in the state of Louisiana. Along with Tony Taylor and Bobby Prescott, McCovey could not play road games in Shreveport because Black players could not lawfully participate with whites.[51] When Shreveport traveled to Dallas in July, McCovey matched a Texas League record when he smashed three triples in a 7–2 win.

Mac's teammates marveled at his talent, including Joe Amalfitano, whom Willie affectionately called "Monk" because of his friend's particularly short haircut. "Willie could run, and we played in a large ballpark," remembers Amalfitano, who played all three of the infield positions other than Mac's first base. "He hit the ball in the gap, and I can still visualize him running. He was always known for his hitting, but he was an above average fielder and he could stretch all the way to second base, which I think added to his nickname. He would shorten your throw because of the length he could get out there to receive the ball."[52] McCovey and Amalfitano routinely discussed defensive strategy in preparation for games, especially if the Eagles starting pitcher struggled to field his position.

Salty Parker knew from their time in Danville that he had a unique talent in his young first baseman. He saw the kid's unquestioned power but also recognized a teachable spirit that occasionally needed guidance. While everyone called McCovey "Stretch" or "Willie Mac," Parker referred to him as "Big One," although his thick Texas drawl emitted something closer to "Biggun." He diligently worked with McCovey on developing a line-drive swing void of focus on the long ball. The homers naturally followed. The two developed a close bond over their pair of seasons together. Sensing a growing narrative swirling around McCovey, Parker called the youngster into his office. "Biggun, you're tall and because you're tall you'll always be respected. You'll always stand out in a crowd. You're not a very outgoing person, and you have an easy going manner. People may interpret that as though you're not caring. But, whatever people say, stay the way you are. Be yourself. Don't ever change or let somebody try to make you something you're not," he advised.[53]

Parker's players respected him because he worked on improving their fundamentals and instilling discipline, which Willie learned about firsthand. McCovey took ill before a road game in Fort Worth. As the team boarded its bus, Willie asked Amalfitano to inform Parker that he would not be making the trip. Amalfitano didn't think that was a good idea. "I'm just a player, and so all of a sudden I'm Western Union," he says with a laugh recalling the story. Parker climbed aboard, and Amalfitano told him that Willie wasn't coming on the trip because he didn't feel well. "What do you mean by that?!" Parker yelled.[54] Mac and he would be having a chat.

Over time, Parker built such a good rapport with his young star that he could give him good-natured grief from time to time, and the team appreciated McCovey's sense of humor about it. "I always thought he would make the big leagues, but with the humidity and temperature being what it was in Dallas, somebody once asked Willie if he was tired. And Salty Parker said, 'Willie gets tired breathing.' It was funny because Willie was so loosey-goosey, you'd think guys could throw fastballs by him, but there was no way," outfielder Dick Getter recalled.[55]

McCovey's jaw-dropping feats drew a copious amount of fans to the ballpark, and, at times, particular members of the press seemed to suggest he was a great young player they should eagerly support. Yet some of the compliments pertaining to his personality and ability to play the game arrived through the framework of race. In one breath, a writer described Willie as having "natural grace" and "tremendous power," while another pointed out that he is "a quiet, unassuming, polite Negro." The implication being that he was "safe."[56]

With a few exceptions like Parker, McCovey generally felt misunderstood by those around him. He *was* introverted. He *was* kind. He *did* hit home runs longer than locals could remember having seen before. But he also had a silly sense of humor that endeared him to others, and he cared deeply about performing well all while being separated from his teammates at every social turn. When he tried to explain himself, it was used to embarrass him. A writer asked McCovey about what he was focused on learning, and the teenager responded by addressing the criticism that he wasn't working as hard as possible. In the midst of his answer, McCovey could not quite come up with the word "lackadaisical." Rather than either spell it out or omit it from the quote, the story included the entire sequence of Willie unsuccessfully trying to remember the word. "'Lot of 'em tell me I'm . . .' He began fumbling for the word. 'They tell me I'm lackadaisy . . . lacka . . .' He abandoned the sixbit word. 'You know . . . they say I'm not pushin' hard enough. But that's just my ways, I guess. But I'm tryin' to talk it up more, now. Still, you don't talk your way on base.'"[57] A seed of distrust with the media was sown deeply within McCovey.

Willie became friends with a number of reporters throughout his long career, but the demeaning tone of certain stories placed a wariness in his heart that he wasn't shy about sharing with his teammates. Other Black, Latino, and Cuban players received similar treatment from the media. Felipe Alou, who became McCovey's teammate in Phoenix the following year, discussed the issue in his autobiography. "Because Latinos either didn't speak English or didn't speak the language very well, we were often made fun of. They would quote us verbatim, but they didn't do that with the American players. They cleaned up their quotes. I saw it as a lack of respect," he wrote.[58]

On July 27, 1957, a coiled Willie McCovey broke for home from third base as part of a double-steal attempt. Anticipating a close play, he extended his legs, hoping to slide home safely. Instead, his spikes caught awkwardly on the baked Texas dirt. The ground refused to give, so his right leg did. A sinewy snap in his knee. A crack in his ankle. The injury haunted him for the rest of his life.

McCovey's serious knee injury required surgery. Remarkably, however, rather than go under the knife, he returned to the lineup in the second week of August, not exactly a move made by a player lacking effort or passion. His leg forced him to miss some games throughout the final six weeks of the season, but McCovey remained productive at the plate. On the verge of being swept in the Texas League playoffs by the Houston Buffs, McCovey drove in the game-winning run in a 1–0 Dallas win. Four nights later, after the Eagles stormed back to force a deciding game seven, Stretch blasted a three-run homer in the first inning to stake Dallas to an early lead its pitchers could not hold. Houston won, 4–3. In the face of adversity, McCovey finished the season with a .281 average, 11 homers, and 52 walks against 52 strikeouts. The injured leg immediately became his focus. The Giants arranged for the surgery to take place in New York. It would be the first of many.

* * *

Following his devastating injury, the Giants assigned McCovey, now 20, to Phoenix of the Pacific Coast League in 1958. The offseason surgery stabilized his right knee well enough for Mac to appear in an impressive 146 games. He hit .319 and smacked 14 homers, but his running days on the base paths had ended. Even though he didn't swipe a lot of bases, McCovey averaged 12 steals a year during his first three seasons of professional baseball. He could run and did so. No longer. He stole only four bases in 1958 and never bested that season total for the remainder of his career. Stretch took care of that problem by doubling 37 times. Who needed to steal second base when you were already standing on it?

McCovey enjoyed his time away from the ballpark. He and new teammate Felipe Alou rented rooms in the same house that was a 20-minute drive from Phoenix Municipal Stadium. The two first met in spring training in 1957. McCovey had gone to Dallas, while Alou split time playing in Minneapolis and Springfield. Alou remembered being impressed by the 20-year-old in camp: "He could run—he was a skinny kid—play a slick first base, hit for average, hit it out of an airport, and hit it *hard*." A year later, they were housemates, and Alou took notice of McCovey's ever-increasing shoe collection, featuring pairs crafted by Florsheim and Stacy Adams. Alou, who sent a notable amount of his paycheck to his family in the Dominican Republic, suggested to McCovey that he stop buying expensive shoes. Willie flashed a big grin at his friend. "You should quit buying cheap shoes, Felipe. You and I are going to make money in the big leagues," he quipped.[59]

For now, they were broke. Anyone looking for Willie and Felipe before a home game could easily find them because the car they bought together for $80 had a radiator that leaked water so badly that it required multiple stops at gas stations between their residence and the ballpark. After two months of this nonsense, McCovey had to take care of the problem by himself, but it was for a very good reason. His friend, teammate, roommate, and carpooling buddy was called up to the majors by the Giants. Alou had to catch a flight so quickly that he didn't even get the chance to talk to Willie, who continued to mash baseballs all season and lead Phoenix to an 89–65 record and the Pacific Coast League championship. Following the 1958 season, Alou presented an idea to McCovey: come play winter ball with me down in the Dominican Republic for the Santo Domingo Escogido Lions. Mac agreed.[60]

In 1958–1959, Escogido featured a dynamic lineup that included McCovey, Felipe Alou, Matty Alou, Manny Mota, and Bill White. There were a couple of older guys on the roster, too. White, a left-handed slugger who had smacked 22 homers in 1956, worked with Mac on injecting more power into his swing by using his wrists more effectively. Additionally, Escogido featured a dazzling 20-year-old pitcher with a unique windup that unleashed an electric fastball whom McCovey met for the first time. "I was a rookie in

1958 when McCovey came for the first time to the Dominican to play for Escogido Baseball Club, and that's how we met," Juan Marichal warmly recalls over six decades later on a calm summer night as he reclined in a rocking chair on the back patio of the Otesaga Hotel in Cooperstown, New York. "I remember him hitting a ball over the right field wall where nobody ever hit a ball before, a long hit, a home run. Right from the beginning he showed that he was going to be a great, great ballplayer."[61]

For all of his success on the field, homesickness overwhelmed McCovey during his initial trip outside of America. Felipe noticed his younger teammate wrestling with the temptation to return to the United States before the end of the winter ball season, so he invited Willie to stay at his home. McCovey moved in with the Alous, and, together, they helped Escogido win the Dominican Winter League championship.

Part II

SUPERSTARS

"IN THE NEWS"

Mobile Economy to Get $5,000,000 Boost . . . Eisenhower Gives Award to Mobile Ship. . . . Great Day for Rookie. . . . 50,000 in Loop Greet '60. . . . Slam for Willie Mac! . . . Cubs' Rally Overhauls. . . . Williams Leads Cubs to Victory. . . . Roger Maris's Record 61. . . . Yanks Win Series. . . . Kennedy Had—Wife Cradles His Wounded Head. . . . Sad Story of Willie. . . . Williams, Cubs Whip Braves. . . . Comprehensive Guide to Vietnam. . . . McNamara's Report. . . . Beatles Have Changed. . . . Unity Made by King. . . . Shocked Nation Expresses Grief . . . McCovey Powers National Squad. . . . Billy Stars on His Day; Cubs Take. . . . Compares with Gehrig. . . . The Hippy Fever—View of the Music Festival. . . . Fading Cubs. . . . McCovey MVP in National

Chapter 3

"Smooth as Velvet"

The dizziness spun Billy Williams's vision in circles. Most concerning, the sensation swirling inside of his head was without any external cause. Following his impressive 1957 campaign, the Cubs assigned Williams to the Class A Pueblo Bruins of the Western League. He started the season off decently, but a series of festering physical ailments made his life miserable and forced him out of the lineup. Williams underwent several medical examinations, but, frustratingly, no concrete diagnosis emerged.

The Cubs' general manager, John Holland, asked Williams to travel to Chicago so that he could undergo a battery of tests at Wesley Memorial Hospital. Initially, nothing. As time moved along, however, Williams learned that he may have suffered from intense bouts of vertigo perhaps caused by the high altitude of Pueblo. His health improved noticeably in Chicago, and Holland reassigned Williams to Burlington of the Class B Illinois-Indiana-Iowa League. Williams appeared in 61 games for the Bees and produced an OPS of .879, including 10 homers.

Following his frustrating 1958 season, Williams anticipated picking up where he had left off at the end of his impressive earlier campaign now that he felt healthy. Once again, he put on a deft performance with his bat. This time, it occurred during a three-week camp for the organization's top prospects that took place in Mesa prior to spring training. A new signee joined Williams in the youngsters' camp. He was an energetic teenager from Seattle who hit everything in sight. Following one particular workout, Ron Santo sat down next to Williams as Rogers Hornsby looked over the young Cubs. "Rogers Hornsby was a person who didn't hold back with anything. There were maybe seven guys in the first row. He looked at the first guy and he said, 'You might as well go home. You won't get by A ball.' He went to the next guy, 'Forget A ball. You won't even get to C ball.' And he went right down the line," Santo recalled.

Hornsby's words changed when his eyes landed on Billy even if his demeanor did not. "You will play in the big leagues. And you could play now," he said. And to Ron, "You can hit in the big leagues right now."[1]

Holland assigned Williams and Santo to San Antonio, where they could be challenged by Double A pitching in 1959. Santo started slowly but really got it going after being threatened with a demotion. Williams performed admirably offensively, but the organization played him at first base a considerable amount. They each batted over .300 and smacked home runs that thudded into the scrabbled Texas dirt beyond the outfield fences. Hornsby's responsibilities included scouting the Cubs' minor league outfits. He was so impressed on seeing Williams again that he wired Holland with a clear message: "SUGGEST YOU BRING UP WILLIAMS. BEST HITTER ON THE TEAM." When asked for confirmation that Billy was the best hitter in San Antonio, the impatient Hornsby spat back to Chicago, "He's better than anyone up there!"[2]

Williams displayed his remarkable bat speed through the first half of the season. He worked hard to learn how his body positioning led to effective hitting mechanics. Williams also diligently applied Hornsby's advice: know where the pitch is located in correlation to the strike zone. Putting it all together established a picturesque batting stroke that inspired those in and around the San Antonio ballclub to dub the 21-year-old "Sweet Swinging."

In late June, Williams was batting .309 and leading the Texas League with 53 RBIs. However, despite his successes in the batter's box, Williams constantly dealt with the despicable racism found throughout the Texas League. Rumors of persistent stomach pain and even a "liver ailment" made their way into local reports.[3] He was not the only African American on the San Antonio team as he had been in Ponca City, but, along with roommate J. C. Hartman, he could neither join his white teammates for meals nor share the same hotel accommodations.

They had to live at the crumbling Manhattan Hotel.

Following a mid-June road game in southeastern Texas, Williams and Hartman attempted to get a postgame meal at a spot where Black players could get food, but it was closed at that late hour. They returned to the team hotel empty handed. On arriving, they recognized that several of their white teammates were eating a late dinner. They informed Missions skipper Grady Hatton of their situation, and he spoke with the manager of the hotel restaurant. Rather than allow Billy and J.C., who had served in Europe as a member of the U.S. Army, to eat alongside them, the restaurant said they had to go back into the kitchen. Angry and humiliated, they ate by themselves.

The combination of racist ridicule and a homesickness for Whistler urged Billy to stop playing professional baseball and return to Alabama. "The despicable and inhumane treatment got to the point where I couldn't take it anymore. . . . I told my dad that I would rather get a job back home doing pretty much anything else than to go through the humiliation I was going through in San Antonio," he wrote.[4] Williams asked Hartman to drive him to the train station in the Studebaker they shared. Hartman initially expressed reservations to Williams about his quitting baseball, but he knew that Billy had made up his mind. On June 16, following the team's return to San Antonio, Hartman dropped Billy off at the depot.

The following day, as Billy's train headed east, the Missions arrived at the ballpark and noticed their teammate wasn't there. Hartman informed Hatton that Williams had left the team. The news that the organization's top prospect had quit baseball was quickly relayed to John Holland, who turned to Cubs scout Buck O'Neil for help. O'Neil, who had known the Williams family for several years, was in New Orleans watching Southern University players. He immediately hopped into his Plymouth Fury and headed to Alabama.

Billy arrived home to a variety of reactions. He remembers that Shirley, his girlfriend, was frustrated that he hadn't called to tell her the news before he showed up. His father, Frank, understood his son's reasoning, but Billy suspected that he was a little disappointed. A day later, Billy sat on the front porch of the family's house when a Fury with Missouri plates pulled up. He knew who drove that car: Buck O'Neil. "So when I showed up at his parents' home, I was as friendly as could be. I shook hands all around, making out like it was a social call. I said nothing about Billy jumping the team. We chatted for a while, and then I took them all out to dinner," O'Neil remembered.[5] Williams recalls sharing his frustrations with Buck that evening. "I just don't want to go through the stuff that I have been going through off the field. You know, waiting for the white guys to bring me sandwiches, staying in separate run-down hotels, and things like that."[6] Buck nodded his head affirmatively as he quietly listened.

The next evening, O'Neil joined the family for dinner at their place. After the meal, he asked Billy to join him on a jaunt over to Prichard Park to watch some kids play baseball. The young ballplayers affectionately swarmed Billy as soon as he approached the field. They bombarded him with questions about playing professional ball and what life was like beyond Whistler. An old friend reminded Billy about crushing baseballs through Simon Brown's windows as kids. Their questions and comments got Billy thinking that perhaps he could deal with the obstacles in front of him after all. The wise O'Neil took in the boisterous scene with knowing eyes. He remained quiet the entire time. Billy decided he would return to the team. "If it weren't for Buck O'Neil, my entire life likely would have turned out differently," he admitted.[7]

Years later, O'Neil was having breakfast alongside J. C. Hartman and writer Joe Posnanski, and the story of Buck's visiting Billy in Whistler

came up in the conversation. Hartman asked Buck about his strategy in taking Williams over to Prichard Park. How was he confident that all of the
kids would respond to recognizing Billy in the excited fashion that they
did? Buck replied that he knew that they all truly loved and admired Billy.
The sublime Posnanski perfectly captured O'Neil's reply to Hartman. "'Of
course'—Buck looked around for a second—'of course, a good scout always
checks things out first. I might have gone out there the night before, you
know, just to be sure.'"[8]

Following a little more than a week away from the team, Williams returned
to San Antonio. Marvin Milkes, the club's general manager, threatened to
fine him for missing games. Billy's response? Try me. Milkes immediately
dropped the idea but informed him that the press would be told that the club
had issued a fine. No one was happier to see Williams back in the clubhouse
than Ron Santo, who never prodded his friend about the circumstances surrounding his absence. "To this day, I'm not one hundred percent certain of
the details of Billy's short-lived retirement," Santo admitted in his memoir
published in 1993. "But it didn't take a genius to figure out the scenario: the
pressure of living apart from the rest of the team, the slurs he encountered
from fans, both hometown and visitors. Billy was a proud man, something
I sensed even on that level. . . . Billy came back without an explanation. I
never sought one. I was probably too embarrassed to inquire. Whatever went
through his mind, though, wound up being a Godsend not only for him, considering the mind-boggling numbers he put up during his major league career,
but for the Cub organization."[9]

The *San Antonio Express and News* reported that "severe headaches"
caused Williams's absence and told readers that he had returned to Alabama
for treatment.[10] Williams did not go out of his way to dispute the report's
claim. In 1974, Williams wrote a book with Chicago sportswriter Irv Haag
and blamed stomach pain and homesickness for his leaving San Antonio for
Whistler without specifically mentioning what happened to him at the restaurant.[11] After years of not discussing it publicly, Williams pointedly addressed
this experience during his incredibly powerful 1987 Hall of Fame acceptance
speech.

Williams's bat proved hotter than the weather for the rest of his time with
the Missions. He continued to lead the Texas League in RBIs and earned
praise from the organization for his sustained performance. John Holland told
Bill Furlong of the *Chicago Daily News* in late July that "Rogers Hornsby
says (Santo) and Williams are the two best hitters in the system."[12] On July
30, 1959, Williams got word that his time in San Antonio was through. The
Cubs were sending him to the Triple A Fort Worth Cats. Chicago had called
up Don Eaddy and promoted Billy to backfill him. Despite arriving just a few
hours before first pitch, Williams, who was back in left field, rapped three

hits for his new team in a 13–6 win. He homered, walked, and tripled in his first three at-bats the following night. Billy Williams was back, and he was putting on a show.

* * *

Willie McCovey spent the early summer months of 1959 walloping baseballs in Phoenix. Did the dry heat help the ball carry? Perhaps a bit, but young Stretch was administering punishment on a grand scale that dwarfed the other power hitters in the Pacific Coast League. Before the season ended, he proved to everyone that no form of weather could suppress the blasts generated by his formidable swing. During the second week of July, Bob McCarthy of the *Sacramento Union* beamed as he discussed McCovey's strong impression on him. McCarthy's comments—as presented anyway—dripped with hyperbolic praise. "I know the Giants don't need another first baseman. They've got a good one in Orlando Cepeda. But I've gotta tell you about their guy in Phoenix. His name is Willie McCovey. And you should see him rammy-cackle that ball! He beat Sacramento with a home run the other night. Wotta wallop! I swear the ball would be going yet if it hadn't hit the right field light tower—50 feet up."[13]

Ah, indeed, therein lay the rub. San Francisco Giants manager Bill Rigney found himself in a tricky spot. Following a 4–3 win over the Pittsburgh Pirates on July 18, Rigney's team sat in first place with a 52–38 record and a three-game lead over Los Angeles. Then the team stumbled offensively and lost seven of its next 10 games to fall into second place behind Los Angeles. The Giants scored a total of 13 runs in those seven losses, and Rigney believed his team needed an offensive boost. The organization's immediate answer to that quandary was crushing the ball in Phoenix, but McCovey played first base, the same position as Cepeda, the reigning Rookie of the Year, who was hitting .320 and had just smacked his 21st homer of the season. Rather than force the issue, Rigney deployed his adept interpersonal skills. He asked Cepeda to change positions to make room for his friend. Years later, Cepeda recounted their brief yet poignant conversation. "One morning I came to the ballpark, and Bill Rigney told me, 'Orlando, Willie McCovey's hitting .400. Do you mind if we put him at first base, and we put you at third base?' I said, 'Go ahead, bring him up!'"[14] Cepeda, who played more than 100 games at third in the minor leagues, alleviated the Giants' concern that promoting McCovey would impact the clubhouse's chemistry.

McCovey's torrid hitting in Triple A made a clear point to the Giants' front office that he was ready for the big leagues. Through 95 games, the 21-year-old destroyed much older Pacific Coast League pitching. Of his 130 hits, 66 had gone for extra bases, including 29 homers. He had nothing left to prove at that level, which forced the Giants' hand. Despite his gaudy numbers, McCovey had been in a recent funk at the plate but felt like he was emerging from the slump.[15] The moment arrived on the cusp of the summer's dog days. Following a doubleheader on July 29, Phoenix Giants general manager Rosy Ryan informed McCovey that the Giants wanted him suiting up for the big-league team the following day. Adrenaline-fueled panic shot through McCovey's bloodstream. It wasn't due to the pressure of performing at baseball's highest level but rather what would happen to all of his record albums. "It never did occur to me they'd send it all to me," he admitted.[16] Music aside, McCovey was caught off guard by being told of his call-up and remained up all night. "I was excited and afraid I'd miss the plane in the morning."[17] The moment tapped deeply into the well of Stretch's psyche, and a gnawing thought in the back of his mind began repeating, "Am I good enough?"[18]

Simultaneously, Rigney was working late in his clubhouse office. His team had just been knocked out of first place by the Philadelphia Phillies hours earlier by a score of 3–1. San Francisco now owned a season-high four-game losing streak. An unhappy Rigney pulled no punches about his team's struggles. "Great pitching—we're getting it, but it's not doing us a damn bit of good. What we need are just doubles back to back. If even one guy starts hitting, everyone might get into the act. One live bat can spark a fire," he assessed.[19]

Perhaps Rigney directed his pointed postgame comments at the front office to ensure the promotions of McCovey as well as José Pagán. Rigney fearlessly played rookies. He embraced their youth rather than holding it against them. Cepeda produced a brilliant inaugural campaign in 1958, and why couldn't McCovey repeat the feat over the final two months of the season? After receiving confirmation of the call-ups, Rigney looked up from his desk with a gleam in his eye and summoned the team's teenage batboy, Mike Murphy, who also assisted Eddie Logan with the postgame clubhouse duties. "Hey," Rigney teased. "We're bringing a big Irishman in tomorrow. Wait until you see this guy." Intrigued, Murphy arrived at the ballpark early the next morning and met McCovey, who had caught a 7:00 A.M. flight out of Phoenix to San Francisco but arrived too late to participate in batting practice. The newest Giant proved to be quite literal to the 17-year-old, although he clearly wasn't Irish. "I thought Paul Bunyan had come to life," Murphy wrote years later.[20]

McCovey asked Murphy for jersey number 44 out of his admiration for Henry Aaron, the Atlanta Braves slugger and fellow Mobile product. Murphy, as he would go on to do for more than 60 years, retrieved everything that the latest addition to the team needed to play baseball. The Giants trickled back into the clubhouse and welcomed McCovey to San Francisco. The rookie flashed a big smile that simultaneously revealed his chipped front tooth and expressed his joy at being in the big leagues.

Rigney informed McCovey that he would be starting at first base and hitting in the third spot of the batting order nestled between Willie Mays and Cepeda. Despite the hype, a tranquil McCovey maintained an even keel. He was all set to make his major league debut against the Philadelphia Phillies and their ace pitcher, Robin Roberts, who had posted half a dozen 20-win seasons through his 11 big-league campaigns, but McCovey's spring training experience gave him confidence for this moment. He just needed to keep doing his thing, but first he needed to find some pants because none were in his locker. His bats had not yet arrived in San Francisco either. He borrowed a pair of pants from Andre Rodgers, who just so happened to weigh 30 pounds less than McCovey. Eddie Bressoud loaned him a bat.

The ballgame itself held notable consequences for San Francisco. At 55–45, the Giants stood just a half-game behind first-place Los Angeles. Meanwhile, Philadelphia was not a good team, but the club was currently hot. The Phillies sat in the National League cellar, but they were in the midst of playing their best baseball of the season. The Phillies had won 12 of their past 15 contests, including the first two games against the scuffling Giants. Roberts aimed to garner his club a sweep.

A small crowd of just over 10,000 spectators filed into Seals Stadium, the Giants' home ballpark, that sunny afternoon notably unaware that it would leave the stadium completely enamored with baseball's newest sensation. Among the fans was four-year-old Mike Norris, accompanied by his mother, aunt, and uncle. The family lived in the Fillmore District of San Francisco and enjoyed several annual visits to Seals Stadium. Norris loved the Giants. He imitated all of their batting stances throughout the summer during intense games of "Strike Out" played with his friends between the buildings of the projects in which he lived. Mike and his family sat together in the outfield bleachers, although the studious youngster made it a habit over the years of finding his way to the seats behind home plate to closely inspect Juan Marichal's pitches, especially the screwball. On this particular day—July 30, 1959—Norris witnessed the major league debut of Willie McCovey. "I was four years old," Norris recalled. "We were sitting in the bleachers, and I remember him hitting a line drive. I didn't know who he was or anything, but they were all talking about him—'this is a rookie!'"[21]

McCovey provided everyone in attendance with a host of moments to gasp at during his first game. His first major league at-bat occurred during the bottom of the first inning. The lithe 6-foot-4 lefty batter now carried close to 200 pounds as he dug into the batter's box, about 30 more than when he first signed with the club in 1955. McCovey wasted no time smacking a Robin Roberts curveball into right field. His first big-league hit was a single off a future Hall of Famer. The Giants scored the first run of the game during McCovey's second plate appearance in the bottom of the third inning, but he did not factor into the play. With two outs and Eddie Bressoud at third base, Willie Mays took off to steal second. Phillies catcher Joe Lonnett threw the ball into center field, allowing Bressoud to trot home, but Mays was caught in a rundown to end the inning. McCovey led off the Giants' half of the fourth and lifted a long fly ball into center field that fell in for a triple. He came home on Willie Kirkland's fielder's choice groundball to second to extend San Francisco's lead to 2–0.

McCovey's third plate appearance resulted in a single, but it was his loudest of the day. He struck a Roberts sinker so solidly that it smote the right-field fence with such force that it left behind some damage. Norris, who had about as good a view of that ball as anybody from his bleacher seat, never forgot that particular at-bat. "McCovey hit this unbelievable line drive to right field, and he hit the wall," he recollected. "I remember it was a wooden wall and a piece of wood chipped off the wall, a nice size piece of wood, too. Then the outfielder came and picked up the ball and threw it back to the infield. I remember that vividly."[22] McCovey's long single drove in Mays from second base as the Giants extended their lead. For the finale of his grand debut, Stretch went the opposite way and tripled into the left-center-field gap to again plate Mays and give the Giants a 5–2 lead. They went on to win, 7–2.

McCovey's dazzling 4-for-4 performance put a smile on his face that, according to *Examiner* sports editor Curley Grieve, "could be compared only with the sunrise." McCovey became the fifth player in major league history to collect four hits in his debut. However, he was the first man to do so with multiple extra base hits and more than one RBI.[23] It was a virtuoso performance in four acts. His flabbergasted teammates and coaches could hardly espouse high enough praise for the otherworldly debut that they had witnessed. Pitcher Johnny Antonelli congratulated his newest teammate on the clubhouse chalkboard with a twist. "Nice going, Stretch! The drinks are on you." As photographers snapped pictures of McCovey in front of the proclamation, Antonelli marveled, "Never—never have I seen anything like that." Bill Rigney, who had opined for more offensive thump just one day earlier, let everybody know how he felt. "Four bullets! How about the way he hit that ball," he exclaimed.[24]

As for McCovey, the experience left him shaking his head. "It was the greatest thrill of my life. I've dreamed of being here. But this—what can I say?" When asked if he was familiar with the next day's starting pitcher for the incoming Pittsburgh Pirates, Harvey Haddix, McCovey replied with a hint of nonchalance that blended together his unique mix of humility and confidence, "You bet—that no-hit performance. He don't scare me. When I'm going good. I hit left handers."[25]

What did Willie Mays think after the game? Although McCovey's other teammates are quoted, reports do not include any comments from him, and that is for good reason. Mays was headed to an appearance before Superior Court Judge Edward Molkenbuhr. Along with his wife, Marghuerite, Mays had received approval for the adoption of a baby boy, Michael.[26]

McCovey left the ballpark with teammates Willie Kirkland and Leon Wagner for a celebratory dinner. They noticed a newsstand outside of a restaurant selling the evening edition of the *Call-Bulletin*, which had splashed McCovey's name across in a bold headline. Seeing it in large font on the publication thrilled him. "I think I bought all the papers that were on that stand," he said.[27]

His magical debut drew a crowd so large the following day that the Giants turned away 4,000 would-be ticket buyers. With the ballgame tied, 3–3, in the eighth inning, Pirates lefthander Harvey Haddix struck out Jack Sanford and Jackie Brandt before walking Willie Mays ("I wasn't going to give that guy anything to hit," Haddix remarked afterward.[28]) Next up: McCovey, hitless in three trips to the plate against the southpaw, who had taken a perfect game into the 13th inning just five weeks prior. Rigney sprung out of the dugout to catch the long-striding McCovey before he reached the batter's box. The skipper quietly informed him that Mays would attempt to steal second base, which meant that a single would score him.

Haddix started McCovey's at-bat by throwing a fastball that hit the inside corner for a strike. Mays broke for second as Haddix delivered his second pitch off the outside corner. Catcher Danny Kravitz's throw sailed wide, and Mays slid in safely. McCovey promptly brought the capacity crowd of 22,871 fans to its feet when he pulled Haddix's next offering fair down the right-field line. Mays scored easily as Roberto Clemente fired a perfect strike to second base to nab McCovey, who tried to stretch his base hit into a double. Sanford retired the Pirates in order in the ninth, and the Giants won the game, 4–3.

"How about that guy! Two days in a row," Rigney trumpeted in the clubhouse afterward.[29]

This is where the movie montage really picks up steam. McCovey ripped two doubles among three hits the following day, a 9–5 Giants win. He belted his first big-league homer, a two-run blast into the right-field stands, to help San Francisco complete a three-game sweep of Pittsburgh and remain in first place a half game in front of Los Angeles. Cue the shot of Pirates manager Danny Murtaugh shaking his head in the clubhouse after the game remarking to reporters, "If anybody had told me that a rookie farmhand would beat me three games in a row I would have put him on a psychiatrist's couch."[30] How was McCovey making it look so easy this quickly? It wasn't just that the pitchers did not have a book on him yet, Rigney believed. The youngster's combination of talent and baseball IQ enabled him to hit the ground running.

"He stands close to the plate. He knows the strike zone at all times. He takes on a short stride. His swing is as smooth as velvet. His power is in the perfect coordination of unusual muscular strength. The rhythm of the swing gives it a touch of beauty," Rigney explained.[31] He went on to add admiringly, "McCovey's hands travel with lightning speed, like a righthand punch thrown by Marciano."[32]

Willie Mays immediately identified Bill White's influence on McCovey and pictured a young Larry Doby when he watched the lefty swing the bat. "He's a wrist hitter. He don't stride much. If you don't stride you gotta be a wrist hitter," noted Mays.[33]

Unsurprisingly, at least as far as these things go in terms of the fallibility of human nature, irritation at the effusive praise McCovey garnered a week into his career earned him sarcastic derision from other corners of the National League. Phillies star Richie Ashburn sounded more than a little annoyed after McCovey's debut. "Four line drives—he looks like the world's greatest hitter. He must be a helluva hitter to push Cepeda off first base," he quipped.[34] One Pittsburgh writer was overheard chirping in the press box after McCovey delivered the game-winning RBI hit in the series opener, "What are you going to do—send him to Cooperstown right now or wait until the end of the season?"[35] Cincinnati Reds catcher Ed Bailey, who would go on to finish the year with fewer home runs than McCovey despite playing in 69 more games, argued, "He's not the great hitter they're painting him to be."[36]

The defending National League champion Milwaukee Braves followed Pittsburgh into Seals Stadium. The Giants took two out of three games to remain in first place as McCovey collected five hits, including the first multihomer game of his career. Following the series, Braves manager Fred Haney heaped praise on McCovey: "That's what makes baseball a great game— some rookie popping up and blazing a trail. He has stirred the imagination of fans east and west."[37]

The confidence of the Giants organization in the team's ability to win the pennant soared. After winning six of seven games following McCovey's insertion into the lineup, San Francisco's record of 61–46 put them one game clear of the Dodgers atop the National League standings. With visions of the fall classic in its head, *Examiner* columnist Dick Nolan reported that the franchise felt confident enough in their first-place position that they commissioned a New York company to produce a mock-up World Series program for $5,000.[38]

McCovey's arrival did present one significant downside for the organization: it moved Orlando Cepeda off his customary first base position across the diamond to third. The spirited competition between Cepeda and McCovey recalled the moment they signed with the Giants, but it always remained compartmentalized on the field—two incredibly talented kids fiercely determined to make it in the big leagues. Both youngsters genuinely liked and respected one another. They just happened to play the same position. Their bond, initially forged at the tryout camp in Melbourne, Florida, in 1955, remained completely unharmed by Cepeda's desire to continue playing first base. He knew that having his friend on the team would improve its offense. "I was playing third base and left field because I knew the way he could swing the bat," Cepeda explained. "Willie never said anything bad. He was very smart. Even though we competed he was still a great friend."[39]

Despite embracing the arrival of McCovey the person, Cepeda quickly soured on his new defensive role. Cepeda had earned the right to be frustrated. The 21-year-old was the reigning Rookie of the Year and a National League All-Star in 1959. Cepeda's success mocked the idea of a sophomore slump, and he was beloved in the city of San Francisco. However, Cepeda's struggles in four games at the hot corner, punctuated by a wild throw that flew over McCovey's head and hit a fan in the stands, left him deeply frustrated. He had been willing to change positions for the team but not embarrass himself. That was a different type of sacrifice altogether and one that wouldn't help the ball club win games. Cepeda admitted to reporters, "I don't like it, but I have to play it. I'll give it 100 percent."[40] Without question, Cepeda was a superior athlete to McCovey, but the infield position change fit like a small glove on a large hand. "A noble experiment," Cepeda called it years later, "that clearly didn't work."[41]

Despite the wobbly defensive arrangement, Bill Rigney piloted the ship forward, hoping that the swelling seas surrounding the situation would calm down. McCovey continued to produce a cavalcade of base hits, and his magisterial home runs took fans' breath away while threatening the cars parked beyond right field along 16th Street. Mike Norris, the young San Franciscan who attended McCovey's debut and was a future big-leaguer himself, marveled, "McCovey would hit it out to right field. It would bounce one time, and then go into the parking lot."[42] On August 28, McCovey played against the Los Angeles Dodgers for the first time on a cool evening in front of more than 66,000 fans at the Los Angeles Memorial Coliseum. After Jackie Brandt struck out to lead off the game, Willie Mays doubled and went to third base on an error by center fielder Duke Snider. That brought McCovey to the plate for his inaugural clash with the hard-throwing right-hander, Don Drysdale, an All-Star who was in the midst of a marvelous season during which he led the National League in shutouts and strikeouts. Drysdale bore a pitch in on Mac's hands, but the rookie fought it off and dropped a double down the left-field line to score Mays. "He got the ball in on me real tight. I was late getting around on it. It was a good pitch," McCovey said after the game.[43] Good pitch, bad pitch, inside pitch, outside pitch: regardless of the pitch, it was the first of many thrown by Don Drysdale over the course of the next

11 seasons that Willie McCovey smacked around the yard. McCovey didn't face Drysdale a second time in this ballgame because Mays's three-run blast in the second inning chased the Dodger hurler en route to a 5–0 San Francisco victory. Newspaper writers outdueled one another to tab McCovey with a nickname that conveyed his incredible start, including the "Phoenix Phenom," "Mister Too-Good-To-Believe," the "Story-Book Swinger," and, of course, "Stretch."

In 1959, the United States admitted Alaska and Hawaii to form a 50-state union, and the National League added McCovey, who, when all was said and done, retired as its career leader in home runs by a left-handed hitter.

* * *

Willie McCovey, smartly dressed in a light-colored polo and dark slacks, flashed his thousand-watt smile while relaxing on a bed as he held a newspaper detailing his exploits on the baseball diamond in his room at the Booker T. Washington Hotel as the photographer snapped away. The *San Francisco Examiner* included the image in a trilogy of stories it ran following the rookie's debut week. The "Booker T.," as the hotel was known, played an integral role in African American culture within the city's Fillmore District, also known as the "Harlem of the West," and Mac spent the remainder of his rookie season immersed in it. The building itself had undergone a transformation from the Edison Hotel and opened its remodeled doors in 1951. The hotel, highlighted by its famous Emperor Cocktail Lounge, hosted a great many Black celebrities over its first decade of operation, especially musicians. Duke Ellington, Nat King Cole, and Dinah Washington could be counted among its guests. James Brown, Little Richard, and McCovey added their names to that distinguished list as the decade continued. Sadie Williams managed the hotel, and Vivian Baxter worked there as a desk clerk. They developed a close friendship. Jaqueline Chauhan, Williams's daughter, spent numerous hours of her youth there. "The hotel had six floors and 125 rooms, with suites in the front of the top floor," Chauhan reminisced. "There were free radios in every room and television sets in each suite. Chartreuse drapes laced the windows and maroon carpets embellished with silver scrollwork covered the floors. Mirrors decorated in peach and silver lined the serving counter." Meanwhile, Baxter's daughter, Maya Angelou, who was known throughout San Francisco as a calypso musician and dancer, in addition to having quite possibly been the city's first Black female streetcar conductor, had recently moved to New York in pursuit of developing her writing career.[44]

McCovey's first week in San Francisco could not have gone much better. He loved being in the heart of the city. He could frequently be found at the movie theater watching several films per day. Additionally, he was enveloped by music and soul food prepared by chef Sam Mines at the Booker T. Through a combination of events, Willie connected with two people who impacted his life forever: Ruth Stovall, a local seamstress and real estate expert who treated him like a son, and Hal Silen, a young attorney who had recently opened up a law practice with Bill Bernstein on Market Street.

McCovey visited Silen and Bernstein, and they quickly reached an agreement by which the Giants would send Stretch's paychecks to them, and they, in turn, took care of his finances. At first, Bernstein, who had focused primarily on criminal law, handled McCovey as a client, but that dynamic imploded after the lawyer ill-advisedly gave out the young ballplayer's phone number. Bernstein's action angered McCovey, who viewed it as a break in their trust. Silen, whose early law practice included some contract work, immediately stepped in and salvaged the relationship, one that the two men maintained for the rest of McCovey's life.

* * *

Boosted by their rookie phenom, the Giants tenuously maintained their grip on first place, but the competitive Chicago Cubs had defeated the Milwaukee Braves, 5–4, on July 28 to climb within 4 1/2 games of the National League lead. Then the bottom fell out. Chicago dropped its next seven games and fell 9 1/2 games behind the Giants. The handwriting was on the wall. The 1959 National League pennant race would be decided by the Giants, Dodgers, and Braves unless the Cubs could mount a substantial rally. Cubs general manager John Holland sought a spark for his sputtering ball club. He hoped that the solution was playing in Fort Worth, Texas. How would that sweet swing of the organization's top prospect play in the major leagues? Only one way to find out. On August 5, Holland placed a call to Fort Worth to speak with Billy Williams, who in his five games for the Cats had rapped out 10 hits in 21 at-bats, including four doubles, a triple, and a home run.

"You've had quite a year, Billy. How'd you like to finish up here?" Holland inquired.[45]

Taken by surprise, Williams found himself in the midst of a remarkable unfolding of events. He was headed to the big leagues several weeks after temporarily quitting baseball. After landing in Chicago, Williams called his father and told him the exciting news. An ecstatic Frank told everyone in Whistler that the Williams family now boasted a big-league ballplayer, although he may not have specified which son had gotten the call in his enthusiasm. "You know how proud your father is. You got a son playing major league baseball," Billy says. "He would go around and he would broadcast it, 'I got a son playing major league baseball now!' But everyone thought it was my brother, Franklin, because he was a better ballplayer, but I just got the opportunity."[46]

In the midst of his own excitement at becoming a member of the Cubs, Williams candidly wondered in his autobiography at the organization's motivation for promoting at that particular moment in time. "I don't know if they moved me through the system so quickly to make me feel good, or because I was swinging the bat so well. But you normally don't get a reward like that."[47]

On the morning of August 6, 1959, Williams left the Sheridan Plaza Hotel and made his way to Wrigley Field. He had been to Chicago previously to receive treatment for his bout with vertigo, but this time he was there as a Cub. Veteran clubhouse manager Yosh Kawano greeted Williams shortly after the latter's arrival at the ballpark. Kawano, unique for his ubiquitous fishing hat, had been working for the Cubs longer than Williams had been alive. He began his tenure as a 13-year-old batboy for the team during spring training in 1935. At 22, Kawano was named visiting clubhouse attendant, a role he served in faithfully before entering the U.S. Army. He earned a pair of medals for his service in New Guinea and the Philippines before returning to the Cubs. The organization tabbed Kawano the new equipment manager in 1953, a job he held for more than 40 years.[48]

After aiding so many players, it was now Billy Williams's turn to receive Kawano's assistance. Kawano handed him a jersey with the number 4 embroidered on it.[49] Cubs manager Bill Schelling wasted no time and penciled him into the lineup to face the Philadelphia Phillies that afternoon. Schelling slotted Williams in the third spot in the lineup between first baseman Jim Marshall and shortstop Ernie Banks, the reigning National League MVP. Williams would play left field, although, curiously, nobody made it a point to apprise him of the notorious winds of Wrigley Field.[50]

Although Williams recognized a few of his new teammates from spring training, he felt a little "strange," and he cast glances at his new teammates to observe how they conducted themselves. Of course, Billy recognized and greeted his friends, Banks and Tony Taylor, whom he had gone out to dinner with numerous times back in Arizona. "After a while, all the veteran ballplayers came up and said, 'Glad you're here,' 'Welcome to the Cubs,' and things like that."[51]

Any sense of a genial mood surrounding Williams's debut for the ball club abruptly vanished during a pregame mishap. The shabby netting attached to the Cubs' cage used for batting practice had a large hole in it. Philadelphia catcher Joe Lonnett struck a ball while taking his pregame hacks that flew through the netting's ripped window and drilled an unsuspecting Banks directly in the stomach as he was playing catch. Banks, who had struck his team-leading 30th homer of the season the day before, crumpled to the field with a thud. He lay on the ground for several minutes doubled over in pain and restarting his breath.[52] It was a scary scene, but there he was, trotting out to shortstop, as Williams ran out to left field in the top of the first inning. Naturally, as is wont to happen in baseball, Philadelphia leadoff hitter Joe Koppe began the game by hitting a groundball to short. Banks threw him out without incident. The next batter, Richie Ashburn, lifted a fly ball in the direction of the new kid. Williams caught it for the second out. Cubs hurler Art Ceccarelli then struck out Ed Bouchee. No runs, no hits, no errors in the top of the first.

The Cubs' offense got right to work against Phillies starter, Jim Owens. Taylor led off the bottom of the first inning with a single that was followed by Jim Marshall's base hit to center field that put runners on the corners with nobody out. Billy Williams strode to the plate focused on putting the ball in play. Owens, meanwhile, wanted to strike him out to keep the possibility of an inning-ending double play in order. The 25-year-old right-hander delivered, and Williams ignited his swing. The bat struck the ball, and it bounced down the first-base line. Taylor raced home from third as the Phillies first baseman, Ed Bouchee, charged the chopper, fielded it, and tagged out Williams, who was running up the line.[53] In his first major league plate appearance, Williams executed a situational at-bat perfectly by driving in a run from third base with fewer than two outs to give the Cubs a 1–0 lead. Phillies pitching prevented him from collecting his first major league hit during his debut, but Chicago put together a two-run rally in the bottom of the eighth inning to win the game, 4–2, and snap its seven-game losing streak. Williams's debut was a winner.

Schelling put Williams right back into the lineup the following day against Pittsburgh, and even though the rookie left fielder went hitless in four trips to the plate, Moe Drabowsky tossed a complete-game shutout as the Cubs won their second straight game, 4–0. Billy collected his second RBI the following day on a groundout, but Chicago lost, 4–3. On Sunday, August 9, the Pirates and Cubs finished their three-game series, and Williams smacked the first two base hits of his major league career. He pulled a ball through the right side in the bottom of the third inning off Pittsburgh's Vern Law and added an opposite-field knock in the bottom of the 10th. The Cubs lost the game, 5–3, but Billy now owned a big-league batting average.

Chicago's latest defeat sunk them into fifth place in the National League standings, 10 1/2 games behind the streaking Giants. After starting Williams for the first four games of his major league career, Schelling decided to utilize him off the bench. Billy started only three of Chicago's final 46 games, although he did appear in 11 other contests, primarily as a pinch hitter. One special highlight occurred on August 19 during the second game of a doubleheader at Connie Mack Stadium in Philadelphia. Williams reached base three times, including the first extra-base hit of his career, a smashed triple into right field. At the moment, the game made some news because Bobby Thomson, most famous for homering off Ralph Branca to clinch the 1951 National League pennant for the Giants, collected the 1,000th RBI of his career. Thomson, now a Cub, launched a two-run homer in the sixth inning, but none of it was enough because the Phillies scored a run in the bottom of the 12th inning to tie the game, 7–7. Rules stipulated that a new inning could not begin after 12:50 A.M., so the statistics counted, but the game did not. It was completely replayed from the first inning onward the following day. Momentary reprieve or not, the Cubs went an uninspiring 17–20 down the stretch and finished the 1959 season with a record of 74–80 (and one!), well off the pace of the National League pennant–winning Dodgers.

The seven and a half weeks that Williams spent in Chicago proved to be a unique challenge for a young player accustomed to playing every day, but a friend from his father's past kept him encouraged. Born in Whistler, Bill Robinson, an infielder, primarily played third base. Around the age of 10, he developed a friendship with an older local kid, Frank Williams. They spent a lot of time together, especially on the baseball field, as Robinson played on the left side of the infield with Williams at first base. When he reached the age of 21, Robinson started playing semipro ball and then earned an opportunity to join the Indianapolis ABCs in 1925, which was the beginning of his 17-year career in the Negro Leagues. He played for teams throughout the country, including the Chicago American Giants and the Birmingham Black Barons. Robinson set down roots in Chicago with his wife, Bernice, after his baseball career ended and worked as a brick mason.

In 1959, the Robinsons made it a point to open their door for their old friend's son. "When I came to Chicago he made me feel at home. He welcomed me," Williams reminisces. "First year I came up here I didn't hit, maybe pinch hit every now and then, but I didn't play. After the game he would be out there waiting on me, so he would take me to the house. His wife would cook a big meal, and we would sit there and have dinner. He would talk about old times that my father and he had growing up in Whistler. So, it was a good time in my life."[54]

Williams faced his longtime friend from Mobile, Henry Aaron, and the Milwaukee Braves several times that season. Following one of the games, Williams noticed Aaron walking with his back to him from a reasonable distance away. Fans called out to him, "Hank! Hank!" He kept moving. "Henry!" Hearing his name hollered at him prompted Aaron to turn around because that is what everyone back home called him. Henry recognized Billy, and the two friends warmly greeted each other.[55]

At season's end, Billy's numbers with the Cubs may not have looked like much on paper (5-for-33 with a triple and two RBIs), but they belied his incredible internal strength of character that allowed him to stick with baseball and reach the big-league club. For months, Billy set aside the cruel effects of racism and tore up quality minor league pitching. He hit .327 and slugged at a .518 clip while striking out only 39 times in 433 plate appearances across two levels. Williams's sublime work in the batter's box portended big things for his baseball career. He had, after all, been only 21 years old for a little over three months when the season ended on September 27.

* * *

The Giants stumbled something fierce in September and gagged away the pennant by losing 11 of their last 16 games. It was their only losing month all year, but it gave the Dodgers just enough room to find a lane and slip by them. While the disappointing finish soured perspective of the season, Willie McCovey's rookie campaign provided thrills for two months straight. His numbers were ridiculous. He smashed 13 homers and drove in 38 runs in only 52 games. Although the small sample size deserves scrutiny, contextualizing McCovey's 1.085 OPS puts his season in some perspective. That mark would have led the National League. Ernie Banks, for example, who won his second consecutive MVP Award in 1959, posted a .970 OPS. It all added up to an extraordinary inaugural campaign for McCovey.

By the way, now that the season is over, if you want a new ride, head on over to the Ellis Brooks Agency and ask for Stretch—he was now a newly minted car salesman. He won't pressure you to buy anything, promise. "It takes time to make a sale," McCovey pointed out.[56]

On November 17, the car dealership's phone rang. The caller asked to speak with McCovey. The representative of the Baseball Writers' Association of America informed him that he had been named the National League's Rookie of the Year by a unanimous vote despite the good inaugural campaign turned in by Maury Wills of the Dodgers. The Giants' lineup now boasted consecutive Rookie of the Year winners (both unanimous) in Cepeda and McCovey.

McCovey was thrilled with the news and talk quickly turned to the damage he would do at the plate inside Candlestick Park, the Giants' new ballpark set to open in 1960. Bill Rigney anticipated 30 homers from his first baseman. McCovey, too, looked forward to next year but for a different reason. He hoped to play without having to wear a brace on his right knee, so his offseason workouts already focused on strengthening his leg. "The doctor tells me I don't need treatments. It's just a question of building up a weak muscle. I'm lifting foot weights to strengthen it," he detailed.[57]

McCovey's tremendous 1959 season gave the Giants an opportunity to compete for the pennant, emblazed his name on the hearts of fans throughout the city, and earned him national acclaim. An extraordinary future seemed inevitable. However, knee pain, inconsistent playing time, and a dearth of power frustratingly derailed 1960 for McCovey like a skipping needle on a vinyl record. That said, he produced a highlight on June 12 against Milwaukee: an impressive grand slam home run, the first of his career, as the Giants routed the Braves, 16–7, at Candlestick Park. That swing of the bat earned Mac widespread praise from everyone who watched the ball disappear into the Bay Area afternoon. Even venerable umpire Al Barlick, a future Hall of Fame arbiter notorious for his impartiality, couldn't hide his admiration for McCovey's stirring homer. "If that ball had gone as far out as it did up, it would still be going," Barlick said admiringly.[58] Alas, it proved to be an exception rather than the rule for Mac that season, and it left him aggravated. "I don't know why I had so poor a year," McCovey divulged a decade later. "The main thing is I had too good a first year."[59]

Chapter 4

Charlie's Lament

Willie McCovey immediately fell in love with the city of San Francisco when he arrived at the end of July 1959. He enjoyed the bustle of the city, ample opportunities to indulge in watching films, and the cosmopolitan demographics of the people. He spent time with his teammates, Leon Wagner, whom Mac played with in Danville, and Willie Kirkland. They shared meals together and could be spotted taking in live music around town. With the season ended and a spot on the Giants' roster all but ensured in 1960, he turned his attention toward finding a longer-term living situation as much as he loved staying at the Booker T. Washington Hotel.

Throughout his life in the Bay Area, McCovey surrounded himself with caring people who looked out for his best interests, and it started with Ruth Stovall and Hal Silen. Stovall took to young McCovey as though he were her own son. She invited him over to her home for meals and conversations. Where he ought to live served as a primary topic, and her experience included time working in real estate, which put an expert in his corner right away. San Francisco in 1960 was not Mobile, but it wasn't a place where McCovey would be welcome to live wherever he wanted. Just three years prior, neighborhood resistance on the west side of the city made purchasing a home by Willie Mays a public issue because its white members did not want a Black family living among them. Fully aware of that situation, Stovall helped McCovey navigate the discriminatory dynamics of the real estate market.

Silen counseled McCovey on financial matters, beginning with the establishment of a budget. For the time being, Silen received McCovey's paychecks from the Giants directly and paid his bills. McCovey continued to sell cars for Ellis Brooks over the winter. He took out newspaper advertisements inviting local buyers interested in purchasing a 1960 Chevrolet Corvair to personally visit him at the corner of California and Van Ness. In the end, he sold only five cars (four if you subtract the one Stretch bought for himself).[1] McCovey also made the rounds alongside several of his teammates at local winter banquets and fundraisers.

McCovey reported to camp in mid-February. Although he put on a show in batting practice, including launching one ball over the Municipal Stadium scoreboard, McCovey struggled at the plate for notable periods during the spring and even got benched at one point by manager Bill Rigney. He snapped out of his funk at the plate by hitting his first home run of the spring against the St. Louis Cardinals in the Giants' 21st game. He cracked another one the next day.

The now 21-year-old was noticeably larger. He started the Triple A season in 1959 around 185 pounds and had been exhorted by Rosy Ryan, former National League pitcher and current Phoenix general manager, to put on more weight. "We found out at 185 pounds he was just not strong enough," Ryan explained to reporters as Stretch took batting practice. "He was doing all his punching to left and left center. When he got that added strength with additional weight, he got the bat around faster and started pulling the ball to right." McCovey's slow start to the spring left Ryan unfazed. He had seen it the previous year. However, McCovey had put on too much weight over the winter. He tipped the Arizona scales at 225 pounds when he reported. Giants hitting instructor Lefty O'Doul did not get the chance to work with McCovey a lot that spring, but he noticed that McCovey "hunched over the plate to far," but he wasn't worried on a macrolevel.[2] Meanwhile, McCovey's quest to shed 15 pounds by Opening Day commenced but it didn't help enough in the end. Nagging injuries plagued his knees and ankles to the point where he required "special shoes" to mitigate his pain.[3] Following a disappointing campaign, McCovey blamed his physical condition for his underwhelming season. "I wasn't underplayed," he lamented. "I was overweight!"[4]

* * *

Billy Williams's eventful offseason culminated in his marriage to Shirley, but his relationship with the Cubs wasn't proceeding quite as smoothly. Despite putting up outstanding numbers in the minors, he hadn't been able to establish any kind of rhythm for the big-league club in his limited playing time. The Cubs frowned on Williams's request for a salary bump, and he was told that some inside the organization did not view him as a sure-fire major league prospect. "I was upset and down on myself. I was trying to prepare for my future, and it didn't look like baseball was going to be it," he said.[5]

Billy sought out Henry Aaron for advice. Aaron was still only 25 years old, but he had just completed his sixth season with the Milwaukee Braves.

Aaron understood that Billy thought he had earned a spot in Chicago, but he cautioned that the Cubs might be working on a plan that would ensure Williams played every day so he wouldn't have to endure another sporadic stint with the club. They bonded over the challenges being a young player presented and the anxieties they could cause. Williams, in particular, tensed up as a result of wanting so badly to succeed.

The conversation buoyed his spirit, and talks with the Cubs started to improve as well. Williams expressed his interest in opening the season with the team's Triple A affiliate in Houston. Playing time lay at the heart of the dilemma. While Williams would be in the lineup every day in the American Association, the Cubs' outfield featured the veteran trio of Frank Thomas, Richie Ashburn, and Bob Will, which left little room for a rookie. For the good of his development, Williams agreed to return to the minor leagues, where he again linked up with familiar teammates: Lou Johnson and Ron Santo. The organization responded amiably by offering him a contract that paid $6,500. On March 28, the Cubs assigned Williams to Houston as part of the team's second-to-last cut of the spring.

The Cubs lost their season opener, 3–2. That contest predicted the future of the team's remaining games. Manager Charlie Grimm was fired after a 6–11 start. Lou Boudreau left the broadcast booth and took over as the team's skipper. Boudreau's installment opened the door for younger players to ply their craft. The Cubs called up Santo, Dick Ellsworth, and Jerry Kendall amongst a bevy of other personnel moves under Boudreau. However, none of general manager John Holland's changes altered the team's losing ways. The team ended July with a 27–39 record.

Writers covering the Cubs started to question their lack of impact prospects. One particularly underwhelmed scribe compared the system's holdings to a patch of weeds. Boudreau expressed disagreement. He had received "good reports" on several outfielders, including Billy Williams.[6] Indeed, Williams was in the midst of producing a sensational season down in Houston amidst the mosquitoes the size of small birds. He slashed .324/.390/.560, and his 26 homers helped the Buffs finish second in the American Association in long balls to the Denver Bears, who enjoyed the advantage of swatting baseballs into the thin Rocky Mountain air. On September 6, the stumbling Cubs called up a dozen prospects, including Williams. He never played a minor league game again.

Williams showed what he could do in the final series of the 1960 season against the Dodgers at the Los Angeles Memorial Coliseum. In three games against Los Angeles, he reached base eight times in 16 plate appearances and drove in six runs as the Cubs took two of the games. Batting in the third spot, Williams delivered three extra-base hits and a keen eye in drawing four walks. In the second game of the series, Williams launched the first homer of his career, a two-run shot in the top of the ninth inning that gave the Cubs an 8–5 lead. They eventually won the game, 10–8, in 14 innings. He followed it up with another blast in the season finale, a solo shot in the top of the first inning. Williams finished the 1960 season with 13 hits in 47 at-bats for the Cubs.

* * *

While Billy Williams steadily worked his way through the hurdles of being a young player on his way to success, Willie McCovey experienced a brutal 1960 season that dimmed the brightness of his instant stardom. The Giants opened the season against the St. Louis Cardinals, who drew the assignment of playing visitor for the christening of Candlestick Park on April 12. The teams worked out in the afternoon prior to Opening Day, and it did not take Cardinals superstar Stan Musial long to recognize that the fans in San Francisco better not get their hopes up to see home runs considering the brutal wind conditions. "They are not feasible in this park—at least not many of them," he said.[7] Despite the presence of Willie Mays, Orlando Cepeda, and McCovey, Musial suggested that the organization bring in the fences. A game hadn't even been played in it yet.

The inaugural game at Candlestick Park brought out a number of dignitaries, including Vice President Richard Nixon. Accompanied by San Francisco mayor George Christopher, Nixon, a former two-time congressman from California, made his way down to the field to greet the players. He exchanged pleasantries with Mays and a few other Giants before encountering McCovey. "They said you had too much weight on you. What happened?" cried Nixon.

McCovey's eyes dropped. "They got it off me, Mr. Nixon."[8]

Stretch doubled in three plate appearances, and the Giants won, 3–1, in the first game at the 'Stick, but it's hard not to think about how the youngster felt after hearing about the criticism pointed at him by some in the organization from the vice president of the United States. His confidence took a few more hits during the season's first week. Although the Giants started 5–2, McCovey went 1-for-20 at the plate over the next six games, although his one hit was a three-run homer against Chicago. His struggles extended to the field. He missed two catchable foul popups in the April 20 game against the Dodgers that incurred restlessness from the crowd and a sharp rebuke from Bill Rigney, who believed in his young player but wouldn't tolerate these mistakes. "I told him to wake up—be more alert," he said. McCovey admitted he needed to start wearing sunglasses in the field.[9] The phone call he had received at the car dealership informing him of his unanimous selection as Rookie of the Year felt like a lifetime ago. Despite the challenges he faced at work, McCovey celebrated good news off the field. He was newly engaged.[10]

A momentary cure for McCovey's ailment at the plate arrived in the form of Dodgers pitcher Don Drysdale on the last day of April. It was Ladies' Night at the Los Angeles Memorial Coliseum, and more than 20,000 women participated in the promotion, which brought attendance that evening to a staggering 85,065. Mac opened the scoring with a solo shot off Drysdale in the second inning. In the fifth, Mays doubled, and McCovey followed with a blast that cleared the right-field wall by a considerable margin, giving San Francisco a 5–0 lead that sent Drysdale to the showers. "It was the hardest hit ball I've ever seen. Counting the roll, it must have traveled 600 feet," Rigney marveled. "Drysdale can be thankful it wasn't a little lower. Had he been in the way of it it might have torn a hole right through him." Despite his early season struggles, Mac's multi-homer game gave him the National League lead with seven round-trippers and 21 RBIs, and his manager guffawed at the early season calls for him to bench Stretch. The best way for McCovey to get on track involved playing every day. "Benching him, as some people wanted me to do, would have been the biggest mistake I ever made," Rigney said.[11]

By mid-July, however, the organization's mood had shifted. The team's winning ways skidded to a halt, and McCovey's inconsistency gave the Giants pause. Perhaps he needed more experience in the minor leagues to regain his stroke from the previous season. The truth is that McCovey couldn't meet the unrealistic expectations he had created for himself in 1959. He knew better than anyone that he wasn't going to hit .350 like Ted Williams, but those expectations haunted him like indefatigable specters. On June 18, a frustrated Horace Stoneham fired Rigney after the Giants were swept at home by the division-leading Pittsburgh Pirates. Rampant rumors hinted at a reunion with Leo Durocher, but Stoneham instead made the stunning choice of turning to Tom Sheehan, the head scout for the ballclub, who also happened to be the owner's friend. McCovey's embarrassment deepened after he drew unwanted headlines two weeks later when Sheehan caught several players breaking curfew in the lobby of the Warwick Hotel in Philadelphia. "Big Tom refused to disclose the names of the transgressors, but it was believed Willie McCovey, who is on borrowed time in the big leagues, anyway, was one of them," alleged the *Examiner* beat writer, Walter Judge. His newspaper plastered McCovey's picture next to the story.[12] To make matters worse, Stoneham, who rarely spoke to the press, made it a point to publicly support his manager in the matter. "McCovey will have to play his way back on the club," he said.[13]

On July 17, the Giants decided to send the scuffling McCovey down to their Triple A affiliate in Tacoma. He had homered just twice and had driven in only nine runs in San Francisco's last 40 games. In a season of very public frustrations, being demoted may very well have been its most disappointing event, compounded by the fact that he learned of his demotion from a reporter. McCovey concealed his feelings and flatly refused to complain about it to his teammates.[14] The story dominated the Bay Area's sports pages and gave writers the opportunity to take the organization to task for failing to meet expectations. Notable local baseball writer Curley Grieve slammed the Giants' lack of cultivation skills as they pertained to McCovey. "He was like a Boy Scout lost in the woods without a compass. Instead of a severe critic, he needed a chaperon and taskmaster. He needed help at the outset and didn't get it. So he lost confidence in himself and departed from the center ring with spirit broken," argued Grieve.[15] The Giants replaced the newly departed McCovey with one of his former Escogido teammates, Juan Marichal, who threw a complete-game one-hit shutout against the Phillies the following day in his major league debut. He struck out 12.

The Giants recalled McCovey at the beginning of August. It was either that or leave him in the Pacific Coast League, per rules, so it was back to San Francisco. A few days later, he contributed a timely pinch-hit two-run opposite-field triple to help the Giants erase a 7–1 deficit and beat the Phillies, 8–7. Despite that knock, McCovey essentially pinch-hit the rest of the season. Just like Williams in 1959 and 1960, Stretch wasn't viewed by the brass as a reliable everyday player. This was going to hurt him financially, and it was already challenging at times to make ends meet living in a city as expensive as San Francisco. "I let you play in the greatest city in the world. What more do you want?" Chub Feeney teased McCovey one day. "I'd like to be able to afford to stay here," Willie responded. One day, McCovey made the mistake of calling Chub by his first name. "Mr. Feeney to you, kid," was the response. On August 11, with the Giants trailing the Dodgers, 3–2, in the bottom of the sixth inning, Sheehan called on Stretch to pinch-hit with two men aboard against Don Drysdale. McCovey's 15th home run of the season landed three-quarters up the right-field bleachers. In the clubhouse after the Giants win, McCovey politely greeted the Giants' executive. "He came over to me in the clubhouse and I said, 'Hello, Mr. Feeney,' and he said, 'You can call me Chub.'"[16]

Despite that bright spot, the end of the regular season couldn't come fast enough. At least McCovey could look forward to working an offseason job more to his liking than moving cars. He agreed to sell threads at the Rochester Clothing Company, but first the Giants traveled to Japan for a special tour of games throughout the country. Reborn, McCovey crushed the baseball. He hit .423 and cracked eight homers in 16 games. He returned to the States loaded down with electronics. Locals gave him a transistor radio for each dinger he hit.[17] He thoroughly enjoyed the sojourn to Japan, and he successfully played himself right off the trade block.

The Giants finished the 1960 season in fifth place with a 79–75 record, a far cry from the preseason expectations for the team, and now the postmortem dissection of the club's failure began intensely. Perhaps the most explosive article exploring the Giants' disappointing campaign was written by a former World War II Marine Corps pilot turned scribe, Roy Terrell, who penned a brutal piece for *Sports Illustrated* in which he obliterated the organization. He started by ripping Horace Stoneham for hiring Tom Sheehan instead of Leo Durocher. Terrell continued by heavily criticizing Giants players, who "have never been a team—only a group of individuals, overpaid, over-publicized, overrated." While pointing his finger at these problems, Terrell vehemently pushed back against the most stunning suggestion he heard for the Giants' struggles in 1960: the racial composition of the team's roster. "In private, when this self-imposed censorship is relaxed, there are several dozen players, coaches, managers, writers and executives who will tell you what is really wrong with the Giants: too many Negroes." No one went on the record with this opinion, but he heard it frequently enough to include this take in the story. "The reason you cannot print it—and mean it—is that it is not true," Terrell, who became the managing editor of *Sports Illustrated* in 1974, concluded about this faulty line of thinking.[18]

Race was clearly on the minds of those who spoke with him, however. One unnamed Giants official told the writer, "Our white players unfortunately have neither the ability to inspire others by their performance nor the personality to pick this team and demand that it put out." Terrell pointed out that the Giants lacked leadership and blamed the white players for neither providing it nor exhibiting a willingness to let a nonwhite player lead.

Speaking at a press conference following the annual gathering of National League owners, Stoneham agreed that the Giants' clubhouse stood to benefit from the presence of an alpha. "Our leader (Willie Mays) is a modest man," said Stoneham. "He doesn't want to get on anybody."[19] Putting the debacle of 1960 aside for a second, Terrell expressed his belief that the team's returning core of Mays, Cepeda, Willie Kirkland, Felipe Alou, Mike McCormick, and Jack Sanford, among others, provided a talented foundation to build on for 1961. He did not mention Willie McCovey.[20]

* * *

Billy Williams and Willie McCovey experienced the crucible of establishing themselves on major league rosters in 1959 and 1960, but, while Mac dealt with a setback sophomore season, "Whistler," as his teammates had taken to calling him, was trending up. The Chicago Cubs invited Williams to spring training in 1961 and put him in the middle of the outfield competition that featured nine other players. The bigger story swirling around the organization involved another change in manager. In fact, it was a complete switch-up of the position in general. Following the 1960 season, Lou Boudreau wanted a multiyear contract to continue managing the team, but Wrigley refused to give it to him. Talk about turnover. In the twentieth century, the Cubs employed 21 managers over 61 seasons. The lack of stability hindered the organization's opportunity to achieve sustained success. Now Wrigley assembled a collection of eight coaches who would lead the Cubs as well as the organization's minor league affiliates, a truly ridiculous idea. It became known as the College of Coaches.

Williams played left field in all 12 of his appearances with the big-league club in 1960; however, the organization wanted to see how he performed in right field during camp to maximize its options once the season started. Harry Craft, one of the Cubs' coaches, noted, "If he can, it will give us a more pliable lineup."[21] General manager John Holland's visions sparkled with thoughts of the Cubs' young outfielders for years to come with Williams, Danny Murphy, Nelson Mathews, and Louis Clark Brock, a 21-year-old outfielder out of Southern University who had signed with the organization the previous August. Williams impressed the Cubs' brass by driving in 25 runs in 23 spring training games and earned himself a full-time job from the outset of the season. He also caught the eye of his teammates. Williams left veteran reliever Don Elston impressed. "There was a guy, the first time you saw him, you said, 'Here's a star.' Billy had so much power. When he hit the ball, it was like a rifle shot," Elston told historian Peter Golenbock.[22]

It was an eventful first two months of the season for Williams and the Cubs. Wrigley tabbed Vedie Himsl to be the team's initial head coach, and he started Williams in right field on Opening Day. Williams went 0-for-4, beginning an early stretch of struggles at the plate for him. Meanwhile, Chicago started the season 5–6, which compelled Wrigley to swap out Himsl for Harry Craft, who piloted the club for 20 games before Himsl was reinstated. Williams bounced back at the plate on May 2 when he connected for the first grand slam of his career as part of a sterling four-hit performance to help Chicago beat the Giants, 9–4. However, National League pitchers continued to find ways to get Williams out, and he was benched again as Chicago dropped 18 of its 25 games in May. He made a number of pinch-hitting appearances over the course of the next two and a half weeks before the Cubs switched things up as they began a series in San Francisco on June 16.

Now under the guidance of El Tappe, the ballclub made several changes with long-lasting implications, beginning with star Ernie Banks. The left knee belonging to the now 30-year-old Banks throbbed as a repercussion of a serious cartilage injury he suffered while in the Army 12 years prior, and it now inhibited his ability to move while playing shortstop. He played a few games in the outfield for the first time in his career but did not take to it. Tappe asked

Banks if he would try first base. He responded positively to the suggestion, and Banks took the field at first base for the first time in his career on June 16 at Candlestick Park. The domino effect of the move opened up left field for Williams, whom Tappe reinserted into the lineup. In the top of the third inning, Billy, batting sixth, launched his second grand slam of the season against the Giants as Chicago won, 12–6, and he never looked back.[23]

Williams and Banks developed a close bond that lasted for the rest of their lives. Banks made it a point to take Williams under his wing and teach him how to be a big-leaguer. They spent considerable time talking about baseball and life, although Billy laughs when recalling how much Ernie deployed his gift of gab. They roomed together on the road for a brief time, but Banks woke up so early in the morning wanting to talk that the arrangement did not last long. One of their proudest moments of the season occurred in June, when the organization hired Buck O'Neil to coach for the ballclub, specifically Banks's work at first base. O'Neil became the first African American coach in Major League Baseball history, but he didn't receive an equivalent ranking with the other coaches. On July 15, 1962, both Tappe and Charlie Metro were ejected in a game down in Houston; this should have put O'Neil on the field as a coach, but it didn't. Pitching coach Fred Martin assumed a new role in the newly shuffled deck that refused to deal with Buck. A lifelong baseball man with an excellent track record of success managing the Kansas City Monarchs, O'Neil remained in the dugout. "Everybody got thrown out of the game, and Buck was still sitting on the bench. Buck was there, and they didn't let Buck manage the club. Ernie and I talked about it, and George Altman was on the club at the time. It didn't happen, and I think that this is one thing that was disappointing to me, to him because he was considered as a coach for the ballclub," Williams says.[24]

The Cubs floundered under the College of Coaches. They won only 64 games and finished 29 games out of first place. What an inaugural campaign for Williams, though. The 23-year-old buried the frustration of his previous season by slashing .278/.338/.484 with 25 homers and 86 RBIs. He earned National League Rookie of the Year honors in December. Williams, Banks, and Ron Santo gave the Cubs a formidable offensive trio to build the ballclub around for years to come.

* * *

Willie McCovey had a front-row seat for a number of Billy Williams's potent offensive performances in 1961. Perhaps his friend's work at the plate reminded him of his own Rookie of the Year season two years prior. However, getting back on track remained stubbornly difficult for Mac, not least of which because the Giants organization hampered his development.

Spotty playing time prevented him from establishing a rhythm at the plate, and the inability of new manager Alvin Dark to reconcile the awkward dynamic of what to do with Mac and Orlando Cepeda compounded the issue. During the offseason, Dark decided that McCovey would start playing some left field to allow Cepeda to play first. Oddly, Dark announced his decision at a hot stove banquet in Fresno. The following morning, McCovey's phone rang. A reporter was on the line wanting to get his reaction to Dark's intention. Stretch expressed his willingness to give it his best effort.[25]

Horace Stoneham provided all of the Giants' hitters with a boost heading into the season when he moved the left-center-field fence in by more than 30 feet and brought the foul poles in 10 feet.[26] Stan Musial had been spot-on the previous season when he pointed out that the fans ought to not anticipate seeing many homers. However, the reconfiguration of the playing field had its intended effect. Cepeda smashed a league-leading 46 homers, and Willie Mays clobbered 40 of his own. McCovey hit only 18 but in far fewer plate appearances.[27]

Dark defended McCovey's play at first base against a significant number of Giants fans who maintained that Cepeda should be permanently installed at the position. Regardless of his public profession, Dark platooned McCovey for large chunks of the season, hampering his development and hurting the team's offense in the process.[28] Dark maintained that players' morale stayed more buoyant when they knew if they would be playing that day, but it's hard to fathom how this situation boosted McCovey's confidence.

McCovey unleashed a modicum of his pent-up frustration in a home game against Pittsburgh on July 13. He struck a long fly ball that curled fair around the foul pole for a home run, except first-base umpire Tony Venzon, following a momentary pause, declared it a foul ball. Angered, McCovey moved in on Venzon and yelled at him that he was blind. During the ensuing argument, Stretch contacted the umpire and was thrown out of a game for the first time in his career. He was incensed. "That ball went fair by over 10 feet," he groused after the game. The Giants went on to win the contest, 2–1, but McCovey's reaction stirred up those around him not accustomed to witnessing such an outburst. Giants third-base coach Whitey Lockman also earned an ejection for arguing the call. Several irked Giants supporters contacted local media outlets to criticize Venzon, including a local fan named Bob Lurie.

McCovey's season dragged on frustratingly. He didn't start another game for more than a month. Although it's difficult to believe it now, Giants fans showered McCovey with boos so frequently that an annoyed Alvin Dark, the skipper who wasn't playing him, issued a rebuttal against their derision. "You don't expect that from home town fans. McCovey doesn't deserve it," Dark said. "And some day those jeers are going to turn to cheers."[29] Even so,

McCovey continued to sit. When he did return to the lineup, Willie scalded the baseball. In August, he raised his average from .243 to .269 boosted by eight multihit games. The Giants never threatened Cincinnati and finished the season eight games behind the Reds despite monster seasons from Cepeda and Mays.[30]

Their first-base competition, compounded by the organization's inept decision making, remained at the ballpark when McCovey and Cepeda left work. In addition to becoming friends, they were now neighbors near San Francisco's Sunset District, and their bond was further strengthened by the danger both faced as minority men in the city. They lived in different flats in the same building and frequently spent time together. A terrifying incident while Mac and Cepeda lived at 48th and Pacheco served as a stark reminder of their realities regardless of how many home runs either of them had hit that day. One night, a sudden ringing of his telephone pierced the quiet and roused Cepeda. "Chico, can you come here?"

Cepeda immediately recognized McCovey's voice, but something in its tone struck him as different. He sensed fear. Willie told Orlando that he was out on a date and had realized that he was being followed by several white men, so he pulled over to call his friend. Cepeda raced out of his flat to meet them.

"Two cars are following me," McCovey told him when he arrived.

"He was afraid," Cepeda recalled. "It was about 1:30 in the morning. He wasn't afraid of nobody, but, you know, three people follow you?"

The followers appeared to be German and pronounced Willie's name in a way that sounded closer to "Billy." Nothing beyond their intimidation attempt seems to have occurred, but that aspect of the strategy seemingly worked, sadly, because the two young ballplayers never forgot this night for the rest of their lives.[31]

While this scary incident brought the two friends closer, Mac and Cepeda shared lighter moments together that also forged their bond. They ate dinner together in New York ("He liked Latin food") and ventured out to various venues for an evening of music ("'Nancy [with the Laughing Face]' . . . he loved that"). Cepeda marveled at McCovey's even-keel demeanor, and while the two young ballplayers intensely battled to see who would be the Giants' first baseman, they enjoyed each others' company. At times, Cepeda felt that the media wanted to stoke personal strife between the two, and he admired Willie for never taking the bait. "Even though we competed we were still great friends. He never said anything bad. He was very smart. They tried to put words in his mouth," Cepeda maintained.

McCovey adored Cepeda. Stretch gifted Chico three brand-new pairs of shoes while purchasing a pair made from alligator for himself. Mac also spoke openly with his friend early in his career. During a game against the

Cincinnati Reds, Jim Maloney was dominating the Giants' batters. McCovey turned to Cepeda and said, "I'm going to get him," and then promptly launched a ball over the right-center-field fence that Cepeda estimates sailed more than 500 feet. Not much more to say than that.

* * *

The 1962 World Series changed Willie McCovey's life in ways he could not have imagined. It had been a wild ride just to reach this point. The Los Angeles Dodgers led the race for the National League pennant by four games as late as September 17, but they collapsed, losing 10 of their final 13 games to finish in a tie with San Francisco. The Giants captured the ensuing playoff by taking two out of three games against the Dodgers, punctuated by San Francisco's four-run ninth-inning rally off of Los Angeles's exhausted bullpen in the finale to give it a 6–4 win and the pennant. McCovey produced a quality season despite appearing in fewer than 100 games, primarily as an outfielder. Offensively, he was great. McCovey slashed .293/.368/.590 and homered 20 times in 262 plate appearances. Defensively, he struggled. Alvin Dark settled on Cepeda as the Giants' first baseman, and he had another terrific season, batting .306 with 35 dingers, but the arrangement left McCovey twisting in the wind, literally, on some days.

On October 4, Giants hurler Billy O'Dell delivered the first pitch of the 1962 World Series from the Candlestick Park mound to New York Yankees shortstop Tony Kubek. McCovey watched it from the dugout. It's astonishing, really, to envision Mickey Mantle, Roger Maris, and Whitey Ford leading the incredible Yankees, winners of nine of the previous 15 World Series played, squaring off against Willie Mays, Orlando Cepeda, and the scintillatingly talented Giants with McCovey benched, but that's the way it was. The Yankees quickly jumped out to a 2–0 lead in the first against O'Dell courtesy of a two-run double by Maris. The Giants tied the score with single tallies in the second and third innings but couldn't push any more runs across the plate and lost Game One, 6–2. Ford went the distance for New York.

With Yankees right-hander Ralph Terry set to start Game Two, McCovey knew he would be in the lineup the following day. The 26-year-old Terry made his one and only All-Star appearance in 1962, a season in which he led the American League with 23 wins and 298.2 innings pitched. He had a bugaboo, however; Terry surrendered a league-leading 40 home runs. Indeed, Dark inserted McCovey at first base and hit him fifth. Cepeda would have to sit this one out.

When McCovey dug into the batter's box against Terry in the bottom of the seventh inning the following afternoon, his team clung to a 1–0 lead. Giants starter Jack Sanford, winner of 24 games during the regular season, had pitched incredibly well, limiting New York to just two hits. Terry rocked and fired a slider to McCovey. Terry thought it was a good pitch located down and in, but the result nullified his effort. "I knew it was gone as soon as I hit it," Stretch said after the game. The towering fly ball sailed beyond the right-field fence and doubled the Giants' lead, 2–0. Sanford, in spite of a tension-filled moment in the ninth inning when Mantle doubled with two outs to bring the tying run to the plate in Maris, held on tight. After observing one of Maris's pregame batting practice sessions, Alvin Dark adjusted the team's defensive alignment by moving Giants shortstop José Pagán to the other side of the second-base bag, thereby giving San Francisco three infielders to defend Roger's pull side. Sanford pitched Maris perfectly, inducing him to hit a ground ball into the shift. Second baseman Chuck Hiller fired the ball to McCovey for the final out of the Giants' 2–0 win. Asked about his impressive World Series clout against the magisterial Yankees, the unflappable McCovey downplayed the magnitude of it all and made more than a few Yankees fans choke on their morning coffee by suggesting to reporters that it was "just like playing against Houston or the Mets."[32] A glowing photograph of McCovey warmly embracing Sanford in the clubhouse greeted viewers on the front page of the *Examiner* the following day. McCovey's electric smile beamed in a joyful moment following so many vexing ones over the past two seasons.

Game Three in the Bronx proved to be a frustrating affair for the Giants, who lost to New York, 3–2. The Yankees moved the canvas out in center field that typically provided the batter's backdrop to make room for more spectator seats. As a result, hitters struggled to pick up the ball all day. San Francisco felt that it was at a distinct disadvantage playing in Yankee Stadium for the first time while the opponent had significantly more familiarity with the surroundings even if the Yankees' hitters likewise scuffled. McCovey, who started the game in right field, also found the windy conditions to be a challenge. Billy Pierce and Bill Stafford kept the offenses at bay through six and a half scoreless innings until the Yankees broke through with a three-run rally in the bottom of the seventh highlighted by a two-run single by Maris. The ball skidded off the grass, and McCovey did all he could to prevent it from getting past him, but the misplay allowed Maris to advance to second base. He scored on a fielder's choice later in the frame to make it 3–0. Giants catcher Ed Bailey hit a two-run homer in the ninth, but it wasn't enough as the Yankees took a 2–1 series lead.

McCovey watched Game Four from the bench as Dark sat him against southpaw Whitey Ford. The Giants broke open a 2–2 contest in the top of the seventh inning when second baseman Chuck Hiller, who had homered only three times all season, popped a grand slam off reliever Jim Coates as the Giants evened the series with a 7–3 win. However, the victory came at a cost. Juan Marichal, who had tossed four scoreless innings, had his pitching hand injured when Ford hit him with a 3–2 delivery on a bunt attempt in the fifth inning. Marichal, who chucked his batting helmet in frustration, was lost for the remainder of the series and never pitched in the postseason again.

New York won Game Five, 5–3, behind Ralph Terry. McCovey collected a single in four trips to the plate with one strikeout, making him 2-for-7 against Terry in the series. The ballclubs flew back west with New York one win away from another World Series championship. However, an incredibly intense storm descended on Northern California and unleashed destructive winds that reached up to 75 miles an hour in some areas and intense rain that caused the deaths of nearly 50 people along the West Coast and indefinitely postponed Game Six.

On Sunday, October 14, following three postponements of the series, the continuing rain forced the Giants and Yankees to move their operations southwest to Modesto, a rural community situated 90 miles east at the northern end of the San Joaquin Valley, for a workout at Del Webb Field. If the place appeared counterintuitive to the bright lights of the World Series, it nonetheless provided something that the city could not at that moment: an arid climate mostly devoid of moisture. More than 4,000 fans packed the bleachers to watch both teams go through the paces following several days of inactivity. Among the throng, McCovey noticed a young lady. Her name was Karen Billingsley, a 22-year-old hairdresser who had spent considerable time in San Francisco working in a salon before moving back home to be close to her family. Locals knew of Karen's stunning looks and affable personality—she had competed in a number of talent and beauty competitions over the years—and both qualities immediately seized McCovey's attention.

She attended the Giants' workout to say hello to Orlando Cepeda, whom she had gotten to know through mutual friends during her time working in San Francisco. Willie watched as they chatted behind the batting cage, and he later asked Cepeda about her. She was a friend who used to live in the city, he replied. McCovey asked him if he would make an introduction. Chico readily agreed, but it would be more than a year until they spoke.

Following a four-day delay, the series resumed at Candlestick Park with the Giants' backs against the wall in Game Six. Dark started Cepeda over McCovey against Whitey Ford, and Chico delivered a three-hit performance highlighted by an RBI double in the fourth inning as part of a three-run outburst that gave the Giants a 3–0 lead. Billy Pierce took over from there and pitched San Francisco into Game Seven with a complete-game performance. San Francisco won, 5–2, and now the 1962 World Series would be decided the following afternoon.

The Giants sought their first championship in San Francisco since moving west in 1958. The Yankees wanted to earn their twentieth. Dark assembled his best offensive lineup with McCovey in left and Cepeda at first.

Ralph Houk countered with his usual lineup anchored by Mantle and Maris. On this day, however, the pitchers dictated terms. The rain allowed both teams to reconfigure their starting rotations to their liking prior to Game Six, which set up a third matchup between Jack Sanford of the Giants and Ralph Terry of the New Yorkers. Each hurler already owned a win in the series, but each had been tagged with a loss as well.

Nearly 44,000 jammed into Candlestick Park for the biggest baseball game in San Francisco's history. They held on to every pitch as the game remained scoreless through its first four innings. The consternation of the moment intensified in the top of the fifth inning, when the bottom of New York's lineup got to work against Sanford. Bill "Moose" Skowron led off with a single to left. Clete Boyer followed up with a single to center that sent Skowron to third. Sanford then inexplicably walked Terry to load the bases for the Yankees leadoff hitter, Tony Kubek, who grounded into a double play that scored Skowron to give New York a 1–0 lead.

The Yankees clung to their slim one-run lead as the game entered the bottom of the ninth inning. Matty Alou led off with a well-executed drag bunt that put the speedy outfielder aboard with the top of the lineup following in his wake, but Terry responded by striking out Felipe Alou and Hiller. That brought Willie Mays to the plate. In his last at-bat, Mays had smoked a line drive down the left-field line that Tom Tresh ran down admirably. It was a good thing, too, for New York because McCovey had followed it up by smashing a triple to center field. All that had occurred in the seventh inning, and now San Francisco was down to its last out. Terry delivered a pitch away from Mays, who went with the location and sent it screaming down the right-field line. Maris, helped by the outfield grass thickened by the heavy rainfall of the previous week, tracked it down and fired the ball to the cutoff man, second baseman Bobby Richardson. All the while, Alou tore around second base and raced toward third. Giants third-base coach Whitey Lockman, sensing Maris's clean play, threw up a stop signal. San Francisco now had the tying and winning runs in scoring position for Willie McCovey.

It was a huge spot for Terry and not only because he found himself embroiled in a difficult game situation. Two years prior, Terry had come out of the bullpen in another Game Seven, this one against the Pittsburgh Pirates in 1960. Terry entered the game in the bottom of the eighth inning and extinguished the Pirates' five-run outburst only to surrender Bill Mazeroski's walk-off homer in the bottom of the ninth after New York had tied the game. "Don't think he wasn't in tough with that Mazeroski thing on his mind. That was a terrific mental thing," Joe DiMaggio later marveled.[33] Yankees manager Ralph Houk popped out of the dugout and headed to the mound for a discussion with Terry. Meanwhile, shortstop Tony Kubek and second baseman Bobby Richardson held an impromptu meeting near the second-base bag. "I sure hope Willie McCovey doesn't hit the ball to you," Kubek told his roommate. Why? "Well, you've already made one error in this series. I'd hate to see you blow it now," he chirped.[34] The meeting on the mound finished, Houk left the field, and the infielders resumed their positions. The stunned Giants could not believe what was unfolding in front of them.

McCovey dug into the box. Was Terry, a right-handed pitcher, really going to face Stretch? Cepeda, who now stood on deck, anticipated that Mac would be walked and that he would soon be striding to the plate with the bases loaded. However, even with visions of Mazeroski scampering around the bases in his head, Terry, fully aware of the magnitude of this moment—"A man rarely gets a second chance like I did"—bore down on facing McCovey, who had homered off him in Game Two.[35] Houk knew that if this move backfired, it would be over for him. "I knew if he got a hit, I was going to be crucified," he admitted to Felipe Alou after the latter joined the Yankees in 1971.[36]

Terry rocked and fired. Mac swung and pulled the ball foul down the right-field line. Terry's second offering appealed to McCovey, who fired his hands and swung. He cracked a line-drive smash that whistled just to the left of Richardson, who snared it—shoulder high—for the final out of the game. The New York Yankees were champions, again. Despondent, McCovey's face, awash with emotion, told the entire tale. He had scalded the baseball only to have it turn into an instant out to suddenly, painfully, end the Giants' season.

After the game, controversy swirled amongst the writers concerning Lockman's decision to hold Alou at third base on Mays's ninth-inning opposite-field double, but those on the field appeared in agreement in the game's aftermath. "Maris is a good fielder with a strong arm. If he bobbled the ball, even for a second, (I'd) have sent Alou home. But Maris handled the ball cleanly," Lockman said after the game. "If I had the same decision to make, I wouldn't change it." Yankee catcher Elston Howard echoed Lockman's read on the play. "I was hoping he'd come in. I wanted to get this thing over with," he said.[37] McCovey concurred. He gave an interview in 2014 following San Francisco's World Series Game Seven win over Kansas City, in which the Royals Alex Gordon did not attempt to score on a three-base error by the Giants. McCovey elicited his deep chuckle when asked about it. "Arm chair managing. I love it," he replied. "In 1962, after we lost Game 7, 1–0, writers were saying that Matty (Alou) should have scored on Mays's double to right field. Now remember, I was up next and Cepeda was behind me. Meanwhile, Maris, who had a fantastic arm, made a great play in right and made a perfect relay to Richardson. Matty would have been out by a mile. I hit a rocket, but, unfortunately, right at Bobby."[38]

Lore tends to develop with the passage of time, but the stories engulfing McCovey's lineout started to take shape immediately. As an overwhelmed Ralph Terry asked for somebody, anybody, to get him a cigarette in the celebratory clubhouse, Whitey Ford hollered, "How'd you like the way I positioned that Richardson for that last out!" Alvin Dark made his way in to congratulate Houk and said, in part, "And, incidentally, you sure steered that McCovey line drive right."[39] For his part, Richardson, whom Felipe Alou recalled sharing his personal faith with any Giant who reached second base during the series, suggested supernatural intuition played a role. "Some strange sense told me to play him toward the first base side. I guess I really was out of position," he was quoted as saying.[40]

Legendary *San Francisco Chronicle* writer Bob Stevens, whose decades of baseball coverage included this series, later talked with Richardson about the circumstances surrounding the play. Richardson said that he had walked toward first base to smooth out some infield dirt following McCovey's foul ball. As Terry determined what to throw next, Richardson swept the spot and looked up only to shockingly realize that his pitcher had already started his motion. Stunned, he froze in place. McCovey then lined the ball right to him, which was close to 10 feet away from where he should have been positioned.[41] Richardson, however, doesn't remember it quite that way. "People often suggest that I was out of position on that play, but McCovey hit two hard ground balls to me earlier in the Series, so I played where I thought he would hit the ball," he explained years later.[42]

Richardson added another layer to the increasingly complex tale when he explained that one of the National League umpires interrupted the entire scene by asking the second baseman for his hat just prior to the pitch. The umpire wanted to give it to his cousin. Suddenly, the ball was screaming toward him and into his glove. It all happened so fast. The whole thing has become one of those blurred baseball stories that blends fact and fiction to create a monumental myth. We'll never truly know which pieces belong to which section.

On December 22, long after the season had concluded and the ballplayers had retired to their winter hideaways, Charlie Brown sat next to his friend, Linus, with his head propped up by his hands solemnly sulking in the pages of America's newspapers. Neither of them move for three panels. "WHY COULDN'T McCOVEY HAVE HIT THE BALL JUST THREE FEET HIGHER?" Charlie screams at the sky with arms outstretched in the fourth and final panel. Poor Chuck, and by Chuck, perhaps it's best to say, *Peanuts* creator Charles M. Schulz, who still wasn't over it five weeks later. Charlie Brown and Linus again sit together in a heavy silence for three panels before America's favorite underdog cries out for the entire nation to hear, "OR WHY COULDN'T McCOVEY HAVE HIT THE BALL EVEN **TWO** FEET HIGHER?"[43] Charlie's lament echoed the sentiment shared by McCovey, his teammates, and the entirety of Giants fandom.

Chapter 5

"See You Down the Road"

Willie McCovey and Billy Williams established themselves as superstars throughout the 1960s, a decade of change for both men and the country itself. McCovey brought a presence to the ballpark and belted breathtaking home runs that left fans, teammates, and opponents alike in awe as he established himself as one of the game's most feared sluggers. Meanwhile, Williams put on a show for the people that featured a barrage of crisply lined doubles and memorable round-trippers. Fans also knew that when they purchased a ticket to a Cubs game, they would see Williams play. He established a stunning consecutive-game streak that captured the respect and admiration of the sport. Each appeared in four All-Star games throughout the decade, including together in 1968. Despite their personal accomplishments, however, the Giants and Cubs did not capture a pennant outside of San Francisco's flag in 1962. Traversing the decade reveals Williams's steady climb to success and exposes the tribulations of McCovey's career, which took a significant step back before he firmly established himself.

It was a transformative time for our protagonists both professionally and personally. Off the field, both men established home lives that remained largely entrenched for decades, interrupted by one move each that proved only temporary. Billy and Shirley Williams had four daughters, who livened their home at 74th and Constance Avenue, which they bought in 1966. McCovey lived in several spots in the city before deciding to build a house in Woodside during the 1970s. Fans of the two left-handed-hitting savants in Chicago and San Francisco adored their franchises' homegrown stars. Williams and McCovey went from young players deserving of a daily place in the lineup to perennial candidates for the MVP Award. They, along with Henry Aaron, also proudly welcomed a new wave of young players from Mobile, Alabama, to the majors.

Willie McCovey formed a deep, personal relationship with the Dudum family in the early 1960s that shaped the rest of his life. They met after Giants owner Horace Stoneham provided Willie Mays with the name of John Dudum, a wholesaler in the linens business who would be a great contact for home goods. Mays invited several teammates, including McCovey, to visit Dudum, whose company served as a primary distributor for Macy's. He supplied McCovey with linens, towels, and the like for his apartment. Although Dudum was not particularly a baseball fan—he spent the vast majority of his time running the family business—the two men quickly formed a close bond. It soon became a ritual for McCovey and Dudum to eat lunch together before night games at Candlestick Park. McCovey got to know John's son, Rocky, who became one of his closest friends. Their presence expanded Mac's Bay Area family, which included Ruth Stovall and the Silens, who continued to look after him with care.

The Dudums' imprint on McCovey's life deepened over the ensuing years. Not only did they befriend him, but John advised him on financial matters and business opportunities in a way that Willie had not previously experienced. Additionally, his deep reluctance to ask for things or insert himself into advantageous off-field opportunities as his celebrity began to grow hindered him in ways that the Dudums, Silen (his de facto agent), and Stovall recognized. They stepped in and assisted him on matters ranging from housing to business advice to friendship. Stretch surrounded himself with good people who put his interests—personal and professional—first. Throughout Mac's career, Rocky traveled to cities around the country where the Giants played road games. He essentially kept the shy McCovey company. Mac liked seeing National League cities during his first few seasons, but he grew more reluctant to venture out as fans increasingly recognized him. He still very much enjoyed, say, dinner with Cepeda or a jazz performance, but he increasingly preferred to stay in his hotel room and order room service.

Surrounded by his supportive cast, McCovey exploded at the plate in 1963 in part because he added to his number of career at-bats against Don Drysdale. The 1962 National League Cy Young Award winner could not get Stretch out for the life of him. Despite McCovey's uneven offensive production through his first three campaigns, he had no issues when it came to hitting Drysdale. Even with his reputation as a headhunter, he never threw at Mac. Robert Creamer of *Sports Illustrated* described McCovey as "a left-handed hitting Paul Bunyan, a legend in a baseball suit" when facing his Dodger rival. By midseason, Stretch had belted nine career homers off of Drysdale in 47 plate appearances.[1] "There was no way he could get Willie Mac out. No way," Juan Marichal shakes his head with a laugh. "He read his book on hitting against him."[2]

Jack Hiatt, who played alongside Stretch for five seasons as part of his nine-year career, explains how McCovey's mind-boggling success against the Hall of Fame pitcher transpired. "All these line drives and home runs. It was every time up. Now, why? Drysdale was a low fastball pitcher. McCovey was a low fastball hitter, and Drysdale didn't make an adjustment. He just kept throwing it down there thinking, 'This will be a ground ball.' Well, it was sometimes, bouncing out there on the highway somewhere because he would tee off on that ball. No one would treat Drysdale like that. Nobody," the former catcher Hiatt explains.[3]

Bill Rigney, Mac's first manager in San Francisco, concurred. "I don't think anybody hit Drysdale harder during those years than Willie McCovey, but Drysdale never backed off, he always came right at them even though Willie kept handing him his lunch," he said.[4]

If his major league debut was his breakout moment, the 1963 season served as McCovey's blaring announcement. He crushed 44 homers to tie Henry Aaron for the National League lead en route to his first All-Star Game appearance. It was no coincidence that he also appeared in a career-high 152 games. Knowing that he would be in the lineup every day simplified his routine and eliminated any uncertainty about his role, although manager Alvin Dark made it clear that McCovey was the team's left fielder with Orlando Cepeda starting at first base. McCovey was not a particularly great outfielder, but he tried and grew comfortable enough to eschew returning to the infield, at least in his mind. The Giants had to get everyone's bat into the lineup regardless of the defensive impact. McCovey had already lost an untold number of at-bats during the first four seasons of his career because the team couldn't find a spot for him. At last, some sort of solution was at hand. As a result, the Giants received explosive offensive performances from McCovey, Cepeda, and Willie Mays, who combined to hit 116 home runs and drive in 302 runs. However, in spite of their success at the plate, the Giants won only 88 games and finished in third place.

Mac's reputation as a hitter grew exponentially around the league. Mets manager Casey Stengel certainly took notice. The Giants were playing New York, and as Stengel was going over the scouting report of San Francisco's hitters with pitcher Roger Craig, he looked up with advice on his mind and pity in his heart. "Where do you think we should defense McCovey?" he asked, "in the upper or lower deck?"[5] McCovey had in fact already homered off Craig twice in a June 1962 ballgame. "If he were using an aluminum bat, he would have killed someone," Craig said.[6]

Out in Chicago, a youth movement was underway. On September 21, 1963, Billy trotted out to left field in the top of the first inning. Billy Cowan, that is. Billy Williams had received the day off after playing in each of the Cubs' 155 games. Milwaukee beat Chicago, 4–0, as manager Bob Kennedy drafted a lineup of only right-handed-hitting batters, who nonetheless went down meekly against Braves lefty starter Warren Spahn. It was the only game that Williams sat out all season, and he did not miss another one for the rest of the decade. He appeared in the team's final six contests, one of which included a homer off Bob Gibson in a Cubs win that eliminated the Cardinals from playoff contention in Stan Musial's final season.

Williams made a deep impression on Kennedy, the skipper who had replaced the College of Coaches. Years later, Billy worked with Bob's son, Terry Kennedy, who spent 14 years playing in the majors. In the meantime, Williams's third full season in Chicago proved to be yet another productive one for the 25-year-old, who was firmly establishing himself as one of the National League's headline players. He hit .286 and drove in 95 runs. He bashed 25 home runs, which tied him with Ron Santo for the team lead. With the presence of the two young stars in the middle of their lineup, along with Ernie Banks, the Cubs capitalized on their offensive talent and performed drastically better than it had in 1962 by winning 23 more games and finishing over .500 for the first time since the 1948 season. At 82–80, the Cubs' youth movement showed promise.

* * *

Family events back home in Mobile impacted McCovey in 1964. The most shocking and distressing was the death of his father, Frank, who passed away in January. Willie traveled south for the funeral. It was a difficult loss for him, and even in that circumstance, the large McCovey family was not able to reunite in full. "Even at the tragedy of my father's death, somebody was missing. I don't know what it was that inspired me to stay with baseball, my family didn't know much about it, they never did get interested in baseball until I started doing well and started getting my name in the paper and being on TV," he lamented.[7] Frank McCovey died without ever seeing his son play a Major League Baseball game.

Saddened by his father's passing and a nagging foot injury that bothered him throughout the season, McCovey had a rough time on the field in 1964. Although he continued to draw walks at an impressive pace, his batting average plummeted. To compound matters, an errant throw during pregame warm-ups in Philadelphia struck him in the head and sent him to the hospital. Things got so bad during the season that fans and writers questioned McCovey's confidence and his ability to sustain success at the big-league level. Halfway through the campaign, a columnist suggested that Mac's season "is sad enough to make a grown man cry."[8]

In the midst of McCovey's discouraging season, life's sun broke through the fog and shone brightly on his personal life. Willie and Karen Billingsley began dating that summer, nearly two years after he had first seen her at the workout in Modesto prior to Game Six of the 1962 World Series. Willie asked Karen if she could fly up to see him. She laughed to herself. The Modesto airport wasn't exactly a hub of commercial air travel, and, besides, Karen couldn't afford it. She could, however, take the bus. McCovey's driver, also named Willie, picked Karen up at the Greyhound station in San Francisco and whisked her away to meet McCovey for lunch. Frequently, Willie the driver and his girlfriend joined Willie the ballplayer and Karen on their dates. It was just as likely to be the four of them together as Willie and Karen alone.

Karen had never been to a professional baseball game before meeting Willie, and he preferred it that way. He never invited Karen to watch him play because the idea of her at the ballpark made him tense. McCovey could not fully control his feelings. "Do you ever get nervous out there in front of all those people?" Doc Billingsley, Karen's stepfather, asked him one day. "Well, yeah," Mac replied with a bashful smile. "Just one person: Karen." After the season, they traveled to Nevada for a quiet wedding ceremony away from the press.

The McCoveys settled in to their spotless dwelling that had been precisely kept by Willie, whose attention to detail left everyone in amazement. "He lived like a king," remembers Orlando Cepeda. "I have never seen anyone so clean. Everything had to be perfect. Everything had to be *here* and *here*. Willie was unique. I've never seen anybody like him." Karen referred to their home as "House Beautiful," and she quickly experienced her husband's immaculate habits. One day, he was sitting down in a chair adjacent to their living room coffee table and noticed something amiss about it. Ah, he saw it. An astonished Karen watched as Willie leaned forward and subtly turned the ashtray an imperceptible amount. "I can always tell when you've been dusting," he mentioned. Looking at the ashtray's new position stunned her. "I couldn't tell the difference," she recalled.

Everyone in McCovey's inner circle knew of his perfectionist tendencies. On opening birthday or Christmas gifts, he would fold the wrapping paper into a perfect shape and set it aside. During the season, McCovey packed his own suitcase for road trips. Heaven help whoever moved something. "He would put one thing on the table, and he would know if someone moved that thing from the place he put it," reflects Juan Marichal. "The way I remember Willie Mac is that he wanted to be perfect."[9] He also obsessed over putting on his uniform just right. "Took forever!" howls Cepeda.[10] McCovey had to look perfect before taking the field, and his teammates gave him plenty of grief about it. As he styled himself in the clubhouse mirror, they walked by and pointed out that one pant leg appeared shorter than the other or that his hat looked crooked. McCovey remained hypervigilant after changing back into his clothes following the game.

"If Mac didn't like something about his pants you can believe the tailor was there the next day taking them in," recalls Joe Amalfitano.[11]

"He was the number one dressed guy. He looked good," Marichal notes.[12]

"He was the best dressed player," says Rocky Dudum. "His shirt had to be smooth."[13]

Jack Hiatt chuckles, "We would go on a trip back east, and it would be humid and hot. He would lose a few pounds. He would come back and a tailor would be there at Candlestick. They would retailor his pants and uniform."[14]

Although his drip was always on point, not many people away from the ballpark saw it. McCovey limited his public outings. Willie and Karen went out to dinner from time to time, but so many parents allowed their children to approach the McCoveys' table to ask for an autograph—Mac could not refuse a kid—that he decided it would just be easier to eat at home. Karen, a private person herself, understood her husband's intensely introverted nature, and she shared his resistance to the occasional overzealousness of the public eye, but their married lifestyle started to impact her. One day, she ran into Cepeda, and they exchanged pleasantries. At one point in the conversation, he asked her, "How's Willie doing?" "I don't know," she joked. "He hasn't talked to me in two weeks!"[15] Cepeda could relate. Mac had always been intensely quiet at home.

McCovey did have something poignant to say one evening when Willie Mays came over to visit. Karen offered Mays dinner, but he politely declined. Instead, he wanted to ask Mac about his offseason plans regarding Alabama. "You going to visit the Old Country?" Mays wanted to know. The words hung in the air for a brief moment before McCovey elicited a low chuckle saturated with amusement. Karen is light-skinned and frequently confused for being white. Willie looked at Mays and, smiling, answered the question with one of his own: "Do you think I'm going to take her looking like that down to the Old Country?" Mays, rarely at a loss for words, didn't respond. McCovey would not be visiting Mobile with his new bride. He lived in California year-round for a reason.[16]

In February 1965, the McCoveys welcomed a baby girl, Allison, into their family. Dad insisted on being in the delivery room when Karen gave birth, an unusual request at the time but one readily granted by the hospital staff. When McCovey arrived home after games that season, as Karen busily prepared dinner in the kitchen, he routinely strode to their bedroom, where he slipped off that day's outfit of alpaca sweater and shoes. He pristinely folded the sweater and placed it in its particular drawer. The shoes he returned to their exact place in the immaculate closet, not too close to his other pairs but not too far away either. With his dress clothes safely returned to their correct spot, he stopped at the entrance of the bedroom where tiny Allison slept. Many nights, as if on cue, when McCovey's shadow filled the doorframe, she naturally awakened from her slumber. "It was almost like magic," Karen remembered. "But I knew it was the Lord."[17] He then entered the room, scooped up his baby girl, changed Allison's diaper—perfectly—and carried his daughter around the house for the remainder of the evening.

Despite the optimism of their marriage's start, Willie and Karen's relationship soon experienced intense tumult that set them on a path toward divorce. They did not argue in front of their daughter, who spent time with the Silen family while the two tried to iron out their differences, but Willie wouldn't talk. The situation could not be mended, and by December 1965, their brief, 14-month marriage ended in divorce. The judge called both attorneys into chambers and encouraged them to settle the situation as far from the limelight as possible. They agreed. Karen, 23, returned to Modesto with Allison, and Willie, nearly 28, went back to living on his own again.[18]

* * *

As McCovey battled for a starting spot in the Giants' lineup, Billy Williams entrenched himself in Chicago. His remarkable consistency became a fixture in the city no different from the wind, river, or pizza. With intense work, he was becoming a stronger hitter by the year. In addition to the opposite-field power he had always possessed, Williams now pulled the ball with pop on command. Nicknamed "Whistler" by his teammates after his hometown, it just as well could have been for the sound the ball made as it screamed off his bat. Williams's remarkable batting style featured his ability to lower himself to the level of the ball as the sphere traveled to the plate and strike it with authority. His opponents watched in awe as line drives jumped off Whistler's bat regardless of the pitch's arc. He also liked to move up on the plate with a runner at first base to increase his ability to pull a pitch on the outside corner through the hole on the right side of the infield. Williams's relentless work in the batting cage developed a lethal swing that infused caution into opposing batteries. It had become excruciatingly difficult to induce him into hitting a ground ball.

Another crucial aspect of Williams's development as a hitter was the amount of time he put into watching film. Beginning in the early 1960s, Barnett "Barney" Sterling worked for the Cubs as team photographer. He also added cinematographer to his duties and recorded the team's at-bats using a 16-millimeter projector. Williams and Banks eagerly took advantage of this new tool and spent many hours studying their hitting mechanics. At one point, they got two projectors going simultaneously so that they could compare their current swings to the ones they had going during hot streaks. Lest anyone think that Williams simply arrived at the ballpark with his swing in a groove, watching these recordings of his at-bats was just one aspect of his relentless work ethic that served as the foundation for his success at the plate.

"We would come out to the ballpark early just before we hit. We had a little room that we would go in, and Barney Sterling would show these films of the past day game. We would look at that," says Williams, who knew exactly what he was looking for. "I wanted to see the stride. My stride should be no more than six inches long—four to six inches—my stride foot. If I got too long I hit a lot of ground balls to second base, and I knew I'm messed up. I had a little area on the Cub uniform where I set the bat, and I would see that from the side. If it's too low, I hit a lot of fly balls to left field."[19]

The veterans' work ethic heavily influenced the clubhouse. In 1964, Williams hit .312 for the season—his first year achieving the .300 mark—and made his second All-Star Game. He set a bevy of new career highs, including 201 hits, 39 doubles, and 33 homers. The Cubs' young guys took notice and followed suit. "Sweet Swinging and all that's true, but no one worked harder at hitting than Billy Williams," says shortstop Don Kessinger, who debuted for the Cubs in 1964. "Many, many times Billy would take the film home with him to watch it. He would take a lot of films of himself hitting in games so he could critique himself. That always meant a lot to me because you see a guy as great as he is work as hard as he does. You just can't beat that."[20]

A star ascending to the highest echelon of the sport has moments along the way that tell the tale of the journey. One such at-bat for the 27-year-old Williams occurred in 1965 against baseball's finest. On an early September evening at Dodger Stadium, the Cubs experienced Sandy Koufax at his best. The Dodgers lefty spun yet another gem in his breathtaking career as he became the first pitcher in Major League history to throw a fourth career no-run no-hit ballgame. His perfect game defeated Chicago, 1–0, despite the valiant effort of Cubs pitcher Bob Hendley, who allowed only one hit himself, in a brisk one hour and 43 minutes. Billy Williams's at-bat in the top of the seventh inning was the closest Chicago came to getting a baserunner aboard against Koufax. Williams worked the count to 3–0 before Koufax threw him three straight fastballs for strikes. Billy never thought of walking. He was up there to swing the bat in the tight contest. "All the time," he insisted. Ron Santo never saw the lefty throw harder. In fact, many players on the field that night agreed that Koufax's velocity increased as the game wore on. "This guy could drive you to drink," Santo told reporters afterward.[21]

Perfect game aside, the 29-year-old Koufax was in the midst of an incredible season. He wound up leading the National League in a bevy of categories, including wins, complete games, innings pitched, and walks plus hits per inning pitched (WHIP). Koufax also struck out a career-high 382 batters on his way to winning his second Cy Young Award. His next start following the perfect game came five days later at Wrigley Field, and Williams, who had produced eight multihit games in his past 10 contests that raised his average to .313, was waiting for him.

Koufax and Bob Hendley locked horns in another dual. The Dodgers southpaw retired Williams on a comebacker with the bases empty in the bottom of the first inning. Three innings later, Williams popped up to second. Billy's close study identified that Koufax had been throwing him a lot of fastballs recently and had twice begun his at-bat with pitches to the same spot. "Sandy had started me off with a fastball away, fastball away and never did throw it inside," he remembers thinking. The game remained scoreless through five innings as Hendley again matched zeros with Koufax. Hendley blanked Los Angeles in the sixth, which brought the top of Chicago's order up against the Los Angeles ace in the bottom of the frame: Don Young, Glenn Beckert, and Williams.

As the three hitters prepared to hit, Williams anticipated that Koufax would again try to sneak a fastball by him on the outside part of the plate. Young walked to the plate while Beckert and Williams got loose in the on-deck circle. Billy turned to his teammate. "Beck, get your ass on base," he told him. "We're going to win this game today." Williams knew better than anyone that it was not the best idea to announce one's preparedness to hit Sandy Koufax's offerings around the yard at will, but his analysis informed him that an outside fastball was on the way. "You never tell anyone you're going to hit a home run off of Koufax," is how he put it years later.

Young led off the inning by hitting a ground ball to second that was mishandled, so he reached on the error, which summoned Beckert to the plate. It wasn't necessarily pretty, but Beck came through. He grounded a ball to Dodgers first baseman Wes Parker, who threw out Young at second. The Dodgers, however, could not complete the double play, and Beckert was aboard as Williams strode to the plate knowing he wanted to attack that first pitch so Koufax couldn't get to his curveball. Koufax went into his motion and delivered. Williams's swing went with the pitch perfectly. His bat met the baseball on the outer part of the plate and sent it scorching toward left field. It landed in the bleachers: 2–0, Chicago. Hendley made Williams's homer stand up as the Cubs won the game, 2–1. The next day, Williams was standing at his locker when he was approached with a gift, a small image of the home run as a memento of the moment. Williams, who notched 17 hits in 68 career at-bats against Koufax, took one look at the tiny photograph and shook his head. "Man, take that thing and blow it up," he roared. "You don't do that to Sandy Koufax, you know." Always a special blend of confidence and humility, Williams wanted that homer captured by the largest iteration of the picture possible. A moment like that didn't happen every day.

It's not much of an exaggeration to state that Billy Williams's life changed forever in 1966. The Cubs acquired two young players who not only helped the organization evolve into a competitive force but also became his lifelong friends, Randy Hundley and Fergie Jenkins. Additionally, the organization moved on from the disaster that was the College of Coaches, a rotating set of managers that proved ill-conceived. The Cubs hired veteran manager Leo Durocher to pilot the ballclub following three years of that failed experiment. As expected, Durocher brought his fiery demeanor and demanding expectations with him to Chicago. General manager John Holland made another important move trading for the 24-year-old Hundley, who established himself as Chicago's everyday catcher. The swap infused the team with more offensive talent and gave the pitching staff someone with whom they could build a daily rapport.

Holland made another key deal on April 21, when he sent veteran pitchers Bob Buhl and Larry Jackson, who had combined for more than 300 major league wins, to the Philadelphia Phillies in exchange for John Herrnstein, Adolfo Phillips, and Jenkins, a young hurler known for his control. Chicago signaled its willingness to engage in a youth movement with the trades for Hundley and Jenkins, whom Cubs scout Rube Wilson called "one of the best minor league prospects in the game."[22]

Jenkins joined a Cubs team that was young and not quite ready to compete. While Durocher brought instant credibility to the post, he couldn't make up for the organization's lack of pitching depth. Williams and Santo were now in their primes, but Ernie Banks turned 35 before the season started. Hundley, along with infielders Glenn Beckert and Don Kessinger, gave Chicago a trio of young 20-somethings to balance the lineup, but it wasn't nearly enough to offset a pitching staff that compiled a team ERA of 4.33, the worst mark in the National League, even though Ken Holtzman showed tantalizing promise as he led the staff with 11 wins in his age 20 season. Durocher gave Jenkins a dozen starts, and the newly acquired control artist won a half dozen ballgames while compiling 182 innings pitched. Otherwise, the pitching staff was an issue. Ernie Broglio, a key piece of the Lou Brock trade, finished his career on a sour note. Plagued by continued arm trouble, he struggled mightily and washed out of the major leagues by season's end.

Williams again posted terrific numbers in 1966. He appeared in all 162 games, but Chicago stumbled to a 59–103 record. The Cubs finished dead last in the National League miles behind the pennant-winning Dodgers. Williams, though continued to make a deep impression on his peers around the game, and the organization's youthful roster presented hope for future seasons.

The adjustment to Durocher proved difficult for some players in the clubhouse, including Hundley, who developed a case of the yips under the stress of his manager's withering criticism. Try as he might, Hundley couldn't throw the ball back to the pitcher accurately. He quickly found a book that calmed his mind down and rediscovered his throwing accuracy, but Durocher's intensity continued to be felt throughout the clubhouse. For his part, Williams got along fine with the team's new manager. "Leo didn't dish out much to Billy," Hundley says. "He knew better than to do that because Billy had a really tough side to him, and I think people knew that he didn't want to cross his path in any way."[23]

During this era, Williams started a unique tradition all his own. Everyone knew about Williams's ongoing consecutive-game streak, but he also developed a reputation around the league for pulling off a signature magic trick. When the hitter ahead of him finished his at-bat, Billy would leave the on-deck circle and spit. He then hit it with his bat. As time went on, Cubs owner Philip K. Wrigley started loading the players up with gum, and Williams incorporated it into his routine. He popped half a stick of spearmint gum into his mouth and chewed it while standing in the on-deck circle. When it was his turn to hit, Williams would walk behind the umpire on his way to the batter's box, spit out the gum, and whack it into the opposing dugout. "It became a psychological thing," Williams explains. "You know you start a tradition and you stay with it. This is why I did that. I never did miss it! That was strange to me and strange to the players. I walked behind the umpire, and I would look over to their dugout. I would spit this half a stick a gum out, and I would hit a line drive. I would see guys ducking and darting and some of their pitchers say, damn! If he can hit that little piece of gum I can't throw him that pitch. It became psychological in my mind that if I hit this little piece of gum I should be able to hit that big baseball. That's why I did it."[24] Many players tried to swat their own gum, but none could replicate Sweet Swinging Billy Williams.

* * *

The inability of the Giants front office to resolve the conundrum of playing McCovey and Cepeda together plagued the organization throughout the 1960s. A future Hall of Famer was forced to play out of position one way or another, if not sit the bench. "We had Willie and Orlando playing first base and neither one could play another position. They tried Orlando in left field to play both of them on the same day. They tried McCovey in left field with Orlando at first. It didn't work," says Marichal. "If we could have had the designated hitter in the National League we would have won a lot of games."[25] The excruciating culmination of the conundrum was close at hand.

McCovey made several adjustments following his frustrating 1964 campaign that reignited his power at the beginning of his age 27 season. He also regained a measure of health. He worked with weights throughout the off-season to strengthen his arms and wrists. Noting that a considerable amount of his power was to left and center field, he traded in his longer bat for a smaller model that allowed him to get to the hitting zone quicker. Increased bat speed would allow him to pull the ball more frequently into the jet stream that blew out to right field at Candlestick Park. He also moved on top of the plate to better reach pitches on the outside corner with complete extension. McCovey's adjustments returned him to prominence in 1965. His average shot up 46 points, he smacked 21 more homers, and he finished tenth in the MVP Award balloting at season's end. It is also worth noting that his body held up throughout the season. Stretch played in a career-high 160 games.[26]

McCovey's trajectory was back on track, and the folks who watched him play on a daily basis recognized his dominance. Ed Montague wasn't your typical vendor working the outfield bleachers. His father, Ed, a longtime Giants scout, played an important role in signing no less than Willie Mays. Now his son paused as one of them strode to the plate. "Every time Mays came up or McCovey came up we'd stop selling and watch them hit. I remember those balls soaring over my head and out of the ballpark into the players' parking lot. (McCovey) hit them nine miles," Montague remembers.[27] On October 1, 1974, Montague the Younger made his major league debut as an umpire and worked home plate for a Padres/Giants game at Candlestick Park. Mac pinch-hit for San Diego in the seventh inning of that game. Montague went on to umpire for 34 seasons in the major leagues before retiring in 2009.

Despite Willie's resurgence, the Giants still could not figure out how to solve the McCovey/Cepeda defensive dynamic that had now haunted the organization for six seasons. McCovey spent 1965 at first base because Cepeda missed most of the year with an injury, but the quandary returned the following year. The on-field saga finally came to an end on May 8, 1966, when San Francisco dealt Cepeda to St. Louis on the same day his bat produced four hits in a victory over the Cardinals. Despite rumors that suggested Cepeda was on his way out of San Francisco, the trade stunned the players. Following the win, Cepeda and Marichal walked up the tunnel toward the clubhouse. Juan put his arm around Orlando's shoulder and told him, "There's no way they're gonna trade you." Just as they entered the clubhouse, a throng of writers and photographers swarmed them. Cepeda had been dealt to the Cardinals for pitcher Ray Sadecki. Marichal recounted the scene in disbelief over half a century later. "That was . . . ," his voice trails off. "He became the most valuable player a year later." Marichal isn't finished. "Every trade we made was so bad you couldn't believe it. We traded Orlando for Ray Sadecki. Felipe Alou for Bob Shaw. Gaylord Perry for Sam McDowell," he chuckles in disbelief.[28]

Despite now possessing the first base position as his own, the trade of his friend saddened McCovey. "Chico, I wish you the best," he told Cepeda.[29] Their bond remained true for the rest of Stretch's life. Cepeda's son, Ali, recognized it whenever the two friends spent time together. "You could feel the love when they saw each other at the games. You could see their smiling faces, and how they would relate when they would get together," he said. "It was something special."[30]

First base was the only truly viable option for McCovey, not least of which because he handled the position adeptly. He possessed a long reach that reinforced his nickname "Stretch" each time he consumed a throw from one of his infielders. He had soft hands and effectively turned the 3-6-3 double play. It also provided some respite from running around the outfield on deteriorating knees. By now, Mac was arriving early at the ballpark to spend time in the whirlpool before getting taped up extensively to play. Despite his ailments, he never complained. The other Giants saw the rigorous pregame routine he went through to make himself available for that night's game, and they admired his positive attitude. "That was tragic what he went through to play," Hiatt says. "They taped him up, and he played every day with those knees that way. Despite that he was the quickest man from first to third on the ballclub. It only took him about seven strides."[31]

McCovey had clouted some impressive home runs throughout the first six-plus seasons of his career: his first three round-trippers during an electric first week as a big-leaguer, the broken-bat line shot off Bob Gibson in 1962, and his World Series blast later that year. But there is no debate—none—about the hardest-struck one. He hit it on September 4, 1966, in St. Louis at Busch Stadium in a 9–2 win over the Cardinals and old friend Orlando Cepeda. The Giants entered the series a half-game ahead of the Dodgers atop the National League, but while the win proved important, it was a ball crushed by Mac that remained an indelible memory for the rest of the lives of anyone in the stadium that afternoon. The Cardinals deeply respected McCovey, including their legendary radio broadcast team. Harry Carey once chuckled as he described Stretch as only he could as "too big to be a man and not quite big enough to be a horse" as Mac strode to the plate from the on deck circle. "His hobby is reading comic books and seeing motion pictures," added Carey. "And hitting," interjected Jack Buck.[32]

With San Francisco ahead, 3–0, McCovey dug into the box to lead off the top of third inning against St. Louis southpaw Al Jackson. Cardinals catcher Tim McCarver called for an off-speed pitch, which Jackson threw. McCovey swung. The noise produced when the bat met the ball stunned everyone, and then the ball simply screamed on a straight line. "There was no trajectory!" McCarver told writer Mike Lupica years later, the sound still resoundingly clear within the banks of his memory. "There was just that sound of the bat on his ball." It eventually slammed into the deck facing or the scoreboard—depending on whom you ask—more than 500 feet from home plate and ricocheted back onto the field. Outfielder Mike Shannon called it the farthest ball he had ever seen hit for the remainder of his life. The homer so impressed Jackson that he called McCovey after the game to congratulate him on the prodigious nature of his achievement. Yet another reason for the people of San Francisco to love and admire Stretch, whom opponents around the league cherished as well. "He was theirs," McCarver noted.[33] In a wild twist, McCovey said he enjoyed his at-bat in the top of first inning when he bunted for a hit against the Cardinals' defensive shift. "I love a home run ribbie but I got to admit there is something special in a surprise bunt when they aren't expecting it," McCovey smiled.[34] He enjoyed the homer, too, especially since it came off a left-handed hurler. Platoon this.

Although the Cardinals' defensive alignment couldn't hold McCovey in the ballpark on this occasion, increasingly during the mid-1960s, opponents deployed shifts to thwart his strong tendency to pull the ball. As Mac dug into the batter's box, third basemen and shortstops would scamper to the right side of second base. Managers Dave Bristol (Cincinnati) and Gil Hodges (New York) weren't above putting one of those infielders in the outfield on the warning track. McCovey nonchalantly shrugged it off. No one could dictate his approach.[35]

While Mac watched his close friend exit the clubhouse for St. Louis in 1966, a new one walked in the door. Twenty-two-year-old Tito Fuentes, who had appeared in 26 games for the Giants the previous year, established himself as an important middle infielder in his first full season with the club. Energetic and talkative, Fuentes made an impression on McCovey. At first, their conversations focused on defensive strategies against opposing hitters, but they gradually evolved into more social engagements. Both loved music, and one night, McCovey rang an awed Fuentes with an invitation to go see Joe Williams, an incredible jazz singer who performed with the Count Basie Orchestra, among others. Fuentes returned the favor by introducing Mac to Latin musicians.

Although opportunities for outings abounded, life on the road in the big leagues could be brutal for minority players. Although McCovey knew where they could (and couldn't) go, Fuentes experienced episodes of racism in which he wasn't allowed to eat at particular restaurants. Certain hotels catered only to white players, and sitting anywhere but the back section of the bus on drives into cities from an airport was discouraged. Fuentes took cues from Mac, Mays, and Marichal on how to act in these situations. On one trip, Fuentes went out to dinner with his roommate, Ollie Brown, a 22-year-old African American outfielder who hailed from Alabama. The two young men were served meals, but after they finished, the restaurant staff ruined their experience by throwing away the dishes so no one else would have to eat off the same plates. They didn't try to hide the sound of them breaking.[36] Mac didn't talk about his experiences much—he never mentioned Mobile—but Fuentes understood all too well what his teammates had endured.

* * *

Imagine driving by a local park in the Mobile area during mid-January and seeing struck baseballs disappear into the morning light like runaway fireworks. Hey, that's Billy Williams of the Chicago Cubs! *Thwack!* Then an enormous man who blocks out the sun climbs into the batter's box and uncoils his vicious swing. *Pow!* Woah, that's Willie McCovey of the Giants. Wait a minute. Is that, wait, is that Henry Aaron? *Crack!* You've now pulled your car over to get a closer look. And Cleon Jones of the New York Mets? Yes. Yes, it is. And Tommie Aaron, Amos Otis, and Tommie Agee, among still others. They've all gathered at this neighborhood diamond to dust off their swings before spring training starts. Now they're clustered in a group sitting on the bleachers. Analyzing, talking, teasing, laughing. *See you down the road*, they say to one another as they begin to collect their things. The tapping of bats together. The crunch of spikes puncturing dirt. The slamming of trunks and the roaring of car engines leave behind a suddenly quiet field cocooned in silence. The pages of the winter calendar seem to turn more quickly, signaling the incoming start of the baseball season. Ferocious battles for the two pennants await. You ask your astonished self, what did I just witness? *See you down the road.*

* * *

Billy Williams returned to Whistler in the offseason during his first five full seasons in the big leagues, but that changed when he and Shirley decided to purchase a home on the South Shore at 74th and Constance Avenue in 1966. The house wasn't too far from where Ernie Banks lived, so to keep things easy, they commuted together to Wrigley Field. They talked pitchers and hitting and family. The ballclub and kids and current events. They had developed into one of the game's most lethal duos and maintained a close friendship. One exciting topic for their discussions involved the continued maturation of Chicago's core as well as the exciting young players added to the club. There was no better example than Fergie Jenkins, who was on the verge of stardom. The 24-year-old control artist admired other National League hurlers, names like Gibson, Marichal, Bunning, and Koufax. To help facilitate reaching their level, Jenkins had formulated several goals to obtain: win 20 games, pitch 250 innings, and strike out 250 batters. The idea was that hitting these targets would help propel the team up the National League standings. Jenkins had a remarkable 1967 campaign in his first full season as a starter. He won 20 games and led baseball with 20 complete games en route to his first All-Star season.

Jenkins arrived in spring training of 1968 ready to build on his success. Jenkins again sat down to write down his goals for the season, but this time, Williams joined him, and a new tradition was born. "Billy said he wanted to hit .300, 100 RBIs, with a certain amount of home runs," Jenkins recalls. "I did the same thing: lead the league in innings pitched, strikeouts, win 20 games and hope that the ballclub propelled itself in the standings."[37] The two friends diligently filled out their notecards with their goals for the season and put them away in their lockers for revisiting at the end of the year. "Even though it's an individual thing that we tried to accomplish, we wanted the team to survive and basically move up in the standings. You had to put your act together. It was a goal that, I thought, if we reach, who knows, it might mean a pennant," Jenkins says.[38]

Williams and Jenkins developed a very close friendship that extended well beyond Wrigley Field, and the bond strengthened as their families grew. Their daughters spent considerable time together. Actually, it was one of the unique characteristics of that group of Cubs teammates. Playing day baseball allowed them time to gather in the evenings. Sunday doubleheaders supplied off days on Monday. The families really got to know one another.

Billy and Fergie quickly recognized that they shared a common love of the outdoors, specifically fishing and hunting, and they went on many adventures over the next few years. Williams had grown up tossing a line in the waters around Mobile, and Jenkins had a similar experience growing up in Chatham, Ontario. They plotted a good number of offseason trips. "Either he would come to Canada, and we'd fish in some of the Great Lakes in Ontario, or I'd go down to Alabama and do some deer hunting," Jenkins fondly remembers.[39]

A number of Cubs fans were local farmers who frequently attended games at Wrigley Field. They happily made their land available to Williams and Jenkins on learning of their enjoyment of the outdoors. "We would go hunting in the farmers' fields all the time," Jenkins points out. The teammates also went fishing together on Lake Michigan whenever they could manage to squeeze in a little free time during the season. Eventually, they reached a point where it became simpler for them to buy a boat together, so they did. They docked it at a small marina during the season and headed out on the open water of Lake Michigan after games.

* * *

The date of April 4, 1968, remains etched in the minds of those who lived through it. On that day, an assassin's bullet took the life of Dr. Martin Luther King Jr. at the Lorraine Motel in Memphis, Tennessee. King, who was in Memphis to show solidarity with local sanitation workers, was shot while on the balcony of the hotel. King's assassination set off widespread rioting throughout the country, including in Chicago, where stores on Madison Street set afire filled the sky with billowing smoke. Seven Chicagoans were killed and more than 1,800 arrested in the days that followed King's murder.

Mayor Richard Daley instituted a 7:00 P.M. curfew for everyone under the age of 21.[40]

The Chicago Cubs were on a tour playing one of their final exhibition games of the spring in Evansville, Indiana, when they received the shocking news of King's death. An hour later, a number of the players prepared to leave the hotel to find a place to eat dinner. Williams and teammate Lou Johnson, the very same player who lost part of his ear in a 1956 car accident that opened up a spot for Billy in Ponca City, headed for the elevator. At one point, its door opened, and they ran into several of their white teammates, including Randy Hundley. Deeply hurting, Johnson ignored them. Meanwhile, Hundley asked Williams if they could speak privately for a moment after they reached the lobby. Williams, also pained and grieving, graciously agreed.

"I am so sorry that this happened," said Hundley referring to King's murder. "I don't know how somebody could do something like this."

Williams answered him bluntly. "This is what we deal with an awful lot."[41]

Hundley's voice trembles as he revisits the events of that day decades later. Johnson pointedly criticized Hundley after being traded to Cleveland in June. Hundley expressed disappointment at never clearing the air with Johnson, who died in 2020. Cubs players, although admittedly close, did not spend extensive time discussing what had happened as an entire group, perhaps in part because no one knew exactly what to say. "We knew they were suffering," Hundley says.

Over the past half century, Williams and Hundley have put their life experiences on the table with one another, and their friendship remains strong. After he retired, Hundley was instrumental in establishing a Cubs fantasy camp, and Williams, along with many others, attended it routinely over the years. They still reminisce together over lunch. Their conversations include a little talk about life as well as their years together in Chicago. Along with the rest of us, they marveled at Williams's 10 career home runs off Bob Gibson, to which Hundley refers with a sharpening voice, "Nobody, and I mean nobody, intimidated him." He means Williams. The outfielder and catcher will stay close for the rest of their lives. "Billy has been very instrumental in our friendship, and I would like to think that I was, too. He was a very gracious person. We've been through a lot of stuff," he says.[42]

* * *

See you down the road turned prophetic when it came to the Mobile sluggers and the All-Star Game. Billy Williams and Willie McCovey became teammates for the first time as professionals during the 1968 midsummer classic, and they were joined by Henry Aaron, which put three locals on the same National League squad for the first time. In years past, two of them had been selected but never three at once. It was the fourth All-Star appearance for Williams, who carried a .274 average and eight homers into the contest. For McCovey, it was the third time he earned the nod, having batted .293 with 20 home runs during the season's first half. Dominant pitching carried the National Leaguers past the American League in a tight 1–0 game at the Astrodome. McCovey and Williams went a combined 0-for-5 in the game but left Houston with a win. It was the sixth straight victory for the senior circuit.

The second half of the 1968 season featured competitive clubs in San Francisco and Chicago, but neither of them could chase down the St. Louis Cardinals, who breezed to the National League crown by nine games over the second-place Giants and 13 ahead of the third-place Cubs. Their age 30 seasons brought more stardom to the diamond. The numbers argued that McCovey and Williams were firmly entrenched in their primes. McCovey, now earning $90,000 a season, clobbered a team-high 36 more homers and walked (72) more times than he struck out (71).[43] As his impressive consecutive-game streak continued, Williams batted .288 and smashed 30 homers, including the 200th of his career. These two were now the batters whom opposing teams looked to stop first with Ernie Banks and Willie Mays now entering the later years of their illustrious careers. That isn't to suggest that they weren't still producing at a high level—Banks homered 32 times in 1968, while Mays struck 23—but both of them were 37, and the Mobile mashers now had everyone's prioritized attention.

On June 25, 1968, Dodger manager Walt Alston preferred that his left-handed starter Claude Osteen face Mays rather than McCovey in a tough situation. With two men aboard in the bottom of the sixth inning, Alston had Osteen intentionally walk McCovey to load the bases to bring up Mays in a 0–0 ballgame. That moment wasn't lost on Stretch. "A lefthanded pitcher walked me, to pitch to Mays," he knowingly acknowledged afterward.[44] In the meantime, Alston's ploy backfired. Mays walked, too, as did Jimmy Ray Hart, to give San Francisco a 2–0 lead. Following a strikeout, a Giants out-fielder making his major league debut dug into the batter's box with the bases still loaded. Bobby Bonds, a 22-year-old prospect from Southern California, launched a grand slam to extend the Giants' lead to 6–0. Bonds's first career homer was one for the record books. It was the first time a player hit a grand slam in his major league debut in the entirety of the 20th century. A notable and exciting ballgame in franchise history, indeed.

The postgame interviews on this night featured Bonds, whose night deserved the well-earned spotlight, but the daily media that covered the Giants frequently turned to McCovey for his thoughts on the club. Over the years, he had grown more comfortable with the press, especially the Giants' radio broadcasters. He liked talking clothes with Russ Hodges. Not just any clothes by the way. The drip. Style was a priority. Stretch developed an especially close personal friendship with Lon Simmons, who, try as he might with McCovey during postgame interviews, typically received the same response to every question: "That's right, Lon." Those who listened to these exchanges throughout the years will recall them well. Mac rarely let Simmons off the hook by providing an in-depth answer, and Lon kept going right back to the well with inquiries. One can imagine the two friends bantering as they sat next to each other on the Giants' charter flights as they always did. "Would you like the seat with more leg room, Willie?" "That's right, Lon."

The story goes that McCovey used a similar line very early in his career— we're talking 1959, 1960, and 1961—with a teammate of his by the name of Hobie Landrith, who participated in postgame interviews, often appearing alongside Juan Marichal. At that time, the format called for two players to converse rather than a broadcaster asking interview questions. With a Saturday Game of the Week on the horizon, Landrith practiced interviewing McCovey, anticipating that they could be on the postgame show. The rehearsals did not go particularly well. "When I ask you a question don't say, 'Yes, sir,' because I'm not that good," was one piece of friendly advice from the catcher to Mac. During their practice sessions, McCovey exasperated Landrith by repeatedly replying to his questions with the same response, "Yes. That's right."

"Mac, you can't *do* that!" Landrith exclaimed.

When the show went on that Saturday, McCovey handled the entire conversation flawlessly and impressed Landrith with his performance. "I think it came off real good," he beamed. "McCovey did a super job and if you've ever heard him I think he has a real future in broadcasting."[45]

That's right, Lon.

Chapter 6

1969

A palpable buzz surrounded the Chicago Cubs entering the 1969 season. Their talented roster engendered high hopes following back-to-back top-three finishes in the National League. In the midst of expectation in the Windy City, a new era dawned for the senior circuit as it added two more clubs: the Montreal Expos and the San Diego Padres. As a result, the twelve teams were divided into two divisions. The Cubs joined New York, Pittsburgh, St. Louis, Philadelphia, and the aforementioned Expos in the newly created East Division. A new playoff format accompanied baseball's expansion. The winners of the National League East and West would play each other in a championship series for a World Series birth, which mirrored the changes in the American League and its two new franchises in Kansas City and Seattle.

Change was also afoot 60 feet 6 inches from home plate due to the outsized dominance of elite pitchers, most famously symbolized by Cy Young Award winner Bob Gibson, who shut down the entire National League in 1968 to the tune of 268 strikeouts and a 1.12 ERA for the pennant-winning St. Louis Cardinals. Consequently, owners decided to shrink the strike zone and lower the mound significantly—five inches—to decrease the pitcher's advantage with the hope of increasing offense. This change, accompanied by the dilution of pitching talent due to the addition of two more franchises, accomplished its goal. National League teams averaged 3.4 runs a game in 1968, but that number jumped up to more than four the following season. None of these noteworthy changes could save National League hurlers from Willie McCovey in 1969.

While an astonishing season awaited Stretch in San Francisco, the Chicago Cubs generated considerable hype as a pennant contender. The ballclub featured a two-time National League MVP in Ernie Banks and four players who had already appeared in at least one All-Star Game: Fergie Jenkins, Ron Santo, Don Kessinger, and Billy Williams. Banks, who loved to wax poetic about any new season, let anyone within earshot know he felt good about the upcoming campaign as he strolled by his teammates toward the batting cage to commence with a spring training workout. "'Yessir, yessir, yessir, the Cubs gonna shine in Sixty-Nine,'" he rhapsodized. "'And how are you, Mr. Billy Williams? And how are those four children? Four children! My, my. I have to hurry up and catch up. And at my age. My, my.'"[1]

Williams felt the tearing of opposing emotions as he prepared for the nearing season. Entering his ninth year, he truly believed that the Cubs had the opportunity to get to the World Series for the first time in his career. The team's situation excited him. Personally, however, he felt increasingly frustrated that his consistent performance was being taken for granted, not least of which because the press frequently used some form of the word "robotic" to describe it. Even the Cubs themselves occasionally added to the problem. "Billy Williams is the only major leaguer to appear in every game played by his team last season. Billy is definitely the strong, silent type. He says little, but does it all," read one team publication. Lost in translation was his work ethic. He relentlessly exerted himself to improve on both the physical and the mental aspects of hitting.

Thousands of Cubs fans lined up at 8:00 A.M. to purchase tickets for Opening Day on April 8 as Chicago hosted the Philadelphia Phillies. The organization sold standing-room-only admission to pack Wrigley Field as tightly as possible. The result was that 40,796 enthusiastic patrons welcomed the Cubbies to the new season. It was a record crowd. Nobody could recall seeing that many people at Wrigley for a season opener. Deron Johnson wasted little time giving the fans pause and the visiting club an early 1–0 lead with an RBI single against Fergie Jenkins, but the Cubs offense—set for a big year—responded with a bang. Banks, now 38 and in his last full season as a player, showed that his bat could still deliver a sting with a three-run homer in the bottom of the frame as his father, Eddie, looked on from the stands. He added another—a solo shot—in the bottom of the third inning. Chicago built a 5–2 lead as the game entered the ninth inning, but Philadelphia staged a three-run rally to tie the game and regained the lead, 6–5, when Don Money doubled in Johnny Callison in the tenth. Rookie Barry Lersch, who had tossed four scoreless innings, was tasked with closing out the contest. The young righthander retired Banks on a fly ball to right but served up a single to catcher Randy Hundley, which ended a string of 10 consecutive retired Cub batters. Jim Hickman was scheduled to hit, but manager Leo Durocher wanted a more favorable matchup, so he went to his bench and called on Willie Smith, a left-handed-hitting reserve outfielder who had been acquired from Cleveland during the previous season for Lou Johnson. "Just a dying quail over third, that's all I want," Durocher muttered on the bench.[2] Smith provided much more than that. After taking Lersch's first pitch, Smith cracked his second offering and sent a scorching line drive over the right-field wall to give the Cubs a 7–6 win. The stadium shook as Smith rounded the bases and greeted his teammates at home plate. The 1969 season was off to a roaring start on the North Side.

The Cubs won their first four games, capped off by a 1–0 walk-off win over the Montreal Expos as Billy Williams drove in Don Kessinger with a base hit in the bottom of the 12th inning. Prior to the game, Williams sat down with David Condon of the *Chicago Tribune* in the freezing home dugout and opened up about being frustrated with the narrative surrounding his public persona. While he felt the excitement about the team's win and was content with his personal contribution, something almost undefinable gnawed at Williams. "I go out, from day to day, to do a job. I do it, and this comes to be taken for granted," he explained. "Hank Aaron of the Braves has been in the same situation. Hank could play the outfield as well as Willie Mays. He could throw as well. All the Braves fans, tho(ugh), just accept this. Meanwhile, because Mays is a colorful player, he pulls in fans at San Francisco."[3]

Williams knew that he neither played the game nor answered questions from the media with the same dramatic flair as Ernie Banks or Willie Mays, but he wanted to be appreciated for his elite abilities—the product of incredibly hard work. He didn't want to be overshadowed all the time. "It's just that if you're not colorful, most writers think they have nothing to write about. Of course writers talk to me in the dressing room. But they know they get better copy from Ernie Banks and Ron Santo. I'm just not too exciting," he admitted.[4]

Condon praised Williams in his column not just for his play on the field but also for his modesty and "keen, subtle sense of humor." Williams was extremely witty, bitingly funny when the moment called for it, and everyone who spent any time around him knew it. Condon noted that Billy did not receive the same level of interest from companies to endorse their products as other players with the same ability. Billy wasn't expressing jealousy or resentment to Condon—he adored Banks as much as anyone—but the tension between his humility and pride in his accomplishments could create internal friction, particularly when he sensed that others disregarded his work ethic or willingness to play through pain during his consecutive-game streak that he began back in 1963. Condon offered a compelling solution: a Billy Williams Day at Wrigley Field when the organization and fans could celebrate him.

* * *

Willie McCovey spent a considerable amount of his offseason reconfiguring his body for the grueling campaign ahead of him. In addition to consulting with orthopedic surgeon Dr. Robert Kerland in Los Angeles throughout the winter months, McCovey worked out several times a week with Bert Gustafson, a Bay Area physical therapist, who helped Stretch not only lower his body weight to 210 pounds but strengthen his arthritic knee as well. Gustafson, who had previously worked with Orlando Cepeda and Jim Davenport, so impressed the Giants organization with his work that he received an invitation to Arizona, where he would work alongside trainer Leo Hughes by designing specialized workouts for the club during spring training.[5]

Business took priority off the field. Following his banner season of 1968, McCovey requested a raise. He had certainly earned one having led the National League with 36 homers and 105 RBIs during the last gasp of the elevated mound. Following the highs and lows of his first decade in San Francisco, Mac had firmly entrenched himself as part of not only the organization but the city itself. The fans amongst whom he lived in the offseason adored him, and Stretch felt an urgency to garner more security during his upcoming contract talks. He, along with adviser Hal Silen, fully understood that his stellar play gave him some leverage in negotiations.

However, the labor situation between Major League Baseball and the Major League Baseball Players Association (MLBPA) over pensions complicated McCovey's situation. Marvin Miller, who joined the MLBPA as its executive director in 1966 following time spent with the steelworkers' union, sought concessions from owners over baseball's pension system. When Miller took over, the pool of pension money had been funded largely by a ratio of television revenue. Unsatisfied, Miller sought to swap out that ratio amount with a flat contribution number in 1967. Negotiations dragged on throughout 1968, and the issue reached a boiling point just as players prepared to report to spring training for the 1969 season. Miller convinced players to boycott, and McCovey was among a significant number who neither signed a contract nor reported to camp on time in a show of solidarity.[6] Miller and the owners reached a palatable solution, but it proved temporary in the end. The contribution amount went up to $5.45 million, and the eligibility requirement for the pension was lowered from five years to four. A veteran player who amassed 10 years of service would now receive $600 every month upon turning 50. Over the ensuing two seasons television revenue spiked considerably, and Miller sought to renegotiate the agreement, which eventually led to the 1972 strike. As the pension negotiations played out in the background, McCovey discussed contract terms with Giants vice president Chub Feeney.[7]

Down at Casa Grande, the new Giants manager, Clyde King, revealed his novel lineup construction for 1969 that featured Willie Mays as San Francisco's new leadoff hitter. Eyeing the idea from a distance, Billy Williams approved of the philosophy behind King's move. "The pitchers are going to be in a hole to Willie before they throw that first pitch. They don't want to start him off with a fastball. The first pitch to him probably will be a curve and right away the pitcher could be behind. Willie will get better pitches to hit," Williams explained.[8] Separating Mays and McCovey lengthened San Francisco's lineup, but it separated the most dynamic back-to-back hitters in the National League. The grand experiment lasted only 11 games.

As Marvin Miller and the owners concluded their negotiations over the pension system, a mad scramble ensued to get the players signed and in camp. Mays, for example, was the first of the Giants' stars to sign, agreeing to a $125,000 contract on February 16, but the team had yet to hold serious talks with McCovey. Discussions dragged on for several weeks, and McCovey decided to report to camp on March 3 without a deal and to continue talks in person. It was immediately clear to everybody that McCovey was in tremendous shape, having lost considerable weight. He moved fluidly and crushed a ball over the center-field fence in his first round of batting practice. Following another week of fruitless conversations with Feeney, McCovey pushed past any personal discomfort he felt with a new strategy and made a rare but savvy move: he went public. "I'd like a three-year contract," he purposefully told a group of Bay Area writers, knowing full well that the report would be splashed across sports pages throughout Northern California. "I need the security. And if I sign for just a year and have another year like I did last season, I'd expect to make as much as anybody on this team." While McCovey justifiably wanted a notable raise, he nevertheless prioritized years over dollars. That said, when a reporter asked him about playing the season for $70,000, he balked. "I wouldn't attempt to play for that amount."[9]

In the midst of this back and forth, McCovey prepared for the season. He had strong hopes that the Giants could contend, especially with young players Bobby Bonds and Jimmy Ray Hart ready to take on significant roles with the team. Finally, after 13 days of negotiations during camp, McCovey and Feeney met in the Giants' clubhouse and hammered out the lingering details of the agreement. They landed on a two-year pact that delighted Stretch. "We each gave in a little and I'm very happy with the contract," he said. Notably, McCovey and Feeney shook hands on a gentleman's agreement that if Stretch outplayed the deal in 1969, the salary of the contract's second year could be renegotiated.[10]

Typically a slow starter, McCovey opened the regular season on a tear. He went 12-for-34 with six homers as the Giants split their first 10 games. Then San Francisco got hot, winning 10 out of its next 11 games to take over first place at the close of April with a record of 15–6. One of the more notable matchups featured longtime foes McCovey and Don Drysdale on April 22 at Dodger Stadium. Stretch singled and scored as part of a two-run rally in the top of the fourth inning, and the Giants led, 5–0, in the fifth when Dodgers manager Walter Alston took Drysdale out of the game rather than have him face

McCovey again. Drysdale, who threw a major league record 58 2/3 consecutive scoreless innings in 1968, was hampered by a torn rotator cuff in 1969 that forced him to retire before the season's close. It was a shocking end to a great career. Drysdale's legendary orneriness helped him out of many a jam over the years, but it couldn't knit together his ripped up shoulder. Drysdale tried a variety of remedies, including taking pain medication from multiple doctors who didn't realize he was seeing other physicians. None of it alleviated the pain, but it did cause other, alarming issues. "I was so drugged up at times that I couldn't see the scoreboard from the mound. I was a walking drugstore," Drysdale admitted.[11]

He made eight more starts, but his arm just wouldn't let him continue pitching, and he announced his retirement on August 11. He was 33 years old. The quantified final damage of their battles was staggeringly lopsided. McCovey belted 12 career homers off Drysdale—the most he hit off of any opposing pitcher—while compiling an OPS of 1.117 in 128 career at-bats. The only batters who homered off of Drysdale more than McCovey were Henry Aaron (17) and Willie Mays (13), but each faced him nearly 100 more times. Don Sutton, a young pitcher for the Dodgers who came up in 1966 and went on to win 300 games during his Hall of Fame career, once asked Drysdale for advice on pitching to McCovey. "Obviously, you haven't seen me pitch to Willie or you wouldn't have asked the question," Drysdale retorted.[12]

Following his retirement from baseball, Drysdale entered broadcasting. In 1973, he began working radio and television for the California Angels. Throughout the 1970s, the Angels conducted spring training in Palm Springs, where owner Gene Autry lived part-time. Their ballpark was originally called the Polo Grounds. One particular afternoon, the Angels hosted the Giants, and Nolan Ryan was on the mound facing Willie McCovey. Well, Stretch homered off the fireballer, sending his friend, Giants broadcaster Lon Simmons, speeding over to the Angels' radio booth. Simmons hollered at Drysdale, "You can't even get him out when you're announcing!"[13]

Returning to 1969, the consortium of National League pitchers couldn't fool McCovey if they tried. If it was over the plate, he hit it out of sight. The next-best solution was to walk him, and they did so at an increasing rate. There wasn't anything McCovey could do about it other than remain patient, but the Giants' lineup did not offer him enough protection to force opposing teams to pitch to him. Maybe every hurler in the National League should have informed McCovey which pitch he was about to be thrown because any other deployed strategy to get him out failed in spectacular fashion. As crazy as it may sound, one superstar in particular used that blueprint effectively out of revenge.

The Giants stumbled throughout May, losing 13 of 21, and entered a three-game series against the visiting Cubs in third place with a record of

23–19 despite McCovey's torrid production at the plate that saw his OPS reach 1.145 over seven weeks into the season. San Francisco took game one of the set against Chicago behind Stretch, whose bat generated three hits, including his 13th homer of the season off the great Fergie Jenkins in the Giants' 5–4 win. Even better than McCovey's game is the story that has circulated for years about the duals between Stretch and Jenkins in 1969. McCovey won this round; however, the future Hall of Fame hurler, truly one of the game's greats, would have his revenge but not before McCovey gave him a hard time about the homer. Prior to one of Chicago's games at Candlestick Park later that year, Jenkins was at the El Cortez Hotel with his roommate Ernie Banks when their room phone rang unexpectedly. Jenkins answered the call, and the maître d' informed him that his car was waiting downstairs. *I never requested a car*, Jenkins thought to himself. "Mr. McCovey has ordered you a car," continued the maître d'. "He wants to make sure you get to the ballpark on time."

Several Cubs, including Jenkins, crammed into the car and headed over to Candlestick Park. On the way over, a plan was devised. "I told Randy Hundley that night when McCovey comes up tell him what's coming. You know for a hitter a lot times they don't want the catcher to say, 'Hey, fastball, look for a fastball.' They'll look back at the catcher and go, 'Come on. What are you doing?' Surprisingly enough those three at bats I got him out," Jenkins said.[14]

Hundley more or less just shook his head and shrugged when thinking about all the ways he tried to get McCovey out at the height of the slugger's powers. "Even if we tried to pitch around him we couldn't get the ball far enough outside or inside or low or high to cause him not to hit the ball. He just wore us out. He was a tremendous hitter. If we could keep the ball in the ballpark we felt very fortunate."[15]

* * *

Billy Williams simply never took a day off. He produced season after season of stellar performances while playing through nagging aches and pains that probably should have taken him out of the Cubs' lineup, but he refused to give an inch. He bore the discomfort without saying a word of complaint. At one point during his consecutive-game streak, Williams fouled a ball off his foot. The next day, the swelling enlarged one of his toes so significantly that it forced him to cut a hole in the toe box of his cleat. A little dab of shoe polish hid his exposed foot, and he kept right on going.[16] His toughness further endeared him to a fan base that loved him for so many reasons. They knew that buying a ticket meant seeing Williams. They adored him for all of the remarkable athletic feats he accomplished on the field, and they revered him for doing them every day regardless of circumstance.

The Cubs took up columnist David Condon's suggestion and honored their own iron man with a day dedicated to celebrating one of their superstars. Billy Williams Day was intentionally scheduled for June 29 between games of a Sunday doubleheader against the Cardinals. Thinking ahead with the assumption that Williams would play every day, he would tie Stan Musial's National League record of 895 consecutive games in game one and then establish a new mark in game two. The only mark beyond that was set by New York Yankees legend Lou Gehrig, who played in an astounding 2,130 straight games. A young Leo Durocher had been teammates with Gehrig in New York for two seasons during that streak, so the Cubs' manager had a personal connection to the record. For Williams to set the National League mark at home against Musial's team was poetic in that special way baseball can be at times. The Cubs organization worked behind the scenes to acquire a number of special gifts for Billy that would be presented to him during the ceremony.

The day arrived with palpable excitement. The Cubs sat atop the National League East 7 1/2 games clear of the New York Mets. Chicago's offense had scored more runs than any other team in the league. Awash with optimism, the buzzing crowd filed into Wrigley Field underneath a beautifully blue summer sky for the memorable occasion. A reporter asked Williams before the game if he would like to reach 1,000. Williams replied with a chuckle. "Well, I'll tell you one thing, this (895) has been a long grind, a long, tough grind, so I've been real fortunate in that way to play this many games. You know, if I could play 1,000 games it would be up to what has happened in the past being real lucky on the field not getting injured while I'm playing out there and just go day by day and trying to do my best."[17]

Williams arranged for his family to be at Wrigley Field to celebrate with him and 41,060 of his closest friends. His mother and aunt traveled to Chicago from Whistler, and Shirley brought the girls, each dressed in replica wool Cubs uniform from head to toe. The opening game featured Bob Gibson and Fergie Jenkins, who battled in a scoreless game until the bottom of the eighth inning, when Williams doubled and scored as part of a three-run rally as Chicago won, 3–1. Cubs fans had stood and cheered their hero each time he walked to the plate. Williams and Musial were now tied.

The festivities for Williams occurred between games. Williams doffed his cap to the adoring crowd as he joined National League president Warren Giles, who presented him with a trophy commemorating the record that was about to be set. The organization and his teammates then showered him with gifts ranging from a car to a washer and dryer set to a watch as the Bleacher Bums along with all the other Cubs fans cheered mightily. The overwhelmed Williams caught himself doing something he had never done before at the ballpark: he cried. "I got emotionally upset up there when they were presenting me with everything. The standing ovations had me thinking back to my rookie year. It really shook me," Williams explained.[18] "It was amazing seeing how much all of the fans loved him," recalls his daughter, Nina, about that day. "I never felt more proud. I think this was the first time that I actually saw my dad tear up."[19]

Billy appeared in his 896th consecutive game in the second game of the twin bill. He didn't just play in it though; Williams dominated. He cracked a first-inning single as part of the Cubs' four-run frame that staked the club to a nice lead early in the contest. Williams then doubled in the second, tripled in a run in the fifth, and then tripled in two more runs in the sixth. He finished the game 4-for-5 with nine total bases, three RBIs, and a 12–1 win.

The entire day brought a deeply felt joy to all of Billy's teammates. After he showered and changed, Banks emerged from the clubhouse and made his way down the left-field line singing to himself. The empty Wrigley Field echoed his refashioned *My Fair Lady* lyrics: "I could have played all day, I could have played all day and still have played some more," he waltzed. Santo, who had played alongside Williams since Double A ball in 1958, shook his head in pure awe at the entire event. "It's just amazing. Billy Williams had a day, then he had another day," he marveled. "You know, he told me he was nervous, and he was. It's the first time I've ever seen Bill nervous."[20]

Williams, who had wondered aloud about the intensity of love for him at the beginning of the season, felt secure in the tight embrace of the organization and his teammates. The fans, who had been going crazy for their team all season, succeeded in expressing how much they admired and cherished him. He was a beloved Cub. Williams tried to articulate with words what his tears had already said so loudly. "You can't explain the feeling when you're up there getting standing ovations like that. I had seen Mickey Mantle's day on television and I thought I was prepared for this. But I wasn't. It was a beautiful day. Just beautiful."[21]

* * *

The Cubs entered the All-Star break with a five-game lead over the New York Mets in the National League East. Meanwhile, the San Francisco Giants found themselves in the thick of things out west. The Atlanta Braves led the division but only by one game over the Dodgers and Giants, who were separated by mere percentage points. Simply put, 31-year-old Willie McCovey was in his prime and putting on an absolute show. In mid-July, McCovey launched his 30th homer of the season, a two-run shot to right field that gave the Giants the lead against the Dodgers in a game they went on to win, 7–3. He was hitting .325 with a National League–leading 30 homers. Mac hadn't hit over .300 since his rookie season, but he seemed like a sure bet to repeat the feat in his 11th year, all of this in spite of nagging knee and hip pain that flared up throughout the season.

McCovey's explosive campaign earned him the starting first baseman's job on the National League All-Star team. Along with Willie Mays and Juan Marichal, Stretch flew east to play in the All-Star Game at RFK Stadium in Washington, DC. It was a special opportunity for McCovey because he was accompanied on the squad by several friends from Mobile. Henry Aaron of Atlanta and Cleon Jones of New York joined McCovey as National League starters. The Cubs sent five players, but, stunningly, Williams wasn't among them, having been edged out for one of the very competitive spots.

Excitement for the game in the nation's capital coincided with a thrilling event for the entire country. The Apollo 11 mission, with astronauts Neil Armstrong, Edwin "Buzz" Aldrin, and Michael Collins, launched from Cape Canaveral on July 16. President Richard Nixon planned on attending the All-Star Game, but the contest was delayed a day by rain, causing the chief executive to hand over his duties to Vice President Spiro Agnew as he headed for the West Coast in anticipation of the astronauts' return to earth. Baseball games in action throughout America paused for a moment of recognition five days later, when Armstrong became the first human to walk on the moon.

Rain washed out the originally scheduled game and allowed McCovey, Aaron, and Jones to spend time together in the clubhouse with their fellow All-Stars. Ernie Banks, who had suffered through so many losing seasons, used the downtime to sing the praises of his contending ballclub. "He goes to everybody's locker talking saying how great the Cubs were," Jones remembers of the man he fondly called the "clubhouse lawyer." "He always made for a fun evening."[22] Aaron, he of 15 consecutive All-Star Game appearances and the Atlanta Braves, hit third and played right field. First baseman McCovey and his National League–leading 30 round-trippers hit cleanup. Jones, the 26-year-old New York Mets outfielder, was in the midst of his finest season as a professional ballplayer. Jones was hitting .341 for the surprising second-place Mets, who trailed the Chicago Cubs by only 5 1/2 games. Jones hit sixth and played left field.

The washout forced the All-Star Game to be played on a travel day. Aaron, McCovey, and Jones lined up along the third-base line during the pregame festivities. "Having three guys from Mobile, not just three guys on the All-Star team, but three starters, everybody was talking about that," Jones recalls.[23] The relentless National League lineup produced a quick 3–0 lead before piling on with an outburst in the third inning against Blue Moon Odom of the Oakland A's. Aaron led off the inning with a single to left, bringing Stretch to the plate. Willie Mac and Blue Moon Odom had a little bit of history in the All-Star Game. Odom had struck out McCovey in the previous season's contest, and Stretch verbalized his intention to get payback as he walked back to the dugout. Fast-forward a year, and McCovey dug into the batter's box on a humid night against the right-hander. Shortly thereafter, he was circling the bases after depositing an Odom offering over the right-field fence for a two-run homer that gave the National League a 5–1 lead. Quipped Odom afterward, "He was a man of his word."[24] But Mac wasn't done. In the bottom of the fourth inning, he took Tigers left-hander Denny McClain deep for his second homer of the game. It was just the fourth multi-homer game in All-Star Game history and the first since Cleveland's Al Rosen struck a pair of them in 1954. McCovey received the All-Star Game MVP Award in recognition of his power display.

The three men who returned from the moon bumped McCovey's MVP performance off more than a few front pages as well as the minds of most Americans from the nation's capital to the Bay Area. Armstrong, Aldrin, and Collins splashed down in the Pacific Ocean to great fanfare, and coverage of the start of their 21-day quarantine took center stage. They were greeted by President Nixon albeit from behind a barricaded enclosure designed to prevent any potential space bacteria from entering Earth's atmosphere. After congratulating the astronauts on their historical achievement, Nixon turned to another pressing matter: the All-Star Game.

"Were you American (L)eague or National (L)eague?" Nixon inquired.

"I'm a National (L)eague man but nonpartisan, sir," Armstrong quipped.

"There's the politician in the group!" laughed Nixon.

"Sorry you missed that game, sir," Armstrong replied.[25]

Nixon hardly minded, and neither did McCovey, who assessed his multi-homer game nonchalantly. "They don't count in the pennant race," he shrugged.[26] If anything, he was a little annoyed because his hip again flared up on the heels of another awkward exchange with a vice president. It had been Richard Nixon back in 1960 at the opening of Candlestick Park; now it was Spiro Agnew, who threw out the first pitch in lieu of the president. "He told me I've got the biggest shoulder swing he's ever seen," McCovey revealed. "I'm not really sure what the Vice President meant."[27] Ambiguity from the White House aside, Johnny Bench, the sensational young catcher of the Cincinnati Reds who nearly matched McCovey's two homers had he not been robbed by Boston's Carl Yastrzemski, made his feelings about Stretch crystal clear. "If they pitched to him all the time, he'(d) have 50 homers now," Bench said.[28]

* * *

All eyes were on Wrigley Field as the season recommenced on July 24. Ken Holtzman pitched the Cubs past Don Sutton and the Dodgers, 5–3, improving Chicago's record to 62–37. The Bleacher Bums, conducted by Cubs pitcher

Dick Selma, cheered vociferously. After playing in front of so many empty seats throughout their careers, Williams and his teammates basked in the glow of playing great baseball in front of large, vocal crowds. Robert Boyle of *Sports Illustrated* observed that summer the electric current jolting the fan base into a frenzy. "To anyone accustomed to what used to be known around Chicago as 'the friendly confines of Wrigley Field,' the screams of the Bleacher Bums and the winning ways of the Cubs must come as a shock," he wrote. The first-place North Siders had firmly placed the Mets and Cardinals in their rearview mirror, and confidence oozed out of them. Ron Santo started to click his heels after wins. The players considered recording an album to forever capture the songs sung throughout the ballpark. Manager Leo Durocher kept his bunch driving toward the dog days of summer. "Everywhere you go people say, 'Hey, what's happened to the Cards?' We're what's happened to the Cardinals," Holtzman told Boyle.[29]

Holtzman's dazzling season hit a crescendo on Tuesday, August 19, on the heels of a notable music festival in upstate New York. Woodstock provided emblematic images of the times, and the Cubs' joyfully celebrating Holtzman's no-hitter against the Atlanta Braves captured the magical season at Wrigley Field. Santo belted a three-run homer in the bottom of the first inning—his 25th of the season—against future Hall of Fame knuckleballer Phil Niekro, and then Chicago turned to Holtzman. The left-handed rotation stalwart, who won 174 games across 15 big-league seasons, initially didn't have a good feel for his curveball, but, nevertheless, he proceeded to dart fastballs in and around the strike zone all afternoon, igniting the increasingly raucous crowd. During each plate appearance, the Brave hitter made contact, and the Cubs' defense retired him. Chicago continued to lead, 3–0, when the incomparable Henry Aaron strode to the plate in the top of the seventh inning.

When Aaron's bat connected with a Holtzman offering, everyone in the ballpark initially thought that the baseball soaring out to left field meant not only the end of the no-hitter but the loss of the shutout as well. Billy Williams sprinted back and to his left toward the spot in the outfield wall where it rounds into a slightly shallower power alley while tracking the ball's flight. His extended glove slapped the ivy to stop his momentum as he ran out of room with the ball high overhead. It was going to be a home run. But the wind was blowing in something fierce that day as it is wont to do at Wrigley Field, and it stalled the ball's momentum before pushing it back toward straightaway left. Williams quickly adjusted by backpedaling along the warning track. He reached up and caught the ball with both hands and fired it back to the infield. "It was gone if it hadn't been for the wind. Just one more foot over, and it was a homer. I was in the vines anyway," Williams said.[30] So many times throughout the history of no-hitters, a defensive play occurs that preserves it and becomes a signature play over the course of history. This catch became just that. The Cubs knew that Holtzman had a real chance to throw one that day, while the Braves sensed defeat. "When that happened, I thought he might get his no hitter," Aaron said.[31] As it turned out, Aaron made the last out of the ballgame—a groundball to second baseman Glenn Beckert—which set off delirium throughout a shaking Wrigley Field. In a scene out of today's college football games, fans stormed the field amidst the Cubs' celebration and caused a momentary adrenaline surge among the throng of revelers. "I was scared," Holtzman admitted afterward. "Some guy was choking me. I thought it was Santo, but I don't know. I was on cloud nine myself."[32] Holtzman's no-hitter was the ninth in Cubs' history dating back to Larry Corcoran of the 1880 Chicago White Stockings and the first one in nearly 46 years of Major League history without recording a strikeout.[33] "I threw about 14 bad pitches and got away with them all," an astonished Holtzman remarked after the game.[34] At 77–45, the Cubs led the National League East by eight games with 40 to go.

Amidst the fervor of their incredible play, an idea percolated: how about making some music? Incredibly, amazingly, awesomely, Cubs players recorded an album during the season. It was neither a one-song effort nor a hit with a B-side. The record, *Cub Power*, included a number of songs featuring Opening Day hero Willie Smith and his teammates. Among the hits, "Hey, Hey, Holy Mackerel" took off in popularity.

Some of the guys—Smith and Banks come to mind—embraced the notion of singing for the masses, while it caused a moment of pause for others. "The Lord gave me a little bit of talent in some areas, but it certainly wasn't in singing," jokes Don Kessinger. Although the team's notable stars had some opportunities to make money through endorsements and other business ventures outside the ballpark to complement their salaries, the bulk of the roster did not. Creating a record together gave the team a unique chance to put a few extra dollars into everyone's pockets. "We had gotten together and decided that it didn't matter how many of us—whether it's eight or ten people that were doing most of that stuff—but that at the end of the year whatever money we had made in that was going to be divided among the whole team. Billy was one of the main people in that because he could have made a lot more than some of us," Kessinger recalls. With the team-first approach quickly agreed on, the players recorded the album.[35] At the end of the day, they didn't make much of anything from it.

* * *

Both the Chicago Cubs and the San Francisco Giants entered September in first place. The Cubs led the Mets by 4 1/2 games, while the Giants clung to a half-game lead over the Dodgers. San Francisco slipped first. McCovey, who entered the month having homered 41 times, had been fantastic all season, but injuries sapped his power. His knee, hip, and wrist, which were hurt while attempting to make a catch, troubled him relentlessly. The Giants beat Montreal twice to open the month before losing seven of their next 10 games as they tumbled into fourth place, a game and a half behind the Atlanta Braves, in the tightly bunched National League West.

The Giants still had one last gasp in them. McCovey reached base three times and scored twice in San Francisco's 5–3 triumph over the Cincinnati Reds in a victory on September 14 that ignited eight wins over a nine-game stretch during which the Giants resurfaced as division leaders. The Giants didn't play bad baseball to close out the season, but the Braves punished them every time they had a hiccup. Led by Henry Aaron and Orlando Cepeda, Atlanta won 10 of its final 11 games of the season. The lone loss was of no consequence because the Braves had already won the division. McCovey's 45 homers and 126 RBIs paced the National League, but, once again, the Giants would not be playing in the postseason.

Much has been written about the New York Mets' incredible 1969 season. That ballclub has been highly praised—and deservedly so. The narrative surrounding that National League East division race has occasionally portrayed the Cubs as having collapsed down the stretch because Leo Durocher played his starters too frequently. Billy Williams didn't buy that line of thinking then and doesn't adhere to it now. The Cubs didn't lose the division title; the Mets won it, he believes. There's no question that Chicago hit a brutal skid at the beginning of September. After winning their first game of the month against the Reds, 8–2, to maintain a five-game lead, the Cubs lost their next eight games and fell out of first place as the Mets revved up. Like Atlanta, New York reached a point where it basically won every day. At least that's how it felt to the Cubs, whose tenuous grip on first place slipped away as the month progressed. "The Mets were unbelievably hot. They played great and every day we went to the ballpark they won again. You don't want to start looking at the scoreboard, but you're also human. I don't want to give the Mets a lot of credit, but I do," confesses Kessinger with a chuckle. "They played great. It wasn't just us they blew right through everybody else."[36] New York wound up winning 23 of its 30 games in September, while Chicago finished the month 8–17. Ron Santo personified the increasing tension within the Cubs' clubhouse. He emitted his deep love for the Cubs throughout the season with heel clicks even though it angered the opposition. Santo's joy was turning sour, and he pressed to turn the Cubs' situation around. Williams tried to loosen his friend up. He pulled a great gag along with Glenn Beckert. They raided Santo's fan mail for one of the many small boxes that contained a baseball sent to him by a fan for autographing. They removed the ball and replaced it with a timer that they had taken from trainer Al Schoonmeir and returned the package to Santo's mail stack. Ron arrived, and Billy casually asked Beckert about the loud ticking noise. Santo reacted frantically and searched until he found the box. Bomb! He raced out of the clubhouse and chucked it out onto Waveland Avenue.[37]

Williams tried every motivational tactic he could think of to exhort the ballclub. He, along with Santo and Beckert, would tell Durocher that a team meeting would be beneficial. At one point, Williams wrote the dollar figure of winning the World Series on mirrors in the clubhouse where his teammates would see it. Nothing worked.[38]

Despite their best efforts, the Cubs fell short. The Mets blanked St. Louis, 6–0, on September 24 to clinch the inaugural National League East title, dashing Chicago's postseason hopes. All the promises built up by their sustained summer success shattered like a jammed bat handle over the season's final weeks. What remains intact decades later are the meaningful memories shared by all the fans who visited Wrigleyville in 1969 as well as the tinge of "what if" that still swirls around that team's fate due to the playoff system during that time period, which admitted only division winners into the postseason. "What I do look back and kind of wish—because we had a very good ballclub for five or six years—that the situation would have been somewhat like it is today," the six-time All-Star Kessinger ponders. "We would have been in the playoffs every year."[39]

The legacy of the 1969 Chicago Cubs will live on in the Windy City forever. Williams's peppering line drives all over the yard, Banks driving in 100 runs, Santo's heel clicks, Holtzman's no-hitter, Selma orchestrating the Bleacher Bums—all indelible memories etched into one of the most scintillating seasons in club history. The players continue to love each other half a century later. "I've never played on a team—I don't believe—that was as close as that group. We all just enjoyed each other," says Kessinger.[40]

* * *

For his incredible accomplishments during the 1969 season, Willie McCovey was named the National League's MVP in November. The result of tilting the game back toward the hitter? Utter devastation by McCovey. In addition to leading the National League in homers and RBIs, he led all of Major League Baseball in OPS for the second straight season with a mark of 1.108. It wasn't just his production that gave opponents pause but also the manner in which he did it. McCovey struck genuine fear into pitchers (and their managers) in a way unique to baseball. In 1969, they just quit pitching to him. Instead, National League hurlers issued a Major League–record 45 intentional passes to Stretch in 1969, which was 12 more than Ted Williams had received in 1957. The sight of McCovey watching four wide ones sail by while his bat rested on his shoulder became a common sight at Giants games. Willie Mays did his best to prevent opposing pitchers from walking Stretch. He would frequently stop at first base when the ball he struck could easily have gone for a double, all in the name of getting Mac a good pitch to hit. Each of the intentional walks genuinely annoyed Stretch after a while, but he understood it. He was in for a bigger dose in 1970. Sparky Anderson, who took over as the manager of the Cincinnati Reds the following season, made sure the trend continued.

Giants owner Horace Stoneham recognized that the team's overreliance on McCovey made life difficult for its offense, particularly in September, when San Francisco struggled. "Willie McCovey had a great year. He played when he was hurt and he never gave up," Stoneham noted before turning to the issue at hand for the front office. "But we couldn't get, and I criticize no one, the protection we needed for McCovey at bat. Had we a good man behind him, they would have been forced to pitch to McCovey."[41]

McCovey always looked the part, but the powder blue suede boots he wore to the press conference discussing his MVP Award were next level. "I've got to dress for the occasion," he smiled. He admitted that signing late had caused him concern going into the season. "Instead, I got off to the greatest start of my career and had my best April ever. Maybe that's what I should do all the time—start late," McCovey joked. He had not taken winning the honor for granted due to the whispers he heard about voters on the East Coast casting ballots for Mets star pitcher Tom Seaver, who wound up finishing second. "I was preparing myself for a letdown the last week or so," he admitted. "That made the news that much better."[42]

The cultural impact of McCovey's 1969 season extended two decades into the future. The popular television series *The Wonder Years*, starring Fred Savage as Kevin Arnold, a teenager growing up during the late 1960s through the early 1970s, referenced it during an episode that aired in 1989 featuring a baseball card trading session between two of the show's primary characters. In season three, set in 1969, Arnold and Paul Pfeiffer, played by Josh Saviano, intensely discuss a swap of baseball cards in which the former offers to swap Juan Marichal and Luis Tiant cards for Pfeiffer's Willie McCovey card. "No, no," Pfeiffer interrupts. "McCovey is off the table." It was, says the adult Arnold, who provides voice-over commentary throughout the show, "the McCovey trade, a common impasse." When Kevin refuses to part with Ted Williams, Paul reiterates that "McCovey is off the table!" The exclamation became a punch line for the actors on set, and Saviano has heard about it from people over the years, including one particularly key player in the potential deal. Saviano, a lawyer and notable sports fan, gave a rare interview to the *Washington Post* and recalled, "People still come up to me, particularly guys my age, and will just say, 'McCovey is off the table!' To the point where

Willie McCovey saw the episode and sent Fred and I a little autographed book of him. It was so cool!"[43]

Meanwhile, the 1969 baseball season gave the city of Mobile the opportunity to boast of being home to several World Champions, an MVP, and one of the league's best players on one of its most exciting teams. Local officials threw a huge bash to celebrate all of their accomplishments. Cleon Jones and Tommy Agee were there, as was Billy Williams.

McCovey, in what would become his customary position on the matter over the years, declined to attend. In fairness to him, Stretch did not travel in January to the annual baseball writers' dinner in Chicago, claiming he was busy tending to "business," but that reasoning seems unlikely.[44] The difficult combination of his troublesome knee and the ill health of John Dudum, with whom he shared such a close friendship, seems like a much more probable cause of his absence. Mobile, however, was a different situation. McCovey retained deeply rooted feelings of contempt for his hometown that did not dissipate. Jones, who has been an active member of the Africatown community for years, pressed his lifelong friend about the issue to no avail. "He had a genuine dislike for the South, in particular Mobile," Jones says. "I probed a lot trying to find out what triggered that, and he never gave me anything concrete or specific that took place. 'I just don't like the South.' Well, none of us like the South you're talking about, but things evolve, things move on, and we have to adjust to what's around us now and the people around us now."[45] That McCovey rejected and Jones returned speaks to the different ways individuals impacted by growing up in Mobile responded to the city in their adulthood. It's complicated, and people see the issue from different perspectives. "Maybe it's not the Mobile you want it to be, but it's different and it's growing in many ways," Jones offers.[46] It wasn't as though Stretch never went back. He visited his family, but Mac always returned quietly. He did not want family members to let it be known that he was in town.

Locals turned out in droves to meet their baseball heroes at the celebration, and they enjoyed returning home and seeing all of the familiar faces. The beaming pair of Jones and Agee feted a throng of excited kids thrilled to meet them. Williams, who frequently took his family back to Whistler during the offseason to visit familiar faces, signed autographs even though the sting of the situation's context gnawed at his competitive genes. Did Jones make sure his fellow ballplayers from Mobile remembered that the New York Mets were World Series champions? "Every day," Jones, who famously caught the final out of the series, happily chirps. "Every day I let them know about it."[47]

Chapter 7

"An Unwilling Constituency of Pitchers"

Receiving the MVP Award was a bright spot during an otherwise challenging time for Willie McCovey physically. As had become his custom, McCovey spent the first month of the offseason consulting with Dr. Robert Kerlan and other medical professionals about his arthritic left knee, which continued to trouble him without mercy. Despite continued work with physical therapist Bert Gustafson, his hip still ached, too. Stretch turned down several media opportunities, presumably to cover the 1969 postseason, to focus on his rest and recovery. Mac did not feel any pressure to pursue a job in the medium, particularly from a financial standpoint. His excellent season assured him of a raise in 1970.

While McCovey unsurprisingly spurned the invitation from Mobile officials to take part in the end-of-year celebration, he also declined the opportunity to attend the baseball writers' dinner in Chicago. The January gala honored the highest achievements in the sport, including the MVPs in each league. McCovey's dear friend, John Dudum, with whom he had eaten lunch before games so many times, was seriously ill. Stretch drew even closer to the family on the verge of losing its patriarch, the savvy businessman who had supplied countless notable hotels and houses throughout the Bay Area with fine linens. Over the 11 years since first moving to San Francisco in 1959, McCovey developed a close kinship with the Dudums, and they embraced him as a member of the family. They grew even closer to one another during this tragic time. "In 1970, my dad died. I took the business over with four of my brothers and my sister," says Rocky Dudum in retracing that year. "All of us got real close to Willie. We gave him an office in our factory. He always had an office with 'Willie McCovey' on it. He would come over because we were right next to the ballpark. He would sit in his office, talk on the phone, do whatever he wanted, and nobody bothered him.

He had his own parking spot. We were one, two, three, four, five, six, and Willie was seven."[1]

In the midst of his personal sadness and physical pain, McCovey received a phone call from Horace Stoneham, who asked if they could meet to discuss his contract to rework the dollar figure for the 1970 season.[2] Stoneham, who was very amendable to rewarding McCovey for his MVP season, cared deeply about his players, and he wanted Stretch to be happy. This negotiation went very differently from the one that had taken place the previous year. Giants vice president Chub Feeney, Stoneham's primary point person (and nephew) in contract talks for years, was no longer with the organization, having been hired as the new National League president at the owners' meeting in December. The diminished tension between the Players Association and owners over the pension issue also made for an amendable environment to talk money. As a result, it took only a 15-minute conversation between the two men to settle on a new pact. Stoneham replaced McCovey's contract with a two-year commitment for what was reported to be $110,000 per season. Stretch trusted that Stoneham would follow through, and the new deal demonstrated that his faith was not misplaced. "They promised me last year I could renegotiate my second year but they didn't have to do it," he said. "They were nice enough to let me renegotiate and I'm satisfied."[3]

Keeping McCovey happy was a no-brainer for Stoneham even if the Giants' financial situation, which was always intertwined with his own, looked increasingly dire under the weight of the relocation of the A's to Oakland in 1968 and significant attendance issues at Candlestick Park. Stoneham's team featured the most powerful left-handed hitter in baseball, and he wanted to keep it that way. "Willie is at the peak of his career," Stoneham rightly noted. "He is the most feared hitter in the game today. I think he's going to have another great season. There's no limit to what he can do."[4] That McCovey now belonged to the $100,000 club in Major League Baseball marked a significant milestone in his career. He became the third Giant to reach that figure, along with Willie Mays and Juan Marichal. Stretch provided superstar play on the field and now earned equivalent compensation. Over the past five seasons—his age 27-through-31 campaigns—Mac's elite run production at the plate included 187 homers and 510 RBIs. Pitchers walked him a ridiculous 428 times, including 97 intentionally. The staggering numbers put his development into perspective. It took him longer to arrive than was necessary, considering how many at-bats the organization thwarted him from getting during his first four seasons, but he had now fully reached superstar status. The fans and factions of the press made life tough for him early in his career. Those days were now long forgotten by most people, and Mac was happy not to relive them.

Mac's biggest foe now was his body. Arthritis had viciously eaten away at the cartilage in McCovey's knee for a decade, creating painful swelling, stiffness, and inflammation. Stretch dedicated himself to a routine of maintenance work, but he could hope to heal only in a situational sense. The foundational issue within his knee was not solvable. McCovey's physical problem was compounded after he arrived at Casa Grande for spring training in 1970. On the very first day of camp, he twisted his knee harshly enough that it necessitated a visit to his longtime physician Dr. Kerlan in Los Angeles at the start of March. Kerlan drained fluid from the knee and prescribed medication to treat its ongoing arthritis if the pain should become unbearable. Unfortunately, it flared up again quickly. On his return to camp, the knee bothered McCovey so intensely that he asked out of the exhibition opener against the Chicago Cubs despite wanting to play. He missed the second game as well. Despite appearing against Cleveland on March 8, something wasn't right. McCovey took a dosage of medicine for his knee and hoped it would calm down.

Although the pain slightly improved, Stretch's overall physical state went from bad to worse on March 12. McCovey struck out twice against Catfish Hunter of the Oakland A's and asked Giants manager Clyde King to remove him from the exhibition game. McCovey couldn't see well out of his right eye. Objects appeared blurry. Adrenaline and panic simultaneously ripped through the insides of the Giants' officials. He immediately visited Dr. Paul Case, who diagnosed McCovey with an inflamed retina and recommended a consultation with Bay Area specialist Dr. Sam Kimura at the University of California Medical Center. Despite all the tumult surrounding his situation, McCovey remained characteristically serene. "I'm not blind yet," he calmly told a group of reporters.[5]

Mac's situation unfolded within the unique context of the Giants' upcoming trip to Japan. Having drawn only 870,000 fans to Candlestick Park in 1969, Horace Stoneham needed to find alternative sources of money. He arranged for his players to travel east for a baseball tour of Japan, providing an opportunity to play exhibitions in front of larger crowds than those typically seen at spring training games.[6] McCovey's ongoing ailment threatened his participation. Japanese officials wanted the MVP of the National League to play, of course, so the unfolding events generated some angst. Did McCovey feel pressure to go on the trip? It seems reasonable to conclude that he felt at least some obligation to go as one of the marquee stars of the league. Beyond the context of the Japan tour, this episode highlights the increasingly intense battle that McCovey was having with his body. Here he had reached the height of his baseball powers as the MVP of the league, yet his physical state was already deteriorating to the point of needing to sit out a game for the purpose of pain management, and he was just 32 years old.

Following a thorough examination, Dr. Kimura concluded that the culprit behind the retina inflammation was the medication Mac had recently been taking to treat his knee. Kimura and Kerlan discussed the situation over the phone and devised a new plan to treat both problems. Kimura was confident that a change in medications would calm McCovey's retina down in short order. His diagnosis proved correct. McCovey ceased taking the pain meds and joined his teammates in Japan.[7]

It would be an understatement to suggest that the tour did not go well for Mac on the field. He battled through his eye ailment well enough to hit a home run during the second exhibition game, but the swelling remained an irritant, and Japan's chilly weather worsened his leg discomfort. One highlight was the time away from the ballpark he spent with his friend Tito Fuentes. They enjoyed the sites and picked up a few words along the way. They had learned a number of Japanese words when they played with Mashi Murakami in 1964 and 1965. Now they gleaned, among other things, "Moshi, moshi," a Japanese phrase used as a greeting when answering the phone. From then on, Mac and Fuentes answered the phone with "moshi, moshi" every time they thought the other was calling.[8]

Following the tour's conclusion, McCovey made a pit stop in California to have his knee drained before returning to Arizona. His legs would need to be at their best because the grass infield at Candlestick Park was being replaced with AstroTurf for the 1970 season as part of a larger makeover to make the stadium more hospitable to its newest tenant, the San Francisco 49ers. The thought was that McCovey needed to be at his defensive best because the new turf would quicken any sharply hit balls off the bats of left-handed hitters. Mac remained unfazed. "The ball will come at you much faster than before but it's only a matter of being ready and reacting quickly enough to field the shot," he pointed out.[9] The real issue was how visiting first basemen were going to protect themselves from him.

* * *

How would the Chicago Cubs respond to coming so close to winning the National League East only to come up short? That was the key question for Billy Williams and his teammates as they reported to spring training in 1970. As McCovey and the Giants boarded their flight to Japan, Williams diligently prepared for the upcoming campaign in his customary style. He ordered bats, closely inspected their grain for any deficiencies, and took account of their weight. Once again, he sat down with Fergie Jenkins, and the two of them mapped out their personal goals for the season.

Team success would have to take on slightly different characteristics this year, as the status of Ernie Banks was changing. The great Banks, in the midst of dealing with the harsh criticism directed at him by manager Leo Durocher, had produced at the plate the past two seasons—55 homers, 189 RBIs—in spite of a painful left knee. He had been playing well, but that knee, originally injured when Banks twisted it decades previously while in the Army, was a snake in the grass waiting to strike. That said, he remained the projected starter at first base.

Despite coming off their exciting 1969 campaign, the Cubs were far from the biggest story in Arizona during spring training. That title belonged to the contract dispute between young Oakland A's slugger Reggie Jackson and owner Charlie O. Finley. Jackson, 23, belted 47 homers in 1969 and wanted a raise that reflected his production. He aimed to procure a salary in the $60,000 range, but the stubborn Finley refused to budge from his offer of $40,000. Jackson lived in the area, having played collegiately at Arizona State. From the start of his career, he developed a number of friendships with veteran players who also spent spring training in the area. They frequently spent time together. "I ate dinner almost every night with Willie McCovey, Billy Williams, and Ernie Banks. And they never let me pay. I was only making maybe $10,000 or $20,000 a year, and those guys were always making $100,000," Jackson told interviewer Charlie Vascellaro in 2021. "It was just a great time for me because I was the kid, and they were teaching me what to do."[10]

The advice given by the elder statesmen included a warning not to get injured because African American ballplayers were not likely to be given bench roles. Choose your words carefully when talking to the media and be wary about whom one associated with. Not doing any of these things could present an unwelcome risk to your career, and they wanted the young star to be successful. Now Jackson found himself in a contract stalemate that drew a lot of attention from media outlets, and he laid out his case for a salary increase. "Who knew whether those 29 home runs were just a one-year thing?" he asked about his 1968 season. "But then I hit 47 and the man has to pay me. I'm more confident in my own talents."[11]

Williams increasingly saw more of Jackson as his holdout lasted well into March. "He was having trouble with Finley one year so I got to know him because right after Ernie and I would get through practicing we would walk out of the clubhouse, and there was Reggie," recalls Williams. "We would go play golf, and I got to know him. We enjoyed it."[12] Eventually, Jackson and Finley reached an agreement that called for a salary of $45,000 and the cost of rent. Williams and Jackson went their separate ways for the season as their ballclubs headed north, but, although they did not cross paths throughout the season playing in separate leagues, their friendship would deepen further several years in the future.

* * *

Billy Williams took his game to new heights in 1970. His season began a bit slowly at the plate, as he opened the campaign 1-for-20, but he adjusted by driving the ball to left field with more frequency. His strategy worked. As many Americans closely monitored the perilous Apollo 13 mission occurring in the sky above them, Williams played in his 988th consecutive game and shone with a four-hit game in Chicago's 5–1 win over Philadelphia on April 15, including the 250th home run of his career, an opposite-field fly ball that carried into the sun-washed bleachers. He followed it up the next day with another multihit game featuring his second long ball of the season in another win over the Phillies. On Friday, April 17, Jim Lovell, Fred Haise, and John Swigert splashed down safely into the Pacific Ocean to everyone's great relief. No respite lay ahead for National League pitchers concerned with facing Williams. That afternoon, he collected two more hits and drove in three as Chicago beat Montreal, 8–7. It was all part of a 10-game hitting streak as the Cubs reeled off 11 wins in a row.

When Ernie Banks's knee pain put him on the disabled list for the first time in his career, Williams picked up the offensive slack. He led the major leagues with a career-high 205 hits and set a new personal best with 42 home runs. It was a sublime performance when Chicago needed it most. The Cubs also lost catcher Randy Hundley to a broken thumb in spring training and then torn knee cartilage in April due to a collision at the plate that allowed him to appear in only 73 games. Losing those two players greatly impacted a Cubs team trying to get over the hump in the incredibly competitive National League East. They finished second to the Pittsburgh Pirates.

Billy Williams's incredible consecutive streak of 1,117 games that spanned across eight seasons and made him the iron man of baseball ended on September 3, 1970, on a rainy day against the Phillies. The Cubs beat Philadelphia, 7–2, but the story was Williams, who hadn't missed a game since September 21, 1963. Late in the ballgame, the crowd, sensing that Williams was not going to appear, chanted, "We want Billy," but he couldn't hear them. Williams was in the clubhouse listening to the broadcast and afterward admitted, "If I had stayed on the bench, I would have started thinking." He understandably felt torn. "Right now I have mixed emotions about it, part relief and part sadness."[13]

After the game, the Cubs walked toward their clubhouse in the left-field corner. The image of Williams running toward them jarred everyone. Still in full uniform covered by a Cubs jacket, Williams jogged past the grounds crew rolling the tarp on his way to conducting an interview. "As we were all going in leaving the field here comes one guy going the opposite way to go on the postgame show which was Billy Williams," remembers Joe Amalfitano, who coached for the Cubs that season. "I'll never forget that."[14] Williams's accomplishment left his teammates and opponents alike in wonder. Decades later,

Billy's streak matters to them as one of the most consequential things they witnessed in baseball. "I think the streak was incredible. Nobody feels great when you come to the park every day. You're going to have to play through things, and to have a streak like that you have to know there were many days that he had to play through either not feeling good or an ankle bothering him or one thing or another, but he never let on he just played. He just played," remarks Don Kessinger.[15]

In the years following the streak's conclusion, Williams frankly discussed the toll it took on him mentally and physically. "I showed up one day and I could hardly stand straight," he confessed to columnist Jim Murray. Williams played through illness, back pain that required cortisone shots, and the risk that playing at less than 100 percent could hurt his team's performance, which meant more to him than anything. "I found myself so exhausted working on the record. I could hardly go from first to third on a long single," he admitted. Baseball didn't notice any slowdown in his performance. The sport was in awe of Williams's achievement.[16]

Billy's incredible 1970 campaign put him in prime position for postseason honors, but the MVP trophy instead went to Cincinnati catcher Johnny Bench. Williams had to settle for runner-up. "I was disappointed, sure, but I wasn't bitter about it," Williams told sportswriter Irv Haag. The voting produced chatter around the game as baseball debates are wont to do. The Cubs won 84 games but missed out on the postseason again. They finished the season in second place, five games behind the Pittsburgh Pirates. Nobody questioned Bench's greatness or his impact on the Reds, who made the postseason, but would Chicago have been a competitive member of the National League East without Williams? One result of this conversation emerged in voluminous praise for Williams. Longtime friend Henry Aaron weighed in on Williams's true value. "He's one of the greatest outfielders I ever played against. It just seems to be Billy's 'thing' to be an all-time, unsung ballplayer. People like Willie Mays and me, and even Cleon Jones and Tommie Agee, who all came from around Mobile, get quite a bit of publicity, but they always seem to bypass Billy in spite of how great he is," Aaron said.[17]

* * *

The offseason banquet circuit gave fans around the country a unique opportunity to hear from some of the most notable baseball stars in the game. Billy Williams appeared at the baseball writers' dinner in Chicago several times over the years, and he attended several during this offseason with Leo Durocher. Williams traveled to a hot stove event in Atlanta to appear alongside, among others, the magisterial ace of the St. Louis Cardinals, Bob Gibson.

During the event, the two men agreed to a dual interview with a local reporter who began the conversation by asking Williams about his contract situation. Billy answered forthrightly. "After you get to a certain point—I'm 32 years old—I feel that I don't have that much more time to play, and you got to collect now. If you do good you got to be paid for it," he said. The interviewer thanked Williams for his honest answer by pivoting to Gibson and asking him a question that would leave any hitter wishing he was somewhere else. "Bob, they call this guy over here the quiet man. What has he done against you? Has he treated you kindly, or have you been pretty tough on him?" As the reporter spoke, Billy vigorously shook his head no as if to say, don't make my life any tougher than it needs to be. "You talking about as far as talking or what?" Gibson retorted. Awkward chuckles. Gibson then backed down—it was only February after all—and graciously showed Williams love. "Oh, there is no doubt about it, Bill is probably one of the best hitters in the league. When I say one of the best I mean of the top three and of course being left handed I would rather pitch against a right hander than face him, so he's done his damage," Gibson said.[18] They would face each other again two months later on Opening Day.

On the cusp of spring training, Billy Williams sought a raise to a six-figure salary. There was just one problem. P. K. Wrigley wasn't exactly the type of owner to hand out a big-money contract. The Cubs had never had a player make a yearly salary of $100,000, and conventional wisdom suggested that Wrigley wanted that trend to continue. Williams didn't have an agent, of course, but he communicated his desire to Wrigley for an upgraded deal. General manager John Holland reached out to Williams, who let it be known that he would be remaining at home instead of reporting to spring training. Following a 10-day holdout, Wrigley agreed to pay Williams what he'd requested, much to Holland's relief. "I'm a little shaky after my first one, but it could not have been a more deserving person than Billy," Holland said. "We're both very happy it's all over."[19] Williams joined McCovey in the $100,000 club.

April 6 could have been colder. Technically, anyway. Practically speaking, it was a pretty miserable day in Chicago. "Similar to something you read in the Bible on Good Friday," says Joe Amalfitano, the Cubs' first-base coach in 1971. "Dark and dreary." Thousands of Cubs fans stridently braved the frigid temperatures and worked their way into Wrigley Field. Although cold weather in April remains a constant theme in Chicago, the weather that day felt closer to a Bears game in December than Opening Day of the baseball season. Already dressed in their warmest clothing, fans stuffed themselves into sleeping bags in a futile attempt to thaw out as their gloved hands clutched cups of coffee whose escaping steam moistened their cheeks and fogged their glasses. The fierce wind blew in off the lake. The conditions, plus the day's starting pitchers, Bob Gibson and Fergie Jenkins, portended a low-scoring contest.

Gibson was coming off a season that featured a National League–leading 23 wins and a minuscule FIP of 2.29, a mark that led all of baseball. Chicago countered with its most domineering hurler, Jenkins, who had recorded four consecutive 20-win campaigns. Jenkins relished personal matchups against Gibson, and facing him on Opening Day proved to be particularly special. Everyone in and around baseball knew about the ferocious battles between Williams and Gibson. Ernie Banks loved to egg on the Cardinals' ace much to the chagrin of his friend. "He always told Bob Gibson as he walked to the mound, 'Billy gonna hit a home run off of you today!' I said, 'Leave that mean son of bitch alone.' Ernie would say that all the time," Williams laughs.[20]

Indeed, each team scored once through the first nine innings as Jenkins and Gibson handcuffed hitters, except Williams, who walked, singled, and hit a laser beam to center field in the eighth inning that Matty Alou plucked out of the air. Jenkins retired the Cardinals in order in the top of the 10th, and Williams was scheduled to bat second in the bottom of the frame. In the dugout, as he prepared to face Gibson for a fifth time that day, Williams strolled by Amalfitano and made a notable declaration. "Joe, I'm gonna get this guy," he proclaimed.[21]

Glenn Beckert grounded out to shortstop, which brought Williams up to bat. Gibson coiled and hurled a pitch toward the plate. Williams's quick wrists fired, and his bat cracked Gibson's offering deep in the air toward right-center field. The crowd exploded with visual joyful shouts of water vapor as Williams's first home run of the season landed amongst the bundled fans to give Chicago a 2–1 win over St. Louis. Amalfitano marveled at the sight. "I've had two guys in my lifetime that went into an at bat saying I'm gonna get this guy here, and that would be Billy Williams and Mr. Mays," says Amalfitano, a 40-year veteran of professional baseball. "Other guys say it, but never do it."[22]

All of the fingers on a hand would be too many to count the number of times Billy made a statement like that before an at-bat, but it happened on this day. "It's one time," Williams recalls. "You have a good feeling, along with everything you see him doing from the start of the game, and then it all comes together at the end when you're hitting. That's what happened."[23]

Jenkins, fresh off career win number 92, lamented giving up the game-tying home run to Joe Torre on a fastball over the plate. "But," he happily stated after the game, "my old fishing buddy took care of everything."[24]

"That was really, really exciting," Williams said.[25]

Williams hit more home runs off Gibson than any other batter: 10. It was an astonishing feat that left his teammates in awe. "Billy would whack that son of a gun and hit it into right center gone, and I mean early in the game when Gibson is throwing missiles," marvels Jack Hiatt, who played alongside Williams in 1970. "The harder he threw the harder Billy hit it."[26]

In the late fall of 2022, just a few days after he had lunch with Williams, Randy Hundley marvels at his teammate's success against baseball's best. It simply cannot be defined by his playing ability alone. "Billy was his own man. He didn't let anybody intimidate him in any way whatsoever, especially opposing pitchers. He stayed in on pitchers that just," Hundley pauses. "I don't know how he did it."[27]

Billy Williams always made himself available to mentor younger players throughout his career, and it continued to be a meaningful practice for him in 1971. Now in his 11th full season at the major league level, Williams continued to be a highly respected veteran player who had reached the upper echelon of performance on the field. As much as he was respected for his work on the diamond, Williams garnered more praise for his presence off the field. Even though Williams had reached superstar status, one would never know it by the way he treated people. "Billy was always available if you wanted to ask him a question," Kessinger says. Williams credits Banks, who had happily helped him when he was a rookie, and now it was his turn to pass along tips to younger players, whether it dealt with a movement on a pitcher's breaking ball or where to eat after the game. They also loved the way Williams made them laugh. "It was a dry wit most of the time, and it was *good*," Kessinger emphasizes.

Billy Williams cracked up his teammates a lot. He enjoyed a good prank as much as anyone—see the Ron Santo timer episode in 1969—and used humor as a way to help everyone in the clubhouse relax. Kessinger recalls one particular ballgame when he couldn't make solid contact against Gaylord Perry's famous spitball. "I was hitting little ground ball after little ground ball," Kessinger, who played with Williams in Chicago for more than a decade, remembers. "Billy's hitting line drives and all that kind of stuff. Gaylord had that quote, unquote super sinker that he threw. In the middle of the game I hit another ground ball. I got back to the dugout and I said, 'Billy, how do you hit Gaylord Perry so good?' And he said, 'Easy. You just hit it on the dry side.'"[28]

In 1971, Bill North, a 23-year-old outfielder, made his major league debut. North, the Cubs' top prospect, was drafted by the organization in the 12th round of the 1969 draft from Central Washington State College. Williams immediately took him under his wing. "He was my mentor," North says. "This is one of the classiest, best individuals, who used to tell me how crazy I was on a daily basis. Somebody that is so dear to my heart. In life you meet some good people, but Billy Williams is the best." Billy wasn't the only Williams who helped North transition to life in the big leagues. "Shirley was my itinerant mama," recalls North. "She made sure I toed the line and made sure I ate."[29]

While he helped his young teammate adjust to life as a major league ballplayer, Williams also imparted baseball wisdom to North. The Cubs once again faced Bob Gibson, and North concluded that the pitcher was hardly pausing between pitches. North turned to Williams and said, "I'm going to step out and slow him down." North, who liked to dig into the batter's box before the first pitch of an at-bat, felt confident in no small part because in the minor leagues, his team had hit Gibson particularly well during a rehab start for the Cardinals' star pitcher. Williams quickly set him straight. "You get your ass in that batter's box and you stay in there," Whistler warned him. "And when you go up there don't do that little thing that you do because Bob Gibson will hit you in your neck, rookie." North warmly laughs thinking back on that quality piece of advice.[30]

Clubhouse rancor, primarily involving manager Leo Durocher, may not have been the direct cause of Chicago's third-place finish in the division in 1971, but it didn't help matters. In late August, the Cubs found themselves in striking position as they drafted behind the National League East–leading Pittsburgh by 4 1/2 games on August 23. The team called a meeting to discuss its current status, particularly the lack of playing time for younger players. Recall that in 1969, Durocher played his regulars without rest down the stretch, resulting in criticism from some corners over the years for the ballclub's collapse. The players continue to credit the Mets to this day in lieu of using fatigue as an excuse. That said, two years later, they attempted to hash out Durocher's resistance to putting his young guys out there. Durocher grew angrier throughout the conversation and then snapped. He yelled at the youthful players for not taking batting practice seriously, Milt Pappas for not executing a pitch as he saw fit, and Ron Santo for wanting a "day" to celebrate himself. The players growled. Santo exploded. Williams held him back. Durocher screamed that he would leave the team. Although Santo and Durocher patched things up, Chicago lost 16 of its next 22 games in a free-fall that landed with a thud in fourth place on September 14. The Cubs were 15 games behind the Pirates, and any postseason hopes were dashed.

In the midst of the Cubs' struggles, owner P. K. Wrigley startled the players by publishing a pointed letter in local newspapers that sought to justify retaining Durocher. Not only did Wrigley stand firm in his decision to keep the manager, but he told everyone that "if some of the players do not like it and lie down on the job," they would be traded elsewhere. He ended the statement with a pointed barb. "P.S. If only we could find more team players like Ernie Banks."[31] Needless to say, the statement alienated the clubhouse. The euphoria generated by Williams's Opening Day homer off Gibson was long gone. The team finished the season at 83–79 and packed up for the winter.

Williams produced the fourth .300 season of his career to go along with 28 homers, but the team was left to again ponder its shortcomings. "When this ad came out, a lot of ballplayers were hurt, a lot of them dropped their chin, and felt unappreciated. Most of them felt our owner didn't think we were giving 100 percent, and we were dejected that he'd say this at this particular time," Williams told a sportswriter a few years later.[32]

* * *

Meanwhile, the 1971 San Francisco Giants featured four future Hall of Famers and sensational right fielder Bobby Bonds, who made his first All-Star Game and led the club with 33 homers and 102 RBIs. The roster included a blend of veteran experience and youthful talent. Willie Mays was now 40. McCovey and Juan Marichal were 33. Bonds, 25, led the younger group, which also included rookie shortstop Chris Speier. The Giants started the season with an outfield of 22-year-old George Foster in left field, Mays in center, and Bonds in right before Horace Stoneham traded Foster to the Cincinnati Reds on May 29 for Frank Duffy and Vern Geishert in another regrettable deal.

San Francisco torched its competition through the first two months of the season, winning 37 of its first 51 games behind Bonds's incredible start. He hit safely in 19 of the first 20 games in which he appeared and finished April hitting .369 from the leadoff spot. Now in his fourth season, Bonds established himself as one of the National League's finest players. Meanwhile, his young son, Barry, together with the children of other Giants players, spent time chasing down home run balls smashed over the fence by these greats of the game. The families all sat in section nine at Candlestick Park, and when McCovey, whose pull-side power made every at-bat a fun adventure, strode to the plate, the kids, including Tito Fuentes's kids, Juan Marichal's daughter, and Bonds, among others, would work their way close to the field in anticipation of a blast of Stretch's bat. "Every time he would come up to bat we would go out there because he used to hit home runs. We would run to see who could get to the ball the fastest," Barry Bonds, who turned seven years old that summer, recalls. "We would get his home run ball in the parking lot, and then we would throw it over the fence to the fans."[33] McCovey's daughter, Allison, did not chase down home runs hit by her dad, but she spent a fair number of her summer evenings at Candlestick Park. She was typically the last one to leave, as her dad's bad knees forced him to ice after the game before leaving the ballpark.

McCovey thoroughly enjoyed being around all the kids. Initially, Stretch's imposing figure struck a bit of fear into them, but the intimidation factor quickly dissolved. "He was so quiet. When we were kids we were scared to talk to him at first, but he was so nice when you went up to talk to him you were like, 'Oh, wow, he's not scary. He's cool.' Then he would play with you all day," Bonds remembers. "He wasn't like Willie Mays. Willie would talk to everybody. Mac was just reserved, but once he got to know you it was the best thing that ever happened." Barry sometimes played with his godfather Willie Mays's glove out on the field, and, on occasion, the Little League first baseman used Mac's left-handed version. In addition to having fun, the diversity inside the Giants' clubhouse made an impression on him. "They were African American ballplayers that were before my time who I looked up to, so having that was special for us African American kids," Bonds says.[34]

The Giants stayed hot through the end of May and held a formidable 10 1/2-game lead over Los Angeles in the National League West entering June. McCovey had missed a week in April but returned to the lineup and went on a tear. His knee was bothering him so badly that it required cortisone, but you wouldn't know it watching him hit. Five times, he produced a three-hit game in May to raise his average to .319. McCovey earned his sixth and final All-Star Game appearance of his career in July. Bonds, Mays, and Marichal joined him in Detroit for the midsummer classic. It's amazing to think that a player of McCovey's caliber was only a six-time All-Star, but such was the competitive environment of the National League in the 1960s and 1970s. The Giants entered the break with a 55–35 record and were six games clear of the Dodgers.

San Francisco maintained a comfortable cushion in the National League West until September, when the team went into an ill-timed tailspin. Eleven losses in 12 games threatened to wipe away all the outstanding baseball the Giants had played during the season's first five months. Don Carrithers pitched San Francisco past San Diego, 4–1, on September 19 as the Giants stabilized themselves, although they remained far from dominant during the season's closing weeks, and the Dodgers vigorously closed the gap. The division title—and its accompanying playoff spot—came down to the final day of the season. Giants manager Charlie Fox handed the ball to Juan Marichal against the Padres, and the future Hall of Famer dominated. Willie Mays doubled in a run to open the scoring in the top of the fourth inning. Rookie slugger Dave Kingman followed Mays's hit with a two-run homer to give San Francisco a 3–0 lead that Marichal, who pitched a complete-game five-hitter, refused to relinquish. With two outs in the bottom of the ninth inning, the Dominican Dandy induced Nate Colbert to hit a bounding ball to shortstop Chris Speier, who fielded the ball and fired it across the diamond to McCovey to give San Francisco a 5–1 win and its first division title since 1962. After catching the final out, Mac ran toward the front of the pitcher's mound to celebrate with his teammates. They were headed to the National League Championship Series.

The Giants faced the Pittsburgh Pirates, winners of the National League East, who were led by Roberto Clemente and Willie Stargell. The Pirates took an early 2–0 lead in Game One against Giants starter Gaylord Perry in the top of the third inning. San Francisco halved the lead in the bottom of the frame thanks to an RBI double by Ken Henderson. The score remained 2–1 in the fifth until Willie McCovey clobbered one of the most memorable homers of his career. Tito Fuentes, who had homered only four times during the regular season, popped a two-run shot off Pirates starter Steve Blass to give the Giants a 3–2 lead. Stunned by serving up a round-tripper to Fuentes, Blass subsequently walked Mays, bringing McCovey to the plate.

Pain afflicted McCovey throughout the 1971 season. He played in only 105 games, his fewest since 1962. His slugging percentage dipped more than 130 points due to the injuries that sapped his strength. Nevertheless, he remained incredibly feared. National League managers intentionally walked him a league-leading 21 times during the season. It was the third consecutive season that McCovey received more intentional passes than anyone else. Cincinnati skipper Sparky Anderson led the charge. After receiving yet another intentional pass, a frustrated McCovey growled at the Reds dugout, "Who do you think I am? Babe Ruth?"

"No," replied Anderson. "You're better."[35]

Flash forward, and McCovey stood in the box against Blass surrounded by cheering fans, who now encircled him after Candlestick Park was enclosed with additional seating as part of the renovation for the 49ers. Blass delivered, and Mac detonated a swing that squared the ball up so solidly that it sounded like a gunshot. Fans roared, teammates erupted from the dugout, and the baseball soared toward right field and into the new bleachers. "You can only hit the ball so hard, but I'd say that one was one of those I hit as far as I possibly could," McCovey would say after the game following the Giants' 5–4 win.[36]

The Pirates bounced back to win Game Two, 9–4, behind Bob Robertson's three home runs. The Giants boarded their cross-country flight to Pittsburgh. McCovey took his usual seat near the front of the aircraft, where a bit of additional room gave his extended cranky knees a small slice of solace. Stretch typically sat next to Lon Simmons, but the play-by-play broadcaster did not take this flight because his duties for the upcoming San Francisco 49ers broadcast required him to be in Philadelphia. Instead, McCovey looked over and saw a completely different person. She was 11-year-old Jaime Rupert, the granddaughter of Giants owner Horace Stoneham, who wanted nothing more than to accompany her family on this trip to Pittsburgh. Initially—as sorry as they were—the completely full flight did not allow her family to provide young Jaime with a seat. Her despondence, however, turned to joy on learning that she could take Simmons's place. So there she sat, next to the tallest of Giants, who was calmly relaxed, as the ballclub flew to the Steel City. On landing, McCovey made Jaime his first priority after the plane touched down and taxied to a stop. "Willie looks at me, takes my hand, and walks me down the stairs of the plane past the people who were cheering and into the terminal where I got together with my family," Rupert reminisces. "The kindness, the gentleness in the middle of this hoopla, and he has the presence of mind to make sure I'm okay. I have never forgotten that."[37]

Game Three featured Juan Marichal and Bob Johnson, an emergency starter who replaced ailing Nellie Briles the day of the game. Johnson arrived at the ballpark anticipating that he might pitch even though he wasn't the scheduled starter. An ailing Briles might not be able to go because of an injury, which could thrust Johnson into the spotlight of the tied series. When manager Danny Murtaugh informed him that Briles could not pitch, Johnson was prepared. He responded by tossing eight innings of one-run ball as the Pirates captured Game Three, 2–1.

On the heels of a well-pitched, one-run contest, Game Four started with a bang. In trying to stave off elimination, the Giants drew first blood against Steve Blass. Ken Henderson opened the game by reaching on an error. Tito Fuentes followed with a single. Blass struck out Mays, but Stretch singled to center to plate Henderson. The Pirates responded in the bottom of the first on Roberto Clemente's two-run single off Gaylord Perry.

Trailing, 2–1, Chris Speier led off the second inning with a solo shot to tie the score. Blass retired Perry before Henderson singled to right field and Fuentes dropped in a base hit between Pirate defenders. Mays popped up to second, which again brought McCovey to the plate with two men aboard. This home run might not have been as show-stopping as the one he hit in Game One, but Stretch's three-run blast gave the Giants a 5–2 lead. But those Pirates refused to back down. Five batters into the bottom of the second inning, the score was tied again courtesy of Richie Hebner, who struck a three-run clout of his own to knot the game at 5.

Following three scoreless innings, the Pirates got to Perry in the sixth. With one out, Dave Cash singled. Hebner grounded out unassisted to McCovey as Cash advanced to second. Clemente delivered a run-scoring single to put Pittsburgh back in front, 6–5. Giants manager Charlie Fox went to his bullpen and called on Jerry Johnson to relieve Perry. Fox then made a crucial decision. Power hitter Willie Stargell had led all of baseball with 48 homers during the 1971 regular season and would finish second in the MVP balloting. He was not a guy one wanted to face in a situation such as this one, yet Stargell had gone hitless in the series thus far, as Giants pitchers had neutralized his bat. Fox, however, preferred to face Al Oliver, a 24-year-old outfielder who had hit .282 during the year. "You have to respect a man of Stargell's caliber, even if he hasn't had a hit for a month," Fox explained.[38] Oliver homered. The Pirates won, 9–4, and advanced to the World Series.

About 100 fans—a nuanced blend of grateful, supportive, and disappointed—greeted the Giants on their return to San Francisco International Airport. McCovey, dressed in a dark sweater layered with a light suit jacket, smiled as they approached him. One young fan carried a scrapbook full of articles about him. Stretch had produced an excellent series at the plate. He reached base 10 times in 18 plate appearances and delivered a pair of notable home runs in substantial situations. But it had not been enough to propel the Giants back to the World Series, and Mac now faced the reality of withdrawal from his cortisone treatment and preparation for yet another surgery on his knee. "Anything will be an improvement," he confessed. "I couldn't go through another season of pain like this." A different type of hurt loomed over him, although he would come to realize it only with the passage of time. He so badly wanted to win a World Series, but McCovey had already played in his last postseason game.[39]

* * *

Chicago Cubs lived a unique life in Major League Baseball for decades. Day games at Wrigley Field began when the ballpark opened on April 23, 1914. The Federal League played at what was called Weeghman Park in those days. The Cubs first took the field at the stadium in 1916 and have called it home ever since. Baseball was played in the park under the Chicago sun for 74 years until the Tribune Company installed lights in 1988.

Billy Williams's career dawned and set well before night baseball in Wrigleyville, which allowed him to spend time with his young family every evening. It was their daily routine when the Cubs played at Wrigley, and he treasured it. The Williams family lived on Constance Street in a South Shore neighborhood that featured doctors and teachers. Although they lived next to families who shared many of the same goals and dreams as they did, it was a volatile time in American history and touched their lives in Chicago. "You just had to turn the television on and you'd hear about what happened today," Valarie Hill reflects. The eldest of Billy's four daughters, she embraces the memories they made living in that house, especially of early evenings spent out front throwing a baseball back and forth with her father before the sun set. Williams eased up a little bit on his kid—he wasn't firing a ball into the cutoff man after all—but not entirely. "He didn't let up on me. He said, 'Don't flinch. Catch the ball.' He would throw it like he threw it—probably not as hard—but hard. It hurt! Putting it into perspective, this is a major league ballplayer, but he found the time and thought it was important for him to spend that time with me," Valarie remembers. "And I loved it."

When asked to describe their dad, all of Williams's daughters referenced the priority he placed on his loved ones waiting for him at home. "Family is and has always been important to my father," says Sandra Simpson. "I think that's from how he grew up and what was instilled in him." Williams transferred the close family dynamic he experienced in Whistler to his own in Chicago. "I always felt protected. I always felt loved," Valarie expresses. "Family was first." As the girls grew older, being outdoors with Dad became a shared pastime, especially while the family lived out west for several years after Williams's playing career concluded. "Julia and I were more the tomboys of the family I guess you'd say. For us it was fishing with Dad. In California we had a pond on our property there, so we would get up in the morning and go fishing with him. We liked to ride the tractors and all that kind of thing," recalls Sandra.

Although Billy's job made him a very public figure around Chicago, he shielded them from the spotlight as much as possible. Notes Simpson, "People will always ask, well, how was it growing up with your father being who he was? To us, he's just Dad." Williams and Cubs fans developed an extremely cordial and respectful relationship during his career. For example, if fans approached them eating dinner at a restaurant, he would politely ask them to wait until their meal concluded to interact. Williams then happily chatted with them afterward. They shared a mutual respect and admiration that established boundaries that allowed Billy to visit public spaces with his young family while also giving him a chance to mingle with people. Valarie: "Chicago fans, especially Cubs fans, good gravy, they will love you forever if you treat them well, if you're respectful of them and understand and appreciate their value. They have always been extremely kind to us and most importantly respectful of Dad." In turn, Williams and his teammates deeply appreciated the love and loyalty of Cubs fans who spent their resources on supporting the ballclub. He thoroughly enjoyed—and still does—talking baseball with fans.

When the Cubs were on the road, Billy would call the house and check in to see how everyone was doing. The girls would say hello and then run off to play. He still calls them about once a week and even sends out the occasional text message, which gains him high praise from his loving daughters. "He's not technical," Valarie says. "At all." Cell phones were still a way off during his career, so calling over a landline had to suffice. While he was gone on road trips with the team, Shirley raised the girls, and when he returned, the family spent a lot of time at Wrigley Field, which made Billy really happy. The girls also made an annual southern summer pilgrimage to Mobile, where they spent several weeks staying with their maternal grandmother to visit both sides of the family. They laugh when thinking back about those trips. "It was hot!" they exclaim in near unison. Want to crank up the air conditioner to cool down? Forget it. There wasn't any.

Growing up, the Williams girls spent a lot of time with the children of other Cubs players. Jenkins's daughters, Santo's boys, "Uncle Ernie's" kids, and Williams's daughters all shared common experiences and friendships throughout the 1960s and into the 1970s. The adults served as additional parents, too. Fergie Jenkins's wife "was like our second mom," Nina Williams points out. The Williams girls attended school during the fall, but Billy and Shirley brought them to Arizona before spring training opened. They enrolled them in a school and hired a tutor in a similar setup to Banks's kids. It was an annual pilgrimage made possible by the business of baseball during that era. One can debate the merits—or lack thereof—of the system at the time, which discouraged player movement, but it undoubtedly allowed the Cubs' core to stay together for a substantial number of years, which gave the families the opportunity to grow very close to one another.[40]

As their daughters grew up, Billy and Shirley exhorted them to pursue their dreams. "My parents encouraged us to do the things that made us happy. They encouraged us to get as much education as we could—go to college—to do the things that make us happy, but, yet, you have to have a work ethic. If you're going to start something you have to finish it. Those are things he taught us," Sandra says. "We're all first generation college graduates," Julia Williams points out. "That was important to our parents to make sure we graduated from college to set that tone. They supported us in our endeavors."

Families of the Cubs weren't the only visitors to the Williams home during his career. Billy frequently invited opposing ballplayers, particularly fellow African Americans, to the house for a meal lovingly prepared by Shirley followed by pool in the basement. These dinners served several purposes. They deepened bonds with friends throughout the game, but it also gave Williams (and other veterans) the opportunity to share their knowledge of Chicago with younger players learning about the social dynamics of cities in the National League. There were places they could go freely without too much concern and other spots they tended to avoid. African American ballplayers throughout the league took turns sharing their tacit knowledge with one another.

The invited guests of 1972 included a pair of young outfielders for the Atlanta Braves, Ralph Garr and Dusty Baker, who were both going full tilt with Williams for the National League lead in batting average. "It was kind of a thing," Baker says of the batting race, "trying to catch Billy." Competition was set aside for these gatherings, not least of which because certain aspects of American society made them required seminars for navigating racial boundaries. "It started in the minor leagues. If you went to the wrong section of town, white or black, you could be in trouble and it happened to us a couple of times, so you always went out with somebody that knew that town on the other side," explains Baker. Williams and Henry Aaron, among others, also exhorted their mentees to play every day with a hunger for success. "Billy,

Hank, and all those guys used to tell us all the time, you've got to stay out of the training room and stay on the field." You didn't want to hand anyone in the front office a reason to give your job away for any reason. "In Chicago, on that north side, he was playing for a lot of the Black people and the Black kids that were watching him and emulating him. I feel it, and I know what they had to feel. I've got nothing but love and admiration for those guys," adds Baker.

Baker and Bill North, who spent more than a decade in the majors and also attended the dinners, name several of the many African American players around the game who hosted them around the league. Aaron in Atlanta. Williams in Chicago. Horton in Detroit. Morgan and Griffey in Cincinnati. Agee in New York. Stargell, Ellis, Oliver, and Clines in Pittsburgh. To name just a few. "The older Black players always took care of the younger Black players. Living conditions weren't always good, and there were some places you couldn't go," says North before he later points out that they verbalized advice what wasn't written down in road trip itineraries. "They put it in words. There were no brochures."[41]

* * *

Billy Williams had played some incredible baseball, but he put on a hitting display in 1972 that left everyone in awe, encapsulated by an 8-for-8 performance during a July 11 doubleheader against Houston. In game one, he collected three hits, including his 17th home run of the season. In the second game, Williams picked up right where he left off with the second five-hit game of his career. He hit another home run (18) and raised his season average to .328. He had awakened that morning hitting .310. He finished it one hit shy of the major league record of nine hits in a twin bill but quipped afterward that the at-bat that produced a sacrifice fly in the opener might have gone his way had the situation been different. "If the man hadn't been on the third base, I might have gone 9-for-9," he told *Chicago Tribune* beat writer Richard Dozer in the clubhouse after the game.[42]

He authored a hitting barrage that resulted in extraordinary statistics. Williams captured the batting title with a .333 average that led baseball. Both Atlanta's Garr and Baker pushed Williams but finished second and third, respectively. Nobody in the game bettered either Williams's .606 slugging percentage or 348 total bases. His 1.005 OPS topped all National League batters. *The Sporting News* selected Williams as Player of the Year. It was a signature season for one of the game's best, but, in spite of all he did on the field, he again finished second to Johnny Bench in the MVP race. The Reds' catcher hit .270 but led baseball with 40 homers and 125 RBIs. Williams wasn't far behind him in either category, though. He hit 37 bombs and drove in 122 runs. The biggest difference was that Cincinnati won 95 games and won the National League West, while the Cubs finished 11 games behind Pittsburgh in the East.

News of again finishing second in the MVP balloting deeply disappointed Williams, who read the news while on vacation with his family in Hawaii. "You say to yourself, 'Try and forget about it.' But it always seems to keep popping up. It makes you think about what Leo said about nice guys," he told Barry McDermott of *Sports Illustrated*.[43] The most troubling aspect of the voting concerned a writer who left Williams off his ballot completely. "I'm ashamed," wrote a disgusted Richard Dozer, "that somewhere in our membership is a baseball writer who didn't do his job when, for a change, it was made easy for him."[44]

The snub sparked an outcry amongst Cubs fans, who inundated publications with complaints. The outcry wasn't aimed at Bench, whom Williams respected and the fans admired, but at overlooking one of baseball's greats in the MVP race for the second time in three years. A particularly peeved supporter echoed the shared sentiments of many. "What does Billy Williams have to do to win the award? Bat .500? Drive in 200 runs? Hit 62 homers?"[45]

* * *

Just like Billy Williams in Chicago, Willie McCovey embraced the role of veteran mentor in San Francisco. McCovey wasn't necessarily as social away from the ballpark due to his introversion, but he sought out young players and took care of them in myriad ways. At spring training in 1971, young John D'Acquisto, San Francisco's first-round pick in 1970, attended his first big-league camp with the Giants. "He was my big brother. I was a nineteen-year-old kid and '71 was my first year with the Giants big league club that I went to spring training. The first guy I met was Willie Mays and then after that I met Marichal. The third guy I met was McCovey, and Mac pulls me aside and says, 'Don't worry kid. I'll take care of you.'" It didn't take long for McCovey to follow through on his word. D'Acquisto recounts in his autobiography the story of his first spring training start at Scottsdale Stadium against the Cubs, who were hounding the rookie in hopes of getting him to make mistakes. Their antics effectively induced D'Acquisto to walk in a run early in the game. McCovey recognized his frustration and walked to the mound. "So, do you know what to do?" McCovey asked in his low, steady voice. D'Acquisto assured him that he did. McCovey encouraged him not to let the boisterous Cubs get to him. The young fireballer promptly drilled Ron Santo in the ribs with his next pitch. After the inning, an impressed McCovey walked up to the young right-hander and said, "Well, I guess you do know what to do."[46]

McCovey's mentorship extended off the field. He emphasized to D'Acquisto the importance of handling the media well. "The media can make you or break you," McCovey advised him. Treat reporters graciously and tell them how you feel during postgame interviews, but always be guarded with what you say. If you've had a bad game, Stretch instructed him, stop, pause, and then respond to their questions.

"You know that's awful deep," D'Acquisto, who followed Mac's advice throughout his career, points out. "It kept me in the big leagues. It really did because then I gained popularity with the media. I was gracious with them, told them how I felt, maybe I was having a bad day, fighting an injury or whatever. I told them the facts about what I felt, and it really paid off in the long run."[47]

D'Acquisto, like most kids who entered the Giants' clubhouse, also received fashion advice from one of the best-dressed players in Major League Baseball. Mac frowned on D'Acquisto's penchant for wearing denim even in the relaxed atmosphere of spring training. "You can't wear jeans," Stretch told him. "You're in the big leagues now." Eyes were watching, so a big-league ballplayer needed to exude class and poise and always look like he's heading out to dinner. D'Acquisto wasn't in the same financial class as McCovey, but the veteran assuaged the kid's concern. A short time later, Giants coach Hank Sauer approached D'Acquisto and handed him a thousand dollars.

Sauer: "Go buy yourself some clothes, and don't say I didn't do anything for you."

D'Acquisto: "Where'd that come from?"

Sauer: "Somebody told me that you had a conversation."

D'Acquisto: "Yeah, we did. Mac?"

Sauer: "Yeah."

D'Acquisto: "Thanks, Hank."

McCovey met D'Acquisto's parents and set their minds at ease. The Giants' players would look out for their son as if they were his big brothers, "and," McCovey added for emphasis, "I'm the big brother leading them all." He soon encouraged his new little brother to buy a red and black suit that D'Acquisto wore the following year in a meeting with the executive director of the MLBPA, Marvin Miller.[48]

The late 1960s and early 1970s featured some of the greatest ballplayers ever seen in Major League Baseball, and Billy Williams and Willie McCovey were at the top of the list. Their exceptional play—built on the foundation of hard work, dedication to their craft, and toughness—amazed admiring teammates, enthralled passionate fans, and rewrote the record books. Although both men prioritized winning over any personal accomplishments, the National League witnessed McCovey's incredible 1968 and 1969 seasons and Williams's 1970 and 1972 campaigns, during which they torched pitching in unique ways even for them. Bill North, who played with both of men, emphasizes why their performances were so special. Implores North, "You've got to understand they did the things that they did with pitchers trying in every situation to pitch around them—to not get into situations where they could hurt them. They did all of those numbers with an unwilling constituency of pitchers that didn't want to pitch to them."

In 1958, Willie McCovey played winter ball for Escogido in the Dominican Republic. His teammates included Felipe and Matty Alou, Bill White, Manny Mota, and a young fireballer by the name of Juan Marichal. *Courtesy of Rick Swig*

Willie McCovey was all smiles after going 4-for-4 against Philadelphia in his Major League debut on July 30, 1959. *San Francisco News - Call Bulletin Photo Morgue, SAN FRANCISCO HISTORY CENTER, SAN FRANCISCO PUBLIC LIBRARY*

The 21-year-old Willie McCovey collected 15 hits during his stunning first homestand as a Giant, including four homers, as he took San Francisco by storm. *San Francisco News - Call Bulletin Photo Morgue, SAN FRANCISCO HISTORY CENTER, SAN FRANCISCO PUBLIC LIBRARY*

Throughout his career, Willie Mac meticulously pored over the details of his uniform as this perfectly ironed sleeve crease indicates. *National Baseball Hall of Fame and Museum, Cooperstown, NY*

Big Mac was traded to the San Diego Padres following the 1973 season. He produced a pair of productive seasons as a marquee star for a young franchise before the relationship soured. *National Baseball Hall of Fame and Museum, Cooperstown, NY*

Willie McCovey alongside three of his closest friends: Franklin Mieuli, who owned the Golden State Warriors for 24 years; Lon Simmons, the Ford C. Frick Award–winning broadcaster; and Bay Area businessman, Rocky Dudum. *Courtesy of Allison McCovey*

Since 1980, the Willie Mac Award has been annually bestowed upon the San Francisco Giant who best represents Stretch's "competitive spirit, ability, and leadership." McCovey's daughter Allison presented LaMonte Wade Jr. with the 2021 Willie Mac Award. © *S.F. Giants*

Billy Williams established himself as mainstay in the Chicago Cubs' lineup in the early 1960s and formed a powerful duo with his close friend Ernie Banks. They carpooled to work beginning in 1966 after Williams permanently settled in Chicago. *Courtesy of the Chicago Cubs and Wrigley Field Archives*

The Chicago Cubs celebrated "Billy Williams Day" with a touching ceremony between games of a doubleheader against St. Louis on June 29, 1969. On that day, Williams, surrounded by his loving family, was showered with gifts of appreciation as he broke Stan Musial's National League record of 895 consecutive games played. *Courtesy of the Chicago Cubs and Wrigley Field Archives*

Ticket buyers could count on seeing Billy Williams in the lineup for nearly seven straight seasons between 1963 and 1970. His streak eventually reached 1,117 consecutive games setting a new National League record. His incredible streak remains the sixth longest in the history of Major League Baseball. *Courtesy of the Chicago Cubs and Wrigley Field Archives*

Billy Williams tirelessly worked on his picturesque swing. He earned a batting title in 1970 and was also well known for hitting his gum into opposing dugouts, a move frequently attempted—but never perfected—by other players. *National Baseball Hall of Fame and Museum, Cooperstown, NY*

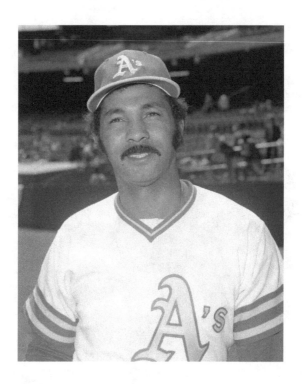

Whistler was traded to the Oakland A's following the 1974 season. In his first American League campaign, Williams hit 23 homers and drove in 81 runs as the A's won the American League West for the fifth consecutive year sending him to the postseason for the first—and only—time in his career. *National Baseball Hall of Fame and Museum, Cooperstown, NY*

During his 1987 Hall of Fame induction speech, Billy Williams delivered one of baseball's finest orations. Forty years after Jackie Robinson broke the color barrier, Williams called upon the sport to "pave the way for true equality." *National Baseball Hall of Fame and Museum, Cooperstown, NY*

Billy Williams remains very close to the Chicago Cubs organization. He frequently attends games at Wrigley Field, and other events like Cubs Convention, where he enjoys seeing longtime friends, including the five fellow Cubs Hall of Famers seen here at the Field of Dreams game in 2022. Left to right: Lee Smith, Ryne Sandberg, Williams, Andre Dawson, and Fergie Jenkins. *Courtesy of the Chicago Cubs and Wrigley Field Archives*

Part III

THERE AND BACK AGAIN

"IN THE NEWS"

Pushes for Watergate Facts. . . . Glenn Will Be Favored in November. . . . Williams Traded to A's. . . . Deletions Are Tantalizing. . . . Knievel Blames Metal Clamping the Parachute. . . . Ageless Mae West Was There. . . . Ford Plea. . . . Saigon Surrendered. . . . New Series of Fuel-Efficient Cars. . . . Ali Defeats Frazier. . . . Winds of the Cold War Swept the. . . . Rejects Senate Cutbacks. . . . Some Men Are Starting to Dress More Comfortably. . . . Voting Rights Wins Extension. . . . Franco Dies. . . . A's Acquire McCovey. . . . Carter Pledges to Support. . . . Activism Mandate

Chapter 8

"He Isn't Dealing with Hamburger People"

The San Diego Padres stunk. The organization had finished last in the National League West from the moment it was born: five years running. Yet, for owner C. Arnholdt Smith, the team's dismal performance was the least of his problems. He ran the United States National Bank, which, in 1973, collapsed. It was the largest bank failure up to that point in American history. Smith faced charges of fraud for his alleged role in a scheme involving illegal purchases using bank funds, and now he needed to offload the team to raise liquidity.

Smith agreed to sell the Padres to Joseph Danzansky, president of Giant Food, Inc., and the former head of the Metropolitan Washington Board of Trade. Danzansky wanted to move the club to Washington, DC, which complicated matters. Sensing an opening, a group led by racetrack executive Marje Everett, who planned on keeping the franchise in San Diego, entered the picture. An exceptionally experienced and talented manager, Everett was the only woman who owned and operated horse racing tracks in the United States, three of them in Chicagoland, before moving west and becoming the director at Hollywood Park in 1972. Everett highly prioritized attendance, and her passion for enthralling fans with an exciting live sporting experience drove her to produce a quality product to create a fun, enthusiastic stadium environment.

Now considering expanding her endeavors into baseball, Everett analyzed the Padres' full situation, and San Diego's lackluster roster dismayed her. She contended that the Padres' dull star wattage needed immediate brightening. Everett maintained that acquiring a heralded player such as Willie McCovey, one of the most feared hitters in baseball, was just the solution the floundering franchise needed to shore up its box office issues. The Everett Group acquired a conditional bill of sale from Smith that put them in pole position to buy the team if the owners rejected Danzansky's bid, which was running into trouble as San Diego officials pushed back against the proposed move to the East Coast.

With the sale of the team still looking promising, Everett tasked Neil Papiano, her lawyer, with approaching Padres president Buzzie Bavasi about her idea to bolster the team. "Why don't you try to get somebody like McCovey?" Papiano not so subtly asked Bavasi.[1] The Padres' veteran personnel man fully supported the idea. With Everett's financial backing, the organization could make moves it never imagined under Smith's ownership. Meanwhile, in San Francisco, Horace Stoneham faced a daunting monetary reality. His family business—the Giants—was struggling financially, and, simply put, he could no longer afford to keep McCovey on the payroll. McCovey maintained his elite status fueled by the power that refused to wane in the face of injuries and age. He hit 29 homers in 1973 and again led baseball with 25 intentional walks. He reminded everyone of his greatness in an early season series against the Houston Astros. Mac hit a game-winning two-run shot in the bottom of the ninth inning to give the Giants a 5–4 win in the series opener. It was up in the air whether McCovey would play the following day, but manager Charlie Fox put him in the lineup. Good call. Stretch homered twice *in the same inning*—an eight-run fourth—to power San Francisco to another win. Mac was so strong that he could even surprise himself. The second homer came off an off-speed pitch that fooled him. "I actually swung onehanded," he admitted.[2] Yeah, the Padres were interested.

A devastated Stoneham knew that he was on the cusp of losing personally and professionally, and he discussed the situation with Willie, whom he deeply cared about. Both men were clear-eyed about the reality of a trade, but neither of them was happy about it. Stoneham wanted to send McCovey to a place where he wanted to go. The Giants' era of the 1960s had been disbanded and sent to various corners of the baseball world. It was now McCovey's turn. Stoneham tried to take care of him as best he could in the midst of this trying time.[3] For his part, McCovey desperately wanted to get back to the World Series. For that reason, San Diego never came up in their discussions. Nevertheless, one night, Stoneham called up Mac and asked him about the Padres. Willie hesitated. They were a cellar dweller without any real hope of reaching the postseason, but he agreed to hear out Buzzie Bavasi, who explained the organization's desire to acquire a marquee player. He also indicated to McCovey that the first baseman could dictate how the contract was drawn up, an appealing notion to Willie, as he wanted to retire a Giant regardless of where the next few seasons took him.[4] McCovey agreed to go, and on October 25, 1973, Stoneham and Bavasi struck a deal that sent Stretch and outfielder Bernie Williams to San Diego for young left-handed pitcher Mike Caldwell.

The injection of money into the 1974 payroll strongly hinted that the Padres were now operating on firmer financial footing, presumably under the auspices of being sold to Everett's group. As a result, Buzzie and his son, general manager Peter Bavasi, acquired four veterans: McCovey, infielder Glenn Beckert, and outfielders Bobby Tolan and Matty Alou, whom they hoped would improve the on-field product and, by extension, appeal to the fan base. The franchise's commitment to improve satisfied McCovey enough to join the Padres, but he expressed his deep frustration at having to leave San Francisco to members of his inner circle. "Willie was mad when he was traded to the Padres," says his close friend Rocky Dudum. "He didn't want to go. He thought he was going to be a Giant all the way through playing ball."[5]

Any tenuous confidence McCovey felt in his new situation was further shaken when he flipped on his radio in early December and learned that the picture had quickly changed. Rather than being sold to Everett's group, the news reported that the Padres' sale to Danzansky would go through after all, and the team appeared headed to Washington, DC. Everett, who had been connected with a bribery scandal involving former Illinois governor Otto Kerner in the late 1960s, proved to be too problematic for Major League Baseball, so the owners approved Danzansky's bid. John Witt, an attorney representing San Diego, threatened litigation as the city held a 20-year agreement between the team and San Diego Stadium, but it still appeared as though the Padres would move to the nation's capital. Insiders knew that Danzansky wanted Minnie Miñoso to manage the team.[6]

"Everything I agreed to hinged on the team being in San Diego. Now I don't know," lamented a stunned McCovey. "Washington is a long way away. And the money I was promised came from Buzzie Bavasi. I understand he may not even be with the team anymore." McCovey had been tossed out of the only nest he had ever known into the chaotic wind of a disjointed franchise. Having not yet signed his contract for the 1974 season only heightened McCovey's level of discouragement. Willie did not want to move to Washington, and he contemplated having his adviser, Hal Silen, explore his ability to reject the trade. One can almost hear him frustratingly muttering to himself as much as speaking with a reporter when he said, "They assured me we'd be playing in San Diego."[7]

As the calendar turned to 1974, the ownership situation remained unresolved. San Diego mayor Pete Wilson wanted the club to stay. Witt readied a breach of contract suit against Danzansky, who thought he had a deal as far back as May. Unable to sell tickets or even point to a playing schedule, the entire situation had become comically ridiculous for the Padres, who still, remarkably, remained up for grabs. However, their fortunes were about to change. In mid-January, a diminutive, lively 71-year-old Chicagoan traveled to San Diego with his lawyers to look at the Padres' financial books.

Satisfied, McDonald's principal shareholder, Ray Kroc, who had retired the previous year, promptly paid C. Arnholt Smith a then-record $12 million for the team and agreed to a new ballpark lease with the city on January 25.[8] And, just like that, the Padres stayed in San Diego. The new challenge invigorated Kroc, and he planned to be in San Diego frequently despite living in Chicago. "I think I'll have about 10,000 times more involvement with the ball club than most of the National League owners do," Kroc said. "You never hear of Phil Wrigley going to Wrigley Field or spring training. That's his prerogative, but if I have something then I'm damned proud of it and I want to be involved."[9]

Kroc's purchase green-lit the Bavasis to move forward with their offseason plans, although they had to hurry with the new season rapidly approaching. Bavasi negotiated a new contract with McCovey, which he signed on February 1. The 1974 contract paid McCovey $115,000, although it included $15,000 in deferred money.[10] Ultimately, McCovey didn't receive a raise, but the agreement nevertheless made him the highest-paid player in the history of the San Diego Padres to that point.[11]

McCovey heartily approved of the Bavasis' next move. They tapped Giants third-base coach John McNamara as the Padres' new manager. "He's my guy," McCovey exclaimed.[12] The personable McNamara had earned McCovey's trust as a sounding board and calming presence in San Francisco, which had countered his deteriorating relationship with skipper Charlie Fox.

From the Giants' perspective, the trade of Willie McCovey to the San Diego Padres, while disappointing, smote an unsuspecting blow only to those fans who hadn't been paying close attention. The franchise's financial struggles made it nearly impossible for Horace Stoneham to justify keeping McCovey's significant salary on the books in light of the opportunity to deploy younger and, more important, cheaper players.[13] McCovey wasn't naïve about his situation; he knew he was as good as gone. Stoneham openly admitted to McCovey that he would probably be dealt to another organization. Their friendship enabled the two men to look fondly at the past while speaking frankly about the future. "It wasn't just an employer-employe(e) relationship," McCovey affirmed.[14]

Moving on from McCovey pained Stoneham, but the business was in such poor condition that he didn't have a choice. The Giants did not generate much revenue through ticket sales. They drew a paltry 834,000 fans in 1973, which put them in the bottom five of major league clubs in attendance. Historian Steven Treder points out that Stoneham was also suffering from pecuniary losses stemming from his real estate investment in Arizona that had failed to develop.[15] The reality of the situation made keeping McCovey impossible. "You know that I'm sad about having traded him, but I was in a position where friendship had to yield to practicality," Stoneham lamented.[16]

Exacerbating the Giants' financial issues, the tension between McCovey and Fox reached a crescendo in July 1973 over a playing time dispute. Ed Goodson had emerged as the Giants' choice to play first base, but Fox could also deploy Dave Kingman or Gary Thomasson. Despite his noted disagreement with Fox during the season, McCovey sought to forgive and forget, and he gently but firmly defended his now former manager following his trade to San Diego. "Actually there weren't that many problems this past season with Charlie. He had some the year before, but mostly with the kids. They're different than they were when I came up and Fox didn't realize how much they'd changed. His views are changing, too, now. There are some writers in the Bay Area who just aren't going to be happy until he's gone. Whatever he does wrong is always going to sound worse," McCovey said.[17]

While McCovey's departure saddened Stoneham, the San Diego Padres organization happily embraced their newest player. Fresh off selecting Dave Winfield, who jumped straight to the majors from the University of Minnesota, with their first-round pick in the 1973 amateur draft, Buzzie Bavasi eagerly received McCovey into the fold. Buzzie immediately wrote McCovey on the day of the trade welcoming him to the team. "I am sure you will like all our people and we will do everything we can to make you happy, and, of course, you know what you can do to make me happy," Bavasi joked. "Seriously, it is good to have you with us and one of these days we will get together for a drink."[18] The letter revealed he still needed to get to know Mac a bit. Stretch rarely, if ever, touched alcohol.

For his part, McCovey's heart remained in San Francisco, but Stoneham's need to make a trade forced him to live with the notion of the slugger suiting up for another big-league club. McCovey had dismissed the idea of playing in the American League because being reduced to a designated hitter did not appeal to him. McCovey initially balked at going to San Diego because he wanted to play for a competitive team. However, the chance to continue playing in the field and Bavasi's respectful willingness to make him the highest-paid player in franchise history persuaded McCovey to accept the trade. "I changed my mind," he admitted. "I hated the idea of not playing with a contender, but the Padres are looking for a 'name' player and I qualify. Sure, I'm sad about leaving the Giants organization. I don't know any other. But I wasn't useful to them anymore. It's a fact you have to face in baseball. I'm not bitter at anybody."[19]

While picturing McCovey ripping line drives in a brown and gold uniform engineered optimism inside many around the Padres, lingering doubts about what he had left in the tank produced its share of skeptics. Local columnist Mitch Chortkoff compared the Padres' situation to that of the city's NFL franchise, the San Diego Chargers; despite acquiring aging stars Johnny Unitas and Deacon Jones, the Chargers sat in last place. "Collecting names alone won't do it," he argued. Buzzie Bavasi vehemently disagreed with Chortkoff and believed that the Padres' pivot signaled that good times lay ahead for the franchise. "It's going to be fun now," Bavasi told him. "We're going to be able to operate like a major league team."[20]

The Padres arrived in Yuma, Arizona, for spring training and were immediately enveloped in McNamara's structured yet laid-back environment. McCovey loved it. He believed in the conditioning drills, and the diminishing pain in his knees confirmed it. The Padres got their work in under the watchful eyes of McNamara's diligent staff. For his part, the new manager made an effort to build personal relationships with the players. The recalibrated vibe, not to mention the increased talent throughout camp, encouraged everyone in the organization. "Nobody here believes the Padres will lose 102 games, as they did in 1973, or finish last in the National League West, the habit of the past five seasons," *San Diego Union* columnist Jack Murphy reported.[21]

With Ray Kroc newly entrenched as the team's owner, the inevitable rebranding of Willie McCovey as "Big Mac" was soon underway. McCovey found himself firmly entrenched as a major league team's biggest star attraction for one of the first times in his career. Although Giants fans affectionately embraced their homegrown first baseman, Willie Mays's superstardom overshadowed McCovey nationally. McCovey did his thing, day in and day out, year after year, in a somewhat understated fashion for the Giants throughout most of the 1960s, but that was not to be the case in San Diego. He was the leading figure for the Padres in 1974.

McCovey willingly embraced his role as franchise ambassador and introduced himself while marketing the team through meet and greets with Padres fans throughout the spring. On Saturday, March 23, McCovey boarded the "Big Mac Bus" and visited an astounding 10 McDonald's locations in a single day to sign autographs. Simultaneously, Kroc created temporary box offices at McDonald's locations throughout the San Diego region to sell season tickets that same weekend. The promotions generated a building wave of interest in the Padres. Local baseball fans felt that a new, moneyed owner and upgraded roster portended good things, and they responded by snapping up tickets at the fastest pace in organizational history.

However, it only took the Los Angeles Dodgers the opening three games of the season to serve San Diegans a dose of reality. The Dodgers swept the Padres by a combined score of 25–2. San Diego limped home to open up a series against the Houston Astros on Tuesday, April 9. One of the largest home crowds in Padres history eagerly filed in to San Diego Stadium to see their new look team. Nearly 40,000 fans hoped that San Diego would demonstrate that the Dodgers series was merely a mirage. Alas, the Astros knocked Padres starting pitcher Steve Arlin out of the game in the second inning as they built a 6–0 lead. This development disappointed the crowd but incensed

Ray Kroc. San Diego scored twice to cut the deficit to four, but Kroc's anger boiled again after trade acquisition Glenn Beckert committed his third error of the nascent season, which allowed the Astros to score in the top of the fifth inning and take a 7–2 lead. This was not how Kroc envisioned the night unfolding.

The game unraveled further for San Diego in the top of the eighth inning. Houston's Greg Gross led off the frame with a single to center off Padres reliever Mike Corkins. Roger Metzger followed by executing a sacrifice bunt that advanced Gross to second base. César Cedeño, who already had a pair of hits and three RBIs in the game, singled to left field to score Gross and extend the Astros lead to 8–2. Kroc fumed. The inning further deteriorated when Corkins's pickoff throw to first base eluded McCovey and allowed Cedeño to scamper all the way to third base. Bob Watson hit next, and he struck a fly ball to center field deep enough to score Cedeño. Houston now led, 9–2. The Padres were getting blown out for the fourth straight time to start the season.

The inning sent Kroc, who admittedly described himself as "hotheaded and proud," over the edge.[22] After Corkins got the third out of the inning, Kroc notified an usher working the owner's box that he wanted to make a statement to the fans. The usher, Denny, quickly got ahead of Kroc as the two made a beeline for the press box and public address announcer John DeMott. Denny arrived first and asked DeMott if Kroc could use the microphone. DeMott quickly assented. "Certainly, it's his crowd," he replied as Kroc materialized in the doorway. DeMott introduced the new owner to the fans and handed Kroc the mic. "Ladies and gentlemen, this is Ray Kroc," the new owner declared over the system to the startled crowd. "I suffer with you." Just as Kroc coiled to hurl another verbal barb, a naked man vaulted over the left-field fence and ran onto the playing field. "Get that man," Kroc screeched into the mic, his voice notoriously rising an octave as his anger exploded. "Arrest him!"

After security hauled the nude gentleman away, Kroc's vexation receded, but only slightly. "There is good news and bad news," Kroc continued over the PA system. "First, the good news. You loyal fans outdid Los Angeles. They had thirty-one thousand for opening night and we have nearly forty thousand. God bless you.

"Now for the bad news. We are putting on a lousy show for you. I apologize for it. I'm disgusted," Kroc derided. "This is the most stupid ballplaying I've ever seen."[23]

Many in the crowd roared their approval at Kroc's assessment of the Padres' poor performance. Other fans laughed in amazement. However, the stunned players stared in disbelief. John McNamara didn't hear Kroc—he was in the middle of a discussion with one of his players—but seemingly everyone else did. The Padres scored three runs in the bottom of the eighth but dropped their fourth straight game to open the season, 9–5.

When Kroc arrived back at his hotel room, the phone rang. His horrified wife, Joan, was on the line. "How could you do such a thing? Were you drunk?" she demanded.

"No, I wasn't drunk," Kroc retorted. "I was just plain mad as hell."[24]

While Kroc became an immediate cult hero amongst Padres fans, his public rant angered and demoralized the clubhouse. For the moment, his brazenness stunned the players. McNamara, now fully briefed on what had transpired, closed the clubhouse to reporters after the game so he could speak with the team. McCovey agreed to represent the players to the media, and he addressed the team's beat writers as his teammates quickly packed up and left the clubhouse. The typically stoic McCovey no doubt felt his blood boiling. The Padres had been publicly humiliated in their own ballpark. On seeing McCovey after the clubhouse reopened, Padres beat writer Phil Collier described him as "(e)motionally disturbed by the events."

McCovey did not mince words. "I wish Mr. Kroc hadn't done that. I've never heard anything like that in my 19 years in baseball. None of us like being called stupid. We're pros and we're doing the best we can," he said. "His words will ring in the players' ears for a long time."[25]

McCovey then offered the Padres' new owner some sound advice about the ugly incident. "Before this is settled, management should come talk to the players," he warned.[26]

Kroc's outburst equally astonished the Astros. Houston infielder Denis Menke, who also happened to be the team's union representative, lambasted the Padres' bombastic owner. "He ruined a big night in this city, for our team as well as his. Neither one of us played well, but those things happen. He made this a bad night for baseball. He isn't dealing with hamburger people, he's dealing with professional athletes," Menke excoriated.[27]

Kroc's eruption generated a lot of reaction from players, writers, and fans. Letters to the editor streamed into the *San Diego Union*, which printed 10 of them on April 13. Many fans wrote in to express their deep displeasure with Kroc for his unprofessional decorum, yet, incredibly, several readers penned ignorant complaints castigating McCovey's reaction to the situation because they erroneously attributed Menke's quote to the new first baseman.

"Willie McCovey, in rebuttal to Kroc's remarks concerning 'stupid play' said (via the press) 'We're not hamburger people, to be talked to that way, we're professional athletes.' Well, then, Mr. McCovey and teammates, perform like 'pros' instead of a bunch of hamburgers," grumbled one letter.[28] Another message complained about the Padres' poor play but again pushed the false narrative that McCovey had made any reference to players being treated as "hamburger people." It read, "Guess who put his foot in his mouth?

It wasn't Ray Kroc. It was Willie McCovey. 'You can't treat us like Hamburger People.' Why not? What makes ball players so different? They get paid, they eat, sleep, etc., just like all of us."[29] The *Union* should never have printed these letters. In doing so, it supported, perhaps unknowingly, the false narrative that McCovey had said something he never did.

Intensely rebuked, Kroc did what he had to do to smooth things over with Commissioner Bowie Kuhn, but he never regretted his outburst. "The answer is hell no! I only regret that I didn't lay it on them a lot harder," Kroc wrote in his autobiography several years later. "It was my insistence, well known to McDonald's employees, that customers receive a quality product for their money. Apparently I was the first owner ever to suggest that players owe top performance to the fans who support them."[30] Kroc referred to the incident in the epigraph of his memoir *Grinding It Out*, published in 1977, to further conjure his reputation as a maverick businessman. "(H)e either enchants or antagonizes everyone he meets," it reads.[31] Kroc's friend, Chicago Bears owner George Halas, found the entire episode hilarious. "Damn, Ray, I've wanted to do something like that for 40 years, but I never had the guts."[32]

Kroc's bluster belies the fact that he did in fact personally apologize to the players, who nobly moved on from the disgraceful episode. Although it remained a favorite talking point for reporters around the league, McCovey and his teammates quickly returned their attention to winning baseball games, a far more important thing to focus on rather than dealing with the tempestuous Kroc. "The media made more out of it than necessary," McCovey later assessed.[33] At least more of it than he wanted them to.

* * *

The Padres lost their first six games of the season before welcoming the San Francisco Giants to town on April 12. The hype around McCovey facing his former team after spending 15 seasons wearing the orange and black colors of the Giants made relatively little news in the media. The story line remained surprisingly muted largely due to the combination of his slow start at the plate and Mike Caldwell's early season performance. Caldwell, the left-handed starter acquired by San Francisco in exchange for Mac, had won his first two starts. After displaying boisterous enthusiasm during the home opener, San Diegans' fiery passion for the new baseball season somewhat fizzled following the team's sluggish start, although the modest increase in early season attendance gave management hope that fans would show up throughout 1974. A crowd of less than 12,000 filed into San Diego Stadium on a Friday night to welcome in the Giants for the series opener. McCovey doubled in three trips to the plate, although he did not factor in any runs. Nonetheless, the Padres beat the Giants, 3–2, to earn their first win of the year.

The win delighted McCovey less because it occurred against his former club and more because it meant that everyone in the Padres' clubhouse could relax. "I'm happy for McNamara. I hated to see him under the gun here so quickly," McCovey told reporters.[34]

The Padres earned a brief respite from their struggles by winning two of three games against San Francisco, but the team's early season misery continued for several weeks. San Diego won the back end of a doubleheader at Cincinnati on April 21, but the victory improved its record to only 4–13, and the team sat firmly in last place in the National League West, having been outscored an astounding 111–42. The optimism that each team felt during the spring fled the Padres as the struggles of the team's pitching staff and the offense's lack of timely hitting frequently produced poor performances. Disappointed with the team's start, McCovey believed that the season remained young enough to retain hope, though he candidly admitted, "I don't go away from the ballpark whistling, laughing and singing." Having said that, "I haven't lost faith in the ball club," McCovey maintained. "I still see the potential."[35]

The Padres were averaging fewer than two and a half runs per game, and McCovey was struggling at the plate. Through the team's first 17 games, Mac was just 9-for-38 with only two RBIs, although he had drawn eight walks. But he was paid to slug in the middle of the order, and a .738 OPS was not the first impression Stretch had hoped to make on his new team. He did not mince words when evaluating his own performance at the plate. "I'm off to a bad start. I've been getting on base but I haven't been hitting when it mattered. I usually start slow, but not this slow. But I'm not alarmed. I feel strong, I still think I'll have one of my better seasons."[36]

As miserably as the Padres played during the season's opening weeks, the team got hot and made Mac look prophetic at least for a moment in time. In a late April three-game sweep of the Philadelphia Phillies, McCovey went 6-for-10 and drew three walks as he boosted his average to an even .300. He had yet to launch a home run, but the base hits helped McCovey settle in further and feel more comfortable with his new organization. He may not have admitted to pressing, but it's hard not to think he felt some pressure to play well. "I kinda washed the first two weeks away as a rut—that really wasn't me. But I really started stinging the ball in the Philadelphia series last weekend. I've got my confidence back and I'm swinging the bat as well as I ever have at any point in my career," he confidently asserted.[37]

Young outfielder Dave Winfield, a 22-year-old phenomenon, joined McCovey in powering San Diego's offensive surge. On May 7, the 6-foot-6 outfielder laced his fifth homer of the season, a solo shot off Philadelphia's Dave Wallace in the 13th inning, to give the Padres a 4–3 lead over the Phillies en route to San Diego's 11th win in 14 games to pull within three games of .500. The young outfielder impressed McCovey.

"I don't like to talk about young players much. It puts too much pressure on 'em. It happened to me after I hit .354 my rookie year. They were comparing me with Williams, with Ruth, with everybody.

"But I'll say this, Dave's as good looking a young athlete as I've ever seen. And with experience, he'll get better."[38]

For his part, Winfield admired McCovey—he had posters of Stretch and Bob Gibson attached to the wall of his college dorm room—and learned from him. "He was my man. He was my friend and role model," Winfield said. McCovey, ever the even-keeled elder statesman, exemplified a calm that served as an example for the rookie. There's a famous story that's been told a number of times of Winfield being tagged out while trying to steal home with McCovey batting against Cincinnati during that 1974 season. Stretch, who served as the kangaroo court judge (as he often did in the later years of his career), issued a fine to his young teammate, who was adjusting to life in the big leagues after making the jump directly from college. Nevertheless, game recognized game. "He had all the talent in the world," McCovey noted.[39]

Winfield acknowledged the bond between the two men during his Hall of Fame speech 27 years later. "I was blessed to have a guy like this on my team," he said before turning around to make eye contact with his longtime friend. McCovey, who had not traveled to Cooperstown for several years due to his health, made sure to attend the ceremony to celebrate Winfield. "There are certain people we have to look up to, role models, people that set the bar higher, people that set standards of life," Winfield emphasized. "That's what he did for me."[40]

Winfield's extra-inning heroics in that early May ballgame against Philadelphia provided a brief moment of joy, but it evaporated in the face of a nine-game losing streak that brought the club back to reality. The Padres simply did not have the pitching required to compete in the tough National League West. McCovey smacked his first home run as a Padre, career number 414, in the midst of the losing streak against the Atlanta Braves, but it proved little consolation for the spiraling club. The Braves handed the Padres their ninth consecutive defeat, an 11–1 whipping, on May 16. The Padres, now 14–25 and again in last place, a significant 14 1/2 games back of the Los Angeles Dodgers, limped into San Francisco to open a four-game series against the Giants the following day.

Manager John McNamara gave McCovey the series opener off and planned to return him to the lineup the following day. McCovey, bundled up in his Padres jacket, greeted his former teammates in Candlestick Park's right field during batting practice. "I'm not playing tonight," Willie joked with them as he smiled. "It's too cold."[41] Everyone was happy to see him, including Giants front-office man Jerry Donovan. "Mac is a warm and understanding person.

We hated to see him go, but he was happy we made a deal for him at San Diego," Donovan said.[42]

Mike Caldwell's sustained performance subdued some of the heartache experienced by Giants fans seeing Mac in brown and gold for the first time. The 25-year-old Caldwell entered the series against San Diego tied for the major league lead with six wins to go along with a 1.66 ERA in his nine starts. McCovey's torrid bat had cooled off after his two-week tear, and he entered the series hitting .204 with just one home run and eight RBIs. Media in both cities dramatized the players' starts to the season and promulgated the view that Giants owner and general manager Horace Stoneham had made a smart deal. "McCovey Who? Caldwell Emerges as S.F. Ace" ran one headline in the *San Diego Evening Tribune*.[43] "When the McCovey trade was made, the Giants picked up a pitcher in the deal named Mike Caldwell. 'Who?' everyone asked," wrote Roger Williams of the *San Francisco Examiner*. "The critics who jumped all over Squire Stoneham in the past have been silenced."[44]

Willie McCovey appeared in the starting lineup for the second game of the series, batting fourth and playing his customary first base. The fans enthusiastically welcomed him. Thousands of kids waved their new souvenir McCovey bats and helmets handed out to them by Giants employees as they entered Candlestick Park. In the top of the first inning, Enzo Hernandez's one-out single allowed McCovey to bat. He strode to the plate from the visitors' on-deck circle for the first time in his life. He faced his former teammate, right-hander Jim Barr. The crowd cheered as Mac sent a fly ball out to right field, but it fell into the glove of Bobby Bonds, a harmless out.

San Francisco took a quick 1–0 lead in the bottom of the first. Bonds, who had spent several minutes reconnecting with McCovey outside the clubhouse the previous night, led off the frame with a double to left off San Diego starting pitcher Steve Arlin. Tito Fuentes sacrificed Bonds to third base before Garry Maddox's sacrifice fly to right plated the Giants' swift outfielder for the ballgame's first run.

The Padres continued to trail, 1–0, entering the top of the fourth inning. Nate Colbert cracked Barr's pitch over the left-field fence to tie the score at one and bring Willie Mac to the plate. McCovey dug into the batter's box, stilled his hands, and coiled as Barr wound up and threw. Stretch tracked the ball and then unfurled his vicious swing. His bat smacked the ball, and it jumped into the frigid Candlestick air out toward left field. It sailed into the stands for an opposite-field homer. Having risen to meet the moment, McCovey circled the bases as his fans joyfully erupted at seeing his opposite-field shot, career home run number 415. The Padres led, 2–1.

In the top of the eighth inning, McCovey batted against Giants reliever Elias Sosa as San Diego clung to its one-run advantage. The right-handed Sosa fired a pitch that was to McCovey's liking, and Stretch swept his bat through the strike zone and blistered the ball again out to left field. Garry Matthews turned and sprinted full speed onto the warning track as he kept his eyes firmly locked on the baseball. Just as he ran out of room to run, the 6-foot-3 Matthews leaped with his outstretched glove, climbing just above the wall. With a loud thwack, the ball smashed into his glove just as the outfielder's body crashed face-first into the fence before he ricocheted back onto the ground in a heap. Somehow, despite gashing the inside of his mouth, Matthews held onto the ball and denied McCovey a multi-homer game. "I was stunned pretty good," Matthews admitted later. "But I wasn't knocked out."[45] The catch kept the Giants' deficit at one run, and San Francisco rallied for three runs off the Padres' bullpen to capture a 4–2 come-from-behind win and spoil San Diego's bid to win McCovey's return to the 'Stick.

The Padres and Giants split a Sunday doubleheader. McCovey sat out the opener, an 8–2 Giants win that featured a complete-game victory for Mike Caldwell. Mac started the second game and blasted a fifth-inning grand slam, the 15th of his career, to help San Diego win, 10–7. McCovey excited Giants fans with his sublime performance at the plate. Although he played in only two of the four games, Mac, who entered the series having homered just once in 34 games, thrilled Giants fans by swatting a pair of dingers (he nearly had a third if it wasn't for Matthews's sensational catch), doubling, and knocking in five runs.

The Padres' series split against San Francisco left them sitting at 16–27. McCovey's homecoming had taken center stage for a few days, but his team's miserable season quickly resumed. San Diego finished the month of May by losing nine out of 11 games, and, although the team considerably improved its play in June, the hapless Padres sank further and further behind in the standings until they again disappeared from view. Despite the optimism of a new, wealthy owner and the acquisition of four veteran hitters, San Diego managed to win only 62 games, matching its woeful total from 1973.

In his first major league season playing outside of San Francisco, the 36-year-old McCovey finished the year with a .253 batting average and 22 homers, which pushed his career total to 435. He produced a .416 on-base percentage and a .506 slugging percentage. Both marks led the team. Perhaps most impressively, he drew 96 walks while striking out only 76 times. McCovey knew he could still perform at a high level, and the numbers proved him correct. The combination of his performance and star power helped the Padres organization draw over one million fans to San Diego Stadium for the first time in franchise history. That mark shattered its previous attendance record of 644,273 set two years earlier.[46]

In the midst of McCovey's successful season in San Diego, he identified going into business with the Krocs as a potentially profitable business opportunity. His close friend and business veteran, Rocky Dudum, encouraged him to ask Kroc about the possibility of obtaining a McDonald's franchise. Joe Morgan, the All-Star second baseman and McCovey's pal, prompted him to do the same thing.[47] The preseason marketing campaign linking Willie Mac with McDonald's wrote itself. The opportunity to purchase his own restaurant appealed to him and would strengthen the relationship between himself and the Padres owner. Mac's adviser, Hal Silen, was a savvy businessman himself. Just one year earlier, Silen partnered with Jerry Seltzer, who was heavily involved with Roller Derby following its founding by his father, Leo, to create Bay Area Seating Services, or BASS, a company that sold advanced tickets to everything from concerts to ski lifts through computer terminals placed in retail stores.[48] McCovey and Silen had dialogued about investment opportunities for many years now, and, following much prompting, Willie conceded that it would be a great idea for him to buy a McDonald's franchise.

The idea was discussed with Ray and Joan Kroc, but they made the prospect too difficult from a practical standpoint. "They said, sure, we'll sit down and go over it with our people," says Silen. "They weren't going to do him any favors on it."[49] At the end of the day, they refused to bend their stipulations for owning a franchise, and McCovey would never live anywhere other than Woodside during the offseason. "We couldn't meet their minimum requirements. The owners had to spend certain time at the place. It just couldn't be. It didn't work. They just sort of brushed him aside on it, so it never came to anything," Silen explains.[50] In the end, it was a missed opportunity for the Krocs to further align themselves with McCovey, especially as his popularity boosted Padres ticket sales.

* * *

Just as the business side of baseball had forced McCovey out of his familiar nest during the 1973 offseason, so, too, did organizational circumstances necessitate that 35-year-old Billy Williams, who produced another All-Star season for a team that finished in fifth place, continue his career elsewhere. The Chicago Cubs announced their rebuild on November 7, 1973, when general manager John Holland dealt second baseman Glenn Beckert to the San Diego Padres in exchange for young outfielder Jerry Morales. The trade was the first of numerous moves that signaled the Cubs' intention to infuse youth into the roster at the expense of veteran talent. The Morales acquisition also made clear the Cubs' intention to replace Billy Williams as the ballclub's everyday left fielder. Williams was not particularly caught off guard by the move—he had taken ground balls at first base knowing he could very well wind up there in recent seasons—but it still bothered him that the organization no longer viewed him as the everyday left fielder. "A ballplayer in the league as long as me has pride, and it hurt to know that I was not going to be the best," he admitted.[51]

More roster upheaval quickly followed. On December 6, the Cubs traded Randy Hundley to the Minnesota Twins for George Mitterwald. Five days later, Ron Santo, whom Billy had played alongside since Double A ball in 1959, was sent to the Chicago White Sox. Infielder Jim Hickman got his moving papers during spring training. He was going to St. Louis. When the Cubs opened the 1974 season on April 9, Williams and Don Kessinger were the only two Cubs from the 1969 team left on the roster. Billy knew that change to the Cubs' roster was inevitable, but it still impacted him to see so many unfamiliar faces entering his 16th season overall with the team. "Sometimes I look around and feel like I'm the one who's on a different ballclub myself," he said.[52]

In the midst of all these trades, Williams sought a second consecutive two-year contract from the Cubs. The new 10–5 rule complicated the negotiation. Players had won the right to refuse a trade after amassing 10 years of service time in the big leagues with the last five occurring with the same club. Williams easily earned that status. As a result, he controlled his destiny. However, P. K. Wrigley and John Holland offered him only a one-year pact. Their back-and-forth went down to the wire. Billy relented and agreed to the one-year offer just prior to the first full-squad spring training workout and went right to work on his footwork at first base. It was uncharacteristic of him to be openly critical of the organization; however, the Cubs' unwillingness to agree on a multiyear contract stung him. "I know John was only doing his job. But still, it was a slap in the face. You keep reading about all this loyalty, you know? And well, after a player's been with one ball club over 14 years and asks for a two-year contract, he feels they'll give it to him," Williams said.[53]

Whistler started the season off hot at the plate. In the Cubs' first eight games, he produced three multihit games and drove in 13 runs. Simultaneously, he tried to make his young teammates feel more comfortable playing on the biggest stage. Williams encouraged rookie third baseman Bill Madlock to think of the sizable Wrigley Field crowds as the same people whom he had encountered in spring training. "There's just more of them, and they've all got coats on," he joked.[54]

Although Williams produced in vintage fashion at the plate despite a lack of protection in the lineup, he made no bones about his struggles with the nuances of playing first base. "I was a poor outfielder when I came up, but I worked at it. That first year I had (11) errors. Well, now I feel awkward again, but I'm learning more and more of the little things every time I play," he pointed out.[55] Two days after making those stand-up comments, he smashed a walk-off homer in the bottom of the 11th inning to beat Cincinnati, 3–2.

On the fourth of July, a report circulated that Oakland A's owner Charlie Finley wanted to acquire Billy Williams to be his team's designated hitter.[56] Finley's timing seemed good. By late June, it appeared that small cracks were growing in Williams's relationship with manager Whitey Lockman, who benched the veteran seven times in a 19-game stretch. Lines that read of dissatisfaction with Williams's play had made their way into the media. The team, now 28–38, in no way, shape, or form would pose a threat in the division. Despite all these dynamics seemingly working in Finley's favor, the Cubs declined to make Williams available. Lockman and Williams met on June 25 and cleared the air. However, in late July, the Cubs removed Lockman and replaced him with Jim Marshall, but it was too late to save the season.

A notable personal highlight for Williams occurred on August 15 against the Houston Astros at Wrigley Field. With Chicago trailing, 3–2, in the bottom of the eighth inning, Billy cracked a single to center field off Astros reliever Ken Forsch. It was the 2,500th hit of his career. Cubs fans saluted him with a loud ovation following the announcement of his milestone achievement. Williams advanced to second base when Andy Thornton drew a walk but then left the game for Jim Tyrone, who entered the game to pinch-run for him. Four days later, Williams's season took an awful turn when he suffered a freak injury. He severely sprained and lacerated his ankle as he hit the first-base bag awkwardly while running out a deflected line drive. He was stretchered off the field and taken to Northwestern Memorial Hospital. The X-ray came back negative, but he needed stitches to reseal his split skin and time to mend the sprain. Despite not being completely healthy, he returned to the lineup in September. When asked if he thought about sitting out the remainder of the year, Williams bristled, replying in part, "I know what people would say if I went home."[57]

In spite of everything, Williams finished the season with a .280 batting average and an OPS of .835 to go along with 16 homers in just 117 games, his fewest played since his 12-game stint in 1960. Chicago bumbled to a last-place finish in the National League East with a 66–96 record. It had been a long year for everyone involved but especially for Billy, who grappled all season with both not being a mainstay in the lineup and a difficult position change. "It's just been a complete loss of a season. The whole season's been that way. I wish I could just wipe the whole thing away, go from 1973 right to 1975 with a new start," he lamented.[58] Nobody wanted to hear Williams say those words more than Charlie Finley.

Chapter 9

Oakland, or "The Sun and Billy Williams"

The headline above the masthead of the *Chicago Tribune* displayed a profound announcement simply: "Cubs Get 3 A's for Billy." After spending 16 years as a beloved Cub, Billy Williams's time playing baseball in Chicago had come to an end even if the trade itself did not come as a huge surprise. On October 23, 1974, in what one columnist called "the most outrageous deal since Esau traded his birthright for a mess of pottage," Cubs general manager John Holland sent Williams to the Oakland Athletics for a pair of relief pitchers, Bob Locker and Darold Knowles, and Manny Trillo, a young second baseman looking to establish himself in the major leagues.[1] Oddly, Locker, who had missed the entire season following elbow surgery, found himself involved in a deal between the Cubs and the A's for the third consecutive offseason.

Despite his adoration for the Cubs franchise and the fans of Chicago, Williams wanted to go elsewhere. "We were going through a transition youth movement—again—and I didn't want to do that. I wanted to be traded," Williams says.[2] He met with Holland, and the two men had a cordial conversation. The organization believed that moving on from the partnership was in its best interest, too. Immediately, a pair of American League teams, Oakland and the Baltimore Orioles, showed interest in acquiring Williams. A's owner Charlie Finley had long envisioned Williams as the perfect candidate to serve as the designated hitter for his team, so he again made overtures to Holland. For his part, Oakland's sustained success enticed Williams, who was eager to play in the postseason. "I agreed to go to the Oakland A's simply because they had won. I wanted to get in a World Series, and because Oakland had won in '72, '73, and '74, I said, this is my good chance. Baltimore called back and wanted me to come up there, but I had made the decision with John Holland," he recalls.[3]

153

The beauty of Finley's pitch was its simplicity: Come on out to California. Bring your bats. Let's go win another World Series championship. Deron Johnson and Jesus Alou served as the team's primary designated hitters in 1973 and 1974. They were solid hitters, but Finley wanted Williams. "When Finley called and wanted me to go out there, I said I could still play. Finley said, 'I don't want you to play. I just want you to hit.' We had Billy North, Claudell Washington, so the outfield was pretty set. Charlie Finley said, 'All I want you to do is hit four times.' That's what I did."[4]

In terms of business, Finley made Williams's decision to accept the trade even easier. He gave Williams the two-year contract with an annual salary of $150,000 that he had sought from Chicago the previous year. Finley's persistent pursuit of the player with 2,510 hits and 392 homers to be in Oakland's lineup paid off, and he was thrilled. "I now have the best designated hitter in baseball," Finley exclaimed.[5]

The A's also received some additional family help, although they probably did not know it. No other organization could match Oakland for its proximity to Billy's older brother, Franklin, who reached Class D in the Pittsburgh Pirates organization but retired following the 1960 season. He lived in Sacramento. The two remained extremely close, and the move would allow them to spend more time together in Northern California during the season.

For all of the consternation Finley caused his players—and he stirred it up haphazardly and incessantly—he maintained a solid relationship with Williams. He made a savvy move in offering a market-value contract, an unheard-of act on his part. Williams, who had known Finley for a long time, understood and accepted the owner's quirks. No one knew better than Williams how Finley had treated Reggie Jackson in the spring of 1970, but it didn't sway him from agreeing to the trade. Billy had been observing and perceiving all sides of the A's owner for a long time. He knew what he was getting into. "Charlie Finley is from Chicago, and many years ago they used to have a baseball writers dinner there. Every year Charlie would be there. I remember Charlie used to bring those orange baseballs. He would wing them out into the audience and tried for so many years to do that. I remember for like two or three years when he would bring those baseballs, so I got to know him real well.

"Charlie was ten years before anybody in this game of baseball. You know the white shoes, the different uniforms, the mule he would bring on the field. It was really something. He was a guy that thought a lot beyond the game of baseball. He tried to get fans in the stands and, you know, he was a guy, I say, who was beyond his years in the game of baseball," Williams explains when reflecting on the A's idiosyncratic owner.[6]

Billy arrived in Mesa during early March with his expanding repertoire of glove types and promptly made himself at home in the A's clubhouse at familiar Rendezvous Park, formerly the spring training home of the Cubs. "Do you have a first baseman's glove, too?" Joe Rudi, the runner-up for the 1974 American League MVP Award, inquired curiously. Well aware of his new teammates' history of quarreling among themselves, Billy joked, "I've got every type of glove . . . I was going to come in here wearing boxing gloves. I'd read so much about you guys I figured let's get it over the first day and have it out one at a time."[7]

One topic dominated conversation among Billy and his new A's teammates during spring training: who would lead Oakland's starting rotation now that Catfish Hunter had signed with the New York Yankees? Finley sparked the predicament when he declined to write a check for the deferred $50,000 payment owed to Hunter, Oakland's ace, to an insurance company to purchase an annuity as part of his 1974 contract. Hunter, who had just helped the A's win their third consecutive World Series championship (not to mention the American League Cy Young Award), and his lawyer appealed to the Major League Baseball Players Association. In December, Hunter won an arbitration hearing that nullified his agreement with Oakland and declared him a free agent. He signed with the Yankees two weeks later. "It's going to be very tough to win without him, very difficult. You just can't expect to get rid of a guy of his caliber and expect to win because pitching is the name of the game," lamented A's third baseman Sal Bando.[8] Williams had hoped to join a team that included Hunter, who had broken his thumb during the 1973 All-Star Game while trying to snag a ball struck by Billy with his bare hand. Instead, he was joining an organization whose owner had just needlessly fumbled away one of the premier pitchers in the sport.

Second-year manager Alvin Dark knew that his team would have to lean on its offense more than it traditionally had now that its former ace would be pitching on the opposite coast. It brought Dark a measure of relief to know that he could rely on his very talented new designated hitter. "Getting Williams definitely added to our attack. We became a better team the moment we got him," Dark said.[9]

Williams experienced an adjustment period with his new team, but a few familiar aspects brought him comfort. He had spent a number of years working out at the A's facility when it had belonged to the Cubs. Oakland star Reggie Jackson and he had been friends for years. Former Cubs Bill North and Ken Holtzman were members of the A's. Billy had known Dark for 16 years dating back to his late season call-up to Chicago in 1959. The 37-year-old Dark was in the twilight of his playing career that season but still posted a .267 batting average and played more than 130 games at third base for the Cubs. He provided young Billy with the number of Milt Stock, a former National Leaguer who lived in Mobile. If you ever need anything, Dark told Billy, reach out to Stock. Dark, who went on to become the controversial manager of the Giants, now piloted the A's. Williams, very aware of Dark's past comments, nevertheless experienced him in a different way. "I found him to be a pretty good guy despite some allegations of him being a racist in earlier years," Billy wrote in 2008. "Maybe he had changed by the time I got there."[10]

With his devastating bat and high-wattage persona, 28-year-old Reggie Jackson led the American League in OPS+ and star power in 1974. The right fielder had already accumulated three championships, four All-Star Game appearances, and a pair of MVP trophies, both earned in 1973, one for the 1973 regular season and the other for his remarkable performance in the World Series. The left-handed hitting slugger would now be protected in the batting order by multiple layers. Dark hit Jackson fourth, followed by righty Joe Rudi, who was coming off a season in which he had led the American League with 287 total bases, and the new lefty, Williams.

Reggie's trust in Billy hearkened back to the spring of 1970, when his contract dispute with Finley led to a lengthy holdout. Williams and Ernie Banks spent a lot of time with Jackson on the golf course that March. The two Cubs commiserated, shared advice, and offered support to the young superstar. Jackson found assurance in his friendship with Williams, and he wanted to maintain it. He asked Williams about rooming next to each other on the road throughout the season. Billy happily agreed. They settled on a setup that featured two adjacent rooms with a door between them to maximize communication.

Recalls Williams, "I saw the way he was going because a lot of people were coming after him wanting him to sign autographs and do different things, so I said, sure. And that's what we did. It was an exciting year. We had a lot of fun. We talked baseball, and when we didn't want to talk baseball, we shut the door and just watched television and relaxed."[11]

On Opening Day, Williams, now wearing number 28, provided the offense that Finley wanted. Batting sixth in the order, he doubled, walked twice, and scored a run to help Vida Blue and the A's defeat the Chicago White Sox, 3–2. The Sox battled back the following day and won, 7–5. In the rubber match of the series, Dark selected rookie right hander Mike Norris to start. Norris, who turned 20 during spring training, was a highly touted flamethrower from the Bay Area. He sat in the Seal Stadium bleachers in 1959 as a young kid on the day Willie McCovey broke into the big leagues with his stellar performance against Robin Roberts and the Phillies. In the interim, Norris developed into a young pitching talent, who Dark and the A's hoped could take pressure off of the pitching staff following the offseason loss of Catfish Hunter. Dark slotted him third in the rotation behind Blue and Holtzman. Dark, who had alienated so many Giants players, especially Orlando Cepeda, while managing that team in the early 1960s had found religion in the interim. Dark wanted Norris on the roster and took to calling him Jeremiah, the name of an Old Testament prophet, because he believed that the Lord had sent him to replace Hunter.[12] Norris lived up to the billing by throwing a three-hitter in his major league debut. The A's offense, led by Jackson, who hit his first homer of the year, and Williams and North, who reached base a combined seven times, provided the rookie with plenty of support in Oakland's 9–0 win.

Following the victory, the A's hopped on a plane for Arlington to face the Texas Rangers. Oakland defeated Texas, 7–5, setting up a clash between sudden frenemies Billy Williams and Fergie Jenkins in the second game of the series. Jenkins, who had been traded to Texas following the 1973 season, was coming off an excellent campaign during which he led the American League with 25 wins. The only way for a starter to amass a significant number of victories is to pitch deep into ballgames. Will 29 complete games work? How about over 328 innings pitched? Yet those astonishing numbers made him only the runner-up in the Cy Young Award voting to Catfish Hunter. In 1974, Jenkins dominated the world champion A's to the tune of five complete-game wins. He allowed a paltry three earned runs in those 45 innings.

The battle between Williams and Jenkins originally commenced in 1965, although it wasn't particularly notable at the time. Jenkins was a rookie reliever for the Philadelphia Phillies in those days, and he pitched out of the pen at Wrigley Field in September. He entered a game in the bottom of the eighth inning with the score tied at 5. Jenkins induced Glenn Beckert to ground out, but then Williams drew a walk, and Ron Santo homered to give the Cubs a 7–5 win. Nearly a decade later, on April 12, 1975, having spent eight years as the closest of friends, the former joint owners of a beautiful fishing boat squared off again. Billy led off the top of the second inning in a scoreless game. Jenkins rocked and fired. Williams went into his famous crouch and smacked Fergie's "impossible low fastball" onto the walkway behind the front section in the right-field bleachers for his first American League home run to help Oakland beat Jenkins for the first time, 5–4.[13] Fergie did get a measure of revenge against the A's 10 days later when he beat them, 2–1, at the Coliseum, but Williams collected both of Oakland's hits, including his second homer of the season. "The next time you give up two hits I may not try to get them both!" Billy teased his friend after the game.[14]

Williams's success against Jenkins may have come from familiarity. During their spring training days with the Cubs, Leo Durocher frequently selected Jenkins to throw batting practice to Banks, Santo, and Williams. He wanted them to face the best stuff possible in camp, and Fergie's pitches more than qualified. As a result, "Billy knew exactly what my pitches were and how they reacted," Jenkins says.[15]

Williams's early season homers aside, it admittedly took him a few weeks to grow comfortable with being a designated hitter. He had run out to the field for many seasons in Chicago. Simply hitting, running the bases, and returning to the dugout required a bit of time for making the necessary adjustments, but, overall, he loved being able to contribute to a contending club along with the newness of experiencing American League cities and ballparks for the first time. Williams, who loves the history of baseball, was thrilled when he got to play at Fenway Park in May. "One of my heroes is Ted Williams who played there. You get a good thrill when you go into those kind of places. . . . It was a thing that was different for me, but it was exciting to go to those cities," Williams remembers.[16]

The A's stacked wins on top of wins and entered their July 12 game against Baltimore with a 53–32 record and a 6 1/2-game lead over Kansas City in the American League West. Their offense faced a stiff test in Orioles ace Jim Palmer, seeking to become the first pitcher in the American League to win 14 games. The A's countered with veteran hurler Jim Perry. Oakland drew first blood during the picturesque Saturday afternoon contest in the bottom of the first inning. Williams coaxed a two-out walk and came around to score on Jackson's opposite-field fly ball that bounced out of Don Baylor's glove. In the bottom of the third inning, Billy popped up, but the cloudless sky momentarily blinded the vision of Baltimore's infielders, and the ball fell in for a single. Then shortstop Mark Belanger booted a groundball hit by Jackson, which set the table for Joe Rudi, who cracked a single that scored Williams. Leading, 4–0, in the seventh inning, the Orioles defense again let Palmer down. Bobby Grich could not locate a popup off the bat of Campy Campaneris that fell to the ground unabated for a hit, and then Bill North drew a walk. This put two men on for Williams, who launched a three-run homer to pad Oakland's lead, 7–0. It was his 12th long ball of the season. Afterward, Palmer was asked to identify the problems he had during the game. "The sun and Billy Williams," he answered.[17]

Oakland built an overwhelming 10 1/2-game lead over the Royals by late July, but the team skidded a little bit by losing six of nine contests, which allowed Kansas City to make up four games in a little over a week. Williams put a stop to the slide by blasting two homers—his 15th and 16th of the season—in support of Vida Blue's complete-game performance as the A's pummeled the Texas Rangers, 10–1. It was Billy's second multi-homer game of the season and the 31st of his brilliant career, but the stubborn Royals hung around into late September.

At last, during an intense week in California that saw President Gerald Ford avoid a pair of assassin's bullets in Sacramento and the arrest of Patty Hearst, the A's finally clinched the American League West title on September 24 by overwhelming the Chicago White Sox, 13–2. It was the organization's fifth consecutive division crown. An exuberant Billy Williams, soaked through with champagne in the clubhouse, was heading to the postseason for the first time. He played a key role in powering an A's lineup that belted 151 home runs, just two dingers behind Cleveland for the most in baseball. "You must have power," said Oakland manager Alvin Dark. "That's what we've got."[18] Jackson led the American League with 36 long balls, and Williams's 23 homers and 81 RBIs helped fuel an offense that offset the loss of Catfish Hunter by scoring 48 more runs than it had in 1974.

In addition to the difficulty of winning without Hunter, getting Williams to the playoffs fueled the joy of the celebration. "Never knew champagne tasted so good!" he exclaimed.[19] After spending a bit more time congratulating his teammates, Williams slipped out of the locker room and headed home to enjoy the moment with Shirley and their girls. He cracked open their doors and told his sleeping daughters that they had won the division, but they smiled at him and said they had learned about it from the news. Billy and Shirley settled in and enjoyed a movie. He was thrilled on two levels. The team won, and, despite taking on a role unique to the American League against unfamiliar pitchers, he contributed to its success. "You hear the saying nothing beats money. But in my case, after all the years and never finishing on top, this beats money," Williams said the following day. The champagne-soaked jersey still hung in his locker from the previous night. He leaned over and kissed it.[20]

The joy of victory, along with the chance to battle the Big Red Machine in the World Series, quickly went up in smoke. The Boston Red Sox swept the A's, 3–0, in the American League Championship Series. Oakland suffered from a number of maladies during the series, but its dearth of starting pitching proved problematic. Hunter was long gone, of course, and Norris, whom Dark thought of so highly, suffered a serious arm injury in April that forced him out of action until late September. Despite his noble comeback, Norris did not pitch in the postseason. Instead, Ken Holtzman valiantly took the ball on two days' rest and tried to keep Oakland afloat in Game Three. Alas, it was not to be. Boston built a 4–0 lead and went on to win, 5–3. Williams went hitless in seven at-bats with a walk. It turned out to be the only postseason appearance of his career.

* * *

While Williams and the A's were winning the American League West, down south, the 1975 San Diego Padres also accomplished something notable: they didn't finish last in the National League West. Led by the remarkable development of All-Star pitcher Randy Jones, San Diego won a franchise-record 71 games. In spite of that improvement, that record still left the Padres 10 victories below .500 and 37 games behind the division champion Cincinnati Reds. Still, it was an 11-game improvement. The team's progress enticed nearly 1.3 million fans to attend its home games.[21] The club finished sixth in the National League in attendance, the highest rank in franchise history.

Manager John McNamara scheduled days off for Willie McCovey in hopes of keeping his aching legs as fresh as possible, and the first baseman responded with his second straight solid campaign as he contributed 23 homers and 68 RBIs at the plate during the season. However, some people around the game believed they saw slippage in his bat speed. The combination of injuries and age appeared to impact his performance in a way not previously seen. No opponent admired McCovey more than Reds manager Sparky Anderson, he of the you're-better-than-Babe-Ruth fame. Late in the season, Anderson expressed his profound sadness at watching McCovey, 37, age before his eyes. "You watch Willie McCovey pop up a pitch that five years ago he would have put into orbit and it hurts," he lamented. Anderson bristled at his own pitchers whenever they proudly mentioned their recent success against McCovey. "I just go up to them and tell them, 'Son, that wasn't Willie McCovey you got out. That was a ghost of Willie McCovey,'" Anderson said.[22]

The Padres organization shared Anderson's sentiment, and general manager Peter Bavasi planned to substantially cut McCovey's salary in a cost-trimming move in spite of Mac's quality 1975 campaign. He had slashed .252/.345/.460, but, nevertheless, Bavasi decided to offer McCovey a contract that cut his pay by 20 percent. He viewed the aging first baseman as a part-time player who could come off the bench or occasionally platoon with Mike Ivie, a promising 23-year-old product of the Padres' farm system. Animosity between McCovey and the Padres organization quickly thickened throughout the offseason and solidified during spring training in 1976.

The Padres' attitude deeply offended Hal Silen, McCovey's lawyer, who expressed his dissatisfaction to Bavasi. It was an open secret that the Padres wanted to phase out Stretch in favor of younger players, who required significantly lower salaries. Everyone concluded that trading McCovey could benefit both sides, and Bavasi gave Silen permission to explore a trade but only with one potential suitor: San Francisco.

Word of the organization's interest reached Mac, and he desperately wanted to return. Bill Rigney, Stretch's manager during his rookie season way back in 1959, had just been reinstalled in that position, so McCovey called him. Rigney transparently told him that he would be used primarily off the bench and as a coach, but he could remain in that role for a number of years. It seemed that even the Giants thought his playing days were numbered, but McCovey, who desperately wanted to return home, hung up and rang Bavasi asking for his release. No, he answered. McCovey fumed. He had hit home runs and brought fans to the ballpark. He felt like he had held up his end of the bargain. The Padres front office had given him three choices:

take the pay cut, retire, or be released. However, now that San Diego knew that the Giants possessed a genuine interest in reuniting with Mac, the release option disappeared from the table. "My value seems to have gone up since they (the Padres) found out the Giants want me back," he noted sarcastically. Mac resented that Bavasi was putting him in a bad spot. They had told him he could be released, especially with a club that would absorb his contract, but now they refused. Always mindful of reigning in his frustrations publicly, McCovey softened his tone, saying, "I don't want to sound like a cry baby. I've always had great relationships with management and I would hate to tarnish that reputation."[23] Ultimately, the trade talks produced nothing. The Padres wanted players from San Francisco rather than just salary relief. Rigney balked, and the trade talk died.[24] An irked McCovey, who nonetheless admitted that he would not have met the Padres' asking price if he was running the Giants, refused to sign San Diego's contract offer and was declared a holdout.

Following several more days of hostilities, McCovey agreed to sign his 1976 contract for $100,000. His 20 percent pay cut meant free-agency freedom at season's end, but he suspected the interested parties would be few. His production would plummet without consistent playing time, and no one knew that better than he did. "When the season ends people will look at my statistics and say, 'He must be washed up. He's 38, you know.' . . . They won't consider the fact that I wasn't playing," he explained.[25]

McCovey showed that his bat still maintained some pop. On May 5, acutely aware that the wind was blowing out to right field, Stretch blasted a majestic first-inning homer that cleared the scoreboard at Parc Jarry in Montreal and bounced into a public swimming pool to help the Padres defeat the Expos, 6–4. Although he admitted to thinking home run for one of the very few times in his career, the distance meant nothing to him. "I've hit balls much harder than that one," McCovey said nonchalantly of career bomb number 482.[26] He then returned to the bench.

* * *

The Oakland A's underwent changes after coming up short in the 1975 American League Championship Series. Charlie Finley hired White Sox manager Chuck Tanner to replace Alvin Dark. Pitcher Mike Norris returned from injury. These moves took a backseat, however, to the earth-shattering trade that occurred on April 2, when Finley sent Reggie Jackson, Ken Holtzman, and prospect Bill Van Bommel to the Baltimore Orioles for Don Baylor, Mike Torrez, and Paul Mitchell in a blockbuster deal. Money lurked at the heart of the trade. Jackson sought a substantial raise, and Holtzman wanted a multiyear deal. None of the A's who headed east had signed their

contracts. Finley defended the swap, but his notoriously thrifty ways under-
cut his claim. "I would have made the deal even if all three of the players
were signed," he argued. "I think that under the circumstances it will turn
out to become one of the best trades we ever made."[27] Money aside, that it
occurred one week before the start of the 1976 season deeply shocked the
players involved. Unsurprisingly, the A's lost 23 of their first 38 games.

Williams started the season slowly. For the first time in his career, his
batting average hovered around .200 into mid-May. His swing established a
groove against the White Sox and Royals. He rapped eight hits in 14 at-bats,
including three homers and nine RBIs, but it did not portend future developments. At 38, the wear and tear of playing nearly 2,500 games across 18
major league seasons revealed itself without reprieve. That aside, Whistler
contributed to the ballclub in ways that remain impactful to this day. The A's
roster was undergoing a sort of youth movement after Finley broke up its
championship core. Billy made it a point to guide the younger players about
everything, from facing certain pitchers to healthy routines to how they could
handle making money. "You know when you come to the big league as a
young kid, you have people who have played in the Major Leagues, who take
the young guy under their wing and try to teach him the ways of life, how the
game should be played, and just tell him what to do and where to go. It was a
thing Ernie (Banks) did for me," Williams explains. "The guys are coming in,
and you want to make sure that you really give them an idea how this game
should be played and *just about life.*"[28]

One of the youngsters to whom Williams gave advice was Norris, who was
20 years old when he made his big-league debut in 1975. Admitted Norris,
"I was just a year and half removed from high school, so I didn't get it yet. It
was just a big party for me, you know?"[29] Williams recognized Norris's ability and consistently encouraged him to develop good habits and warned him
against making questionable choices, and he didn't hesitate one day to let the
young pitcher know that he wasn't meeting his expectations.

"One day he comes up to me and he says, 'You know what? I'm going
to stop wasting my breath on you.' He loved to fish. He would go out on
the Delta and go fishing before the games. He said, 'One day I might be
out there on that Delta and my boat tips over, and then I go down once, and
come back up. I go down again, and come back up. The third time I'll be
going down going, 'I wasted my last breath on that damn Mike!'" Norris
laughs.[30]

For all of the different challenges moving to the American League presented Williams—new role, new pitchers, new umpires—one of his greatest
delights was playing in unfamiliar stadiums, including Fenway Park and
Yankee Stadium. On August 3, it was Billy's turn to play tour guide for his
teammates on a road trip to Chicago. The Windy City's two teams almost

never played home games on the same day, but the schedule featured a Cubs doubleheader against Philadelphia with the A's battling the White Sox that night. The situation provided a unique opportunity. "I invited Gene Tenace, Joe Rudi, and several other guys over to Wrigley Field because they had heard a lot about it. They had seen it on television, but they hadn't been there. You're talking about an exciting time that they had over there looking at the ballpark. We always had thirty to forty thousand fans. It was a little different for them, but they really, really enjoyed it. It was exciting for them to see Wrigley Field," beams Williams.[31]

* * *

By 1976, the San Diego Padres front office no longer believed that Willie McCovey could help the ballclub. Although Mac had led the team in home runs and RBIs during his first two seasons in a Padres uniform, not to mention providing the franchise with some veteran star power, they concluded it would be best for the organization and player to part ways. McCovey's .203 batting average and seven home runs suggested on paper to Bavasi that the bat had slowed down, but Willie strongly felt that sparse playing time hindered his effectiveness. After blasting a homer over Candlestick Park's center-field fence, just his fourth of the season, on June 24, McCovey declared, "I think I still could hit 35 or 40 home runs in a season if I played every day. I haven't lost my power."[32] By mid-July, McCovey had essentially been relegated to pinch-hitting appearances, and a separation between organization and player was clearly in the cards.

As fate would have it, McCovey would soon be reunited with his friend from Mobile. Sensing an opportunity, Charlie Finley swooped in and acquired McCovey for cash on August 30. It seemed like an odd move from a personnel standpoint for Oakland considering that Williams already provided left-handed pop off the bench, but Finley could never have enough designated hitters. On hearing the news, Mac lashed out at the Padres organization. "People talk about racial discrimination but I was discriminated against because of my age," he contended.[33] It had already been a very long and frustrating season for him, and Finley made things worse by informing McCovey that he must pay for his own plane ticket to join the team in the Bay Area. The requirement stunned both Mac and Silen, who recommended that his client take the organization to arbitration over the matter. McCovey, who didn't want to rock the boat with his new team publicly, declined his adviser's advice. He would play out the season and become a free agent. In the end, Willie shelled out several thousand dollars to pay for the move. Finley's thriftiness may have saved him a few bucks, but it caused intense resentment in his team's newest acquisition.[34]

McCovey compartmentalized his feelings and joined the A's. With only five weeks remaining in the season, Oakland had significant ground to make up. They trailed the Kansas City Royals by eight games in the American League West. Stretch arrived in the East Bay on August 31 and sat behind home plate in a stylish denim suit as Oakland lost to the New York Yankees, 2–1. One of the sweetest benefits of coming to Oakland was the unique chance to play with his longtime friend Billy Williams. After the game, McCovey went down to the A's clubhouse to greet him. They spent time catching up, talking about their seasons and speaking to the media. "Don't laugh. Billy really was my idol," Mac ardently expressed.[35]

The young players on the team marveled at seeing the two superstars together. Willie immediately joined Billy in mentoring anyone on the team who wanted to ask questions. It was especially meaningful to Norris, who had witnessed McCovey's major league debut. When he slept as a kid, Norris experienced a recurring dream of sitting in the Giants' dugout amongst his baseball heroes. The dream always closed with McCovey asking him when he was going to pitch. Then Norris woke up. Now sharing an actual big-league dugout, Willie sometimes caught Norris staring at him. "What's wrong, Mike?" Mac asked. "This is unbelievable," Norris gushed. "I used to dream about you guys, man, and here I am on the same team with you."[36]

While exciting on a personal level, manager Chuck Tanner explained that their reunion would cost them both playing time. Mac made his first start as a designated hitter the following night against the Yankees. Williams was not in the lineup. The crowd of 8,881 welcomed Mac back to the Bay Area with a rousing ovation that genuinely moved him. The machinations of management in San Diego and Oakland suggested to McCovey that he wasn't valued, and it hurt him. McCovey flew out to left field in his first American League at-bat, but hearing those cheers from the crowd resuscitated him on a deeper level. "It just felt good to be around some people who appreciate my ability," he said after the game.[37] Stretch picked up a single in the fifth, but it didn't factor into any of the A's runs. Oakland won the ballgame, 5–0.

The two stars rarely played in September. During the team's final 29 games, McCovey started only seven games and Williams just once. They combined to drive in one run. Oakland managed to win 17 of its final 30 games, which got them within striking distance of the Royals, but Kansas City held on to win the division by 2 1/2 games. One bright spot occurred on October 2 against the California Angels. Trailing, 8–7, with one out in the bottom of the ninth inning, Tanner sent up Williams to pinch-hit, and he pulled a ball into right field for a single. It was the 2,711th and final hit of his fabulous career. Williams left the field for a pinch-runner. McCovey followed with a pinch-hit single of his own before being replaced by Bill North. Ken McMullen then singled to center to tie the game, 8–8. Oakland won the game,

9–8, on a Gene Tenace base hit in the bottom of the 14th inning. The following day, Tanner penciled McCovey into the lineup for the season finale, but he refused to play out of disgust for not being used more frequently. He didn't hold back his frustration at the decision. "If they couldn't play me when it meant something, why play me in a meaningless game? I deserve more than that after the career I've had."[38]

The inordinate adjustment of becoming a designated hitter after so many years of playing in the National League proved challenging for both players. Williams had a standout first season in Oakland, but he finished the 1976 campaign with a .211 batting average and .659 OPS, both career-low marks—his cup of coffee in 1959 notwithstanding. "I think I could play some more, but I can't go through another season like the last one. It was too much sitting around and too much being the designated hitter," he told A's beat reporter Ron Bergman in mid-November.[39] McCovey echoed his close friend's sentiment. He wanted an immediate return to the National League. "The people over there know what I can do. Plus the fact that I want to play both ways. If I stay here, I'm going to be typecast only as a designated hitter," he said.[40] Ultimately, the one definable joy found by Williams and McCovey during an otherwise disappointing September 1976 was the chance to play alongside each other, a far cry from being a couple of kids from Whistler and Down the Bay. "It was a thrill for me, and I know it was a thrill for him to just enjoy our time playing baseball with the Oakland A's," Williams says of that fond memory.[41]

* * *

At one point, the sun conspired with Billy Williams to win a ballgame against the great Jim Palmer, but its latest message conveyed the setting of his time playing professional baseball. Neither the Toronto Blue Jays nor the Seattle Mariners selected him during the expansion draft, most likely due to cost, and Williams already knew that the A's were set to release him. The idea of retirement swirled in his mind throughout the six weeks that followed the end of Oakland's 1976 season. The idea of suiting up for an expansion team did not bother him, but he wanted to play in the field again. In the midst of the bustling early offseason activity within the sport, he decided to hang up his spikes for good. Walking away appealed to him. He could spend more time with his family and fish with Franklin whenever and wherever he wanted. Williams contacted a local real estate agent who helped him locate a lovely 10-acre plot with a fishing lake in Loomis, 25 miles northeast of Sacramento. The family spent another year living in Walnut Creek while building a home on that land and then settled into their new furnishings, where Billy, Shirley, and their four girls spent the next five years. The 38-year-old

Williams amassed stunning numbers during his majestic 18-year career. He slugged 426 homers, drove in 1,475 runs, and, between September 22, 1963, and September 5, 1970, played in 1,117 consecutive games. Williams retired from the game as one of the most admired and respected players to have ever donned a uniform.

Although he wished his dear friend all the best in retirement, McCovey's baseball journey was not yet complete. The sour note produced by the 1976 season bothered him, and he still hoped to reach 500 career home runs. However, there were some questions about whether Mac could find a baseball home where he could clout another 35 round-trippers. One organization valued him above all others and wanted to see how much Stretch still had in the tank. Bob Lurie, the new owner of the San Francisco Giants, had watched the developments surrounding Mac's career with great interest. A reunion made a lot of sense for both parties.

Chapter 10

The Birth of History

As Willie McCovey played out his tumultuous 1976 season in San Diego and Oakland, the San Francisco Giants experienced a wild ride of their own. In January, the franchise was on the precipice of leaving California for Canada. Horace Stoneham, hampered by financial challenges for years, could no longer afford to keep the team that he had owned since inheriting it from his father, Charles, in 1936. The fate of the Giants had been in limbo for nearly a year. Stoneham required a loan from the National League to meet payroll obligations during the 1975 season. It was only a matter of time before a new owner would need to be found. Although Stoneham wanted the team to stay, Labatt Brewing emerged as a serious buyer and reached an agreement to purchase the franchise for $13.25 million in January 1976 with an eye toward relocating the team to Toronto. Hopes of keeping the team in the Bay Area appeared slim.

Bob Lurie, a commercial real estate mogul and longtime Giants fan, decided to pursue a purchase of the team. Lurie had attended games at Candlestick Park for years and loved the ballclub as much as anyone. He couldn't imagine the Giants anywhere but San Francisco. George Moscone, who had just been elected as San Francisco's newest mayor in November, encouraged Lurie to get involved. While Moscone fought the sale of the team, he simultaneously connected Lurie with Bob Short, the former owner of the Texas Rangers, in hopes that the two men could join forces and make a competitive bid with the appeal of keeping the team local. Lurie and Short agreed to counter the offer made by the Labatt Brewing officials. Lurie, however, had his doubts about the partnership. "Short let me know, 'I know everything about baseball. You don't know anything, but with your money we can do well,'" Lurie recalls.[1]

If Short sounded like a challenge to work alongside to Lurie, the other National League owners confirmed it. They didn't really want to deal with him either. They informed Lurie and Moscone that garnering an approved sale required Short to be sidelined as a minority investor who couldn't vote on league matters. Short wouldn't have it. The partnership dissolved on March 2. Needing a fellow investor to make the dollars work, Lurie appeared out of time despite assistance from influential people throughout the league. "Walter O'Malley tried to be a big help," Lurie points out. "He hated the idea that the Giants and Dodgers rivalry was going to disappear."[2] Lurie asked National League president Chub Feeney for another 48 hours to identify another partner. Feeney's response: I'll give you five.

While most people can't claim to have seen lightning strike out of a clear sky, a few individuals have experienced it, and that's exactly what happened to Lurie, Moscone, and the Giants. As the minutes slipped away, the phone rang at the mayor's office, and Moscone's executive assistant, Corey Busch, answered it. On the line was a one Bud Herseth. Who? Nobody had any working knowledge of him, but he immediately caught Busch's attention. Herseth, a rancher from Arizona, expressed interest in joining Lurie's bid for the team. Moscone quickly linked Herseth and Lurie, and the two men agreed to split an $8 million bid for the team down the middle. The Giants stayed in San Francisco.

As the team prepared for the upcoming 1976 season—now just weeks away—Lurie traveled to Arizona as the owner of the team he had loved for so long. The miraculous intervention of Herseth saved the day, but Lurie soon discovered that it might not be a long-term arrangement. "We went down to Scottsdale for spring training, and I went to his office and he let me know that his favorite thing to do was go in the woods and shoot jackrabbits. I said to my wife, this partnership will not last, and it didn't," says Lurie.[3]

The Giants played a forgettable 1976 season. They won 74 games and finished in a distant fourth place in the National League West. Despite having talented players on the roster, San Francisco landed 28 games behind the division champion Cincinnati Reds. Any potential excitement around keeping the team in San Francisco failed to materialize at the ticket office. The Giants' failure to draw fans to the ballpark meant finishing last in the National League in attendance. Hampered by the abysmal conditions of Candlestick Park, the team needed a jolt to reinvigorate the fanbase. Lurie had briefly tried to bring Willie McCovey back to San Francisco after taking over the club, but those negotiations with the Padres went nowhere. Lurie decided to revisit the idea after the season. "I know that he really wanted to bring Willie back," Busch says of his boss. "He just couldn't stand the idea of Willie McCovey playing in another team's uniform and certainly not retiring in another team's uniform."[4]

Reuniting Mac and the Giants wasn't just about bringing back a player to swing a bat for his former team, however; reacquiring Stretch would reconnect him with the city that he knew and the fans who adored him. Imagine if the team had moved to Toronto and McCovey's career had spun in an unknown direction outside of the Bay Area. His greatness could have floated through baseball history without an anchoring point. Instead, Lurie and Herseth's purchase of the team engineered Mac's return to San Francisco, and tens of thousands of fans would soon experience the joy of a heartfelt reunion with their beloved homegrown star. It wasn't just a reunion for sentimentality. McCovey entered the campaign leading all active major leaguers with 465 career home runs. Multiple clubs offered McCovey a contract during the offseason, but he ignored them all after the Giants offered an incentive-laden one-year pact. "The quality of the man and the ability of the player," Lurie responds when asked why bringing McCovey back into the fold was so important to him. "He was such an outstanding player. He was a hero in San Francisco, and I was just delighted to have the chance to bring him back. I can't say enough nice things about Willie."[5] McCovey's return to San Francisco was made official on January 6, 1977, with a caveat: he had to earn a spot with the club during spring training. Despite not having the guarantee of making the team, Mac happily signed the deal.

Nothing would be handed to Mac, but Stretch was very confident that first-year manager Joe Altobelli would have a spot for him after the two discussed the matter during the offseason. If he didn't make the team, McCovey would be given the option of remaining with the organization in a nonplaying capacity. For his part, Stretch was thrilled with the opportunity. Willie was returning to the franchise he loved, his close friends, familiar golf courses, and close proximity to Warriors games. "I don't want to say that I hated to leave the Giants because I played in a nice city and made good friends in San Diego. I look at it as having been in pleasant exile for three years," said Stretch. "But this is where I belong. My home."[6]

McCovey was back in the spot where he felt most comfortable, and he scoffed at the talk that his bat was washed up at the age of 39. "That kind of talk really bothered me. It wasn't that I lost my ability, it was just that I wasn't playing very much. Also, after the way they treated me down there I have to admit I didn't have much incentive," he said.[7] Despite his public display of confidence, deep down, McCovey wondered just how effective he remained.

Soon after returning to the Giants, Mac joined teammates Gary Lavelle, Mike Sadek, Jim Davenport, and Pat Gallagher, the organization's new director of marketing, on a hot stove banquet tour. They all jumped in a station wagon and spent hours driving throughout the Central Valley making various stops along the way, including Fresno. Gallagher, who was new to working in baseball following his time in the theme park industry, remembers being a little intimidated sitting next to Mac, but the two men got to talking about formerly living in San Diego and soon developed a warm friendship. "I used to think of him like a Redwood tree," says Gallagher. "He didn't say much, but you knew he was there. I just think there was that strength."[8] Following the caravan, McCovey turned his attention toward the season's start in Arizona.

McCovey rejoined a Giants organization that looked very different from the one he had spent 17 years with. The Giants entered the 1977 season having refashioned their offense around slugger Darrell Evans, acquired in a trade with the Atlanta Braves the previous season; Bill Madlock, who was coming off back-to-back batting titles with the Chicago Cubs; Jack Clark, a budding young star; and McCovey, who earned his old job back by hitting close to .300 during spring training. It was evident that he belonged on the roster, and Mac's new teammates were thrilled to have him. His physical presence resonated throughout the clubhouse, and his leadership gave them a north star. "If you played on the other team you were scared of him, and when you played on the same team as him it was, well, this is the ultimate gentleman," states Evans, who had competed against Stretch since his first cup of coffee in the big leagues in 1969.[9] McCovey and Evans quickly established a friendship with the former affectionately calling his new teammate "Doody" after the latter's resemblance to the Howdy Doody character.

The Giants won three of their first six games during a season-opening road trip before returning to San Francisco to open the home portion of the schedule against the Los Angeles Dodgers on April 15. Sensing the fans' excitement stirred by McCovey's arrival home, management asked the returning hero to wait until all of his teammates were introduced before being announced to create a special moment between the player and his fans. The large crowd at Candlestick Park jumped to its feet and roared as number 44 emerged from the dugout. Despite reaching base twice, Mac and the Giants lost the game, 7–1.

Loss aside, this day was all about McCovey being back in San Francisco. The fans who had grown up watching him throughout the 1960s could now turn to their children and point to one of their heroes and say, there he is, big Willie Mac. He was San Francisco's own; the star that shined in the city following the team's move west. His return brought a deep joy to the fan base and gave it a new sense of self. McCovey uniquely represented the team's presence in the Bay Area, and his return brought about a birth of history for fans who now looked back on their fandom through the full-circle prism of McCovey's career. Mays, Marichal, Cepeda, Perry: all these great players were gone, never to return, but the first homegrown star—the one with the deepest bond of all—was back. Historian Lincoln Mitchell, who grew up in San Francisco and has authored several books on the Giants, vividly remembers McCovey's homecoming and the meaning it held for so many. "If you talk to people who are in their mid- to late 50s, McCovey was this connection to the past," Mitchell observes. "When Lurie brings McCovey back the Giants finally understand that they have a history in San Francisco that they can talk about, and McCovey is part of that living history. *And* he continues to hit."[10]

Did he ever. Typically a slow starter, McCovey began the season a house afire. Through San Francisco's first 10 games, McCovey pounded out 12 hits in 34 at-bats, including two homers, and was hitting the ball as hard as ever. Opponents shifted their infielders toward McCovey's pull side to stifle his success. "It didn't matter to him because he hit the ball so hard on a consistent basis he hit it through them," marvels former outfielder Terry Whitfield, who was also a newly minted Giant in 1977. In addition to his incredible power, McCovey continued to use his knowledge to set up pitchers early in games by intentionally fouling off a pitch he hoped to see in the late innings with the outcome on the line. It was something that all the Mobile guys did, and it left their teammates in awe. "The guy would come back and try to do it again, but he was a little bit tired and that's when McCovey would kill him. He had a book on everybody mentally," Whitfield says.[11]

It wasn't a stretch to suggest that life and death could still be on the line with McCovey at the plate. Pun intended. Opponents certainly thought about it. "It was pretty scary at times getting on base in front of him and then having him come up. You're ninety feet away with no glove on," Evans points out. "I remember we were playing in Pittsburgh against the Pirates and back then the AstroTurf fields were very thin with almost no padding and were worn out. We were playing the game, and it had been raining. When that ball hits that wet turf it just stops spinning and speeds up, actually. I happened to walk and Willie Stargell is playing first—another one of the great people—and I get down there, and he goes, 'Hey, Doody. What are we going to do here?'

"'What are you talking about?'

"'Listen here. You want to take my glove because I'm going to be standing behind you and trying to hide from Mac.'

"Standing there at first with no glove on was a scary proposition."[12]

Joe Morgan, who developed a close friendship with McCovey over the years, echoed Stargell's sentiment. The Reds' Hall of Fame second baseman told a great story about the glove he used to play second base. "Pete Rose once looked at my small glove and said, 'You'll need more protection than that when McCovey hits.'"[13]

For all that Mac brought to the Giants lineup, he provided the clubhouse with even more. His rock-solid leadership was defined by quiet confidence, selflessness, and more than a few laughs. Mac's imposing presence capped the intensity of any disagreements among his teammates. "We didn't have to worry about having any fights," Evans quips.[14] They also didn't have to think very long about who would serve as the leader of the team's kangaroo court.

Before he was traded to San Diego, McCovey was elected by the clubhouse to lead the court. The Giants' clubhouse featured high-wattage star power throughout the 1960s and 1970s, but there was no question who would be the judge. "That's the respect he had amongst everyone," says Chris Speier, who played alongside McCovey from 1971 through 1973 and again in 1977.

Now the judge was back. McCovey played up the role to the hilt. He was notorious for donning a mop head and robe to oversee the proceedings. Stretch sat in a chair placed in front of his locker with "The Judge" scripted on it.[15] He never hesitated to hit a teammate with a fine. Those were issued for everything from sleeping to tardiness with all the funds going toward an end-of-the-year team party. It was all in good fun and played an important role in keeping the team together during the long season. "Of course, the guy that we wanted to be—the funny one, the one that we took kidding from and we could give kidding to him—became the kangaroo court judge because that's the kind of personality you had to have," adds Evans.[16]

McCovey loved to joke around with his teammates, and the batboys didn't escape unscathed either. One time, he sent one on an errand to find Eddie Logan, the Giants' clubhouse manager, with a request for the key to the batter's box. Late in the 1973 season, Giants outfielder Gary Thomasson told the new kid working as a batboy, Mario Alioto, to ask McCovey for a frozen rope. "He laughed so hard," Alioto, who went on to work in the Giants organization for over four decades, recalls of Stretch's reaction. The next day, Alioto and another batboy took a piece of rope, froze it in an ice tray, and presented it to Mac. They joked about that funny story for many years. "Yes, he was a great star," Alioto says, "but he was light hearted, too."[17] All kidding aside, McCovey also embraced the serious side of leadership. He noticed that Terry Whitfield was facing some challenges with public speaking. Wanting to help but in a respectful way, Mac contacted someone he thought could help and made a connection without wanting any recognition. "He did it in a subtle way, but I knew where it was coming from," Whitfield says.[18] When the team needed to reconfigure its lineup late in the 1977 season to ensure that Evans got more at-bats, McCovey approached Bill Madlock, who had been playing well at third base, about changing positions. "I moved to second base because McCovey asked me," Madlock, who took over the position full-time in 1978, explains. "I wasn't considering it until Mac asked me to do it."[19]

McCovey's teammates also witnessed his daily battle against knee pain. They never heard about it, however, because he never complained. He showed up early every day with the intent to be a difference maker. Stretch's teammates fed off his dedication. "He was always an intimidating force no matter what. We felt good when he was playing. We didn't expect him not to be Willie Mac. It was like, hey, he's one pitch away from killing somebody," Evans says. Tito Fuentes witnessed Mac's routine for 11 seasons in both

San Francisco and San Diego. "He never complained about being sore, and I know his knees were in bad shape, but McCovey never said, 'I don't want to play,'" he says. Fuentes so admired Mac that in 1977—the first season he played on a different team than his friend—he asked the Detroit Tigers for number 44 on signing with them in free agency. Fuentes wore it for the rest of his career. He never did mention it to his friend; he didn't have to. "Willie's smart enough to know why."

Players, coaches, and managers weren't the only ones who appreciated McCovey's class. Umpires, too, held him in high regard. Shortstop Chris Speier considers the time McCovey came up to him prior to a game and asked for a bit of patience. "Hey, kid, my knee is really bothering me," the first baseman told Speier. "Give me a little time to get there on a ground ball hit to you." Happy to help, Speier scooped up a routine ground ball and took a little hop to give McCovey time to get to the bag. One wasn't quite enough, so Speier took another small hop and then whipped the ball to first for the out. Same thing happened again. Later in the ballgame, Speier reached first base, and the umpire had a question for him. "Can you get rid of the ball quicker? You're making every play a bang-bang play." Speier, knowing the real reason for the delayed throws, quipped, "Why don't you go tell McCovey that he needs to get there quicker."

"Oh, no. That's okay," was the response from the sheepish arbiter. "You just keep doing what you're doing. Not a problem."

Recalling the story, Speier notes the feeling McCovey engineered inside everyone. "It was just respect."[20]

McCovey homered for the first time at Candlestick Park since returning as a member of the Giants on May 1 against Philadelphia. It was his fifth homer of the season and the 470th of his career. With each long ball, he reached closer to becoming the most prolific left-handed home run hitter in National League history. He now only trailed Stan Musial (475), Eddie Mathews (503), and Mel Ott (511). However, the team's uneven play prevented it from being serious contenders in the National League West. Despite Mac's return, the Giants finished just 8–11 in the season's first month. The team showed flashes at times—San Francisco won six of seven games in late May—but then it stumbled in this case, losing six of its next seven.

While the team's results proved inconsistent, a rejuvenated McCovey turned back the clock and produced his best season in years, highlighted by a record-setting performance on June 27 against the back-to-back World Series champion Cincinnati Reds at Riverfront Stadium. This day illustrated why Reds manager Sparky Anderson loathed pitching to the guy. The game began ominously for San Francisco. The Big Red Machine was in control, leading, 8–1, after three innings. In the top of the fourth, Madlock hit a two-run homer to pull the Giants a little closer, 8–3. The fifth inning belonged to McCovey.

Evans tripled to lead off the frame and scored on Gary Thomasson's sacrifice fly. That brought up Mac, who took Reds starter Jack Billingham deep for his 12th homer of the year to bring San Francisco closer still, 8–5. The Giants batted around as one after another hitter reached base, chasing Billingham and tying the ballgame when Evans was hit by a pitch with the bases loaded. Thomasson subsequently got plunked, too, which stunningly gave the Giants a 9–8 lead. McCovey strode to the plate with the bases loaded to face Reds reliever Joe Hoerner with the opportunity to break his tie with Henry Aaron for most career grand slams by a National League hitter. McCovey always looked up to Aaron. Their Mobile connection strong. A pair of 44s. As he so often did throughout his career, Mac delivered. He crushed a grand slam that turned the record book into a ringing slot machine. The Giants had now scored 10 runs in the inning and led the Reds, 13–8, on their way to a win. In hitting this slam, McCovey set a new National League mark with 17 and in doing so became the first player in major league history to homer twice in an inning two times in his career. It was no wonder his jubilant teammates lifted Stretch off the ground in bear hugs when he returned to the dugout after circling the bases for the 478th time. The moment brought McCovey's thoughts back to Mobile, to playing for the Black Bears and admiring Aaron. "(W)hen I came to the big leagues, I insisted on wearing his number, 44. Breaking one of his records is an honor," said McCovey, who was also thrilled by the impressive comeback victory.[21] Stretch also noted that he wasn't the only local Mobilian who felt that way about the Hammer. "I remember Billy Williams trying to start a movement that would have had all the guys from Mobile wearing 44 on their uniforms. And at one time there were quite a few of us," he recalled during the postgame media scrum.[22]

Mac wasn't finished in 1977. In August, Mac smashed the final grand slam of his career against Montreal to extend his new National Lague record to 18. He knocked in five runs in both games he hit slams during the season. For context, McCovey hadn't driven in five runs in a game in seven years. The Giants celebrated Willie McCovey Day on September 18. His mother, Ester, made the long trip from Mobile to be by his side. The Giants showered Mac with gifts, highlighted by a new car. His close friend, Golden State Warriors owner Franklin Mieuli, gave Stretch a lifetime pass to watch his favorite team. Mac received a basset hound puppy that he later appropriately named "Homer." When handed the microphone, Stretch thanked everyone, especially his mother, whom he jokingly asked, "Do you still think I should've been a lawyer?"[23]

Mac celebrated his day with a divine moment in the bottom of the ninth inning. With the game tied, 2–2, McCovey lined the game-winning single to left-center field (the opposite way!) to plate Derrel Thomas for the walk-off win. Even though the years had rolled by, it was as though times had never changed. After the game, Giants manager Joe Altobelli poignantly expressed the veteran first baseman's greatness. "Some things get blown out of proportion but not Willie McCovey," he said.[24] Stretch's stunning performance caught the imagination of Giants fans young and old in 1977. The team drew nearly 75,000 more fans than it had in 1976, an increase of 10.5 percent, even though it finished 75–87.[25]

McCovey's phenomenal campaign earned him the Comeback Player of the Year Award. He received 17 out of a possible 22 votes to capture the honor for his remarkable season. The numbers were impressive. In his age 39 season, McCovey appeared in 141 games, homered 28 times, and drove in 86 runs. One would have to go all the way back to 1970 to find the last season in which he had played in more games and had driven in more runs. He pondered his campaign at home in Woodside with his young dog, Homer, by his side. Ultimately, in a classic case of two things being true at the same time, the award left McCovey feeling both satisfied and frustrated. "It's always great to have a good year. This, I guess, is a recognition of that fact and, in that regard, I'm happy. I hope I never will be in the position again of being eligible for the award," he said.[26] The most important thing in his mind that the season resolved was his ability to navigate the season from a physical standpoint while playing at a high level. He was now ready to pursue career glory on a historical scale. Stretch was ready to chase his 500th home run.

* * *

The news proved so tantamount in the Bay Area that it relegated every other story below the fold of the front page of the *Oakland Tribune* on March 16, 1978. "Kuhn Expected to OK Giants' Deal for Blue," shouted the headline with an adjacent photo of the (soon to be) former A's electric left hander staring down the reader as he followed through on a pitch. It was big baseball news, but it was huge in the Bay Area. Vida Blue, the three-time All Star who had captured the baseball world's imagination as a rookie in 1971, had been traded to the San Francisco Giants by Charlie Finley following a protracted contract dispute. The return was substantial, at least on paper: seven players—equivalent to one for each full season Blue had pitched in Oakland—and $300,000. When reached by Tom Weir of the *Tribune* in his hotel room at 3:30 in the morning, Blue reacted by noting it was way too early for putting together his thoughts on the deal. "Just write something Vida Blue might say, and make it look good," he said.[27]

While Vida stayed mum for the moment, Giants executives couldn't stop talking about the blockbuster deal. General manager Spec Richardson, who had stayed up until the early hours of the morning waiting for Finley to call with an acceptance of the deal, expressed his willingness to revisit Blue's contract after pulling off the trade for one of baseball's most captivating stars. Joe Altobelli could not hide his excitement. "When you get a pitcher of Blue's class you really have yourself someone," he gushed.[28] The Giants needed to get the permission of commissioner Bowie Kuhn to complete the deal in light of Finley's exploration of relocating his team to Denver, but no one believed it would be a problem. There was also an odd dynamic of the Giants potentially playing some of their home games in Oakland. Neither issue prevented the trade from going through. At the end of the day, the Giants needed to bolster their starting rotation, and Richardson delivered.

Buoyed by acquiring Blue, the Giants felt a sense of optimism that they could contend. McCovey concurred about the team's prospects and also felt rejuvenated about his own abilities. Now sitting on 493 career home runs, the 40-year-old McCovey, who was set to begin his 20th major league season, could see the finish line of reaching rarified air. "It's always been my goal to hit 500 homers, but I was beginning to wonder if it would be possible the way things were going until this year. Now I'm sure I'll be able to do it," he said.[29]

McCovey and Blue had already met in Oakland, where they spent the final weeks of the 1976 season together, but their time in San Francisco established a bond that remained true for the rest of their lives. Blue's clubhouse locker was established next to Mac's, and the two became fast friends but not without a little initial hesitancy from Vida. "Big Stretch," Blue begins when considering his longtime friend, "he was a genuinely humble person, and I was lucky to have him be a part of my life. They put my locker next to his after the trade from Oakland. I was a black cat who lost one of his lives but got it back. Mac had an open heart and open door policy. If you needed something he would try to get it for you."[30]

Unanimously known for his generosity, McCovey remained somewhat elusive on road trips. He mostly kept to himself, but Stretch thoroughly enjoyed going out with his teammates on occasion. Blue was thrilled when Mac started calling him up. They enjoyed lobsters at one of Stretch's favorite dinner places in New York City. Music always made for a great night. McCovey always took care of a friend. "He paid for everything," Blue recalls. Vida always stayed ready to reciprocate McCovey's generosity, but he couldn't recall a time Stretch asked for anything. "I was on 24/7 standby, but he never wanted nothing from nobody. He just wanted to be respected." Vida Blue pauses, his voice still in the silence, and then, "These tidbits are priceless in my life. I am getting chills talking about him."[31]

The Giants started the season in moribund fashion, splitting their first 20 games to finish April in third place behind Los Angeles and Cincinnati. McCovey homered three times during the season's opening month, but then he scuffled through a 13-for-67 spell, ironically as the team heated up and took over first place in the National League West. However, his only homer of May was important. In a key series against the Dodgers late in the month that drew huge crowds to Candlestick, McCovey smacked a three-run shot off Doug Rau—the 497th of his career—to help the Giants win the series opener, 6–1, in front of 43,646 exuberant fans. The surprising San Francisco Giants were now 27–14 and in first place. The Giants continued to maintain their pole position in the division through late June, when they visited Atlanta. McCovey had added a pair of long balls to his career total earlier in the month, and he now stood on the precipice of legendary status with 499 career homers.

McCovey's resurgence in San Francisco drew the attention of media around the country. The dynamic of the situation was remarkable. Mac, now 40, had returned to the city that loved him and had turned back time with a hitting display that reminded everyone of, well, a younger Willie McCovey. It was also beginning to strike everyone that McCovey just might play a few more years as he so frequently noted he wanted to do. Reaching the 1980 season would mean that McCovey played in four decades. It all now seemed not only possible but also plausible. The mutual love and appreciation between McCovey and the city of San Francisco deepened during this time. His leaving and returning engineered a swell of affection that further endeared him to a place that already loved him so much. McCovey willingly revealed his emotions on the subject—something he rarely did—as he expressed the depth of his own appreciation for the opportunity to return. "I love San Francisco and the people of the Bay Area," McCovey told Ron Fimrite of *Sports Illustrated* in April. "I think people there consider me a part of the city. San Francisco is identified with certain things—bridges, the fog, the cable cars. Without bragging, I feel I've gotten to the place where people are thinking of me along those lines. I'd like to think that when people think of San Francisco they also think of Willie McCovey. It's where I want to be, where I belong. I hope the people love me a little in return."[32]

June 30, 1978, was unsurprisingly a sweltering 95-degree day in Atlanta as the Giants and Braves squared off in a doubleheader. McCovey led off the top of the second inning against southpaw Jamie Easterly, who got ahead in the count, 0–2. The third pitch of the at-bat proved to be the money ball. Mac connected with a fastball and scorched it on a line toward left field. As he broke out of the batter's box, his helmet nearly flew off, and as he clamped it down, the ball sailed over the fence. It was a joyous jog from there. McCovey broke into a big smile as he rounded the bases with his trademark trot, head still and elbows high. He became just the 12th player in major league history to hit 500 home runs. His teammates were thrilled. They had made shirts that read "500 for 44" and waited for this moment in baseball history. "It was a bullet to left like a right-handed hitter had pulled it," marvels Vida Blue.[33] The Braves soured the moment slightly by winning both ends of the doubleheader, but the day was all about celebrating the great Willie Mac.

The Giants thrilled their fans for a few more weeks before stumbling in August and falling out of first place. McCovey's beautiful moment in Atlanta would be remembered over the years, but the season did not play out as he had hoped from a team perspective. By mid-August, Mac was hitting only .220, and in September, he again lost playing time to Mike Ivie, whom the Giants had acquired from San Diego. Despite its strong start to the season, San Francisco finished 89–73, six games behind the division champion Dodgers.

Now in the twilight of his career, McCovey took on a reduced role the following season. He split first-base duties and provided pop off the bench as a pinch hitter for the 1979 squad. Veteran center fielder Bill North, who signed with the Giants as a free agent in the offseason, remembers pitchers taking no notice of McCovey's age. "They still feared him for what he might do," North says. Stretch's 15 additional homers attested to that truth.

Even if his bat speed was waning, McCovey's star power remained as bright as ever. Immaculately dressed, McCovey's presence at any social gathering took it to new heights. Stretch invited his new teammate for an evening on the town after a home game, and the event impressed a lifelong memory on North. "Mac got me hooked up with high society in San Francisco," North recalls of the party. "I met Baryshnikov."[34] Another time, Dodgers owner Peter O'Malley invited Giants owner Bob Lurie and team executive Corey Busch to join him in his box for a game between the rivals along with several other guests. The group included the incomparable Cary Grant, gray haired, bespectacled, and, as it turns out, a big baseball fan. Busch and Grant got to talking, and the actor mentioned that one of his favorite players was Willie McCovey. Busch offered to introduce him to Stretch after the game, and Grant excitedly accepted the invitation. "Cary Grant was as excited to be in a big league clubhouse to see all these ballplayers as the ballplayers were to see Cary Grant," Busch remembers. McCovey, who had always been a huge fan of the movies, and Grant were thrilled to meet each other. "There was this mutual admiration," says Busch. "It was incredible for me to watch someone of the magnitude of Cary Grant, who was just in awe of meeting Willie McCovey. It was a real special moment."[35]

The 1979 Giants won only 71 games during a disappointing campaign. Manager Joe Altobelli was fired in September and replaced by third-base coach Dave Bristol. The results weren't much better in 1980, when the team won 75 games. Actually, in some ways, things got worse, particularly for McCovey as he entered his 22nd season. Stretch understood that the end of his baseball career was near even as he did all he could to delay its close. He was, however, very pragmatic about his situation. "When you get to be 42 years old it's not so much a case of a player retiring as it is of them retiring you," he admitted.[36]

Instead of being celebrated for appearing in four decades in the major leagues, McCovey found himself in the crosshairs of Giants management. In the midst of the team's struggles in 1980, Bristol called a team meeting and aired out the players. He shocked Bill North by calling out McCovey in front of everyone for not driving in enough runs. "You talk about somebody getting pissed off, and it wasn't Willie McCovey. It was me," North fumes. Sharp criticism inappropriately directed at their leader stirred up the clubhouse. The team never had a chance. ("Bristol knew he had made a mistake," North states.[37]) The damage was done. It was clear that McCovey's stature had slipped with certain members of the organization, including general manager Spec Richardson and, at times anyway, Bristol. Rumors began reaching McCovey that his time with the Giants might end before the season concluded. Awkward silence from the front office seemed to infuse these whisperings with credibility. McCovey bristled. Mac knew that he wasn't playing well; he admitted as much himself. "The fans are not seeing the real me," he lamented as his average hovered around .200, but Mac maintained that his abilities were not diminishing. His bat wasn't slowing, his knees weren't interfering with his fielding, and his long strides still translated on the bases. "I know the lack of skills is not going to be the thing that's going to force me into retirement," McCovey tried to convince Blake Green of the *San Francisco Chronicle* and himself simultaneously.[38] Fear of the unknown prevented McCovey from being completely honest with himself, but that does not exonerate how the Giants treated him in the final days of his career. The organization wanted to get young players in the lineup consistently, and Richardson approached McCovey with the news. The Giants wanted to move on from him. The declaration cut McCovey to the core. "This was a shock to Willie. Why did Spec Richardson do that to Willie? Willie never hurt anybody. It just came out of nowhere," exclaims Rocky Dudum, McCovey's close friend who was with him when word came down that he was going to be released.[39]

Deeply wounded, McCovey arrived at Candlestick Park on June 22 with the intention of announcing his retirement during a pregame press conference. Before meeting with the media, Mac sat alongside his longtime adviser and friend Hal Silen in the office of Giants executive vice president Corey Busch. "I asked Willie how he felt. He looked at me. Here's this big, strong, athletic man, and he looked at me and said, 'I'm scared to death.' And I go, really, what are you scared of? And he says, 'Corey, ever since I can remember from the time I was a young boy all I did was play ball every summer. I've played ball all my life, and honestly I just don't know what I'm going to do,'" Busch remembers. "It was a very touching moment for me. It's one of those moments when you realize that these heroes are people just like the rest of us."[40]

Everybody said all the right things at the press conference that afternoon, but McCovey's insides churned throughout the ordeal. If ever there was a time when he followed his own advice about stopping and intentionally considering his words with the media, this was it. McCovey responded to a reporter's question about emotions surrounding this announcement with something shy of the truth. "No," he replied earnestly. "Not a bad day at all."[41] Two things can be true at the same time. He could publicly acknowledge his remarkable career while privately wrestling with the hurt that swirled within him when the thing he had dedicated his life to no longer wanted him. He now faced having to refashion his identity. Maybe not a bad day for Stretch per se but nonetheless a very difficult one. McCovey rarely held back from the media if he wanted to express his feelings on a particular topic, but he blocked his agony from escaping into public view on this day. However, those close to him, away from the camera's glare and the reporters' notebooks, knew better. "He wasn't doing good, you know. He was still playing good ball. That's what we couldn't understand," Dudum reveals before turning to the subject of Spec Richardson. "He should never have let him go. He could have waited until the end of the season."[42]

McCovey would play two more weeks and conclude his playing career at the All-Star break. Bob Lurie expressed how difficult it was for him to accept McCovey's retirement, but the organization would keep him in the fold to work for the franchise in several off-field capacities. Lurie explained his perspective on McCovey's unusual midseason retirement to Ira Kamin of the *San Francisco Examiner*. "He'd been thinking about it and we talked about it, then he came up to the office and said it's time to talk about it. We talked about it for several days. How to do it. He wanted to do it fairly immediately. So we decided to do it early. So he said how about after the All Star break. We said fine," Lurie said.[43] The situation—and some of the statements that accompanied it—confused more than a few people on the outside. It left some members of the team scratching their heads. Regardless, McCovey was now on the doorstep of retirement, but he wasn't quite yet done creating magical moments on the baseball field.

A week later, the Giants hosted the Dodgers for a Sunday doubleheader. McCovey was not in the starting lineup for the first game, but when catcher Milt May doubled in Darrell Evans in the bottom of the sixth inning to tie the score at three, it seemed increasingly likely that he could be called on to pinch-hit in the late innings. Sure enough, the ballgame remained deadlocked into the bottom of the ninth. Second baseman Rennie Stennett led off with a single against Dodgers reliever Bobby Castillo. Rich Murray, a young player whom the Giants wanted to see more of at first base, popped up. Castillo then struck out Johnnie LeMaster to set the scene. Dave Bristol turned to Stretch, who was ready. A bolt of energy surged through the more than 50,000 fans at Candlestick Park as McCovey walked to the plate and dug into the batter's box. The first two pitches from Castillo resulted in a 1–1 count. McCovey waited patiently for the third offering with his coiled bat ready to strike, a subtle timing tick of lifting his front foot the only sign of movement. Castillo threw a fastball that caught a little too much plate, and McCovey unleashed a smooth stroke that firmly met the ball and sent it soaring out to the right-center-field gap. Stennett immediately raced toward second as the ball bounced twice and hit the outfield fence. Dodgers center fielder Derrel Thomas gathered the ball and threw it back to the infield as quickly as he could, but it was too late to prevent Stennett from sliding home safely as McCovey downshifted into second base with the game-winning hit. The Giants poured out of the dugout to congratulate McCovey, whose final career extra-base hit gave San Francisco a 4–3 win over its archrival. McCovey's pinch-hit double gave the fans a chance to fill his ears with the cheers for that afternoon and days gone by, and they cascaded their beloved first baseman with gushing adoration. His reaction revealed no emotion; the muted look of serenity on his face belied the context of the moment. Emotions in control to the end.

The sustained cheers, some of which were belted out by those who had seen his debut in 1959 and by many more who had not, continued as McCovey and his teammates left the field. They coalesced into a chant of "We want Willie!" as the players collected their things in the dugout and walked up the tunnel to the clubhouse. The sustained noise pulled McCovey back out after several minutes. He doffed his cap by its orange bill in acknowledgment of the ovation—a memory for all that would remain regardless of how the final few games of McCovey's career played out.

Lincoln Mitchell describes how that day puts the relationship between McCovey and Giants fans in perspective. "McCovey at 42 seemed like 142 not because he was ancient looking but because he just had played forever. He's a four-decade guy. He goes 4-for-4 off Robin Roberts when Jack Kennedy is some minor senator from Massachusetts. He hasn't even really started running in the primary yet. That's how long ago this was, and now it's 1980. He's hitting a double off the wall at Candlestick Park. He just played so long that bond was so intense," Mitchell explains.[44]

The final start of McCovey's career occurred in his final home game on July 3 against Cincinnati. Bristol told reporters early in the week that he would start Stretch on Thursday. Knowing that this would be their hero's last appearance in San Francisco, thousands of fans throughout the Bay Area made their way to the ballpark to say good-bye. The vivid memory of all those Giants fans lined up to get in still resonates with Corey Busch more than 40 years later. "The last game he played at Candlestick we had over

17,000 people buy tickets at the gate that day. That's a huge walkup. You're never prepared as a ballclub to try to sell that many tickets at your ticket windows the day of the game. A lot of people didn't even get in until about the third inning. The lines were so long," Busch says. "It's just another tribute to the way San Franciscans responded to Willie McCovey."[45]

Many people throughout the Bay Area began their morning by reading McCovey's own words in a first-person article published by the *San Francisco Examiner*. Mac encapsulated all he needed to say in his first two lines. "San Francisco is my home. It means home to me." He named several reasons he loved the Bay Area so much and concluded with another poignant thought. "The people of San Francisco have accepted me as one of their own and made me feel at home."[46] McCovey's focus on the importance of home cannot be overemphasized. McCovey lived amidst a love and peace on the West Coast in a way that the South never pretended to offer him. There was a reason he intentionally used the word "home" three times early in the piece.

Their reciprocated connection fueled fans that afternoon who cheered McCovey's every move, especially his RBI single in the bottom of the third inning that gave the Giants a 3–1 lead, the game itself but a footnote. Mac basked in the ovations but admitted surprise at the attention he received from the national media. He had long thought that his career went unnoticed outside of California—that he had homered for all these years in relative obscurity.

Willie McCovey woke up with a sick feeling on July 6. Perhaps it was the flu. Maybe nerves caused it. Perhaps it was a combination of the two. He would have remained in his hotel room if he wasn't playing in his final major league game later that afternoon at Dodger Stadium. Naturally, Stretch kept news of his queasiness to himself. No one needed to know. Once again Mac was called on to pinch-hit, and he came through in the top of the eighth inning. After receiving a notable ovation from the Dodger Stadium crowd, he struck a sacrifice fly to center field that plated Jack Clark and gave the Giants a 4–3 lead. McCovey acknowledged the loud cheers of the Dodgers' fans by lifting both arms in the air before ducking into the dugout and disappearing like one of his towering homers lost in the San Francisco fog. When reporters reached his locker after San Francisco's 7–4 extra-inning triumph, it was empty.

McCovey retired the most prolific left-handed home run hitter in National League history. He also owned a number of prestigious major league records, including career grand slams (18) and number of intentional walks in a season (45). His 521 home runs placed him ninth on the all-time list and assured him future membership in the National Baseball Hall of Fame. His longtime friend Willie Mays suspected that it would be a while before McCovey would be able to get away from baseball and settle into retirement. "It's taken me five years," Mays admitted to veteran newspaper writer Stephanie Salter of the *San Francisco Examiner*. "Knowing Mac, it may take him a lot longer."[47]

Lurie and the Giants didn't wait long to award McCovey with the club's highest honor. The organization retired McCovey's number 44 during a ceremony on September 21, making him just the fifth Giant to receive that honor as he joined Mel Ott, Carl Hubbell, Willie Mays, and Juan Marichal. Additionally, McCovey's friend Pat Gallagher helped the Giants create a new honor to bestow on one of the team's players at the end of each season. It would be given out annually to a player who best exemplifies "competitive spirit, ability, and leadership" on the ballclub. They called it the Willie Mac Award, and players, along with McCovey himself, voted for its recipient. Jack Clark won the inaugural prize. Over time, the award became a staple of the late season Giants calendar, and it has been bestowed on more than 40 Giants. McCovey remained heavily involved in the process for the rest of his life. Along with casting a ballot for his personal choice, McCovey annually took the field to present a plaque to the winner during a pregame ceremony as his health allowed. Following Mac's passing in 2018, his daughter, Allison, took up the mantle of presenting the award. Recipients have frequently cited the Willie Mac Award as one of their most prized honors when reflecting on their careers.

Darrell Evans, 1983 Willie Mac Award winner: "What a great honor . . . he had such an infectious smile, and he was always just a humble guy. Everybody just loved being around him."[48]

Chris Speier, 1987 Willie Mac Award winner: "I think, and I can say this truthfully, that probably means the most to me of anything that I've ever done, World Series ring, All Star Games. That award—because it's named after that man, Willie McCovey—that means the most to me of anything, and the way it was voted by the players because of who he was and what he represented. I cherish that."[49]

In recent years, the organization has included fans in voting for the winner as well as honoring a player and volunteer from each of the more than 80 baseball leagues included in the organization's Junior Giants program.

In mid-December 1980, McCovey took the unusual step of briefly returning to Mobile for a celebration of his career. He wore a plaid, double-breasted suit and greeted fans on "Willie McCovey Day," but all was not right. "When he was here for that parade, he just wasn't comfortable," recalls Cleon Jones. "He couldn't wait for the next flight."[50]

* * *

While Willie McCovey returned amidst great fanfare to San Francisco and completed his playing career, one had to drive only a little over two hours northeast of the Bay Area into the heart of agriculture-rich California to find Billy Williams enjoying retirement in Loomis, a small town outside of Sac ramento where the outdoors beckoned. Williams happily answered its call. He cast a line into nearby lakes and any other body of water that teemed with something to catch. His daughters, who were quickly growing up, also fished and occasionally rode the lawn mower that trimmed the grass on the property. It was an idyllic scene far from the cramped realities that come with living a city life, the bright lights flipped on by a baseball season replaced with sunshine that lit up wilderness trails rather than 90-foot base paths and postgame interviews.

The Williams family embraced this setup, but then an old friend called. In 1978, Bob Kennedy, who had managed the Cubs for several years following the College of Coaches debacle, called Williams with a request. He wanted Billy back with the Cubs to work with the organization's minor leaguers. Kennedy assured Williams that in exchange for two years of working with those players down on the farm, he would have a place on the major league coaching staff. While he missed the game after being in it for so long, Williams wouldn't have agreed to return in just any situation. The unique combi- nation of the Cubs, Kennedy, and a guarantee of promotion was too good to pass up, so Billy Williams became a Chicago Cub, again.

One of the most pressing issues Williams addressed over the next two sea- sons involved an unhappy minor league pitcher from a town in Louisiana so small that stoplights were hard to come by who faced a critical decision. At 6-foot-5, Lee Smith could throw a baseball through a brick wall, but his arm talent appealed to the organization out of the bullpen rather than in the starting rotation. But Smith bristled at the idea of becoming a relief pitcher, a posi- tion that played a much smaller role at the big-league level in the late 1970s than today. There were a few exceptions: Goose Gossage and Rollie Fingers come to mind. Most starting pitchers, however, especially touted ones in the minors, viewed themselves in the mold of workhorses who worked deep into games rather than relievers called on to bail out a struggling starter.

Originally drafted by the Cubs in 1975 after being scouted by the same Buck O'Neil who played such an instrumental role in saving Williams's career, Smith spent four seasons as a starting pitcher in the organization before being told about its desire to turn him into a reliever during the 1979 season while he was pitching for Chicago's Double A affiliate in Midland, Texas. Smith, who dreamed of becoming the next Fergie Jenkins, Bob Gib- son, or Don Newcombe, wasn't interested. Throwing quality starts would be the fastest way to getting promoted to Chicago, he thought. The deeply frus- trated Smith, who grew up loving basketball, decided to quit baseball rather than accept the new role. His primary dream had always been to play college hoops anyway. As the team prepared to leave for a road trip, Smith packed his bags and went home.

The organization caught wind of the situation and asked Williams to visit the hard-throwing 20-year-old. Billy believed that Smith possessed unique talent and was convinced that the young pitcher's ability would translate well to the shifting landscape of the sport. Williams also understood the emotional dynamics involved in wanting to return home during the season. Billy drew on his own circumstances in 1959, when he left the San Antonio team for Mobile, and the crucial visit from Buck O'Neil that played a pivotal role in his return to baseball. "C. B. Davis, who was the farm director, sent me down there, so I kind of smoothed that out from the experience that I got from Buck O'Neil. We got him to continue to pitch because (manager) Randy (Hundley) was going to make him a relief pitcher, and he wanted to be a starter. I told him that the way the game is going now you're going to be used as a relief pitcher, and that's how you can make your money. So, he made a decision to go ahead and do it after our conversation, and everything worked out," says Williams.[51]

Smith went on to have an 18-year major league career. "Somehow—I don't know how—Billy saw that the whole realm of Major League Baseball was about to change with this relief pitching thing," Smith says years later. "Billy said, 'Man, I see the game changing. This relief pitching thing is going to take on a bigger role in how teams go about setting up their pitching staffs.' I didn't think about that. I was thinking about the right now." During their conversation, Williams declined to mention that he had decided to leave the San Antonio club in 1959 albeit for much different reasons. "I didn't know up until a couple of years ago that Billy actually thought about quitting," Smith adds.[52] Their conversation proved revelatory, and Smith returned to Midland. He reached the majors in 1980 and never looked back. Williams spent a notable chunk of the 1980s working for the Cubs, so the two men remained in a familiar circle until 1987, when Smith was traded to the Boston Red Sox. They remain friends today.

Lee Smith finished his major league career with a record 478 saves. In the quarter century since his retirement, only Mariano Rivera and Trevor Hoffman have surpassed his mark. His remarkable career concluded with enshrinement in the National Baseball Hall of Fame in 2019. Smith turned to Williams during his induction speech and thanked him for that conversation. "Thank God for Mr. Billy Williams," Smith said, eliciting a chuckle and shake of the head from his friend. "He knocked some sense into me."[53]

After seeing his excellent work with kids in their minor league system, the Cubs followed through and promoted Williams to the major league coaching staff for the 1980 season. He had an immediate impact. Veteran first baseman Bill Buckner reported to spring training still feeling the effects of a severe

ankle injury in 1975, along with the ramifications of a broken finger he suf
fered during the 1979 season finale. Williams helped Buckner make a few
adjustments that helped put him back on track. "With Buckner, it's just a
matter of moving the lead shoulder, keeping the top of the body tilted—not
falling back on the ball as he's going into it," Williams explained.[54] Buckner
went on to hit .324 and win the National League batting title. For Cub hitters
not named Buckner who might find themselves struggling at the plate, Williams suggested a remedy that had worked for him many times over during
his career: watch the current iteration of a Barney Sterling classic. "When I
was in a slump I used to take a pitcher of tea down to the basement and look
at movies. I had films of myself when I was hitting well and other films of
myself when I wasn't," he said. Williams encouraged his hitters to compare
their swings in good times and bad to identify the mechanical problems.
For Billy, it was usually dropping his hands or taking too long of a stride.
That said, he also stressed the other important aspect of being a great batter.
"There's a lot to be said for the mental part of it, too," he stressed.[55] Each of
these conversations revealed aspects of Williams's tireless work ethic.

After three seasons in Chicago, Williams accepted the hitting coach position with the Oakland A's in 1983. Among Williams's pupils during his three
seasons in Oakland was veteran outfielder Dusty Baker, who soaked up Williams's philosophies in 1985. "He would always tell us to save something for
the end of the swing because that's how Sweet Swinging Billy Williams was
known to hit," Baker recalls. In addition to punctuating the follow-through
that made him so unique, Williams emphasized to Baker a mind-set driven
by the goal of being a special hitter. "Dusty," Williams would say. "They
would come to watch Ernie Banks, but they would go home talking about
me." Williams wanted each player to create his own identity based on his
own success as he had done throughout his 18-year career. Baker has passed
along that mind-set throughout his own extensive experience as a hitting
coach and manager. "I try to tell my guys the same thing," Baker points out.
"I say, you want them to go home—they came to see whoever the stars are
on the team—but they're going to go home talking about you, so you start
your own reputation."[56]

Williams returned to the Cubs in 1986 for two years before taking a hia-
tus from coaching. He came back in 1992 as Chicago's hitting coach and
remained an instructor for the next 10 seasons. One of the key moments
for the organization during Williams's first year back with the club was a
trade on March 20, when the Cubs dealt veteran George Bell to the cross-
town Chicago White Sox for reliever Ken Patterson and a young outfielder
named Sammy Sosa. There was just enough time before the end of spring
training for Williams to get a close look at his newest batter. It quickly
became clear that pitchers wanted to attack the inside part of the plate against

the right-handed-hitting Sosa. "They ran the ball in, and he got jammed. He looked over at me. He knew I was the hitting coach. I said, 'Don't look at me. Look at the pitcher. We'll work on it tomorrow,'" Williams says. "I saw him and I knew what he was doing right away." Sosa was getting himself jammed because his movement brought him too far toward the plate. Williams and Sosa spent countless hours in the hitting cage, refining his approach by keeping his head down and driving the ball to right-center field. "I never threw the ball inside to him," explains Williams. "I just stayed outside. I wanted him to go that way. He had the power."[57] Pitchers who countered with a slow curveball would find it smoked to Sosa's pull side. Sosa raised his batting average 57 points to .260 but saw his first season on the North Side abbreviated when a pitch broke his wrist in June. Another injury in August sidelined him for the rest of the season.

The two worked together relentlessly. Williams sought ways to keep Sosa motivated. When Billy learned that Sosa was a big Roberto Clemente fan, Williams, who played against the Pittsburgh star for years, emphasized it. "He wanted to be like Clemente. I used to walk along in Pittsburgh and see a picture of Clemente. I would get it to give it to him just to inspire him," he says.[58]

Six seasons later, Mark McGwire and Sosa engaged in a home run dual that captured the country's attention. Sentiment surrounding the context of that chase has significantly changed over time, of course, but in the moment, it was one of the biggest stories in America. Throughout that summer, McGwire, a larger-than-life stoic, smashed herculean moon shots while the jovial Sosa injected the chase of Roger Maris's single-season home run record of 61 with a unique enjoyment as he launched soaring fly balls all over the place. As McGwire closed in on Maris's record, Hall of Fame president Jeff Idelson traveled to St. Louis Cardinals games to collect artifacts for the museum should the record be broken. On September 8, 1998, McGwire lined a homer that just snuck over the left-field wall for number 62. He hit it against the Cubs at Busch Stadium. Sosa ran across the field and congratulated McGwire in one of the chase's more memorable scenes.

Having honored McGwire for setting a new mark, Idelson spoke with Sosa, who was sitting on 58 home runs, about the Hall of Fame's interest in his artifacts if (when) he, too, broke Maris's record. The Hall wanted Sammy to be appreciated for his accomplishments as well. Sosa promised Idelson that if he hit number 62, that jersey would go to Cooperstown. So Idelson peeled away from the Cardinals and began following the Cubs. Sosa hit number 59 on September 11 at Wrigley Field against the Milwaukee Brewers. He blasted number 60 the following day as the Cubs eyed their first postseason berth since 1989. The huge crowd that packed Wrigley Field on September 13 for the series finale against the Brewers witnessed Sosa crack not one hut two homers, the second a towering fly ball that carried onto Waveland Avenue, to pass Maris in Chicago's 11–10 win. In the jubilant clubhouse after the game, Idelson patiently waited for the media to finish interviewing Sosa before approaching him about the jersey. Sosa was wearing his undershirt with the uniform in a nearby basket. Yosh Kawano, the longtime Cubs clubhouse manager, had taken it. Idelson told Kawano that the jersey was going to Cooperstown, but he declined to give it up. "Yosh, I can't go home empty handed, or I won't have a job," Idelson told him. Kawano responded by wheeling it back into the equipment room, where the president was not allowed to go. Feeling a sense of panic creep into his chest, Idelson turned to Billy Williams, now Chicago's bench coach, whom he had gotten to know well over the years.

"Billy, you've got to help me out," he implored.

"Fear not," Williams replied.

He went back into the equipment room and had a lengthy conversation with Yosh, who gave him Sosa's jersey.

"Here you go," Williams said to Idelson as he gave him the memento. "Take this back to Cooperstown where it belongs."

Whistler isn't just a member of the Hall of Fame but also one of the museum's curators. "If it weren't for Billy Williams I don't know that Sammy Sosa's jersey ever would have made it there," says a grateful Idelson.[59]

Part IV

ENSHRINEMENT

"IN THE NEWS"

Super Sunday for Bears. . . . Explosion Set to Delay but Not End Shuttle Program. . . . Giants' Youth Movement. . . . Comet's Journey through. . . . Soviets Report Nuclear Accident. . . . Roger Craig Spins Magic. . . . Rain Can't Spoil McCovey's Hall. . . . Reviewer Gives "Platoon." . . . Iran-Contra Hearings Begin. . . . Cub Great Billy Williams Joins Hall Today. . . . Dawson's Hitting Sparks. . . . Thatcher Re-elected. . . . "Mr. Gorbachev, Open This Gate, Tear Down This Wall." . . . Griffey Selected Number. . . . Giants Win West for First Time since. . . . Keep Eye on Young Grace. . . . "Won't Be Long before He's Here," Williams. . . . Giant's Clark Ready for Postseason. . . . Battle of the Bay. . . . In Face of Horrific Earthquake. . . . Cubs, Giants Face Off in Wild Card. . . . Bumgarner Steller in Relief as Giants Win Third World. . . . Series Champion Chicago Cubs!

Chapter 11

"A Time for Reflection"

The playing careers of Willie McCovey and Billy Williams may have been in the rearview mirror, but retirement opened new avenues for each of them to continue influencing the game of baseball. Both entrenched themselves with their longtime organizations—everything felt more aligned with them in San Francisco and Chicago—if in different capacities. Williams stayed in the game as an on-field coach and front-office adviser, while McCovey worked for the Giants in a variety of capacities before he and the team drifted apart prior to reconciling. Their organizations experienced success on opposite ends of the 1980s. The Cubs won the National League East in 1984 before losing in the National League Championship Series to the San Diego Padres in five games. Meanwhile, the Giants stumbled through the decade before a wave of young talent revitalized the franchise and helped it win the National League West in 1987. Through it all, Williams and McCovey remained beloved staples of the two fan bases. They were more than just great ballplayers; they had become iconic figures whose presence spanned generations. Williams, with the exception of his two short stints in California, and McCovey remained entrenched in their communities following retirement. Fans saw them all the time whether it be at local restaurants, golf courses, or the ballpark.

Although their experience playing baseball together in the big leagues consisted of just a handful of games in Oakland at the end of the 1976 season, Williams and McCovey became ultimate lifelong teammates when both received election into the National Baseball Hall of Fame for their incredible accomplishments. Their impact on the game would be forever enshrined in the majestic Valhalla of Cooperstown, the only appropriate conclusion to their playing careers. McCovey marked the occasion with a gracious speech that displayed his humble nature. Williams, too, kindly thanked many people who helped him on his life journey, but he also pointedly challenged baseball to be honest with itself about its lack of racial progress. The 1980s saw both men reach a new stage of life. Each turned 50. Their daughters were quickly becoming adults. They no longer produced the flame of played baseball, but they were keepers of it. Reflecting on this era of their lives reveals how their iconic status continued to heighten well after Williams and McCovey had hit their last homer and driven in their final run.

* * *

A few days before his 48th birthday, McCovey received "the call." Congratulations, he was told, you've been elected to the National Baseball Hall of Fame. Jubilation. His name now had a new adjective for the rest of his life: Hall of Famer Willie McCovey. Mac received votes on 346 out of 425 ballots. He became just the 16th player to be elected on the first ballot, excluding the five inaugural members and Roberto Clemente, who was enshrined in 1973 following his tragic death. McCovey hopped on a plane and flew to New York, where he was introduced the following morning as part of the Class of 1986. He didn't sleep. "It's great to be thought of as an all-time great. It's not only an honor for me, it's an honor for all of San Francisco," he said.[1]

The election thrilled McCovey, who happily invited all of San Francisco to celebrate with him. He was proud of his accomplishments in the game of baseball, and having them validated by the voters meant a great deal to him. Although enveloped in joy, McCovey nonetheless felt a sting of sadness that he would not be joined by his friend Billy Williams, who fell just four votes shy of election. McCovey had recently spoken with Henry Aaron, who shared his hope that his two friends from back home would join him in Cooperstown. "I was a little disappointed because all of Mobile anticipated us going in together," Stretch admitted.[2]

The clouds above Cooperstown blotted out the sun and dripped rain on the gathered crowd on August 3 as Willie McCovey, dressed in a light gray suit over a mauve shirt, headed over to the National Baseball Hall of Fame with all of his family and friends alongside him. Well, almost everyone. His brother, Clauzell, thought they were meeting at a different spot and had to catch a ride with some fans driving over to the museum. Included in the 21 Hall of Famers who attended the ceremony was Ted Williams, a longtime friend of McCovey, who had first started asking the famed Red Sox savant about hitting at the outset of his career. Williams effusively praised McCovey. "I knew he had a chance to be an outstanding slugger the first time I saw him in Arizona in 1960. He had a good swing. He was much stronger and bigger than I was starting out," Williams said.[3]

McCovey addressed the crowd for a little over 11 minutes. He had to slightly scrunch his shoulders when he referred to his notes because he was so much taller than the podium. "You know, I've been thinking. Even though it's raining it's still a perfect kind of day for me," he said. "Standing here on this stage celebrating the pinnacle of my life and my career. The one reason it seems so right today is because it's the summertime and it's Sunday. Sundays and summertime only mean two things to me. That means it's a time for baseball, and it's a time for families." Willie felt elated at being surrounded by so many who loved him: from his mother, Ester; daughter, Allison; and siblings, Frances and Clauzell, to those who "adopted" him throughout his career, including Ruth Stovall and Charlotte Kahn. Hal and Helen Silen, Bob and Connie Lurie, Franklin Mieuli, and the Dudum family sat among the riveted throng soaking in McCovey's speech. Horace Stoneham could not attend due to illness, but Chub Feeney was there representing the family. "Come to think of it," said McCovey, who was also sure to thank his friend Lon Simmons, "I'm not sure how I ever got to be known as a loner when I was actually surrounded by so many special, loving people."[4]

McCovey carefully took time to thank all of them for being there and supporting him throughout his career. "I've been adopted, too, by all the thousands of great Giants fans everywhere and by the city of San Francisco where I've always been welcome. And like the Golden Gate Bridge and the cable cars, I've been made to feel like a landmark, too," he said, looking up with a smile. McCovey neared the close of his remarks by expressing his deep appreciation for his newest family. "And now I have become a player on the most distinguished team of all. It's a new family in a way. A family of men whose accomplishments in baseball and in life set them apart from all others, and I am truly honored and blessed with this ultimate adoption, if you will, by the game that I played so hard and loved so deeply." On finishing, the crowd, as it had so many times before, belted out cheers for McCovey as it stood and applauded.

* * *

Billy Williams had come excruciatingly close to joining McCovey in the Hall of Fame in 1986, his fifth year of eligibility, but he fell a few votes shy of election. The feeling in his camp was that 1987 would be his year, and they were right. Valena McCants, the teacher who spent notable energy keeping an eye on Billy and Shirley all those years ago, spoke for everyone in Whistler when she described the love everyone felt for him and the unified dream of his hometown. "If Billy makes it to the Hall of Fame, I have to feel that the whole community will feel as if it has accomplished something right along with him," she said.[5]

All of Whistler rejoiced on January 14, when Williams received the call informing him of the life-changing news. Longtime baseball writer Jack Lang told Williams that he was now a Hall of Famer. "Beautiful," Williams offered. "Beautiful. Lovely. It was a long wait, but it was worth it."[6] He received 354 votes on 413 ballots—86 percent—and cruised to election. Chicagoland celebrated, too. The Chicago Bulls honored Williams prior to their game against the Philadelphia 76ers. He snapped photos with a new Illinois license plate that featured his Hall of Fame designation. Williams received a note from President Ronald Reagan congratulating him. The Cubs would make Billy just the second player in franchise history to have his number retired during a ceremony that summer.

One of the most poignant aspects of Williams's election in 1987 was that baseball would be celebrating the 40th anniversary of Jackie Robinson breaking the color barrier in Major League Baseball. Williams considered that commemoration as he began to think about his induction speech. In the meantime, to celebrate on Opening Day, the Cubs arranged for Shirley to throw out the ceremonial first pitch to Billy as the kickoff starter to the new season. She was both excited and a little nervous about it, so they practiced together in the backyard for a few days.

Eager anticipation for the 1987 season was rocked the night before Opening Day when Al Campanis, the vice president of player personnel for the Los Angeles Dodgers, appeared on ABC's *Nightline* with Ted Koppel and made a series of outrageous comments about the abilities of minorities in baseball. What made the interview especially scurrilous was that it aired on the heels of a segment highlighting Robinson breaking the color barrier. A teammate of Robinson when the two men played together for Montreal of the International League in 1946, Campanis stated that he believed that African Americans "may not have some of the necessities to be, let's say, a field manager or perhaps a general manager." Koppel immediately pressed Campanis about believing that sentiment. "Well, I don't say that they're—all of them—but they certainly are short. How many quarterbacks do you have? How many pitchers do you have that are black?" Koppel cut him off and compared these comments to the same "garbage" being said about players in the past.[7]

Billy and Shirley were watching the interview at home. "What is this guy saying?" a deeply troubled Williams asked aloud. "You can't say that kind of stuff." They were dismayed at what they were hearing. "It was just something I could not believe," he said later. Williams knew many incredibly intelligent Black ballplayers who would be excellent managers—Maury Wills was just one name that immediately came to his mind—let alone himself.[8] Williams, too, personified the very best candidates for any of these jobs. His experience, knowledge of the game, unquestioned leadership skills, and devotion to the sport had earned him one of these opportunities, but it hadn't happened.

Williams had played at the highest level, coached at the big-league level for two different organizations, and had visions of possibly becoming a manager or working in an organization's front office. He had also just piloted an instructional league team for the Cubs. Nevertheless, Campanis's despicable comments seemed directed at a person with Billy's exact résumé, and it would be naïve to think he was the only front-office official who held these viewpoints. "The ironic thing is that every game is dedicated to Jackie Robinson this season in memory of this being the 40th year since he broke the color line with the Brooklyn Dodgers, and here comes a statement from a Dodger official like this," Williams told Fred Mitchell of the *Chicago Tribune*.[9] At one point during the *Nightline* interview, Koppel responded to another comment made by Campanis regarding the lack of Black news anchors. Koppel suggested that it was due to a lack of opportunity (because white executives did not want to relinquish their power) rather than a disparity of talent. Williams agreed, telling Mitchell, "I think a good point was brought up. Prejudice exists because of power. Whites don't want to give up the power of being the general manager or the owner or the manager. There is prejudice in baseball, and it shouldn't be."[10]

Williams wasn't alone in publicly denouncing Campanis's comments. His longtime friend Henry Aaron, who was not only baseball's all-time home run leader but even more aptly, at this moment, the vice president of the Atlanta Braves, was incensed. "You'd have to say this is [the] feeling from all the owners. Mr. Campanis has been in that position a long time. As long as you have men like that in those positions, it will be like this," Aaron said.[11] Campanis, who had said the quiet part out loud, was fired by the Dodgers within 48 hours.

The following day was a big one for baseball and for the Williams family. It was Opening Day, and the celebration of Billy Williams's election to the Hall of Fame began. A significant traffic jam on Lakeshore Drive caused by an accident delayed Shirley's arrival at Wrigley Field. She made it just in time and threw out a successful first pitch to her husband in front of an adoring crowd. The season was ready to commence.

* * *

The game of baseball has produced its share of extraordinary speeches throughout the decades, including Lou Gehrig's "Luckiest Man" speech at Yankee Stadium in 1939; Ted Williams's Hall of Fame speech in 1966, during which he expressed his deep hope that great Negro League players of the past would be enshrined in Cooperstown; and Jackie Robinson exhorting the sport to make more racial progress, specifically by hiring a Black manager, at Riverfront Stadium in 1972. These are a notable few, and Billy Williams's

Hall of Fame acceptance speech on July 26, 1987, stands alongside them as one of the great addresses in the sport's history.

Inspired by Robinson's anniversary, Williams knew early in the process of composing his speech that he wanted to address racial inequality in the game he loved. He had certainly spoken out at particular times in the past, but the platform of this ceremony was something altogether different. The eyes of the baseball world would be upon him on induction day. In preparation, Williams asked a mutual friend to reach out to Albert "Happy" Chandler, who served as commissioner of Major League Baseball from 1945 through 1951. Chandler, a seasoned politician from Kentucky who served as both a governor and a U.S. senator, had assumed the mantle of the commissioner's office from Judge Kenesaw Mountain Landis following World War II.

In Chandler's first year at the helm, a monumental change in baseball had occurred. Brooklyn Dodgers general manager Branch Rickey had sought to sign the first African American ballplayer in major league history. Chandler supported Rickey during that process. During his six-year tenure, Chandler proved to be such a proponent of the players that the owners declined to give him a second term. Now, 40 years later, Williams sought to learn more details about how Robinson signed with Brooklyn.

The big weekend finally arrived. The magnitude of it all struck Williams when a large van with the Hall of Fame emblem splashed across it arrived to pick up his family and shuttle them to the Hotel Otesaga. The energy of the moment was palpable, and it was a bit challenging for him (for all of the inductees, really) to stay present in the moment. "Everything in '87 is a blur," Williams confesses. "You come up here, and the family is going around. The wife is making sure people have places to stay. You're so excited about it. You watch baseball. You watch good players being inducted into the Hall of Fame, and now you're saying that you're one of those guys. So, the following year you come up, and you find out what the hell you did last year," he laughs.

Williams entered the Hall of Fame alongside Catfish Hunter, the pitcher he missed out being teammates with in Oakland, and Ray Dandridge, a wonderful third baseman who spent the vast majority of his career starring in the Negro Leagues. Williams began his speech under the clear sky by thanking, among others, Lilly Dixon, an educator from Whistler whose words were etched into his mind as deep as anything. "Good, better, best. Never let it rest. Until the good is better, and the better is best." Williams admitted that he did not fully grasp all of her meaning as a young kid, but Dixon's phrase resurfaced again and again with a driving force that motivated him at the deepest level. "These few words were the driving force behind my desire to succeed," he said.

Reflection. The vital motif of Williams's speech. He walked listeners through his past: Whistler. Mobile. Chicago. Oakland. Chicago, again. The places that shaped him, full of people who did the same. Donning a dark blue suit with light pinstripes, a red tie, and white ribbons—Cubs colors—Williams turned his focus to the key figures who played important roles in breaking baseball's color line in 1947. "If it weren't for the courage of three great men, forty years ago, I might not have the opportunity to have played 18 years in the big league and stand before you today," noted Williams. He pointed out the important roles played by Rickey and Chandler in Robinson's signing with the Dodgers. "Two of them are no longer with us today," he added, noting the passing of Rickey and Robinson before looking directly at Chandler. "But I would personally like to thank you, Happy Chandler, for your outgoing and steadfast support in the game of baseball not only as commissioner but from year to year coming up here and getting involved in these annual ceremonies. Thank you, sir."

Williams then vulnerably recounted the difficulties faced by African Americans in baseball over the past 40 years. He told the crowd about his experience in 1959 of being denied the ability to eat a meal with his white teammates in Texas. "As we traveled up and down the highway on the road I had to be taken to a private home. I couldn't stay at the hotel with the rest of the team. I think most of you agree at this time that wasn't right," he said as the crowd applauded in agreement.

"These injustice wasn't fixed by Major League Baseball. They had to be fixed for all minorities years later by the government. This ceremony today is a reason to celebrate, but it is also a time for reflection, a time to examine the game's strength and weaknesses by improving what is good and correcting what is bad. Yes, the road is rocky and long, but the time to pave the way for true equality is now. The next courageous step rests with the owners of 26 major league ballclubs. They can make the difference, but by not looking at the color of a man's skin but by examining his ability, talent, knowledge, and leadership. If this is the land of opportunity then let it truly become the land of opportunity for all.

"The question has been raised in the recent months by the media about the participation of Blacks and other minorities in decision making positions in baseball. The issue wouldn't have come up *if* every job in baseball was open to every creed, race, and nationality. But this is not the case. We minorities for the past four decades have demonstrated our talents as players, now we deserve the chance and consideration to demonstrate similar talent as third base coaches, as managers, as general managers, as executives in the front office, and, yes, owners of major league ballclubs themselves."[12]

Williams's speech hit a crescendo with a call to action. "Plans and words can be transformed into actions and deeds. We ask for nothing less, but we seek what is just," he implored before reflecting a bit further on his life in the speech's closing moments. On finishing, the crowd responded to Williams with a standing ovation. His powerful words left an indelible impression on all who heard them that day, including his own family. "His speech was very different," his oldest daughter, Valarie Hill, remembers. "I was proud that he took that chance to speak out because that wasn't something he had done historically throughout his career, but he had a platform and he used it effectively."[13]

The allure of Cooperstown has brought Williams back time after time over the years. He loves the history of baseball and annually treks east in July to learn more in addition to seeing longtime friends. The Hotel Otesaga has long hosted the Hall of Famers during induction weekend. A picturesque building situated on the southern end of Otsego Lake, the hotel offers a special setting for players and their families to return to year after year. Williams is no exception. He annually attends and especially enjoys interacting with all of the living history and welcoming new members to the club. "The climax of the whole thing is Sunday evening when you introduce and see all those great players on the podium up there," Williams smiles. "Guys that you faced, guys that you played with, guys that you played against, guys that you read about, guys that you followed through the years. It's a lot of stuff that goes through your head. It's great."

Sitting on a couch inside the lobby of the Hotel Otesaga, he directs his attention to a very distinct large conversation chair that seats up to four people conveniently located near the main entrance, where the elder statesmen who don't move as well as they once did can set up shop. "It's a chair where many, many Hall of Famers sit. They can see guys coming in, see guys going out, and you will holler at them," Williams says. He always enjoys entering the lobby to see who's around. One time, Billy had a long conversation with Monte Irvin, who told him about the great Josh Gibson. Another year, Williams spoke at length with Chandler about the details of Robinson's rookie season."[14] Another year, Williams made it a point to seek out former Dodgers shortstop Pee Wee Reese, who had been enshrined in 1984. Williams had heard the story about Reese showing support for Robinson in Cincinnati by putting his arm around his teammate for all to see in the face of intense prejudice. Williams expressed his appreciation to Reese.

Williams's impact continues to be felt around this idyllic town for reasons beyond the scope of his on-field accomplishments. Billy and his wife, Shirley, participated in countless events over the years, whether it be a golf outing or a promotional event for the museum. Now in his mid-80s, Williams is a firmly established elder statesman who is held in the highest regard. "He's adored and appreciated by fans and players alike, and the Hall of Famers really look up to him and respect him. They know that he embodies character, integrity, and sportsmanship and has something to say that matters," explains former Hall of Fame president Jeff Idelson.[15]

The election of Willie McCovey and Billy Williams to the National Baseball Hall of Fame put the proper respect on their incredible careers. Neither man prioritized the public relations game during their careers, but then again, they didn't need to. Their play did all the talking. Vida Blue put it well. "Better to be seen and not heard. Be the ultimate teammate," Blue gushed about the mantra of both men. "They got their justice when they landed in Cooperstown."[16]

* * *

Willie McCovey would have played baseball for the rest of his life if his body had held up, but, as every athlete knows, Father Time remains undefeated. Mac had always enjoyed playing golf, and he turned to it more frequently to get his competitive fix. Stretch could drive the ball a long way. Returning to the Giants had made his living situation simple and again put him in close vicinity to the courses that he loved to play. Mac once again lived full-time in the Woodside home he had built. He happily remained there in retirement.

One important shift in his life involved his daughter, Allison. Willie had spent some time with her over the years—on one particularly fun day, they met a newborn cub at the large-cat exhibit inside Marine World Africa, U.S.A., named after the slugging first baseman when she was in junior high—but they had mostly been apart throughout his career. His travel schedule during the season, combined with Allison living with her mom in Hayward, made things challenging. Willie felt comfortable laughing with his friends at work, but his introverted nature could produce some social distance at times. Mac intentionally patterned his stoic nature after his own father, Frank, who had once admonished his son's baseball playing as akin to gambling. Willie's siblings said their brother reminded them a great deal of their father. It was a double-edged sword. On the one hand, mimicking his father kept trouble away, which was very beneficial for someone so intensely in the public eye, yet it also created the by-product of an emotional distance that could isolate him from family members. Compounding matters, those in McCovey's inner circle have always believed, was his childhood experience in the South. He quickly learned that survival there required adherence to certain codes or ways of doing things. It exacerbated his already shy nature. People close to McCovey throughout his life believe that the damage inflicted by the horrific racist incidents he experienced and witnessed never left him.

Retirement created space for Willie and Allison, who turned 15 the year he retired, to get to know each other. Her picture had sat on his nightstand for years, but now time afforded a fresh opportunity. They saw each other with increasing frequency over the years, including taking a trip to Hawaii to celebrate Allison's high school graduation. McCovey rehabbed a knee to walk her down the aisle after initially fearing that he might have to do so in a wheelchair. These bigger events went smoothly, but he struggled to maintain the day-to-day connection with his daughter, which required additional communication and emotional expression. He didn't really know how. His intense introversion included a disinterest in talking about growing up in Mobile. "My dad was a very quiet person, and some of it brought up bad memories for him, and I can see why considering the era that he grew up in," Allison says. One time, she mentioned to him that she wanted to see where he grew up. "Well, there's a highway through it," he responded abruptly.[17]

In recent years, Allison learned more about her dad's history and traveled to Mobile for the first time in 2023. "I just said, you know what, I'm going to go. Life is short. Tomorrow's never promised. It's something on my bucket list. I'm going to go down there," she decided.[18] Passionate about learning and connecting with people, she wanted to absorb everything, especially the cultural and social differences between the West Coast and the Deep South. The McCoveys warmly embraced her, including some she had never met, and she spent extensive time talking with her relatives and visiting sites around the city. She is now ideating about a future Mardi Gras float that would both commemorate her father and celebrate all of the Mobile Hall of Famers, who will have their waterfront statues revealed in short order.

* * *

If one of the more memorable aspects of Willie McCovey's life and career is his return to the San Francisco Giants in 1977, then one of its more puzzling oddities is how they drifted apart again. While Billy Williams remained embedded in the Chicago Cubs organization throughout the years, the same could not be said for his Mobile counterpart. The good news is that the story of this life chapter includes a very happy ending, but it took a while to get there. The relationship between McCovey and the Giants went well throughout the late 1980s and the opening of the 1990s. He was around a lot and readily shared his expertise with Giants players.

One particular player who soaked in McCovey's advice during the late 1980s was Will Clark, a fellow left-handed-swinging first baseman who also hailed from the South. Mac gladly shared his knowledge with Clark whenever asked, and the two formed a close friendship over the years. "I trusted what he said deeply," Clark says. They talked about anything and everything from establishing the proper mind-set to hitting at Candlestick Park to playing the same position. "One thing that he talked about was take your front foot and stretch towards the baseball. That way your head, your arm, and your glove were right in line with the ball and over the top of your knee, foot—you could actually stretch further. That was one of the bits of advice that I used that he gave me. I used it extensively," explains Clark, who continues to preach this exact point to young players in his current role as a special assistant in the Giants front office.[19]

As Clark's career unfolded, it quickly became evident that he embraced pressure-filled situations and even thrived in them. His confidence and clutch hits became a staple of the organization's resurgence. The Giants won the National League West in 1987 and captured the pennant in 1989. Clark came through for San Francisco in the biggest of moments. He inquired about Mac's mind-set during intense situations. Stretch's message to Clark boiled down to engaging one's emotions so as not to become overwhelmed by them. Absorb the moment without being amazed by it. "Willie Mac and I got along so well because we were first basemen. We talked about when the big situation comes up, how you separate yourself? How do you not get caught up in the hype? The fans going crazy, and how do you go about doing your job?" Clark recalls. "Some of the advice that he gave me was just absolutely unbelievable, and it came true."[20] The base hit off Mitch Williams. The grand slam off Greg Maddux. Clark delivered incredible moments throughout his career, and his number 22 now resides retired alongside 44.

Despite this success, the Giants seemed to be living on borrowed time in San Francisco as the 1990s commenced. Giants owner Bob Lurie encountered similar issues with the franchise that Horace Stoneham faced, primarily Candlestick Park, a baseball stadium lashed by cold weather, wind, and fog. Lurie asked Bay Area voters to approve public funding for a new stadium on four occasions and was refused each time. In 1992, Lurie reached an agreement with a group from Florida to sell the team, which would then be moved across the country. Pressed to respond quickly, a local group of investors, led by Walter Shorenstein, put together an offer of their own. The group included Safeway CEO Peter Magowan and Larry Baer, who worked at CBS. On November 10, the National League owners voted, 9–4, to reject the Florida bid, thereby reopening the process. The local group received unanimous support throughout baseball to purchase the franchise at the winter meetings. The Giants stayed in San Francisco.[21]

Over the ensuing years, distance grew between McCovey and the organization. Perhaps matters were made a bit more complex after McCovey pled guilty to tax evasion in 1995 stemming from an autograph show appearance in Atlantic City six years prior for which he collected a cash payment. He paid the taxes and received two years of probation along with a $5,000 fine.[22] He was horrified by what happened, and it never strayed far from his thoughts. Hal Silen drove down to visit Willie, and one day, Stretch held up some cash that he had received to sign baseballs. "You see what this is?" McCovey asked, voice rising. "There's eight hundred dollars here. I am going to declare it."

"I know you will," Silen gently replied.[23]

What exactly happened between Mac and the Giants during the 1990s? "I'm not sure," Silen admits. "Somehow he came out of the spotlight of what was going on."[24] The distance hurt McCovey, but he kept it tucked inside where it wouldn't draw unwanted attention on himself. The feeling didn't dissipate, however. Instead, it gnawed at him until he couldn't keep it to himself much longer. In the meantime, the Giants finally got the stadium approval they had so long desired. Magowan's group accomplished the unthinkable in 1996: it secured $170 million in bank loans, supplemented by $121 million in corporate sponsorships, to support a privately funded waterfront ballpark in San Francisco to be called Pacific Bell Park. Construction on the stadium began the following year with an eye toward opening in 2000.[25] Candlestick Park would no longer be an albatross hampering the franchise. Plans called for a statue of Willie Mays to greet visitors outside the main gate of the park, but a notable honoring of McCovey was initially missing—that is, until *San Jose Mercury News* columnist Mark Purdy drove by the site in 1999 with construction well underway. It struck him that the China Basin Channel, the body of water beyond where the right-field wall was being built, would be just the spot where McCovey's notoriously long blasts would land. "The next move, then, is obvious," Purdy wrote in his column that appeared in the *Merc* on May 9, 1999. "Why not rename the channel after McCovey?"[26] He kicked around several possibilities, including the likes of "McCovey Channel" or "McCovey Run," but, ultimately, it was "McCovey Cove," a splashy moniker born from a conversation between Purdy and fellow Bay Area sportswriter Leonard Koppett, that emerged as the favorite.[27] Purdy approached Larry Baer with the idea of naming that area of water after McCovey, and the Giants' executive was very much open to it while acknowledging that McCovey and the organization had drifted apart. Purdy wrote several more columns expressing the need to honor McCovey, who thanked the writer for his support.

When he was eight years old, Larry Baer met Willie McCovey at the Home Savings and Loan on Geary Boulevard in the heart of San Francisco. Stretch, who occasionally worked at the bank in a promotional role before night games, allowed Baer to sit on his lap. A few decades later, Stretch feigned regret. "Mac blamed me for his bad knees," Baer jokes.[28] Baer's father took him to games at Candlestick Park, and they frequently sat down the right-field line. They were in the stands when McCovey homered against the Pirates in Game One of the 1971 National League Championship Series. It fell to him to mend the relationship between the organization and the city of San Francisco's most popular player. "Willie was a very proud person," Baer notes, "and wasn't going to be out tooting his own horn or asking for things necessarily."

With the urgency of the issue fully revealed, Baer, who was named the executive vice president of the Giants in 1992, drove down to Woodside and talked with McCovey over lunch. The two spoke candidly about the crux of the matter. Baer expressed his desire to see Willie as a Giant. Stretch expressed his interest to be a part of the organizational family, and there wasn't a good reason why he wasn't. Baer sums it up succinctly: "We just basically said, we're going to agree to agree here."[29] By August, it was a done deal. The water beyond the walkway bordering the right-field wall would be called "McCovey Cove." Stretch had expressed his fear to Purdy that he had been left behind, forgotten like an old, unneeded relic from the past; he now relaxed in relief. The cove changed everything. "The ice has finally been broken," Stretch said.[30]

The magical ballpark opened the new millennium on April 11, 2000. Its breathtaking views of the Bay Bridge, open water, and Oakland hills thrilled fans. On May 1, Barry Bonds, whom Mac had adored since Barry ran around the clubhouse as a youngster, launched a ball over the right-field wall and into McCovey Cove for the first regular-season "splash hit" in the stadium's history. Giants television play-by-play broadcaster Duane Kuiper incorporated a new twist on his signature home run call. *"He hits one high, he hits one deep, McCovey Cove, outta here! And Big Mac loved it."* Thunderous applause rained down from the home crowd, and a spine-tingling baseball moment was born. The moment played out as sublimely as anyone envisioned. Twenty-three seasons later, Lamonte Wade Jr., winner of the 2021 Willie Mac Award, smashed the team's 100th "splash hit" into the water. It's a signature aspect of the stadium that remains an enthralling component of Giants baseball. "McCovey Cove was the perfect inspiration," Baer reminisces. "Give Mark credit for it. We took it and ran with it. Number one. That's where balls would go, if he were still playing. Number two. Willie would come and sit at games and sit down in the broadcast area looking toward his cove or waterway."[31]

The public address announcer's box was three doors down from McCovey's suite at the new ballpark, and that seat was filled by Renel Brooks-Moon, a local radio personality whom the Giants hired in 2000. She grew accustomed to seeing Mac, usually in the elevator going up to the stadium's press box level. However, they remained surreal moments for Brooks-Moon, who grew up going to Giants' games at Candlestick Park with her baseball-crazed family during the 1960s. "It took me years before I got up the nerve to even speak to him," she admits, "because I revered him so much." For his part, McCovey enjoyed listening to Brooks-Moon's morning radio show and began to talk to her about it. He would reference a joke she told on the air or ask about a particular song that he had heard. "The fact that he listened to my show and shared that with me blew my mind. It was like coming full circle. I was in your audience as a little girl, and now you're in my radio audience as an adult. It's a trip," Brooks-Moon exclaims. "That broke the ice."[32]

Their friendship developed as Brooks-Moon, the first African American female public address announcer in Major League Baseball history, and Mac continued to interact on the way to their close proximity booths. "He was so proud of me, along with Mr. Mays," Brooks-Moon says as her voice catches with emotion. "They were so proud of me. . . . It just means so much to me. These are my childhood heroes. They could have never imagined me sitting in a PA booth on a microphone when they were playing, nor could my grandfather, who followed Negro Leagues barnstorming teams in Texarkana, Texas." Brooks-Moon had the opportunity to introduce her mother to McCovey. She, too, loves baseball and proceeded to tell Mac all the stats from his big-league debut against Robin Roberts and the Phillies. Mac looked at Renel with smiling eyes. "Ah, ha," he teased, "I see where you get it from."[33]

Once again rewoven into the fabric of the franchise, McCovey remained closely connected to it for the rest of his life. In addition to continuing his participation with the annual Willie Mac Award, he was actively involved in two of the organization's most important initiatives: a golf tournament designed to raise money for the Giants Community Fund and Junior Giants, a baseball and softball program for Bay Area kids, who participated free of charge. McCovey embraced the ideas. He loved golf and had started a tournament that supported the March of Dimes during his playing career. The urgency around his involvement in these initiatives intensified in 2008, when the Great Recession struck the economy. This newly unleashed economic event catastrophically slayed budgets the world over and facilitated a new, deep bond between player and organization.

Giants executive vice president of business operations Mario Alioto, who began his career with the team as a batboy in 1973, engaged with Giants Community Fund executive director Sue Petersen in a dialogue about ways to enlarge the organization's charitable arm in the wake of the economic crisis. Seeking to combine the franchise's efforts with those of one of its most hallowed players quickly emerged as a natural and exciting approach. Alito served as a communication bridge between Petersen and a cheerful McCovey, who immediately embraced the new blueprint. "We all wanted to be a part of the solution," Petersen recalled about those conversations. "It wound up being very easy to join forces."[34] Fruitful strategy sessions between Alioto, Petersen, and McCovey resulted in the birth of the Willie McCovey Golf Classic, a tournament held at TPC Harding Park that would simultaneously raise money for the Giants Community Fund and honor one of baseball's all-time greats.

The purpose of the tournament coalesced around a singular focus: we need your help! As the economic crisis deepened, McCovey knew its dreadful impact on Bay Area youth. Public school sports budgets faced deep cuts and family dollars spent on extracurricular activities teetered on the brink. Now was the time to voice a call to action for local fans, businesses, and vendors to support this new charitable endeavor.

As the Great Recession raged into 2009, the Giants asked McCovey to partner with them again on a new annual campaign for Junior Giants, the flagship program of the Giants Community Fund, called the "Stretch Drive." It was clear that after spending the 1990s adrift from the franchise McCovey loved so much that the Giants organization, with a special nod to Alioto and Petersen, longed not just to partner with Stretch but also to warmly embrace him again. "I wasn't fully aware of what had happened between Willie and the organization until Mario explained it to me," said Petersen, who, before joining the Giants in 1993, worked on special projects for public schools as part of the San Francisco Education Fund. "It was gratifying for me to see him honored."[35]

McCovey returned the hug. His name was on the event, and Stretch did everything possible to ensure its success. He spent hours signing various items to be given out by the Giants as gifts for drive donations. In addition to providing television interviews, McCovey happily agreed to meet and greets with individuals who supported the "Stretch Drive" at its highest levels. Giants manager, Bruce Bochy, who did not frequently call for team meetings, did just that after McCovey expressed a desire to speak with the players about how much the event meant to him. McCovey passionately told the team about growing up in Mobile without baseball equipment or proper playing fields. He wanted to ensure that Bay Area kids did not suffer the same fate. The "Stretch Drive" gave all of them the opportunity to provide youth the chance to learn about teamwork, competition, and leadership through playing baseball. In the decade and a half since, the Willie McCovey Golf Classic and "Stretch Drive" events have raised more than $2.5 million for the Giants Community Fund.[36]

* * *

The years started to roll by with Willie McCovey again a fixture with the Giants. He had frequently attended games at Candlestick Park during the late 1990s and now transitioned to the new ballpark, where he sat in his box wearing that familiar orange and black cap with the interlocking "SF." Peter Magowan, Larry Baer, and Mario Alioto made sure that McCovey retained his quality view of the playing field from his Candlestick Park perch when the new stadium opened in 2000. He was at different times a sounding board for the front office, an adviser for players, and a kindhearted waver to fans—a storyteller, an observer, a presence. He was Willie McCovey. Mac was there even as his eroding legs made it more difficult by the season. Arthritis, infections, and pain bit into his knees and feet like striking snakes. There had been more surgeries. At one point, a doctor talked with Mac about amputation. He wouldn't have it. Those close to him knew the intensity of his pain, yet the joy he got from being around the Giants fed his soul in a unique way, so he continued to commute from Woodside to the corner of Third and King.

That didn't mean Mac didn't disagree with the organization at times. Always attuned to equality, McCovey noticed that fewer African Americans were on major league rosters, and it deeply bothered him. So many outstanding Black players in his generation had set an incredible standard within the game, but it struck him as problematic that progress seemed to be stalling. One year, late in spring training, McCovey learned that San Francisco was on the cusp of announcing its regular-season roster. Stretch was well aware of which players were in the running for each spot on the team, and, frankly, its projected composition troubled him. McCovey expressed his disappointment to Baer, who had just returned to the Bay Area from Arizona, over the phone. "I love the Giants so much," McCovey told him, "but I'm embarrassed about something. I don't think we're going to have a single Black player on the 25-man roster." Baer acknowledged that he was right.[37] "The lack of African American players in the league is something Willie called out a long time ago," Baer, who refers to that conversation with McCovey as "one of the best calls I ever received from him," contends.[38]

Stretch also kept a running dialogue about all things Giants with Bobby Evans, who joined the organization in 1994 and filled myriad roles for the franchise before being named general manager of the club in 2015. On getting the post, Evans received a call from McCovey, who offered his congratulations. Mac continued to phone Evans with high praise for successes and questions about moves he found less than ideal. "I think it was done out of care for all of us on the baseball side, just to make sure that we knew he was watching and get some of his perspective," Evans says. "As an executive, you really value those conversations." Sometimes that meant discussing Mac's concern about the lack of diversity in baseball and at times in terms of the Giants' roster. McCovey and Evans built a great foundation of trust and support over the course of their nearly quarter century together with the franchise. "He always spoke with the heart of a fan and the experience of a player. He had both," Evans says. "He always balanced it and ultimately was never coming down on us or coming down on the club. He always had an intention to help and support. I felt that for many, many years as we got to know each other and converse on these things."[39]

McCovey continued to attend games in person as frequently as possible. He felt so at home there inside the confines of the ballpark. He spent many an evening sitting in Mike Murphy's office visiting with current players and telling stories. On quite a few occasions, Willie Mays was there, too. Evans was among many visitors who stopped by Mac's box to say hello during games. Former teammates loved to check in on him to see how he was doing, but they made it a point not to stay for long. They didn't want to bother him too much. Everyone also knew how seriously he took watching the ballgame. It was best to catch him between innings. He very much remained on the quiet side, yet McCovey went night after night to be next to baseball, yes, but also around the people who make the game what it is. They knew and understood him from decades gone by in that special way that old friendships are fashioned by time.

One thing McCovey handled with class, even if he was tired of talking about it, was the conversation around the at-bat that ended the 1962 World Series. It stuck to McCovey like dirt caught in his spikes for the rest of his life. Sometimes it seemed like the narrative surrounding that line drive drowned out any talk about the 3,885 times he reached base. In 2000, the New York Yankees dropped by Pacific Bell Park on April 1 for an exhibition game against the Giants. It was the first time the teams had faced each other in 38 years. McCovey agreed to participate in a pregame ceremony alongside Ralph Terry, the pitcher on the mound all those years ago, even though it celebrated a moment he never did recall all that fondly. The two men participated in a pregame press conference, and McCovey, sporting a Giants cap, allowed reporters to ask him about the moment—again. "Even now, I run into somebody who remembers that line drive. Even if I wanted to forget it, people wouldn't let me forget it," he admitted.[40]

When the Yankees returned to San Francisco for a three-game series in 2007, there was McCovey again, this time alongside Bobby Richardson, who despite his initial hesitancy at attending, traveled across the country to participate in the reunion. Richardson made it known that he would not have let Mac hit. "If I was the manager," said the second baseman, who coached the University of South Carolina to the national championship game in 1975. "I would have walked him."[41] McCovey and Richardson threw out first pitches before the ballgame and shared a collegial conversation afterward.

Then San Francisco started winning, stunningly so, and conversations about postseason baseball in the city would never be the same. In 2010, McCovey underwent back surgery during the summer, which kept him away from the ballpark. He kept an eye on the team as he recuperated, and when the Giants squared off against the Texas Rangers in Game One of the World Series, he joined fellow Hall of Famers Orlando Cepeda, Juan Marichal, Monte Irvin, and Gaylord Perry with the assistance of a walker. Fans soaked in Giants history personified. McCovey was thrilled. The Giants fell behind, 2–0, before storming back to win, 11–7. San Francisco went on to capture its first title since moving west.

McCovey rode through the downtown parade and received a ring from the organization. Finally, a championship. Joy in winning mixed with a dash of relief that future conversations may relieve him of having to talk about 1962. The Giants' winning ways continued even as McCovey's physical ailments grounded away at his ability to remain independent. San Francisco won a second World Series in 2012. McCovey was thrilled. Two years later, as the Giants marched toward yet another title, a serious infection forced Stretch into the hospital. Still, he closely followed the Giants' postseason exploits and triumphantly returned to the ballpark during the National League Championship Series. He again appeared on the field alongside the Giants' Hall of Famers during a pregame ceremony prior to Game Three of the 2014 World Series. San Francisco won it all—again.

* * *

Billy Williams's final season in the Chicago Cubs dugout was 2001. He retired from coaching having spent 31 seasons in a Cubs uniform, a franchise record. Only 64 years old, Williams continued as part of the Cubs' brain trust but in different roles for the front office. He sat next to executive Andy McPhail for years, providing input on the ballclub. Quite a few of his teammates maintained relationships with the organization as well, in particular, Randy Hundley, who had managed in the Cubs' minor league system, and Ron Santo, who called games on the radio alongside Pat Hughes. It kept the longtime friends in a familiar circle. There were other activities that kept everyone connected. Hundley's fantasy camps in Arizona played an important role. They not only provided fans the opportunity to play a little baseball alongside the ballplayers whom they had long admired but also gave those guys and their families the chance to annually see each other. Williams was sure to be there. "He enjoyed coming to the camps. Needless to say I was very proud to have him there," Hundley says.[42] The Cubs offered cruise experiences for fans, and it was quite a thrill for fans to meet Billy Williams, Ron Santo, and Fergie Jenkins (among others) and their families on those outings as well. Their friendships are defined by loyalty and love for one another. And that leads us to an important situation that needed to be remedied: Santo was not a member of the National Baseball Hall of Fame.

Ron Santo played professional baseball for 16 seasons. He signed with the Chicago Cubs as a teenager in 1959 and was assigned to their affiliate in San Antonio. One could say he spent the next 15 years alongside Billy Williams before being traded to the White Sox for the 1974 season, but it's more accurate to say they spent the rest of their lives with each other. They were different in a variety of ways—Santo was loquacious, Williams leaned subtle—but winning drove the two competitors something fierce. Their bond was strong because it was built over time through shared experiences, such as time in 1966 that Santo, a type 1 diabetic, batted with the bases loaded against the Dodgers as his blood sugar dropped. The first pitch he saw appeared as three baseballs coming at him. That's how intensely his body was being affected. He swung at the one in the middle and sent it into the Wrigley Field bleachers for a grand slam. Santo nearly ran over Williams, who was jogging around the bases in front of him, as he hustled around the bases to get back to the clubhouse for sugar. Other experiences were road trips to Mexico as minor leaguers playing in air so thick with humidity that you felt as though you might choke on it; Santo, upset about something of course, in 1969; and Williams trying to alleviate his teammate's stress with practical jokes, including that time they put a ticking timer in a package near Santo's locker.[43]

Williams and Santo played together in more than 2,000 major league games. They're an iconic pairing in the game's history. Yet, in spite of hitting 342 home runs, playing in nine All-Star Games, and winning five Gold Glove Awards, all while fighting through juvenile diabetes, Santo passed away in 2010 without being enshrined in Cooperstown alongside Williams, Jenkins, and Ernie Banks. The following year, the Golden Era Committee was established to consider candidates who played between 1947 and 1972. Among the eight Hall of Fame players selected to participate on the 16-member committee was Billy Williams.

Santo had hoped to be elected before he passed away. On several occasions, television cameras were present in his home on the day the Hall of Fame released the voting results. It ended in disappointment for him each time. A determined Williams pushed to make sure that the Golden Era Committee results would produce a different result. He was thrilled when the final tally added up to Santo's admission.

Vicki Santo, Ron's widow, felt a spike of adrenaline when her phone rang. She picked up, and on the line was Jane Forbes Clark, the chairman of the Board of Directors of the National Baseball Hall of Fame, with the news everyone had longed to hear: Ron Santo had been elected. Clark wasn't alone on the call. Accompanying her on the line was Billy. "We did it," Williams told Vicki. "We got him in."

"It was just so cool," says Vicki Santo. "I thank Billy a million times over."[44]

Wrigleyville celebrated—if with a somber note of sadness. "The one thing, of course, is he's not here to enjoy it, but his family will," Williams said. "He long awaited this, and we're all happy. I know I'm happy, his family is happy, the fans of Chicago are happy."[45]

Santo raised tens of millions of dollars for the Juvenile Diabetes Research Foundation throughout his life, and, in the years that followed his passing, Williams and Jenkins continued to support the Ron & Vicki Santo Diabetic Alert Dog Foundation. They have made appearances and signed autographs to help raise money for the charity driven to help diabetics monitor their blood sugar levels through trained dogs. Although sad that his friend wasn't there to enjoy the moment, Williams was overjoyed that Santo was finally in. "They loved each other. They had a ball," Vicki says. "That's what friendship is all about."[46]

* * *

Williams's role with the Cubs in the city of Chicago has shifted over the years. As a player, his bat did the majority of the talking. Williams hasn't gotten the credit he deserves for frequently speaking with the press throughout his playing career. First Banks and then Santo provided extroverted answers that expounded on game situations or their feelings on particular topics. Williams may have been labeled as "quiet," but most people are quiet in comparison to the unique loquaciousness of Banks and Santo. Perhaps he doesn't typically talk extensively about his feelings, but the fact is that Williams has a beautiful way with words, exemplified by his Hall of Fame speech. Williams's expressions of mourning were especially poignant when he spoke following the deaths of his close friends. He began as a player/hero, then moved into the role of teacher/mentor, and now he is the wise counselor who provides grieving Chicagoans respite and comfort. "You look at a little kid coming from Alabama. You look at a guy coming from Seattle, Washington to join up in San Antone and of all those years playing together it was just an enjoyable thing to know him. He is going to be a great loss to Chicago, a great loss to baseball fans and of course to the city. He's been around here a long time and a lot of people got the chance to know him and really enjoyed his work, I think. He's certainly going to be missed by many, many people here in Chicago and the baseball world," Williams said following Santo's passing while also noting that the Juvenile Diabetes Foundation had moved closer to finding a cure because of his friend's work.[47]

In 2015, Banks passed away, leaving a huge hole in the hearts of his friends, family, and fans. Williams again provided words of solace to the mourning community. His voice carried strong and sure throughout Fourth Presbyterian Church during the memorial service. "Do not mourn the death of Ernie Banks," he began, "it's to celebrate a life, a joyous life, and this is what he was all about. Ernie has been the cornerstone not only of the Chicago Cubs but the city of Chicago, and those who have met Ernie, I think they still remember the joyous smile that Ernie had."[48] He recounted the warm greeting he received from Banks on meeting him in Arizona for the first time and carpooling with his friend beginning in 1966. These guys were more than just teammates. They established a large Cubs family and shared the joys and challenges not only of baseball seasons but also of life.

The Cubs went on to win 97 games and earned a playoff spot with a wild-card berth in 2015. Chicago, led by Jake Arrieta, who had dominated all season, shut out the Pittsburgh Pirates, 4–0, to advance to the National League Division Series. More magic followed. Chicago knocked off the St. Louis Cardinals in four games to advance deeper still into the postseason. Williams loved the environment around the team. New manager Joe Maddon infused the organization with his unique leadership qualities. The players responded by coming to Wrigley Field full of energy, which was reciprocated nightly by boisterous crowds. "This is how it should be," Williams said.[49] The New York Mets, however, the franchise that had denied the Cubs in 1969, again thwarted the dreams of Wrigleyville. They flexed their muscles in a four-game sweep. In the year of losing Banks, the Cubs' run came up just short of the World Series. It paved the way for the most incredible season had by the organization in more than a century, for the following year a dream was realized.

The 2016 Cubs erupted out of the gate and produced one of the club's finest regular seasons in team history. Chicago won five of six games during its season-opening road trip before returning to Wrigley Field for the home opener on April 11. Williams, Fergie Jenkins, and Ryne Sandberg threw out ceremonial first pitches before the Cubs beat the Cincinnati Reds, 5–3. Building on the success of the previous campaign, Chicago stayed hot. First baseman Anthony Rizzo launched eight home runs in the Cubs' first 19 games, a first for the organization since Billy had accomplished the feat in 1970. Chicago impressively won 25 of its first 31 games and built an 8 1/2-game lead in the National League Central. The Cubs never looked back.

The Cubs were the first team in baseball to clinch a division championship on September 15 but hungered for more. Williams fully believed in the group's chances to win it all, which was exciting if bittersweet. "The one thing you regret is that two of my teammates, Ernie Banks and of course Ron Santo, (are) not here to enjoy what's going on because, really, deep in my mind, I think we can go all the way because we have that ballclub now," he reflected.[50] The Cubs' combination of power and pitching led them past San Francisco and into the National League Championship Series against Los Angeles. The Dodgers took two of the first three games before the Cubs roared back with three consecutive wins to clinch their first World Series appearance since 1945. Williams's first thoughts were of Banks and Santo as a sweeping wave of euphoria swept over Wrigley Field. They would face Cleveland.

There will be a treasure trove of books, documentaries, and specials that detail the 2016 World Series for years to come. It was a dramatic series of big moments punctuated by a dousing of rain that Cubs fans will never forget. Chicago lost three of the first four games in the series, and hope that the club could snap its 108-year drought dimmed. Williams stayed close to the proceedings, including throwing out another ceremonial first pitch and attending all the games. The Cubs staved off elimination by winning Game Five, 3–1, and forcing the series back to Cleveland. Then their offense exploded. A three-run first inning followed by a four-run outburst in the third put them up, 7–0. Chicago won, 9–3, to force a seventh and deciding game.

Afterward, Williams, even though he was a bit under the weather, celebrated the win back at the hotel along with a substantial number of members of the organization who were brought on the trip. The Cubs needed to win only once more to capture the championship that had eluded them for more than 100 years. In a game full of twists and turns, Chicago won the World Series the following night in extra innings. At long last, the Cubs were champions.

In the chaotic aftermath of winning, an elated Williams shared his joy with family, friends, fans, and members of the organization. People sought him out to share their excitement. The Cubs had won, which meant that, in a way, Billy, Ernie, Ronnie, Fergie, Randy, and all of their teammates were victorious, too. "It was exciting. Not only did we excite the fans in Chicago, but so many people around the world were fans of the Chicago Cubs," Williams said.[51] Cubs president of business operations Crane Kenney noted that it was a cathartic moment not only for the team's supporters but also for all of those who loved Williams. "Everyone needed to have their time with Billy to talk about the importance of the championship to him and his generation of players," he points out.[52]

Celebrating the Cubs' first World Series title in 108 years provided notable happiness for Williams even as he mourned the recent Alzheimer's diagnosis that was cruelly affecting his beloved Shirley. The two were always by each other's side in full support. Throughout his baseball career, Shirley fully underpinned her husband and daughters by establishing the foundation for their family home life, which was vital considering how frequently he was on the road. Baseball can be a challenging vocation for wives, but she thoroughly enjoyed being part of the Cubs family, and everyone in and around the organization adored her.

Now, in the midst of sadness, Billy remained close to his beloved bride and ensured that she received the best care possible. It could be challenging at times to sort through all the information about caregiving and her prognosis, but he remained steady with purpose through it all for her and their four daughters, who shared admiration for their father. "Going through that his only focus was on making sure that mom was comfortable, felt loved, and was taken care of. That was his only focus. Any decision that was made had to meet that criteria," Valarie says. "He would always say, 'You took care of us for so long, now it's time for us to take care of you,'" recalls Nina Williams. Julia Williams affirms, "What sticks out to me is the commitment he showed to our mother. She was suffering through Alzheimer's for seven years, and he never left her side. He wanted the best for her." "It was just extraordinary to see," Hill adds. "It was tough but there was a comfort level because we knew that we were all in this together and that we were going to make sure that she was going to feel loved during the time she had left on earth. That was the message that he drove and that we rallied around."[53]

Billy was constantly at Shirley's side throughout her years-long battle with Alzheimer's. She was courageous to the end. Shirley Williams passed away on December 23, 2021. They were married for 61 years.

Chapter 12

Narratives

The legacies of Billy Williams and Willie McCovey are encapsulated by public memory monuments that will endure for generations. The Cubs and Giants retired their numbers. McCovey's 44 adorns a deck facing of Oracle Park overlooking left field. A flag bearing Williams's number 26 proudly flies from atop the right-field foul pole at Wrigley Field. Near each ballpark stands a statue of their likenesses, both swinging with power and grace. Plaques in Cooperstown boast of their achievements in a manner neither man ever would—heaps of humility before an ounce pride, team accomplishments above any individual accolades. Over the years, McCovey and Williams have been thought of as quiet men, which seems to suggest a sort of disconnection or passive nature, but nothing could be further from the truth. Deeply insightful, engaging, and caring men, they simply refused to engage in self-promotion. Thankfully, we have public memory to remind us of their professional greatness. Rather than talk about themselves, they much prefer to talk about you—look you in the eye and ask your name, where you're from, and how you're doing.

Willie McCovey's legs allowed him to play golf for a little while yet. He frequented Lake Merced Golf Course, where he obliterated tee shots. Stretch typically played his rounds solo. He didn't necessarily like being referred to as a "loner" in those years, but his social life could reflect otherwise at times. Solitude brought him comfort. It reduced uncontrollable variables. Onlookers at the Bay Area course most certainly knew who he was but refrained from interrupting him—everyone, that is, except for Joe Yick. One day, Joe spotted McCovey's cart and turned to a caddy with the request to add his bag to it. The caddy hesitated. Yick insisted. His round with McCovey commenced, and that was the beginning of a beautiful friendship.

If Mac wanted to talk, Yick provided a listening ear. Quite often, they played in pressure-free silence. Stretch warmed up to Yick. He never showed any sign of displeasure that Joe had invited himself along for that initial round. The fact is that after a while, Stretch seemed to appreciate it, and they became close friends. Yick, a successful Bay Area restaurant kitchen expert, gifted McCovey a special gold coin ball marker that commemorated the former's Hall of Fame induction. One time, Yick received a frantic call from Stretch. He had accidently reached into the wrong pocket when getting change for a parking meter only to accidently grasp that special coin, and, well, could Joe contact his friend at the city to retrieve it from the belly of the meter? Not a problem. That ball marker was saved, and a classic story between the friends was born.

McCovey Cove served as the primary piece of public memory for the Giants' slugger at Pacific Bell Park until 2003, when the organization paired it with a 9-foot statue of Willie Mac unleashing his powerful swing at the newly minted McCovey Point at China Basin Park, created by the sculptor William Behrends. It was dedicated at a lavish ceremony on May 4 that featured family, friends, and former teammates, including Willie Mays, Gaylord Perry, Hobie Landrith, and Tom Haller. Overwhelmed with emotion as the speakers lauded him with praise, McCovey uncharacteristically found himself on the verge of tears, much as he had been during his Hall of Fame speech. That the Giants again gave back to him in this way meant the world to him. Mac had cornered the market on this slice of topography, and it will always declare his place in Giants' lore. Many people have admired the cove and sculpture alike over the past two decades. Barry Bonds captures the essence of their experiences. "A family is going to take their kid who wants to be a baseball player and walk by this statue that says, 'Willie McCovey.' There is a history behind that statue forever. He will always be remembered as long as that stadium and statue stay up there," says Bonds. "Someone is going to say, 'Who's that, mom? Dad? Who's Willie McCovey?' There's going to be a story behind it. Everyone growing up is going to know who Willie McCovey is forever."[1]

As the years went by, McCovey's physical ailments mounted, and playing golf became a part of his past. Losing his physical strength disappointed him, but he braved the pain and frustration as well as one could. He never complained. Ever. There were more surgeries, knees and back, numbering into double digits, too many to count it seemed, and his mobility became truly limited due to the chronic pain. Stretch shrugged it off as best he could. "Not many athletes play pain-free," he pointed out to a reporter with a smile. "Mine was just more than normal."[2] Dusty Baker contextualizes the physical toll that an athlete endures as a result of a successful career. One can easily visualize McCovey as Baker shares this wisdom: "If you played this game long enough you left something on the field," he says. "If you go out there and dig that field up you're going to find a bunch of backs, elbows, arms, knees, ankles. There's something that you're going to leave on that field. If you don't leave this game with something kind of ailing you for life that meant that you are really, really lucky or you didn't play much."[3]

In the midst of these physical challenges came several emotional lifts that deeply impacted McCovey's personal life over the last decade of his life. The first occurred in 2008, when Barack Obama, a senator from Illinois, became the first African American elected president of the United States. After all he had suffered growing up in Mobile, McCovey was thrilled to see the nation elect Obama. And, wouldn't you know, Obama was the country's 44th president. The perfect number. Eight years later, the president wiped away McCovey's conviction with a pardon. It was deeply meaningful to Stretch— a man who avoided trouble at all costs—to see that episode from his past resolved in that manner.

McCovey connected with lifelong friends and established several business ventures during his retirement years. The reality for professional athletes who played in the 1960s is that, while the money was good, their career earnings don't come close to what we see today. McCovey continued to work extensively with the Dudum family. He retained an office, and it was very common to see him there. In 2003, McCovey and the Dudums teamed up to open a unique dining experience based on Stretch's illustrious career. The eatery, aptly named McCovey's Restaurant, was situated on California Avenue in Walnut Creek and was open for 11 years. It offered a lively place to watch sports, especially the Giants, and enjoy the "521" burger, 44 ounces of angus beef, under the purview of autographed jerseys and bats, which kept an eye on the dining room from their lookout spots. McCovey had a private dining room but could frequently be spotted chatting with customers. Additionally, Hal Silen involved Willie in a successful farming venture featuring pistachios. Living close to lush California agriculture, pistachio trees presented a health-conscious snack with a growing market. McCovey joined Silen, along with two doctors. They dubbed themselves the "Pistachio Giants," and the successful venture remains alive today.

McCovey remained close to the Giants throughout these years. The front office continued to use him as a sounding board, and he offered his advice to players seeking counsel. Stretch also told stories. You were in for a treat if you saw him in the office of his close friend, clubhouse manager Mike Murphy. In January 2018, the Giants threw McCovey a huge celebration for his 80th birthday at the ballpark. Those close to Stretch filled the bustling room and greeted the guest of honor, including Terry Whitfield, who laughed when recalling how his impromptu expression of love for his dear friend went about as well as expected. "I came over there, and I said, 'Hey, Willie, how are you doing?' and I gave him a kiss on the forehead. Right after I gave him a kiss on the forehead Barry came beside me and gave him a kiss on the cheek, and he looked at us and said, 'Come on, what's going on here?!'

"We said, 'We love you, man.' I knew he didn't like stuff like that, but I did it anyway," laughs Whitfield.[4]

Never a fan of overt affection, McCovey treasured his connections with both of them. In a reflective moment about his career, Mac once admitted to Whitfield that perhaps a bit of stubbornness had cost him at the plate. "If I would have just gone to left field a little bit more no telling how many more home runs I would have hit."[5] McCovey also cherished his friendship with Bonds and ardently supported him at every turn. No one who attended that gathering has forgotten it. At one point, Mays shared several stories. Mac drew laughs from the crowd when he took the microphone and jokingly suggested that a few mistakes had been made in them. The fun vibes emanating from the Giants' royalty filled the room.

In August 2018, McCovey married Estela Bejar in a ceremony appropriately held inside the Giants' clubhouse. The two had been together since first meeting in 2010, when Bejar became McCovey's caretaker. Willie admired Renel Brooks-Moon's work on the radio and as the Giants' public address announcer, so he asked her to host the wedding, and she was thrilled to do it. The celebratory event featured some dancing with Stretch and Estela as the focal points. Although now confined to a wheelchair, McCovey smiled as guests twirled around the center of the room to the song "Love Train" by the O'Jays. He wore a dark suit jacket with a peach-hued shirt and tie. A Giants cap adorned his head. "It was an incredible day," Brooks-Moon recalls.[6]

As much as the Giants' new waterfront ballpark became a staple of the franchise, it was enhanced by McCovey's nightly presence. One of the coolest things about the stadium was that players and fans alike could look up and see McCovey taking it all in above the playing field as he watched from his box. His being there brought a gravitas to the proceedings. His stature elevated the Giants' brand while connecting generations of fans from the 1950s through the 2010s. Stretch stayed in the Bay Area for the rest of his life because he loved it so much. Although expressing his emotions didn't come naturally, he grew so comfortable with his affection for the region that, on this topic, they flowed easily. The place and its people had embraced him since his youth, and baseball was the vehicle that connected them all. Mac enjoyed the cheers, but he lived to love and be loved by family, friends, and fans alike. He shared his egoless gentleness with so many people during the years, which is why it was so discordantly stark when his health took him away from the ballpark, the box empty without the Gentle Giant.

Several months after the wedding, McCovey was admitted to Stanford Hospital, his once fiercely strong composition ebbed away by illness and injury. His daughter, Allison, frequently visited him to get updates and communicate with the doctors. Estela was there, too, by his side. At one point, Joe Yick provided him with meals. A bevy of those close to McCovey visited him, including Joe Morgan, his longtime friend and fellow Hall of Famer. On October 31—Halloween Day, orange and black—Willie McCovey, who had traveled across time and space from a working-class neighborhood in Mobile, Alabama, to immortality in San Francisco, passed away with his family and friends at his bedside.

* * *

In the same manner as McCovey, Billy Williams's retirement never precluded him from watching his team play. For years, Whistler drove from his home to Wrigley Field and watched the Cubs, usually in a suite alongside Crane Kenney, the team's president. Kenney, who decorated that space with photos of Williams, has spent many years observing the minutiae of ballgames alongside the Hall of Famer. Williams pointed out to him how watching the last-second movement by middle infielders, along with a catcher's foot positioning, indicates the pitch that is about to be thrown. Visitors who dropped by to say hello were stunned to realize that they were in Williams's presence, and Billy made them feel right at home by asking their names and about their lives. His infectious smile and warmth were as genuine as that sweetest of swings. "They can't get over the humility of an icon," Kenney notices.

In recent years, Williams wasn't at the ballpark as frequently. Snarling traffic made it a bit more challenging to get into the city. Knowing that he never asks for anything, Kenney offered to send a car for Williams whenever he wanted to come to a game. He accepted and makes it a habit to attend at least all Friday home games. Part of what continues to make Wrigley Field so special is his presence. And because Williams is so frequently there, so, too, in a way, are all of the Cubs he played alongside. "He's the touchstone to that generation," Kenney says. Members of the organization make it a point to check in with Williams to see if he needs anything. They all go out to dinner a few times in the offseason to catch up, reminisce, and talk about the current goings-on around the Cubs.

While Williams maintains close relationships with members of the front office, he also remains dear friends with Fergie Jenkins and Randy Hundley, among so many others. His phone rings during an interview. It's José Cardenal. They are all sure to find Whistler whenever they drop by Wrigley Field. Kenney has observed these reunions for two decades. "Billy is the godfather.

He is the chairman," he says. "When any player visits town, especially who played close to his era, they come in and pay their respects to Billy, and they'll sit in our suite and watch with him. And when they all get going and start talking about hitting you just want to be a fly on the wall. It's fabulous."[7] Williams's close relationships with his former teammates has fostered an environment that allows vital aspects of Cubs' history to be told. Renowned sportswriter Ron Rapoport interviewed Williams while he was working on his terrific biography about Ernie Banks. Not only did he agree to be interviewed, but Williams connected Rapoport with former teammates to help tell Banks's story. "Billy's a wonderful guy," Rapoport says, "and takes his responsibilities in this area pretty seriously."[8]

Williams remains a constant at Cubs Convention, an annual hot stove gathering that takes place each January in the Windy City and serves as an unofficial kickoff for the new season. Fans love seeing him, and he enjoys mimicking that sweet swing for them. On his 80th birthday, surrounded by his grandchildren, Williams sang the "Seventh Inning Stretch" at Wrigley Field, proving that he could not only swing a bat well but also carry a tune. It's in moments like these that we see this special man connect generations, young Cubs fans seeing in person an individual whom so many of their grandparents watched play baseball in days gone by. "That's Billy Williams," they say, and it opens the door to a whole lot of wonderful stories. And that's a line people throughout Chicagoland have uttered for scores of years now. Everyone who grew up there and went to the ballpark saw him play because if there's one thing that Billy Williams did throughout his career, it was have his name in the lineup every single day. Then he went out there and put on a show. The consistency of his career has generated a sense of familiarity, and that notion has evolved into complete adoration.

Williams's impact on the organization is on full display at Wrigley Field. In the same manner the Giants did for McCovey, the Cubs produced two key monuments of public memory that present the high esteem in which the franchise holds Williams. A flag on the right-field foul pole unfurls in the wind to reveal his number 26, which was retired in 1987. There's a funny story about that flag, actually. The Cubs always wanted to retire number 31 to honor Hall of Famer Fergie Jenkins but waited until after another Hall of Famer, Greg Maddux, who also wore it, retired so that both pitchers could be commemorated. In 2009, the Cubs prepared for two ceremonies. Both Jenkins and Maddux would be recognized with individual flags featuring 31. Nervous engineers expressed concern about how the additional flags might impact the wind load on the foul poles when intense gusts off the lake really got going. They suggested producing a slightly smaller set of flags to compensate. That sparked an idea. Now Williams doesn't talk about himself in a braggadocio manner and never trumpets his accomplishments, yet he is fiercely proud of the career that he fashioned over 18 seasons. It means a lot to him that his hard work resulted in election to the National Baseball Hall of Fame. He also has a marvelous sense of humor, which set the table for an amusing meeting.

Kenney got a smaller flag bearing 26 the size of, say, one you might see waving on a used car and kept it for the right moment. Shortly thereafter, he ran into Williams and casually mentioned that the flags needed to be shrunk down to accommodate the pair of 31s.

"What do you mean?" Williams asked.

"Well," Kenney responded. "Too much wind load. The foul poles are old."

"How much are you going to shrink them?" inquired Billy.

Kenney pulled out a handkerchief-sized 26 and held it out. "They're going to be this big," he smiled.

Williams stared at him. "No, they're not," he retorted.[9]

In 2010, more than five decades after he first joined the ballclub as a young outfielder, the Cubs dedicated a second Williams tribute: a statue of his likeness outside of Wrigley Field. Accompanied in the front row by Shirley, Billy listened as Cubs dignitaries shared their heartfelt congratulations. The 1969 Cubs held a mini reunion. Fans who gathered around the dedication site saw Ernie Banks, Fergie Jenkins, Randy Hundley, Glenn Beckert, and Ron Santo, who recounted the notable story about Rogers Hornsby dismissing all of the Cubs' minor league prospects except for two—Williams and Santo—who he believed could hit in the big leagues immediately. In his remarks, Billy thanked his family for their dedicated support. He looked directly at his wife with emotion etched throughout his loving face and said, "I couldn't have made it without you, Shirley, and the family that I have. Great people."

* * *

Public memory tributes to Williams and McCovey outside of Chicago and San Francisco reveal the national impact of their lives and careers. The most prominent of these honors resides in upstate New York on the walls of the Plaque Gallery at the National Baseball Hall of Fame and Museum, where only one percent of professional baseball players are permanently enshrined. More than 17 million people have visited the museum since it first opened in 1939. Positioned on the southern end of Main Street, a thin strip of avenue filled with quaint shops and charming restaurants, it has extensively expanded over the past eight decades. Through the end of 2024, its most hallowed room features 346 plaques—one for each Hall of Fame member—where visitors can see the chiseled faces of the game's greats and read about their accomplishments. Guests are thrilled to see the remarkable tributes to Stretch and Whistler, but those plaques also reflect something back at onlookers, a younger version of themselves. "Invariably, fans travel to Cooperstown to find the past," illuminates Jeff Idelson, who worked at the Hall of Fame for over two decades. "They want to experience the past, and what they invariably will do is end up in their own past. It's uncanny how anybody who comes to the Hall of Fame will find something that's very relevant to their experience or their childhood."[10] Being enshrined in the Hall just one year apart means that the plaques of these two hitting savants are affixed to walls within the gallery mere steps from one another.

* * *

While public memory of the contributions made by Willie McCovey and Billy Williams to their ballclubs stand in the form of statues in San Francisco and Chicago, respectively, a movement to similarly honor them in Mobile began to take shape under the guidance of their longtime friend—and former opponent—Cleon Jones around 2017. Jones has long been an established figure in Africatown, a community established by the descendants of the *Clotilda*, the last slave ship to arrive in America in 1860. In 2019, the *Clotilda* was discovered when its wreck was found in the Mobile Delta. This earth-shattering news shone a bright light on the city and its history. In 1860, Timothy Meaher had financed captain William Foster's trip to Dahomey, a nation located on the west coast of Africa, on this ship. Foster returned a few months later with 110 enslaved human beings, a number of whom participated in the establishment of Africatown on receiving their freedom following the end of the Civil War.[11] Local conversations pertaining to race, economics, and public memory following the discovery of its sunken wreck suddenly became national news. Several books and a documentary followed. Public memory in Mobile took on a heightened level of importance. "Our conversation now—it's not cocktail parties behind closed doors—we're talking on the world stage," says Mayor Sandy Stimpson.[12]

Baseball fans know Cleon Jones as the clutch-hitting left fielder who caught the final out of the Miracle Mets' World Series championship season in 1969. However, closer to home, Jones's visibility is predicated on volunteering to paint fences, landscape yards, and cultivate historical memory of the place where he still lives, frequently while donning a Mets cap. Originally, Jones developed an idea of honoring the region's unique baseball tradition through the creation of a legends exhibit. The city of Mobile has produced more Hall of Fame baseball players per capita than any other city in America, and it's not close. Jones first met one of Mobile's future Hall of Famers at the age of 12, when Henry Aaron visited his school in 1954.[13] In 1969, Jones played for the Mets alongside a pair of Mobilians, Tommie Agee and Amos Otis. The National League All-Star team that season featured three starters from Mobile, of course: Jones, Aaron, and McCovey. The rich tradition of baseball in Mobile was part of Jones's life from the start, and he saw to it that community discussions continued around commemorating these great ballplayers. The discussion concerning the honoring of Mobile's rich baseball history took further shape during the 2021 mayoral race. For years, Mobile has grappled with the best way to tell its story through sport. A park was renamed after Aaron, and its centerpiece included stone slabs dedicated to prolific Hall of Famers, including McCovey and Williams. On January 25, 2021, just a few days following Aaron's passing, Mobile officials unveiled preliminary plans for a Hall of Fame Courtyard positioned next to Cooper Riverside Park on Water Street, which runs adjacent to Mobile Bay. This location would not only honor them but also generate an additional tourism spot by the waterfront.

The rich legacy of outstanding ballplayers from Mobile is well known throughout the baseball ranks, if some fans around the country occasionally benefit from a gentle reminder that it is one of the cradles of the game. The players' reputation around the sport preceded them, and all the opponents of Mobile's finest knew they were about to face some of the most prodigious talent and intellect the sport had to offer. "Those guys could hit, but they were also really smart," raves Bill North. "They looked bad on a pitch in the third inning to get that pitch in the eighth inning. They would swing at it like they were fooled. Then that guy in the eighth inning when you've got somebody on base this guy thinks that he can get you out with that pitch, and you're sitting there waiting for it."[14]

Memorializing the incredible accomplishments of Mobile's five National Baseball Hall of Famers—Satchel Paige, Aaron, McCovey, Williams, and Ozzie Smith—struck everyone as a wonderful idea. Additionally, Robert Brazile Jr., who was enshrined in Canton as part of the Pro Football Hall of Fame in 2018, is also to be honored with a monument. A confluence of forces altered Jones's vision a bit, but the thesis of the project remains intact. Public money arrived in the form of an $8 million allocation from Governor Kay Ivey as the city's share of oil and gas leases, and Stimpson wanted to develop Mobile's underutilized waterfront, specifically Cooper Riverside Park.[15] Stimpson; Danny Corte, executive director of the Mobile Sports Authority; and Matt Anderson, who leads the city's Civic and Cultural Affairs office, relied heavily on Jones's input for the baseball aspects of this newly designed project.

Rightfully, the discovery of the *Clotilda* took center stage over the next several years, but the drive to develop the courtyard continued. Conversations between Mayor Stimpson, Jones, and other officials continued at City Hall. Inspired by the Field of Dreams statues at the Negro Leagues Museum in Kansas City, Jones developed a similar concept of players positioned on a baseball diamond. There was hardly a city, if any, that could compete with Mobile's starting nine, let alone one of similar size.

There are many ways for a place to remember its history. Preserved historical sites seek the protection of physical structures deemed worthy of remaining intact. Paintings and artifacts capture a sense of time and place that is not our own. Statues play a prominent role throughout America, reminding onlookers of past events, deeds, and people. They have played a particularly notable role in the South, specifically in its remembering of the Civil War. Statues produce narratives, and they have played a role in Mobile's public memory for more than a century. Amidst a dozen statues unveiled throughout the South in 1900, the highest number in history up until that point, a monument of Confederate admiral Raphael Semmes was unveiled to Mobilians on June 27.[16] Dozens of sculptures followed suit in the community over the ensuing decades to the point that now the Mobile Museum of Art features a sculpture trail map that details a walk anyone can take to see a wide variety of works. The Semmes statue stood high over the intersection of Royal and Government streets for many years before Stimpson had it removed in 2020.

* * *

Once Mobile officials determined that the Hall of Fame courtyard project would move forward, they put out a national call for artists. The process was rigorous. Typically, an artist's qualifications, along with a sketch, would suffice as a starting point. However, this particular call requested that finalists produce a rendering of how the courtyard might look, drawings of all six statues, and a scale model of the Henry Aaron monument. It caught the attention of Brett Grill, a former professor at the University of Missouri with experience in several mediums, who now specializes in sculpture. He knew immediately that he wanted to take a run at getting the job. Sculptors are frequently asked to work on a project in its later stages of construction, but this gig, which was early on in its process, invited the artist's voice to participate at the decision-making table. The subject matter also galvanized him. "I grew up just loving baseball, collecting ball cards, and these are the guys whose cards I coveted but could never afford with my paper route money," he says.[17]

Grill's notable qualifications, including public works featuring presidents, first ladies, athletes, and coaches, impressed city officials, who selected him as one of the 14 finalists. On learning that he was part of the final group, Grill traveled from his home base in Michigan down to Mobile for his first visit to the city. He spent hours surveying the waterfront area near the convention center to get a sense of the space. While his camera snapped photos, Grill drank in the atmosphere of the area. "One of the things I was quick to notice in being there was how entrenched in sport the community is. The restaurant life and the bar life downtown is something that is rooted in athletics and is energized when there's a big event down there," Grill describes it before turning his attention to the city's history at large. "In walking around the area there are a lot of public plaques and statues that sort of tell the long history of Mobile, but there isn't yet a celebration of this super rich and deep athletic history that it has."[18] Grill returned home and began work on a maquette, or model statue, of Aaron.

In December 2021, the panel tasked with selecting the artist for the courtyard project chose Grill. Three months later, he returned to Mobile and was introduced to the public during a press conference featuring Billye Aaron, wife of the late Henry Aaron, who said, "I don't know what more I can say than to say, 'thank you,' so much for making this a reality." Previously, her husband's childhood home was moved and turned into a museum dedicated to the life and career of Hammerin' Hank as part of the city's early preservation of its baseball history. Mayor Stimpson revealed Grille's scale model of Aaron—which would eventually reach 9 feet in its final form—and clips of his career were shown to onlookers. The city also announced that Canfor Southern Pine had made a $150,000 donation to the project.[19]

Participating in these early stages of the project was a unique opportunity for Grill. He joined designers and architects brought in by the city for early discussions about how the entrance into Cooper Riverside Park would look. This process generated excitement that the final product would look fluent rather than disjointed. Everyone's voices were meshed together from the start.

Now about those statues. Grill determined Aaron's pose during the scale-building process, and Paige's piece would replicate his unique pitching motion. Grill then turned his attention to McCovey and Williams. He pored over all the videos and photos of them that he could find. Grill discovered what so many of Mac's contemporaries knew about him. In his landmark book *Ball Four*, Jim Bouton described what it was like to witness Stretch take batting practice. "A group of terrorized pitchers stood around the batting cage watching Willie McCovey belt some tremendous line drives over the right-field fence. Every time a ball bounced into the seats we'd make little whimpering animal sounds," he describes.[20] Half a century after Bouton wrote those words, Grill embraced the same idea. "McCovey wears his athleticism on his body in a way that not all of them do," Grill notes. "He was just an athletic specimen. You get a sense of that from the photos. Just so strong." He designed the McCovey statue to present the great power hitter late in his swing, watching and twisting toward first base as he prepares to run down the line. Using what he calls "little moments of chaos" in the way McCovey's uniform lays, Grill's piece captures the majestic nature of Stretch's power that frightened so many of his opponents.

Being known as "Sweet Swinging" Billy Williams focused Grill's attention on the Hall of Famer's smooth stroke. Initially, he identified the image of Williams's bat meeting the ball as a great point of reference to use, but a conversation with the man himself changed his mind. While talking through the idea, Williams mentioned that his follow-through made the swing more of his own. The focus of the piece shifted, and a beautiful image emerged. "His body is torqued in a way that—post-swing—it does reveal the sweetness of it," describes Grill. "Not only are we appreciating the twist of the recoil after the ball has been struck, but he's also gazing at the ball as it's flying wherever it might have gone. So, the sweetness is doubled in a way."[21]

If all goes according to plan, the statues of Aaron, Paige, McCovey, and Williams will be mounted along Water Street and unveiled to the public in the next few years. These monuments will not only capture the historical accomplishments of these outstanding baseball players but also point toward their lives as examples of what young Mobilians can dream of accomplishing. They will stand for years to come as part of the community's fabric. Visitors will see one of the greatest pitchers in the history of the sport, an amazing shortstop, and Mobile's most prolific long-ball trio: Aaron (755), McCovey (521), and Williams (426). "It so happens that they hit 1702 home runs, and Mobile became a city in 1702," Cleon Jones says with a smile. "Now you've got something interesting in your book already."[22]

Whistler may have been annexed by Prichard, but those residents who still live there take deep gratification in its existence, along with other people who join them in sharing local pride, and will not have to journey very far to see their own superstar immortalized in sculpture. The significance to Williams and the community runs deep. "He came from humble beginnings, and there are a lot of great athletes who came from humble beginnings, but you get the sense that he will never forget the lessons that he learned in Whistler, Alabama from his teachers, his parents, from the older amateur ballplayers who taught him the right way to play the game," observes longtime *Chicago Tribune* reporter and columnist Fred Mitchell, who first met Williams in 1983. "All these people remain etched forever in his mind, and I think that's what guides him on a day-to-day basis. He never has forgotten what they did for him, and we all see the finished product of what that means."[23]

Jones remembers being in high school and running into Williams, who encouraged him to keep playing baseball to the best of his ability. "He would tell me, 'They're watching you. Everybody knows about you. Keep up the good work,'" Jones says. Williams wanted Jones to maximize his potential as the older ballplayers had hoped for him when he was growing up. "It was like one big family," Jones says of the area. "Whatever happened to you happened to me, and everybody knew about it."[24]

However, for Willie McCovey's family and friends, news of the statue courtyard initially stirred up some mixed feelings. One of the few things McCovey willingly vocalized over the years was his distaste for the experience he had while living in Mobile, and that feeling was further solidified in later years after his retirement. At one point, city officials reached out to McCovey and expressed their desire to honor him. The exact year remains a bit hazy (although it occurred well before the current group of officials entered office) in the recollections of those involved, but what happened is clear as day. McCovey, who could no longer fly alone due to his physical limitations, requested funds for his friend Rocky Dudum to travel with him for assistance. The officials rebuffed his request, so a miffed McCovey stayed at home. His mother, Ester, accepted the award on his behalf. Jones, for one, had hoped Willie would give Mobile an opportunity to show that it had undergone changes in his later years, but Mac felt that he had already given it a second chance. There was some thought that he had returned home only for family funerals after he settled in California, but he did quietly visit his relatives on a few occasions, especially if the Winter Meetings were held in Florida.

There are a wide range of individual experiences and viewpoints in Mobile on the topics of its history and public memory. There are sure to be many conversations in future years around who benefits from increased tourism dollars as a result of this statue attraction, especially as it expands. For his part, the mayor acknowledges this tension while remaining hopeful that this new courtyard will give the families of the honored a place to celebrate their loved ones. "I hope it warms them up to the city of Mobile," Stimpson says, "and what they think about this city."[25]

In spite of this tumult, Allison McCovey believes that her father would ultimately welcome being celebrated where he grew up. "I know Woodside became his home, and I can understand all the reasons why, but he was from Mobile. His family was from Mobile. I think he would like a tribute to him as well as the other players," she says.[26] He would be especially pleased to be a symbol of encouragement to children, especially African American kids, growing up in the area. The statues can serve as a reminder that Mobile's own accomplished these incredible things, and so, too, can they.

* * *

Narratives tell us a lot about how a person's life is viewed by the society in which they lived it. Notable stories that reflect the depth of an impact made by a life inform us about who should be remembered. Legacies tell us as much about another person's accomplishments as much as they enlighten us about what we value. The legacies of Billy Williams and Willie McCovey convey their depth of commitment to their craft, kindness, and humility. Their careers require study beyond the simplistic conclusion that they were great athletes who played in the shadows of bigger stars. They deserve appreciation in their own right. The history of baseball cannot be told without including Billy Williams and Willie McCovey, even though they are the last two people on Earth who would suggest it. "Willie was a very humble man. He was not in the least a self-promoter. He was not flashy. His style of play and his personality did not draw attention to him. I think those are all things that probably conspired to keep him from being as well known and well appreciated as a ballplayer than he was," says former Giants executive Corey Busch.[27]

"I was in awe of him and then I got to know him," recalls Chris Speier, McCovey's fellow infielder in San Francisco. "I was more in awe of who he was as a person and how he carried himself and what he represented and how he represented the game of baseball. Not just by what he did on the field, but what he did off the field. All the lives that he touched. I don't see how you could ever not talk about baseball and McCovey in the same sentence. I don't know how you do that. I don't think you can."[28]

The Chicago Cubs franchise has been around for nearly 150 years. Wrigley Field first opened its doors the same year World War I started, and the Cubs moved in two years later. The sheer aggregate of the organization's history is voluminous. So when Crane Kenney says about Billy Williams, "He's everything to this place," it means something staggeringly special.

The Cubs of Williams's generation were and remain a tight-knit group. "Billy was a very instrumental part in all of that. He was the perfect type of player to have on our ballclub. He was pretty quiet. He didn't say much to anybody. Just went out and did his job," Hundley says. "He did the best he could every single day. He was just an inspiration to all of us."[29] Williams's teammates never stopped being amazed at his feats. They talked about them inside the clubhouse after the game but had to do so without the man of the hour. "Billy wouldn't be in the conversation because he wouldn't talk about it," Hundley points out.

Don Kessinger describes how being around Williams on a daily basis motivated the Cubs. "Billy was a guy who was doing what he loved to do, and he did it as good as anybody," Kessinger says. "He could inspire you. It was by his actions not so much what he said. He was just a great teammate."[30]

Considering the careers of McCovey and Williams together may initially produce a moment of pause, but the more one asks around about them, the more clearly the distinct parallels of their legacies emerge. For starters, both humble superstars let their bats do the talking. "I never heard them complain or brag. I'm not kidding you. I've never heard either one of them—or Hank— I never heard them brag, *ever*," emphasizes Dusty Baker.[31]

"You know when you used to drive that stick shift?" asks Bill North, who played alongside both of them. "You could save gas that way. Those guys were high performance stick shifts—that's a brand new thought right there—you know rather than electric cars. They had big engines, too, boy, and they would roar."[32]

Most importantly, their legacies challenge all of us to stand up for what is right. Billy Williams called for reflection in his Hall of Fame speech as he asked those running the sport to think about the state of opportunities for minorities in the game of baseball. McCovey made personal phones calls to Giants officials seeking accountability to a diversity commitment. Reflection brings awareness and understanding and can lead to change. Contemplation on stories, statistics, and memories facilitates a deeper appreciation for these two men as ballplayers, but it goes further when considering what they've asked others to ponder. Both Williams and McCovey spoke directly to the challenging status quos they faced throughout their careers on and off the field.

As we reflect on their lives, let us ponder the questions they asked. According to the Institute for Diversity and Ethics in Sport at the University of Central Florida, the number of American-born Black ballplayers on Opening Day major league rosters to begin the 2022 season fell 6.2 percent, which is the lowest recorded number since the study started in 1991. Additionally, not a single African American player suited up for the World Series between the Houston Astros and the Philadelphia Phillies in 2022. There have been a few positive developments. African Americans comprised four out of the first five draft picks in the 2022 MLB Draft for the first time in history. Each of those four players played in the DREAM Series, one of several programs supported by Major League Baseball focused on diversity. Williams spoke passionately about Black ownership of teams. In recent years, Hall of Famer Earvin "Magic" Johnson (Los Angeles Dodgers), three-time NFL MVP Patrick Mahomes (Kansas City Royals), and Karen Daniel (Kansas City Royals), an incredibly successful businesswoman, have purchased stakes in big-league clubs.[33] However, there remains far more work to be done.

As for McCovey and Williams themselves, the connection between those two kids born a few miles apart in 1938 never wavered. Billy and Shirley of Whistler, always and forever people of uncommon consistency, annually sent a reminder of their bond to the affable Willie, their friend from Down the Bay, in the mail each holiday season. "I can always count on a Christmas card from Billy and Shirley," McCovey said appreciatively. "Just like clockwork."[34]

Epilogue

Bobby Richardson Calls

In January 2024, with this manuscript on the verge of completion, I missed a call while driving home after teaching class. Notable remnants from a morning snowstorm still lay heavy on the roads, and the sun's rays reflected sharply off the ice. On pulling into the garage, I glanced at my phone. It hadn't recognized the number. Perhaps it's the paranoid teacher in me, but I haven't ever returned an unrecognized call. Limited upside. Yet, in that moment, an unusual gnawing scratched inside my brain, so I pressed the callback icon and listened as the line rang twice. I had to catch my breath when a kindly voice with a gentle Southern accent answered, "This is Bobby Richardson." Oh, the questions that immediately raced through my mind. *Were you surprised Houk let Terry pitch to McCovey? How hard did he actually hit it? How did you end up in that exact defensive position?* I wanted to blurt all of them out at once. Instead, the moment called for restraint, and he very nicely agreed to speak with me early the following week.

Bobby Richardson entered the 1962 World Series having fashioned the finest campaign of his career. Fresh off his third All-Star Game appearance, the 27-year-old second baseman led the American League with 209 hits and formed half of the "Milkshake Twins" with his double-play partner, shortstop Tony Kubek. He might have been the MVP of the American League that season had it not been for that good friend of his, Mickey Mantle, who bashed 30 homers and led the sport with an OPS of 1.091. Richardson settled for MVP runner-up as well as the second of what was to become five consecutive Gold Glove Awards.

Richardson had produced this standout season heading into the World Series against San Francisco. The Yankees were looking to repeat as champions, having knocked off the Cincinnati Reds in five games in 1961, which had somewhat soothed the sting of being upset by Bill Mazeroski and the Pittsburgh

231

Pirates in 1960, a World Series for which Richardson was named the MVP.
The Yankees and Giants split the first six games of the series, setting up their
Game Seven showdown at Candlestick Park. Quick recount. New York leads,
1–0, in the bottom of the ninth inning. With Ralph Terry pitching, Matty Alou
leads off with a bunt single for the Giants. Terry rebounds by striking out
Felipe Alou and Chuck Hiller. Down to the final out, Willie Mays doubles to
right, sending Alou to third. As Willie McCovey strides to the plate, Yankees
manager Ralph Houk emerges from the dugout and walks to the mound to
confer with his pitcher. With first base open, and McCovey having already had
notable success against Terry in the series, surely the Yankees would walk him.

While Houk and Terry conversed, Richardson explains to me, he was having a discussion of his own. "I walked over to Kubek . . . we were standing
together with Willie Mays. We were talking about it. 'Do you think he's
going to walk him?' And I said, 'Well, I sure would.'

"Tony looked at me and said, 'Well, I sure would hate to be you. Left
handed hitting McCovey. You've already made one error in this series. Hate
to see you blow it now.' Then he laughed. Mays laughed. That's what I was
thinking about when I was going back to my position."

Houk and Richardson were close—"a lifelong friend, and the best coach I
ever had" is how the former Yankee infielder describes his manager. *Knowing him as well as you did, what was your reaction to Houk's decision to let
Terry pitch to McCovey?* "I was very much surprised," he admits.

The tension mounted after the first pitch of the at-bat. McCovey smacked
Terry's initial offering far down the right-field line but pulled it very much
foul. Richardson took immediate notice. "He decided to pitch to him, and I
played where I ordinarily played for him but then he hit a ball, a line drive to
right field that was foul, but it was hit hard enough to go out of the park, and
I could tell he was way ahead in his swing. And I said, 'You know, I need
to move over.' I just—my instinct—moved me over another five, six feet,
something like that. And I think that's when Ralph looked around."

To Terry's dismay, Richardson had noticeably shifted away from his original spot. Terry took several steps off the back of the mound to redirect his
teammate, but he suddenly stopped. "He thought I was playing him way too
much in the hole, and he started to move me back over toward second base.
He changed his mind and didn't say anything to me." Terry chose to trust
Richardson's experience.

On the next pitch, Mac hit that line drive right at him.

Ironically, Richardson's thoughts were focused on second-base umpire Al
Barlick. He had asked for Richardson's hat as a gift for his cousin. On secur-
ing the final out of the Series, Bobby handed his cap to Barlick and then gave
the baseball to Terry. Joyful delight in New York. Crushing sadness in San
Francisco.

The sting of that agonizing loss lingered with those Giants and their fan base. The most famous at-bat of Willie McCovey's illustrious career was to become, of all things preposterous, an out. Any of those National League–record 18 grand slams, his homer in the 1971 National League Championship Series against Pittsburgh, yet another extra-base hit off Drysdale—they all frustratingly existed in a shadowy purgatory created by that lineout and the possibility of what might have been. Several years later, Rawlings, the glove company, asked Richardson to present Joe Morgan with a Gold Glove Award during an offseason ceremony. Other players attending the honors gathering, including Willie Mays, who, on hearing that the former Yankees second baseman was nearby, beckoned him over to chat.

"He said, 'Richardson, I want to talk to you. Come over here. I can't see. Let me hold your hand, so I'll know where you are.' He held my hand, and he said, 'I want you to know that if it had been me on first base when I hit that double to right field I wouldn't have stopped at third. I'd have scored, and we'd have won that game. And I said, 'You probably would have. You wouldn't have stopped'"—Richardson breaks into a knowing laugh recalling Mays's sincerity as well as his speed—"'I understand that. You're probably right.'"

* * *

Willie McCovey and Bobby Richardson, forever entwined in baseball lore, encountered one another briefly in Cooperstown when the latter presided over the prayer of dedication during Hall of Fame weekend. However, they didn't really speak to one another until 2007. The Giants faced the Yankees in interleague play 45 years after the famous World Series and wanted to host a reunion. Richardson, who lives in South Carolina, initially declined the invitation but changed his mind after receiving a call from Alvin Dark, who managed the 1962 Giants, asking him to attend.

Richardson retired following the 1966 season after a very successful career spent entirely in a Yankees uniform and expresses his deep gratitude for the opportunity to play for New York. The Yankees have always deeply appreciated him and invited Richardson to old-timer's games until the travel became too cumbersome to navigate. His deep spirituality compelled a significant number of his former teammates to request that Richardson conduct their funerals, which he humbly has, including Mantle's. This request to travel to San Francisco was unique in the sense that it honored a moment and two men beyond just one organization, and Richardson values the nostalgia germinated in baseball's past. He himself has long remembered meeting Stan Musial as a 12-year-old kid and the meaningful autograph he received from him. Richardson expressed his deep appreciation to Musial for that gesture years later and patterned his own meticulous signature after the readable style of "The Man's."

McCovey and Richardson headlined a banquet the evening before they were scheduled to appear together at AT&T Park. McCovey had already arrived when Richardson walked into the room. Stretch was ready with a joke when the two competitors greeted one another. "I bet your hand is still hurting," he quipped. "You hit it hard," Richardson acknowledged. The following day, June 24, 2007, McCovey and Richardson appeared together on the field for the first-pitch ceremony while sporting the hats of their respective franchises, which they deeply loved and represented so well for so many years. The crowd cheered for both men. When speaking about that weekend, it's evident that Richardson is glad he heeded Dark's advice and attended it in spite of any initial misgivings. "I just enjoyed being with him, talking with him, and we had a good time," he says of Stretch.

Eleven years later, just a few months before McCovey's passing, Richardson discovered a large envelope amongst his mail. It had been sent to him from California. He opened it, and out slid a photograph. It was a snapshot of Willie Mac, who had signed the picture to Richardson with the inscription, "To my friend." Both knew Gaylord Perry well, and it was he who had provided Mac with Richardson's address. The package was completely unexpected, but its significance was not lost on the recipient. "I think he just chose, let's be friends," Richardson concludes.[1]

Acknowledgments

A project of this magnitude requires the help of many selfless individuals, who contribute both the time and resources to contribute in significant ways, and this book proved to be no exception. I am incredibly grateful to the dozens of people who assisted me over the past several years and hope that they find satisfaction in this story of two men who have left enduring impressions not only on the baseball diamond but also, more importantly on the communities in which they have lived for so many years.

My greatest of thanks to the two most instrumental people who made this project possible: Billy Williams and Allison McCovey. Williams recounted his life and career with me during a notable number of interviews. His incredibly sharp memory transported me to times gone by and the moments that defined his career and character. Williams's passion for baseball, sense of humor, and engaging storytelling always make for a memorable conversation. I have been very fortunate to have had the incredible experience of working with him. Thank you, Mr. Williams.

Allison McCovey partnered with me to explore her father's life, and working with her has been an honor for me. Although I regret beginning this book after Stretch passed away, one of the true joys of researching Willie's life was having her join in the interviews of people who knew him well. Many of those conversations she helped arrange. Her generosity, kindness, and curiosity made this a much better book. Thank you, Allison.

Each of the families was very generous with their time, and I am grateful for their insights. My deepest thanks to Billy's four daughters—Valarie Hill, Nina Williams, Julia Williams, and Sandra Simpson—who joined me for a group interview. The conversation permeated with their love for family. I am so humbled and appreciative of their participation, as I am for Jeran Simpson, who kindly coordinated that communication. The McCovey family benevolently met with me as well. A special thank-you goes out to Clauzell McCovey, Frances McCovcy, Dr. Carolyn Campbell, Tony McCovey, and Marissa Patrick. Special thanks to Marva Malone and Angelina Guillot.

Special appreciation goes to Karen Billingsley, who spent several hours speaking with me at a coffee shop and then a few more later on over the phone when I had a few follow-up questions. She is an incredible storyteller, and I am so grateful that she shared stories about life with Willie.

Both the Chicago Cubs and the San Francisco Giants organizations have been incredibly supportive of the project. I want to especially thank Crane Kenney, Jim Oboikowitch, Ed Hartig, and Pat Manaher in Chicago. They were all very generous with aiding this book. Special thanks to Colin Faulkner, on whose idea Billy Williams became part of this book. In San Francisco, Larry Baer, Mario Alioto, Sue Peterson, and Renel Brooks-Moon magnanimously shared special memories of Mac. Bobby Baksa and Missy Mikulecky kindly provided their time to facilitate interviews and assist with photographs.

The City of Mobile has been great to work with throughout my research. The Mobile Public Library and Local History and Genealogy center provided crucial primary sources for early chapters. Matt Anderson of the Civic and Cultural Affairs office was incredible. I sent him way too many e-mails, and he kindly answered every one of them. He's also responsible for the interviews with Cleon Jones and Mayor Sandy Stimpson. Many thanks, Matt. Also, much gratitude to Jones and Mayor Stimpson for their contributions to this story.

The National Baseball Hall of Fame remains an invaluable resource for all baseball historians. Thank you, Cassidy Lent, for providing helpful research files.

A very special thank-you to all the interviewees for this book. Your friendships with Willie McCovey and Billy Williams provided unique stories and insights about these two special people. Thank you Joe Amalfitano, Dusty Baker, Barry Bloom, Vida Blue, Barry Bonds, Corey Busch, Orlando Cepeda, Will Clark, John D'Acquisto, Rocky Dudum, Diane Dwyer, Bobby Evans, Darrell Evans, Tito Fuentes, Pat Gallagher, Brett Grill, Jack Hiatt, Randy Hundley, Jeff Idelson, Fergie Jenkins, Cleon Jones, Don Kessinger, Gene Locklear, Bob Lurie, Marty Lurie, Juan Marichal, Bill Madlock, Lincoln Mitchell, Ed Montague, Masanori Murakami, Mike Norris, Bill North, Ron Rapoport, Bobby Richardson, Jaime Rupert, Vicki Santo, Hal Silen, Lee Smith, Chris Speier, Terry Whitfield, and Joe Yick.

A special thank-you to my friends from the annual NINE Conference who read portions of this manuscript, gave advice, and offered encouragement: Willie Steele, Justin Turner, Rob Garratt, Steve Treder, and Yuriko Romer, who also kindly set up an interview with Mashi Murakami. Emma Visker and James Robertson also generously supplied feedback.

Several websites contributed mightily to researching stories and statistics. Thank you newspapers.com, retrosheet.com, and baseball-reference.com for the incredible information.

Rick Swig benevolently made his remarkable collection of Giants photographs available for this book, for which I am so grateful.

I want to share a special word of gratitude to Fred Mitchell and Irv Haag, both of whom worked with Williams on previous books from which I drew on to broaden the scope of this story. It was an honor for me to interview Mitchell, a legendary Chicago sportswriter, for this project and meet him at the 2023 SABR Conference in Chicago.

I have long held that John Dos Passos is the greatest of American writers. Let's debate. But, before we do, I want to acknowledge my appreciation for the way his work has deepened my love of language. I dedicate the "In the News" segments that appear before each section of this book to him and his influence on both my research methods and my writing.

My heartfelt appreciation to the team at Rowman & Littlefield, led by Christen Karniski, for supporting this project.

A special word of gratitude to God and my family. All I know is steadfast love and support from my parents. They encouraged me from a young age to pursue my interests. They were the first to read this book in its entirety, and it is very appropriately dedicated to them. Thank you, Reagan, for your love and encouragement for more than two decades. Your sacrifices make my writing possible. Stanley! I'm finished. Let's go run around outside for a while.

Notes

PREFACE

1. "Willie McCovey, Hall of Famer and Giants Legend, Dies at Age 80," October 31, 2018, https://www.espn.com/mlb/story/_/id/25138329/willie-mccovey-san-francisco-giants-legend-dies-80, accessed October 31, 2018.

CHAPTER 1

1. Willie McCovey as told to Marc Myers, "House Call," July 25, 2017, https://www.wsj.com/articles/hall-of-famer-willie-mccovey-on-his-loving-childhood-home-in-the-segregated-south-1500994846, accessed January 21, 2023.

2. Marva Malone and Angelina Guillot in discussion with the author, August 7, 2022.

3. William Warren Rogers, Robert David Ward, Leah Rawls Atkins, and Wayne Flynt, *Alabama: The History of a Deep South State* (Tuscaloosa: University of Alabama Press, 2018), 466.

4. James Hutton Lemly, *The Gulf, Mobile, and Ohio: A Railroad That Had to Expand or Expire* (Homewood, IL: Richard D. Irwin, 1953), 8.

5. Lemly, *The Gulf, Mobile, and Ohio*, 3, 4, 8.

6. Lemly, *The Gulf, Mobile, and Ohio*, 175.

7. Clauzell McCovey described his father's "wheelman" role in an interview with the author. Willie McCovey stated his father repaired its tracks.

8. Willie McCovey as told to Marc Myers, "House Call."

9. Marva Malone and Angelina Guillot in discussion with the author, August 7, 2022.

10. Marva Malone and Angelina Guillot in discussion with the author, August 7, 2022.

11. "How Whistler Got Its Name," Vertical File, "Cities—Whistler, History," Mobile Local History and Genealogy Center.

12. Johnnie Andrews, "Whistler Had Its Golden Era after the Civil War Ended," *North Mobile PEOPLE*, March 8, 1984; Vertical File, "Cities—Whistler, History."

13. Johnnie Andrews, "Whistler Had Its Golden Era after the Civil War Ended," *North Mobile PEOPLE*, March 8, 1984; Vertical File, "Cities—Whistler, History."

14. Jonnie Andrews, ed., *Whistler Town Directory* (Prichard, AL: Historic Prichard Development Commission, 1976), 2. Located at the Mobile Public Library: Local History and Genealogy, Vertical File, "Cities—Whistler, History."

15. Billy Williams (The HistoryMakers A2007.010), interviewed by Larry Crowe, January 16, 2007, The HistoryMakers Digital Archive, session 1, tape 2, story 1. Billy Williams describes his father's work as a stevedore in Mobile, Alabama.

16. Billy Williams in discussion with the author, May 6, 2022.

17. Billy Williams (The HistoryMakers A2007.010), interviewed by Larry Crowe, January 16, 2007, The HistoryMakers Digital Archive, session 1, tape 1, story 5. Billy Williams describes his father's family background.

18. Billy Williams in discussion with the author, January 10, 2023.

19. Hank Aaron with Lonnie Wheeler, *I Had a Hammer: The Hank Aaron Story* (New York: HarperTorch, 1991), 28.

20. Billy Williams in discussion with the author, May 6, 2022.

21. Clauzell McCovey in discussion with the author, March 15, 2022.

22. Billy Williams in discussion with the author, May 6, 2022.

23. Billy Williams, "Baseball Questionnaire," William J. Weiss, July 27, 1956. Billy Williams and Irv Haag, *Billy: The Classic Hitter* (Chicago: Rand McNally, 1974), 45–46.

24. For more information on Whitley and the rebuilding of MCTS, see Nick Tabor, *Africatown: America's Last Slave Ship and the Community It Created* (New York: St. Martin's Press, 2023), 137–40.

25. Nick Peters, *Willie McCovey: Stretch* (San Francisco: Woodford Publishing, 1988), 5.

26. Mike Mandel, *SF Giants: An Oral History* (self-published, 1979), 76.

CHAPTER 2

1. Clauzell McCovey in discussion with the author, March 15, 2022.

2. Cleon Jones in discussion with the author, July 26, 2022.

3. Arnold Hano, "The Arrival of Willie McCovey," *Sport* 47, no. 6 (June 1969), 66.

4. "As the Editor Views It," *Mobile Journal*, August 14, 1959, 1.

5. Adrian Burgos Jr., *Cuban Star: How One Negro-League Owner Changed the Face of Baseball* (New York: Hill & Wang, 2011), 250.

6. Clauzell McCovey in discussion with the author, March 15, 2022.

7. See Burgos, *Cuban Star*, 158, 183–85.

8. Hano, "The Arrival of Willie McCovey," 66.

9. Orlando Cepeda in discussion with the author, July 15, 2022.

10. Orlando Cepeda in discussion with the author, July 15, 2022.

11. "A Cool Cat Named McCovey," *Sports Illustrated*, August 17, 1959.

12. Carl T. Hall, "'Jack' Schwarz—Signed McCovey for Giants," February 24, 2005, https://www.sfgate.com/bayarea/article/Jack-Schwarz-signed-McCovey-for-Giants-2727802.php, accessed July 13, 2023.

13. Hall, "'Jack' Schwarz."

14. Hank Aaron with Lonnie Wheeler, *I Had a Hammer: The Hank Aaron Story* (New York: HarperTorch, 1991), 61–62.

15. Furman Bisher, "Another Giant Named Willie," *Atlanta Constitution*, May 23, 1955, 7.

16. "Sandersville, Douglas Split State Crown," *Macon Telegraph*, September 5, 1955, 6.

17. Dr. Carolyn Campbell in discussion with the author, July 13, 2023.

18. Billy Williams in discussion with the author, May 6, 2022.

19. Angela Levins, "Vintage Photos and 10 Fun Facts of Mobile's Baseball Past on the BayBears Opening Day," https://infoweb.newsbank.com/apps/news/document-view?p=WORLDNEWS&sort=_rank_%3AD&fld-base-0=alltext&maxresults=20&val-base-0=%22but%20Henry%20came%20around%20our%20house%20on%20Monday%20for%20his%20pay%22&docref=news/1549E74AB1303960, accessed June 26, 2023.

20. Aaron, *I Had a Hammer*, 32.

21. "Hank Never Forgets His Old Friend!," *Mobile Press Register*, July 12, 1970, 3-B.

22. "TUCKER," *Mobile Register*, May 11, 1972, 1-G.

23. Billy Williams in discussion with the author, May 6, 2022.

24. Billy Williams in discussion with the author, May 6, 2022.

25. Billy Williams in discussion with the author, May 6, 2022.

26. Larry Tye, *Satchel: The Life and Times of an American Legend* (New York: Random House, 2009), 20.

27. Tye, *Satchel*, 44.

28. Billy Williams in discussion with the author, May 6, 2022.

29. Billy Williams in discussion with the author, May 6, 2022.

30. Eddie Curran, "Laughter and Tears Fall on HOF Inductees," *Mobile Register*, April 6, 1990, C-1.

31. Billy Williams in discussion with the author, May 6, 2022.

32. Billy Williams Hall of Fame player file.

33. Billy Williams in discussion with the author, May 6, 2022.

34. Billy Williams and Irv Haag, *Billy: The Classic Hitter* (Chicago: Rand McNally, 1974), 52.

35. Billy Williams in discussion with the author, July 23, 2022.

36. Williams and Haag, *Billy*, 53.

37. Billy Williams in discussion with the author, May 6, 2022.

38. "Porter Reveals Pills Preceded Park Gunplay," *Daily Oklahoman*, February 18, 1958, 16.

39. Bill Casto, "Two State Witnesses Are Called at Trial of Ponca City Man," *Ponca City News*, February 17, 1958, 8.

40. Bill Casto, "Verdict Reached This Afternoon at Newkirk Court," *Ponca City News*, February 18, 1958, 10.

41. Casto, "Verdict Reached This Afternoon at Newkirk Court," 10.

42. Several newspaper accounts in the *Daily Oklahoman* claimed that Johnson took four pills, but other articles in the same newspaper stated that Johnson testified at trial that he took eight of them. See "Ponca City Porter Is Acquitted in Shooting," *Daily Oklahoman*, February 19, 2023, 8, for example of eight pills.

43. "Ponca City Porter Is Acquitted in Shooting," 8. Johnson testified that one of the Ardmore players, presumably Coy Smith, called him "an insulting name," which escalated their argument.

44. Jessica McKirahan, "News Staffer Calls Gunplay Firsthand," *Tonkawa News*, August 12, 1957, 1.

45. "Ardmore's Baseball Team Manager Shot before Crowd of 400," *Ponca City News*, August 9, 1957, 1.

46. Billy Williams in discussion with the author, May 6, 2022.

47. Casto, "Verdict Reached This Afternoon at Newkirk Court," 1.

48. Billy Williams in discussion with the author, May 6, 2022.

49. "Second Base, One Outfield Spot Remains to Be Decided Finally," *The Bee*, April 9, 1956, 10.

50. Lorin McMullen, "Eagles Have Secret and Murray's Got It," *Fort Worth Star-Telegram*, 19.

51. "Dallas Beats Sports Again," *Fort Worth Star-Telegram*, May 10, 1957, 36.

52. Joe Amalfitano in discussion with the author, May 4, 2022.

53. Willie McCovey Hall of Fame speech.

54. Joe Amalfitano in discussion with the author, May 4, 2022.

55. Robert Wilonsky, "Baseball Legend Willie McCovey Has Died; Here's a Look Back at His One Season in Dallas," https://www.dallasnews.com/opinion/commentary/2018/11/01/baseball-legend-willie-mccovey-has-died-here-s-a-look-back-at-his-one-season-in-dallas, accessed March 1, 2023.

56. Bill Rives, "The Sport Scene," *Dallas Morning News*, April 2, 1957.

57. Rives, "The Sport Scene."

58. Felipe Alou with Peter Kerasotis, *Alou: My Baseball Journey* (Lincoln: University of Nebraska Press, 2018), 64.

59. Alou, *Alou*, 55.

60. Alou, *Alou*, 55–56.

61. Juan Marichal in discussion with the author, July 23, 2022.

CHAPTER 3

1. Peter Golenbock, *Wrigleyville: A Magical History Tour of the Chicago Cubs* (New York: St. Martin's Press, 1996), 364.

2. Billy Williams and Irv Haag, *Billy: The Classic Hitter* (Chicago: Rand McNally, 1974), 30.

3. For example, see "San Antonio Regular Quits," *The Pantagraph*, June 19, 1959, 13.

4. Billy Williams with Fred Mitchell, *Billy Williams: My Sweet-Swinging Lifetime with the Cubs* (Chicago: Triumph, 2008), 5.

5. Buck O'Neil with Steve Wulf and David Conrads, *I Was Right on Time: My Journey from the Negro Leagues to the Majors* (New York: Fireside, 1996), 211.

6. Williams, *Billy Williams*, 9.

7. Williams, *Billy Williams*, 18.

8. Joe Posnanski, *The Soul of America: A Road Trip through Buck O'Neil's America* (New York: William Morrow, 2007), 86.

9. Ron Santo with Randy Minkoff, *Ron Santo: For Love of Ivy* (Chicago: Bonus Books, 1993), 129.

10. "Williams Returns to Missions," *San Antonio Express and News*, June 27, 1959, 18.

11. Williams and Haag, *Billy*, 59.

12. Bill Furlong, "Cub Farm System Doesn't Brighten Future," *Fort Worth Star-Telegram*, July 20, 1959, 18.

13. Prescott Sullivan, "Sullivan's Low Down," *San Francisco Examiner*, July 10, 1959, 33.

14. Orlando Cepeda in discussion with the author, July 15, 2022.

15. Curley Grieve, "Sports Parade," *San Francisco Examiner*, August 6, 1959, 31.

16. John Shea, "Willie McCovey: Anniversary Memories," *San Francisco Chronicle*, July 8, 2009.

17. Curley Grieve, "McCovey: Hero of New Saga," *San Francisco Examiner*, August 7, 1959, 35.

18. Arnold Hano, "The Arrival of Willie McCovey," *Sport* 47, no. 6, 67, 1969.

19. Curley Grieve, "SF Wastes Hurling," *San Francisco Examiner*, July 30, 1959, 24.

20. Mike Murphy with Chris Haft, *From the Stick to the Cove: My Six Decades with the San Francisco Giants* (Chicago: Triumph, 2020), 54.

21. Mike Norris in discussion with the author, June 5, 2023.

22. Mike Norris in discussion with the author, June 5, 2023.

23. See https://www.baseball-reference.com/blog/archives/5741.html, accessed June 10, 2023.

24. Curley Grieve, "Never Forget It: A Great Day for Rookie," *San Francisco Examiner*, July 31, 1959, 20.

25. Curley Grieve, "Sensational Debut: Grieve: McCovey's Day," *San Francisco Examiner*, July 31, 1959, 23.

26. "Mays Adoption Gets Final OK from Court," *San Francisco Examiner*, July 31, 1959, 23.

27. Murphy, *From the Stick to the Cove*, 55.

28. Curley Grieve, "Grieve: Willie Mac Gives Scribes Eyeful," *San Francisco Examiner*, August 1, 1959, 19.

29. Grieve, "Grieve," 19.

30. Curley Grieve, "Willie Mc Gets Standing Ovation for Memorable HR," *San Francisco Examiner*, August 3, 1959, 27.

31. Grieve, "Grieve," 19.

32. Hano, "The Arrival of Willie McCovey," 68.

33. "A Cool Cat Named McCovey," *Sports Illustrated*, August 17, 1959.

34. Grieve, "Sensational Debut," 23.

35. Curley Grieve, "Is Willie Real? Rivals Gripe," *San Francisco Examiner*, August 1, 1959, 17.

36. "Willie McCovey, Movie Fan, Big Help for Coast Giants," *The Southeast Missourian*, August 25, 1959, 5.

37. Grieve, "Sports Parade," 27.

38. Dick Nolan, "The City," *San Francisco Examiner*, August 3, 1959, 21.

39. Orlando Cepeda in discussion with the author, July 15, 2022.

40. Grieve, "Sensational Debut," 23.

41. Orlando Cepeda with Herb Fagen, *Baby Bull: From Hardball to Hard Time and Back* (Dallas: Taylor Publishing, 1998), 69. For more of Cepeda's thoughts on moving to third base, see Ron Fimrite, "Orlando Cepeda and San Francisco Fell in Love in 1958: The Romance Wavered but Never Died," *Sports Illustrated*, October 16, 1991, https://vault.si.com/vault/1991/10/16/the-heart-of-a-giant-orlando-cepeda-and-san-francisco-fell-in-love-in-1958-the-romance-wavered-but-never-died, accessed June 8, 2023.

42. Mike Norris in discussion with the author, June 5, 2023.

43. Sid Ziff, "The Inside Track," *Los Angeles Mirror*, August 29, 1959, 9.

44. Jaqueline Chauhan, "Remembering the Booker T. Washington Hotel," https://www.reimaginerpe.org/20-2/chauhan, accessed June 11, 2023. See also "Maya Angelou, Streetcar Conductor: The Full Story," https://www.streetcar.org/maya-angelou-streetcar-conductor-the-full-story, accessed June 13, 2023.

45. Williams, *Billy*, 60.

46. Billy Williams in discussion with the author, May 6, 2022.

47. Williams, *Billy Williams*, 17.

48. Paul Sullivan, "Clubhouse Legend: 'King of Wrigley Field,'" *Chicago Tribune*, June 27, 2018, 3-1.

49. Williams, *Billy*, 62.

50. Williams, *Billy*, 62–63.

51. Williams, *Billy*, 62.

52. Richard Dozer, "Cubs Win, 4–2, to End 7 Game Losing String," *Chicago Tribune*, August 7, 1959, 46.

53. Allen Lewis, "Cubs Win after Phillie Miscue in 8th, 4–2," *Philadelphia Inquirer*, August 7, 1959, 28.

54. Billy Williams in discussion with the author, May 6, 2022.

55. Howard Bryant, *The Last Hero: A Life of Henry Aaron* (New York: Anchor Books, 2011), xi.

56. Walter Judge, "Now Needs Agent: McCovey NL '59 Rookie," *San Francisco Examiner*, November 18, 1959, 39.

57. Judge, "Now Needs Agent," 41.

58. Curley Grieve, "It Looked Like a Pop Fly . . . Zoom!," *San Francisco Examiner*, June 13, 1960, 59.

59. Hano, "The Arrival of Willie McCovey," 68.

CHAPTER 4

1. Dick Nolan, "The City," *San Francisco Examiner*, February 22, 1960, 29.

2. Curley Grieve, "McCovey's Batting Slump Causing Little Concern," *San Francisco Examiner*, March 26, 1960, 35.

3. Stephanie Salter, "McCovey Memories: Quiet Power," *San Francisco Examiner*, July 1, 1980, 55.

4. Art Rosenbaum and Bob Stevens, *The Giants of San Francisco* (New York: Coward-McCann, 1963), 147.

5. Billy Williams and Irv Haag, *Billy: The Classic Hitter* (Chicago: Rand McNally, 1974), 66.

6. Edward Prell, "Boudreau 'Sift' Bolsters Cubs," *Chicago Tribune*, July 24, 1960, 80.

7. "Too Big! Move the Fences In for More HRs: Musial," *San Francisco Examiner*, April 12, 1960, 49.

8. Clint Mosher, "Nixon Stars on Sidelines, Praises Giants Play," *San Francisco Examiner*, April 13, 1960, 7.

9. Curley Grieve, "Gilliam Took Siesta—Alert Mike Cashed In," *San Francisco Examiner*, April 21, 1960, 45.

10. Nolan, "The City," 29. See also Karen Billingsley interview with the author, April 19, 2022.

11. Prescott Sullivan, "The Low Down," *San Francisco Examiner*, May 2, 1960, 61.

12. Walter Judge, "Giants' Curfew Violators Caught," *San Francisco Examiner*, July 4, 1969, 49.

13. Walter Judge, "Sheehan Is 'In' for Rest of '60," *San Francisco Examiner*, July 6, 1960, 43.

14. Orlando Cepeda in discussion with the author, July 15, 2022.

15. Curly Grieve, "Sports Parade," *San Francisco Examiner*, July 25, 1960, 51.

16. George Vecsey, "McCovey's Toughest Opponent," *New York Times*, January 10, 1986, A19.

17. Nolan, "The City," 27.

18. Roy Terrell, "Old Pals in a Cold Wind," *Sports Illustrated* 13, no. 13 (1960), 83.

19. "Leo? Not This Season," *San Francisco Examiner*, July 20, 1960, 51.

20. Terrell, "Old Pals in a Cold Wind," 80–89.

21. Edward Prell, "Frank Thomas Holds Key to Career of Three Cubs," *Chicago Tribune*, March 12, 1961, 40.

22. Peter Golenbock, *Wrigleyville: A Magical History Tour of the Chicago Cubs* (New York: St. Martin's Press, 1996), 369.

23. Ron Rapoport, *Let's Play Two: The Legend of Mr. Cub, the Life of Ernie Banks* (New York: Hachette, 2019), 65, 170.

24. Rapoport, *Let's Play Two.* See also Billy Williams in discussion with the author, July 23, 2022.

25. Jim McGee, "Remembering McCovey . . . the Biggest Giant," *San Francisco Examiner*, June 30, 1980, 59.

26. Steven Treder, *Forty Years a Giant: The Life of Horace Stoneham* (Lincoln: University of Nebraska Press, 2021), 241.

27. Cepeda had 263 more plate appearances than McCovey. Mays had 285 more plate appearances than McCovey. Source: Baseball-Reference.com.

28. See "Dark Says: McCovey's Defense OK," *San Francisco Examiner*, March 25, 1961, 37, and "Strategy Remains the Same," *San Francisco Examiner*, April 21, 1961, 61.

29. Grieve, "Sports Parade," 57.

30. See Curley Grieve, "Players, Umpires Boil—But KO'd Hoak Calm," *San Francisco Examiner*, July 14, 1961, 52. See also Charles Einstein, "Top of the Town," *San Francisco Examiner*, July 15, 1961, 35.

31. Orlando Cepeda in discussion with the author, July 15, 2022.

32. Don Selby, "'Series Just Like Playing the Mets,'" *San Francisco Examiner*, October 6, 1962, 43.

33. "Yankees Sing It: 'Bye, Bye, Baby,'" *San Francisco Examiner*, October 17, 1962, 54.

34. Scott Fowler, "Former Yankees Great Bobby Richardson Opens Up on Mantle, Maris and Why He Retired at 31," *Charlotte Observer*, https://www.charlotteobserver.com/sports/sports-legends/article273683250.html, accessed August 9, 2023.

35. Rosenbaum and Stevens, *The Giants of San Francisco*, 192.

36. Felipe Alou with Peter Karasotis, *Alou: My Baseball Journey* (Lincoln: University of Nebraska Press, 2018), 121.

37. Walt Radke, "The Moment of Decision in the Ninth," *San Francisco Examiner*," October 17, 1962, 55.

38. "Q & A with Hall of Famer Willie McCovey," https://baseballhall.org/discover-more/stories/baseball-history/q-and-a-willie-mccovey, accessed August 19, 2023.

39. "Yankees Sing It," 54.

40. See Alou, *Alou*, 122. See also Rosenbaum and Stevens, *The Giants of San Francisco*, 192.

41. Corey Busch in discussion with the author, March 10, 2022. Bob Stevens relayed his conversation with Bobby Richardson to former Giants executive Corey Busch.

42. Len Pasculli, "Bobby Richardson," https://sabr.org/bioproj/person/bobby-richardson, accessed August 19, 2023.

43. Charles M. Schulz *Peanuts* strip, *Evening World-Herald* (Omaha, NE), December 22, 1962, 11; Charles M. Schultz, *Peanuts* strip, *Evening World-Herald* (Omaha, NE), January 28, 1963, 11.

CHAPTER 5

1. Robert Creamer, "Big Willie's Private War with Cousin Don," *Sports Illustrated*, July 1, 1963, https://vault.si.com/vault/1963/07/01/big-willies-private-war -with-cousin-don, accessed July 6, 2023.

2. Juan Marichal in discussion with the author, July 23, 2022.

3. Jack Hiatt in discussion with the author, October 7, 2022.

4. Ross Newhan, "Dodgers Feel the Pain of Death Again: Reaction: Fiery Drysdale Is Remembered as One of the 'Last of the Angry Pitchers,'" *Los Angeles Times*, July 4, 1993, https://www.latimes.com/archives/la-xpm-1993-07-04-sp-10094-story .html, accessed October 6, 2023.

5. Bud Poliquin, "A Little Rain Can't Prevent McCovey from Shining," *San Diego Evening Tribune*, August 4, 1986, 50.

6. Nick Peters, *Willie McCovey: Stretch* (San Francisco: Woodford Publishing, 1988), 16.

7. Mike Mandel, *SF Giants: An Oral History* (self-published, 1979), 76.

8. Fred Claire, "The Claire View: The Sad Story of Willie McCovey," *Progress-Bulletin* (Pomona, CA), June 9, 1964, 16.

9. Juan Marichal in discussion with the author, July 23, 2022.

10. Orlando Cepeda in discussion with the author, July 15, 2022.

11. Joe Amalfitano in discussion with the author, May 4, 2022.

12. Juan Marichal in discussion with the author, July 23, 2022.

13. Rocky Dudum in discussion with the author, July 14, 2022.

14. Jack Hiatt in discussion with the author, October 7, 2022.

15. Orlando Cepeda in discussion with the author, July 15, 2022.

16. Karen Billingsley in discussion with the author, April 19, 2022.

17. Karen Billingsley in discussion with the author, April 19, 2022.

18. Hal Silen in discussion with the author, May 23, 2022. See also "Divorce Suit Is Filed by McCovey," *Modesto Bee*, December 23, 1965, 10.

19. Billy Williams in discussion with the author, May 6, 2022.

20. Don Kessinger in discussion with the author, July 10, 2023.

21. Charles Maher, "Even Koufax Admits Game 'Nearly Perfect,'" *Los Angeles Times*, September 10, 1965, 48.

22. Richard Dozer, "North Siders Get 3 from Philadelphia," *Chicago Tribune*, April 22, 1966, 65.

23. Randy Hundley in discussion with the author, November 17, 2022.

24. Billy Williams in discussion with the author, June 13, 2023.

25. Juan Marichal in discussion with the author, July 22, 2022.

26. Jack Hiatt in discussion with the author, October 7, 2022.

27. Ed Montague in discussion with the author, February 28, 2023.

28. Juan Marichal in discussion with the author, July 22, 2022.

29. Orlando Cepeda in discussion with the author, July 15, 2022.

30. Ali Cepeda in discussion with the author, July 15, 2022.

31. Jack Hiatt in discussion with the author, October 7, 2022.

32. "San Francisco Giants vs. St. Louis Cardinals, June 8, 1962—Baseball Radio Broadcast," May 25, 2013, https://www.youtube.com/watch?v=1Ss9E2L1IMI, accessed March 12, 2024.

33. Mike Lupica, "'I Can Still Hear That Sound,' MLB's Loudest HR?," January 10, 2022, https://www.mlb.com/news/willie-mccovey-s-hardest-hit-home-run, accessed June 15, 2023.

34. Jack Haney, "Surprise Tactics Please McCovey," *San Mateo Times*, September 7, 1966, 43.

35. Mandel, *SF Giants*, 90.

36. Tito Fuentes in discussion with the author, February 15, 2023.

37. Ferguson Jenkins in discussion with the author, March 15, 2023.

38. Ferguson Jenkins in discussion with the author, March 15, 2023.

39. Ferguson Jenkins in discussion with the author, March 15, 2023.

40. "Facts on Rioting," *Chicago Tribune*, April 8, 1968, 7.

41. Randy Hundley in discussion with the author, November 17, 2022.

42. Randy Hundley in discussion with the author, November 17, 2022.

43. Arnold Hano, "The Arrival of Willie McCovey," *Sport*, Vol. 47, no. 6, 64.

44. Hano, "The Arrival of Willie McCovey," 64.

45. Mandel, *SF Giants*, 71.

CHAPTER 6

1. Billy Libby, "Why They Call Ernie Banks Baseball's Beautiful Man," *Sport* 47, no. 6, 54.

2. George Langford, "Record 40,796 See Cubs Win in 11th," *Chicago Tribune*, April 9, 1969, 74.

3. David Condon, "In the Wake of the News . . . ," *Chicago Tribune*, April 12, 1969, 65.

4. Condon, "In the Wake of the News . . . ," 65.

5. Jack Hanley, "Giants Will Rehire Physical Therapist," *Daily Independent Journal* (San Rafael, CA), January 31, 1969, 35.

6. Dick O'Connor, "Ten Years Make Big Change in Giants' Willie McCovey," *The Peninsula Times Tribune* (Palo Alto, CA), November 21, 1969, 28. McCovey told the press after the season, "But I wasn't going to sign this spring until the pension thing was settled. I told the Players Association that I wouldn't sign."

7. Charlie Bevis, "A Home Run by Any Measure: The Baseball Players' Pension Plan," https://sabr.org/research/article/a-home-run-by-any-measure-the-baseball-players-pension-plan/#:~:text=The%20boycott%20of%20the%20spring,four%20years%20rather%20than%20five, accessed October 17, 2023.

8. "Mays Draws Applause as Leadoff Man," *Chicago Tribune*, March 11, 1969, 52.

9. Blaine Newnham, "McCovey Seeking Security," *Oakland Tribune*, March 11, 1969, 33.

10. "McCovey Gets 2-Year, 85G Contract," *The Press Democrat* (Santa Rosa, CA), March 14, 1969, 11. See also "McCovey Inks Pact," *The Argus* (Fremont, CA), March 14, 1969, 13.

11. Don Drysdale with Bob Verdi, *Once a Bum, Always a Dodger* (New York: St. Martin's Press, 1990), 197.

12. Art Spander, "McCovey's Cousin," *San Francisco Examiner*, January 3, 1986, 67.

13. Spander, "McCovey's Cousin," 67.

14. Fergie Jenkins in discussion with the author, March 15, 2023.

15. Randy Hundley in discussion with the author, November 17, 2022.

16. Fergie Jenkins in discussion with the author, March 15, 2023.

17. "Cubs Legend Billy Williams on Reaching 1000 Games Played Consecutively," March 25, 2010, https://www.youtube.com/watch?v=gXa5NB18-6A, accessed March 12, 2024.

18. George Langford, "Cubs Hail Billy's Day with Hit Show," *Chicago Tribune*, June 30, 1969, 85.

19. Valarie Hill, Nina Williams, Julia Williams, and Sandra Simpson in discussion with the author, April 12, 2022.

20. George Langford, "'Cubs Kicked Hell Out of Us,'" *Chicago Tribune*, June 30, 1969, 86.

21. Langford, "'Cubs Kicked Hell Out of Us,'" 86.

22. Cleon Jones in discussion with the author, July 26, 2022.

23. Cleon Jones in discussion with the author, July 26, 2022.

24. Chris Haft, "The Legend Who Dominated D.C.'s last ASG," July 16, 2018, https://www.mlb.com/news/how-mccovey-dominated-washington-s-last-asg-c286189744, accessed October 10, 2023.

25. "'Gee, You Look Great,' Nixon Tells 3 Returning Astronauts," *Chicago Tribune*, July 25, 1969, 4.

26. "It's Year of the Big Bat," *San Francisco Examiner*, July 24, 1969, 58.

27. "Veep Joins Praise for McCovey," *San Francisco Examiner*, July 24, 1969, 58.

28. "Veep Joins Praise for McCovey," 58.

29. Robert Boyle, "Leo's Bums Rap for the Cubs," *Sports Illustrated*, June 30, 1969, https://vault.si.com/vault/1969/06/30/leos-bums-rap-for-the-cubs, accessed October 10, 2023.

30. Wayne Minshew, "It's 0-0-0! Holtzman No-Hits Braves," *Atlanta Constitution*, August 20, 1969, 1-C.

31. Wayne Minshew, "Another Sandy Koufax," *Atlanta Constitution*, August 20, 1969, 1-C.

32. Minshew, "Another Sandy Koufax," 1-C.

33. "Sad" Sam Jones of the New York Yankees tossed a no-hit, no-strikeout game against the Philadelphia A's at Shibe Park on September 4, 1923.

34. Minshew, "It's 0-0-0! Holtzman No-Hits Braves," 5-C.

35. Don Kessinger in discussion with the author, July 10, 2023.

36. Don Kessinger in discussion with the author, July 10, 2023.

37. Peter Golenbock, *Wrigleyville: A Magical History Tour of the Chicago Cubs* (New York: St. Martin's Press, 1996), 412.

38. Jerome Holtzman, "No Holler Guy, Williams Still Led," *Chicago Tribune*, July 27, 1987, 23.

39. Don Kessinger in discussion with the author, July 10, 2023.

40. Don Kessinger in discussion with the author, July 10, 2023.

41. Roger Williams, "Stoneham's 1969 Review," *San Francisco Examiner*, October 5, 1969, 50.

42. James K. McGee, "McCovey Is Named MVP," *San Francisco Examiner*, November 20, 1969, 39, 41.

43. Sonny Amato, "The Chat," *Washington Post*, https://www.washingtonpost.com/archive/sports/2006/08/07/thechat/745b55c0-e720-4dba-a39f-94fc9c399ebe, accessed October 18, 2023.

44. Richard Dozer, "1,000 Fans Have Gem of a Time at Diamond Dinner," *Chicago Tribune*, January 12, 1970, 64.

45. Cleon Jones in discussion with the author, July 26, 2022.

46. Cleon Jones in discussion with the author, July 26, 2022.

47. Cleon Jones in discussion with the author, July 26, 2022.

CHAPTER 7

1. Rocky Dudum in conversation with the author, July 14, 2022.

2. Rob Garratt, *Home Team: The Turbulent History of the San Francisco Giants* (Lincoln: University of Nebraska Press, 2017), 82.

3. James K. McGee, "Brief Talk, Big Payoff for McCovey," *San Francisco Examiner*, January 16, 1970, 47.

4. McGee, "Brief Talk, Big Payoff for McCovey," 47.

5. "M'Covey Eye Responds to Treatment," *Sacramento Bee*, March 15, 1970, 71.

6. Steve Treder, *Forty Years a Giant: The Life of Horace Stoneham* (Lincoln: University of Nebraska Press, 2021), 349–50.

7. There is an extensive amount of media coverage concerning McCovey's knee and eye problems during spring training of 1970. Cited here is an article written by Jim McGee, who covered the Giants for the *San Francisco Examiner*, that notes the conversation between Dr. Kimura and Dr. Kerlan. One mystery that remains unsolved is exactly when—and for how many days—McCovey took the medication for his knee. It is clear, however, that the pain became so intense that McCovey felt it necessary to take. Jim McGee, "McCovey OK for Japan Trip," *San Francisco Examiner*, March 17, 1970, 49.

8. Tito Fuentes in discussion with the author, February 15, 2023.

9. Roger Williams, "The Changing Game," *San Francisco Examiner*, April 8, 1970, 60.

10. Charlie Vascellaro, "'The Inequities Still Are Large': A Conversation with Reggie Jackson on Baseball and Race," October 6, 2021, https://globalsportmatters

.com/opinion/2021/10/06/inequities-still-large-q-and-a-reggie-jackson-baseball-race, accessed June 1, 2023.

11. Ron Bergman, "Reggie Arrives, Still Unsigned," *Oakland Tribune*, February 23, 1970, 29.

12. Billy Williams in discussion with the author, June 13, 2023.

13. Bob Logan, "Cubs 1/2 Game Out! Mets Today," *Chicago Tribune*, September 4, 1970, 49, 52.

14. Joe Amalfitano in discussion with the author, May 4, 2022.

15. Don Kessinger in discussion with the author, July 10, 2023.

16. Jim Murray, "Steady Billy Williams Left His Burden in Dugout," *Tampa Bay Times*, April 15, 1971, 47. Murray wrote for the *Los Angeles Times*. This column was syndicated.

17. Billy Williams, "Baseball Questionnaire," William J. Weiss, July 27, 1956; Billy Williams and Irv Haag, *Billy: The Classic Hitter* (Chicago: Rand McNally, 1974), 141.

18. "St. Louis Cardinals Bob Gibson and Chicago Cubs Billy Williams Interview (Feb. 6, 1971)," October 24, 2022, https://www.youtube.com/watch?v=ZnbYbxqtX4k, accessed. July 15, 2023.

19. George Langford, "Williams Signs $100,000 Pact," *Chicago Tribune*, February 26, 1971, 53.

20. Billy Williams in discussion with the author, May 6, 2022.

21. Joe Amalfitano in discussion with the author, May 4, 2022.

22. Joe Amalfitano in discussion with the author, May 4, 2022.

23. Billy Williams in discussion with the author, May 6, 2022.

24. George Langford, "41,121 See Cubs Win Opener in 10, 2–1," *Chicago Tribune*, April 7, 1971, 57.

25. Billy Williams in discussion with the author, May 6, 2022.

26. Jack Hiatt in discussion with the author, October 7, 2022.

27. Randy Hundley in discussion with the author, November 17, 2022.

28. Don Kessinger in discussion with the author, July 10, 2023.

29. Bill North in discussion with the author, June 14, 2023.

30. Bill North in discussion with the author, June 14, 2023.

31. "The Wrigley Papers," *Chicago Tribune*, September 4, 1971, 45.

32. Williams and Haag, *Billy*, 150.

33. Barry Bonds in discussion with the author, September 23, 2023.

34. Barry Bonds in discussion with the author, September 23, 2023.

35. Chris Haft, "The Legend Who Dominated D.C.'s Last ASG," July 16, 2018, https://www.mlb.com/news/how-mccovey-dominated-washington-s-last-asg-c286189744, accessed November 11, 2023.

36. Bucky Walter, "Perry Strong-Arms Bucs, 5–4," *San Francisco Examiner*, October 3, 1971, 52.

37. Jaime Rupert in discussion with the author, July 8, 2022.

38. Bucky Walter, "Year of the Fox Ends on Downbeat," *San Francisco Examiner*, October 7, 1971, 57–58.

39. Walter, "Year of the Fox Ends on Downbeat," 57–58.

40. Valarie Hill, Nina Williams, Julia Williams, and Sandra Simpson in discussion with the author, April 12, 2022.
41. Bill North in discussion with the author, June 14, 2023.
42. Richard Dozer, "Relaxed Williams Helps Cubs Split," *Chicago Tribune*, July 12, 1972, 77.
43. Barry McDermott, "Bend an Ear to Billy's Music," *Sports Illustrated* 39, no. 4, 31.
44. Richard Dozer, "Baseball under the Glass," *Chicago Tribune*, November 10, 1972, 61.
45. Raymond J. Vince, "Sound Off, Sports Fans," *Chicago Tribune*, November 10, 1972, 61. Vince's letter to the editor is one of a number published by the newspaper in this featured section.
46. John D'Acquisto in discussion with the author, July 26, 2023.
47. John D'Acquisto in discussion with the author, July 26, 2023.
48. John D'Acquisto in discussion with the author, July 26, 2023.

CHAPTER 8

1. Buzzie Bavasi with John Strege, *Off the Record* (Chicago: Contemporary Books, 1987), 152.
2. Bucky Walter, "Bradley's Salute: McCovey 'Fantastic,'" *San Francisco Examiner*, April 13, 1973, 61.
3. Jaime Rupert in discussion with the author, July 8, 2022.
4. Willie McCovey, as told to William Flynn, "Willie McCovey: In His Own Words," *San Francisco Examiner*, July 4, 1980, 49.
5. Rocky Dudum in discussion with the author, July 14, 2022.
6. Bavasi, *Off the Record*, 148.
7. "McCovey's Not Pleased with Result," *San Diego Evening Tribune*, December 7, 1973, 78 (D4).
8. Phil Collier, "City, Kroc OK Stadium Lease; Padres to Stay," *San Diego Union*, January 26, 1974, 35 (C1).
9. Collier, "City, Kroc OK Stadium Lease," 35 (C1).
10. Peter Bavasi to Jan Willis, letter in the possession of the author. McCovey's lawyer Hal Silen kept a copy of this letter written by Bavasi to Willis, the Padres' controller. In it, Bavasi states, "The alteration in the deferment schedule as described above applies only to Willie's 1974 contract calling for $115,000.00."
11. Phil Collier, "Padres Sign McCovey," *San Diego Union*, February 2, 1974, 25.
12. Jack Murphy, "McNamara's Band Playing by Ear," *San Diego Union*, March 1, 1974, 32.
13. Wells Twombly reported the dollar amount of Willie McCovey's salary in his column. Wells Twombly, "Horace Made the Best Deal He Could," *San Francisco Examiner*, October 28, 1973, 32 (C2).

14. Jack Murphy, "Murphy Exemplifies Things to Come," *San Diego Union*, February 28, 1974, 62.

15. Steven Treder, *Forty Years a Giant: The Life of Horace Stoneham* (Lincoln: University of Nebraska Press, 2021), 393–94.

16. Bucky Walter, "McCovey Traded Away by Giants as 49ers' Brodie Calls It Quits," *San Francisco Examiner*, October 26, 1973, 53.

17. Twombly, "Horace Made the Best Deal He Could."

18. Bavasi to McCovey, October 25, 1973.

19. Twombly, "Horace Made the Best Deal He Could."

20. Mitch Chortkoff, "McCovey, Alou, Money on Hand Somehow," *San Diego Evening Tribune*, October 26, 1973, 100 (D6).

21. Murphy, "McNamara's Band Playing by Ear."

22. Ray Kroc with Robert Anderson, *Grinding It Out: The Making of McDonald's* (New York: St. Martin's Paperbacks, 1987), 45.

23. Lisa Napoli, *Ray & Joan: The Man Who Made the McDonald's Fortune and the Woman Who Gave It All Away* (New York: Dutton, 2016), 141–42. There are conflicting accounts of the exact sequence of events involving Ray Kroc's comments that night, but they are all very similar. I selected this version because the Krocs' biographer, Lisa Napoli, received it from the public address announcer, John DeMott, admittedly during an interview that took place 40 years after the scene occurred.

24. Kroc, *Grinding It Out*, 182.

25. Phil Collier, "Kroc Rips Club on P.A. as Astros Romp, 9–5," *San Diego Union*, April 10, 1974, 32 (C1).

26. Collier, "Kroc Rips Club on P.A. as Astros Romp, 9–5," 37 (C6).

27. Collier, "Kroc Rips Club on P.A. as Astros Romp, 9–5," 37 (C6).

28. "Readers' Viewpoint," *San Diego Union*, April 13, 1974, 26. This quote comes from a letter written by Gordon Williams of San Diego.

29. "Readers' Viewpoint." This quote comes from a letter written by Clell Wharton of San Diego.

30. Kroc, *Grinding It Out*, 185.

31. Kroc, *Grinding It Out*, 185. The full epigraph reads, "He searches through his competitors' garbage cans—he scolds his San Diego *Padres* over the P.A. system—he either enchants or antagonizes everyone he meets. But even his enemies agree there are three things Ray Kroc does damned well: sell hamburgers, make money, and tell stories."

32. Bavasi, *Off the Record*, 155.

33. Roger Williams, "McCovey Expects to Regain HR Touch," *San Francisco Examiner*, May 18, 1974, 28.

34. Bucky Walter, "Padres End Famine at Giants' Expense," *San Francisco Examiner*, April 13, 1974, 27.

35. Jack Murphy, "He's Not Whistling but Mac Holds Hope," *San Diego Union*, April 23, 1974, 25.

36. Murphy, "He's Not Whistling but Mac Holds Hope."

37. Phil Collier, "McCovey Laughs, Thinks of Future," *San Diego Union*, May 4, 1974, 38.

38. Joe Hamelin, "Gum Card Mirrors Winfield's Rapid Rise, *San Diego Union,* April 28, 1974, 117.

39. John Shea, "Winfield's Original Mentor/McCovey Taught Young Padre Well," June 3, 2001, https://www.sfgate.com/sports/article/Winfield-s-original-mentor-McCovey-taught-young-3315001.php, accessed July 13, 2023.

40. "Dave Winfield Delivers Hall of Fame Induction Speech," December 11, 2013, https://www.youtube.com/watch?v=8E0_nlijk4E, accessed September 15, 2023.

41. Williams, "McCovey Expects to Regain HR Touch."

42. Roger Williams, "How Willie Mac Helped Make Lowly Padres a Big Draw," *San Francisco Examiner*, May 17, 1954, 54.

43. Steve Bisheff, "McCovey Who? Caldwell Emerges as S.F. Ace," *San Diego Evening Tribune*, May 17, 1954, 83.

44. Williams, "How Willie Mac Helped Make Lowly Padres a Big Draw."

45. Roger Williams, "Matthews Fights Fence to Save Giants," *San Francisco Examiner*, May 19, 1974, 40.

46. "1972 San Diego Padres Statistics," https://www.baseball-reference.com/teams/SDP/1972.shtml, accessed February 17, 2022.

47. Rocky Dudum in discussion with the author, July 14, 2022.

48. Hal Silen in discussion with the author, June 9, 2023. See also Sam Whiting, "Jerry Seltzer, Co-founder of BASS Tickets and Promoter of Roller Derby, Dies at 87," https://datebook.sfchronicle.com/entertainment/jerry-seltzer-co-founder-of-bass-tickets-and-promoter-of-roller-derby-dies-at-87, accessed July 24, 2023.

49. Hal Silen in discussion with author, June 9, 2023.

50. Hal Silen in discussion with author, June 9, 2023.

51. John Husar, "Our Man in Motion," *Chicago Tribune*, May 3, 1974, 65.

52. Husar, "Our Man in Motion," 65.

53. Cooper Rollow, "'Billy the Classic Hitter' on Way to the Stores," *Chicago Tribune*, June 2, 1974, 83.

54. Cooper Rollow, "Reaction to Kroc's Outburst Surprisingly Mixed," *Chicago Tribune*, April 14, 1974, 59.

55. Husar, "Our Man in Motion," 65.

56. David Condon, "In the Wake of the News," *Chicago Tribune*, July 4, 1976, 63.

57. Robert Markus, "Cubs Already Mapping Spring Drills," *Chicago Tribune*, September 26, 1974, 81.

58. Markus, "Cubs Already Mapping Spring Drills," 81.

CHAPTER 9

1. Robert Markus, "Talent Rich Athletics Get Richer Off Poor Cubs," *Chicago Tribune*, October 25, 1974, 47.

2. Billy Williams in discussion with the author, June 13, 2023.

3. Billy Williams in discussion with the author, June 13, 2023.

4. Billy Williams in discussion with the author, June 13, 2023.

5. Richard Dozer, "Bidding War Came Too Late for Williams," *Chicago Tribune*, November 10, 1976, 62.

6. Billy Williams in discussion with the author, June 13, 2023.

7. Ron Bergman, "Boxing Glove Not Needed by A's New DH," *Oakland Tribune*, March 3, 1975, 29.

8. Ron Bergman, "Hunter Awaits Offers," *Oakland Tribune*, December 17, 1974, 36.

9. Dave Newhouse, "Dark Says A's Facing Biggest Challenge," *Oakland Tribune*, February 9, 1975, 35.

10. Billy Williams with Fred Mitchell, *Billy Williams: My Sweet-Swinging Lifetime with the Cubs* (Chicago: Triumph Books, 2008), 161.

11. Billy Williams in discussion with the author, June 13, 2023.

12. Mike Norris in discussion with the author, July 16, 2023.

13. Ron Bergman, "A's Still Exciting, Winning, Angry," *Oakland Tribune*, April 13, 1975, 23.

14. Ferguson Jenkins in discussion with the author, March 15, 2023.

15. Ferguson Jenkins in discussion with the author, March 15, 2023.

16. Billy Williams in discussion with the author, June 13, 2023.

17. Ron Bergman, "Claudell's Career Uncertain," *Oakland Tribune*, July 13, 1975, 25.

18. Ed Levitt, "It Wasn't All Baseball," *Oakland Tribune*, September 23, 1975, 35.

19. Ron Bergman, "At Last! A's Clinch Sweetest Title," *Oakland Tribune*, September 25, 1975, 39.

20. Ed Levitt, "Bubbles and the Stork," *Oakland Tribune*, September 26, 1975, 39.

21. "1975 San Diego Padres Statistics," https://www.baseball-reference.com /teams/SDP/1975.shtml, accessed February 17, 2022.

22. "Reds: Playoffs Ahead," *Ledger-Enquirer* (GA), September 9, 1975, 2.

23. Phil Collier, "McCovey Feels Like Pawn in Padre-S.F. Talks," *San Diego Union*, March 11, 1976, D-1.

24. Phil Collier "McCovey Can Rejoin Giants—If Price Right," *San Diego Union*, March 10, 1976, C-1.

25. "McCovey's Plea: Role as Regular," *San Diego Union*, April 13, 1976, C-1.

26. "Padres' Two Homers Stop Expos, 6–4," *San Diego Union*, May 6, 1976, 58.

27. Ron Bergman, "Jackson, Holtzman Dealt to Orioles," *Oakland Tribune*, April 3, 1976, 33-E.

28. Billy Williams in discussion with the author, June 13, 2023.

29. Mike Norris in discussion with the author, June 5, 2023.

30. Mike Norris in discussion with the author, June 5, 2023.

31. Billy Williams in discussion with the author, June 13, 2023.

32. "Reitz Birthday Nearly Perfect," *Oakland Tribune*, June 25, 1976, 45.

33. Dave Cheit, "McCovey in A's Colors Tomorrow?" *The Berkeley Gazette* (CA), August 31, 1976, 14.

34. Hal Silen in discussion with the author, June 9, 2023.

35. Ron Bergman, "A's Need Super Mac," *Oakland Tribune*, September 1, 1976, 39.

36. Mike Norris in discussion with the author, June 5, 2023.

37. Ron Bergman, "McCovey Big Hit with Fans," *Oakland Tribune*, September 2, 1976, 27.

38. Ron Bergman, "Mac Homesick for Old League," *Oakland Tribune*, October 5, 1976, 37.

39. Ron Bergman, "Williams Leaves Baseball," *Oakland Tribune*, November 10, 1976, 40.

40. Bergman, "Mac Homesick for Old League," 37.

41. Billy Williams in discussion with the author, June 13, 2023.

CHAPTER 10

1. Bob Lurie in discussion with the author, April 30, 2022.

2. Bob Lurie in discussion with the author, April 30, 2022.

3. Bob Lurie in discussion with the author, April 30, 2022.

4. Corey Busch in discussion with the author, March 10, 2022.

5. Bob Lurie in discussion with the author, April 30, 2022.

6. Glenn Schwarz, "McCovey Belts 'Em, Vows to Bat Cleanup," *San Francisco Examiner*, March 3, 1977, 47.

7. Frank Cooney, "McCovey: Now I'm Really Home," *San Francisco Examiner*, March 31, 1977, 57–58.

8. Pat Gallagher in discussion with the author, August 17, 2022.

9. Darrell Evans in discussion with the author, September 2, 2022.

10. Lincoln Mitchell in discussion with the author, March 9, 2022.

11. Terry Whitfield in discussion with the author, June 6, 2023.

12. Darrell Evans in conversation with the author, September 2, 2022.

13. Darrell Evans in conversation with the author, September 2, 2022.

14. Darrell Evans in conversation with the author, September 2, 2022.

15. Stephanie Salter, "McCovey Went Out in His Typically Competent Style," *San Francisco Examiner*, July 4, 1980, 49.

16. Darrell Evans in discussion with the author, September 2, 2022.

17. Mario Alioto in discussion with the author, June 7, 2023.

18. Terry Whitfield in discussion with the author, June 6, 2023.

19. Bill Madlock in discussion with the author, November 14, 2022.

20. Chris Speier in discussion with the author, June 19, 2023.

21. Glenn Schwarz, "It Was a Real Big Mac Attack," *San Francisco Examiner*, June 28, 1977, 46.

22. "McCov' Hit Slam with Sore Wrist," *San Francisco Examiner*, June 28, 1977, 46.

23. Stephanie Salter, "McCovey Provides His Own Postscript," *San Francisco Examiner*, September 19, 1977, 55.

24. Salter, "McCovey Provides His Own Postscript," 55.

25. Attendance numbers courtesy of baseball-reference.com (https://www.baseball-reference.com).

26. "McCovey Sees Both Irony and Honor in Being Comeback Player of the Year," *The Muncie Star* (IN), November 5, 1977, B3.

27. Tom Weir, "Kuhn Expected to OK Giants' Deal for Blue," *Oakland Tribune*, March 16, 1978, 14.

28. Stephanie Salter, "Giants Get Blue for Players, Cash," *San Francisco Examiner*, March 16, 1978, 69, 75.

29. George Vass, "Veteran Players Zero In on Career Targets," *Baseball Digest* 37, no. 2, 28, 1978.

30. Vida Blue in discussion with the author, May 21, 2022.

31. Vida Blue in discussion with the author, May 21, 2022.

32. Ron Fimrite, "The Cable Cars, the Fog—and Willie," *Sports Illustrated*, April 17, 1978.

33. Vida Blue in discussion with the author, May 21, 2022.

34. Bill North in discussion with the author, June 14, 2023.

35. Corey Busch in discussion with the author, March 10, 2022.

36. Larry Pope, "McCovey's Last Days Not Over," *Asheville Citizen-Times*, June 8, 1980, 5B.

37. Bill North in discussion with the author, June 14, 2023.

38. Black Green, "An Inside Look at Willie McCovey," *San Francisco Chronicle*, May 16, 1980, 26.

39. Rocky Dudum in discussion with the author, July 14, 2022.

40. Corey Busch in discussion with the author, March 10, 2022.

41. Bob Stevens, "Willie to Retire, but Stays a Giant," *San Francisco Chronicle*, June 23, 1980, 51.

42. Rocky Dudum in discussion with the author, July 14, 2022.

43. Ira Kamin, "The Last Days of Willie McCovey," *San Francisco Examiner*, September 14, 1980, 507.

44. Lincoln Mitchell in discussion with the author, March 9, 2022.

45. Corey Busch in discussion with the author, March 10, 2022.

46. Willie McCovey as told to William Flynn, "Willie McCovey: In His Own Words," *San Francisco Examiner*, July 4, 1980, 47.

47. Stephanie Salter, "McCovey Memories: Quiet Power," *San Francisco Examiner*, July 1, 1980, 55.

48. Darrell Evans in discussion with the author, September 2, 2022.

49. Chris Speier in discussion with the author, June 19, 2023.

50. Cleon Jones in discussion with the author, July 26, 2022.

51. Billy Williams in discussion with the author, July 23, 2022.

52. Lee Smith in discussion with the author, November 11, 2022.

53. "Lee Smith's Hall of Fame Induction Speech," July 21, 2019, https://www .youtube.com/watch?v=r-RkjJ7WUq0, accessed September 24, 2023.

54. Clifford Terry, "Hustling Along with the Cubs' Buck," *Chicago Tribune*, May 18, 1980, 192–93.

55. Cooper Rollow, "Cub Batters Need Film Cure: Williams," *Chicago Tribune*, May 30, 1980, 37.

56. Dusty Baker in discussion with the author, May 28, 2023.

57. Billy Williams in discussion with the author, May 6, 2022.

58. Billy Williams in discussion with the author, May 6, 2022.

59. Jeff Idelson in discussion with the author, June 12, 2023.

CHAPTER 11

1. Glenn Schwarz, "Willie Mac's Grandest Slam," *San Francisco Examiner*, January 9, 1986, 1.

2. Schwarz, "Willie Mac's Grandest Slam," 18.

3. Harry Jupiter, "It Was a Wonderful Day for Remembering," *San Francisco Examiner*, August 4, 1986, 58.

4. "Willie McCovey 1986 Hall of Fame Induction Speech," November 17, 2014, https://www.youtube.com/watch?v=I0lpdpzgvwI, accessed November 5, 2023.

5. Fred Mitchell, "Williams' Hometown Waits for Sweet Call," *Chicago Tribune*, January 14, 1987, 51.

6. Jerome Holtzman, "Hall Opens to Williams," *Chicago Tribune*, January 15, 1987, 53.

7. "Al Campanis Cancels Himself on National TV," June 21, 2019, https://www.youtube.com/watch?v=DFb5kEnWnKk, accessed December 28, 2023.

8. Billy Williams with Fred Mitchell, *Billy Williams: My Sweet-Swinging Lifetime with the Cubs* (Chicago: Triumph, 2008), 183.

9. Fred Mitchell and Ed Sherman, "Campanis' TV Comments Shock, Dismay and Anger Cubs' Williams," *Chicago Tribune*, April 9, 1987, 70.

10. Mitchell, "Campanis' TV Comments Shock, Dismay and Anger Cubs' Williams," 70.

11. Sam McManis, "Campanis Says He Apologizes for Comments," *Los Angeles Times*, April 8, 1987, 37.

12. "Billy Williams Delivers Hall of Fame Induction Speech," *YouTube*, uploaded by MLB, 10 November 2015, https://www.youtube.com/watch?v=s9_pQskXfAc.

13. Valarie Hill, Nina Williams, Julia Williams, and Sandra Simpson in discussion with the author, April 12, 2022.

14. Billy Williams in discussion with the author, July 23, 2022.

15. Jeff Idelson in discussion with the author, June 12, 2023.

16. Vida Blue in discussion with the author, May 21, 2022.

17. Allison McCovey in discussion with the author, February 19, 2024.

18. Allison McCovey in discussion with the author, February 19, 2024.

19. Will Clark in discussion with the author, June 30, 2023.

20. Will Clark in discussion with the author, June 30, 2023.

21. Historian Rob Garratt has written extensively about the history of the Giants franchise in both New York and San Francisco. I have notably relied on his account for this retelling of this sale by Bob Lurie to Peter Magowan's group. Rob Garratt, "San Francisco Giants Team Ownership History," last revised September 5, 2018, https://sabr.org/bioproj/topic/san-francisco-giants-team-ownership-history/#_ednref57, accessed January 7, 2024.

22. Lynda Richardson, "Baseball Hall of Famer Is Sentenced in Tax Case," *New York Times*, June 8, 1996, https://www.nytimes.com/1996/06/08/nyregion/baseball -hall-of-famer-is-sentenced-in-tax-case.html, accessed January 7, 2024.

23. Hal Silen in discussion with the author, June 9, 2023.

24. Hal Silen in discussion with the author May 23, 2022.

25. "Major League Sport Stadium/Arena Referendums," 2001, https://law. marquette.edu/assets/sports-law/pdf/sports-facility-reports/referenda.pdf.

26. Mark Purdy, "Honoring Him Wouldn't Take a Stretch—Give McCovey Proper Salute," *San Jose Mercury News*, May 9, 1999, 1D.

27. Purdy, "Honoring Him Wouldn't Take a Stretch," 1D.

28. Larry Baer in discussion with the author, July 18, 2023.

29. Larry Baer in discussion with the author, July 18, 2023.

30. Mark Purdy, "Giant's Big Splash—Home Runs at Pack Bell Park to Set Sail for McCovey Cove," *San Jose Mercury News*, August 26, 1999, 1A.

31. Larry Baer in discussion with the author, July 18, 2023.

32. Renel Brooks-Moon in discussion with the author, September 1, 2022.

33. Renel Brooks-Moon in discussion with the author, September 1, 2022.

34. Sue Petersen in discussion with the author, May 20, 2023.

35. Sue Petersen in discussion with the author, May 20, 2023.

36. Sue Petersen in discussion with the author, May 20, 2023.

37. Larry Baer in discussion with the author, July 18, 2023.

38. Larry Baer in discussion with the author, July 18, 2023.

39. Bobby Evans in discussion with the author, August 31, 2022.

40. Frank Blackman, "This One Old Out Just Keeps Going and Going," *San Francisco Examiner*, April 2, 2003, 75.

41. "Giants Notebook: Villain Greeted as Hero in Reunion," June 25, 2007, https://www.mercurynews.com/2007/06/25/giants-notebook-villain-greeted-as-hero -in-reunion, accessed November 20, 2023.

42. Randy Hundley in discussion with the author, November 17, 2022.

43. John Branch, "In Cubs' Luckless Lore, the Story of a Baseball Life," *New York Times*, October 3, 2008, https://www.nytimes.com/2008/10/04/sports/baseball /04santo.html.

44. Vicki Santo in discussion with the author, July 27, 2023.

45. "Santo Elected to Hall of Fame," *Boulder Daily Camera*, December 6, 2011, https://www.dailycamera.com/2011/12/06/santo-elected-to-hall-of-fame, accessed January 15, 2024.

46. Vicki Santo in discussion with the author, July 27, 2023.

47. "Billy Williams Remembers Ron Santo," January 21, 2011, https://www. youtube.com/watch?v=bS2Olg_ceQA, accessed June 14, 2023.

48. "Video: Billy Williams Speaks at Ernie Banks Memorial Service," January 31, 2015, https://abc7chicago.com/ernie-banks-funeral-memorial-service-billy-williams /498983, accessed January 13, 2024.

49. Paul Sullivan, "Opening Day Is Here, and Nothing Else Matters," *Chicago Tribune*, April 4, 2016, A8.

50. Billy Williams as Told to Steve Rosenbloom, "Tell Me a Story," *Chicago Tribune*, September 22, 2016, 3-3.

51. Jon Shestakofsky, "Loveable Cub: Billy Williams Parlayed a Textbook Swing and Unwavering Consistency into a Plaque in Cooperstown," https://baseballhall.org /discover/lovable-cub, accessed December 10, 2023.

52. Crane Kenney in discussion with the author, June 27, 2023.

53. Daughters' interview.

CHAPTER 12

1. Barry Bonds in discussion with the author, September 23, 2023.

2. Sam Whiting, "Willie McCovey Recalls '62 Series—50 Years Ago," March 25, 2012, https://www.sfgate.com/giants/article/Willie-McCovey-recalls-62-Series -50-years-ago-3432936.php, accessed January 20, 2024.

3. Dusty Baker in discussion with the author, May 28, 2023.

4. Terry Whitfield in discussion with the author, June 6, 2023.

5. Terry Whitfield in discussion with the author, June 6, 2023.

6. Renel Brooks-Moon in discussion with the author, September 1, 2022.

7. Crane Kenney in discussion with the author, June 27, 2023.

8. Ron Rapoport in discussion with the author, March 17, 2023.

9. Ron Rapoport in discussion with the author, March 17, 2023.

10. Jeff Idelson in discussion with the author, June 12, 2023.

11. Ben Raines, *The Last Slave Ship: The True Story of How* Clotilda *Was Found, Her Descendants, and an Extraordinary Reckoning* (New York: Simon & Schuster, 2022), 69.

12. Sandy Stimpson in discussion with the author, July 19, 2023.

13. Creg Stephenson, "Hank Aaron's Fame Stretched Worldwide, but He Was Always Mobile's Homegrown Legend," January 22, 2021, https://www.al.com/ sports/2021/01/hank-aarons-fame-stretched-worldwide-but-he-was-always-mobiles- homegrown-legend.html, accessed June 1, 2023.

14. Bill North in discussion with the author, June 14, 2023.

15. John Sharp, "Hank Aaron Statues Displayed as Part of 'Hall of Fame' Court- yard Concept in Mobile," December 6, 2021, https://www.al.com/news/2021/12/hank -aaron-statues-displayed-as-part-of-hall-of-fame-courtyard-concept-in-mobile.html, accessed July 20, 2023.

16. Ryan Best, "Confederate Statues Were Never Really about Preserving His- tory," July 8, 2020, https://projects.fivethirtyeight.com/confederate-statues, accessed November 2, 2023.

17. Brett Grill in discussion with the author, June 19, 2023.

18. Brett Grill in discussion with the author, June 19, 2023.

19. John Sharp, "'This Bands Communities Together': Hall of Fame Courtyard, Hank Aaron Statue Project Unveiled in Mobile," March 17, 2022, https://www.al .com/news/2022/03/this-bands-communities-together-hall-of-fame-courtyard-hank -aaron-statue-project-unveiled-in-mobile.html, accessed November 24, 2023.

20. Jim Bouton with Leonard Shecter, *Ball Four* (Hoboken, NJ: Howell Book House, 1990), 385.

21. Brett Grill in discussion with the author, June 19, 2023.

22. Cleon Jones in discussion with the author, July 26, 2022.

23. Fred Mitchell in discussion with the author, May 16, 2023.

24. Cleon Jones in discussion with the author, July 26, 2022.

25. Sandy Stimpson in discussion with the author, July 19, 2023.

26. Allison McCovey in discussion with the author, January 15, 2023.

27. Corey Busch in discussion with the author, March 10, 2022.

28. Chris Speier in discussion with the author, June 19, 2023.

29. Randy Hundley in discussion with the author, November 17, 2022.

30. Don Kessinger in discussion with the author, July 10, 2023.

31. Dusty Baker in discussion with the author, May 28, 2023.

32. Bill North in discussion with the author, June 14, 2023.

33. Richard E. Lapchick, "The 2023 Racial and Gender Report Card," 2023, https://www.tidesport.org/_files/ugd/ac4087_3801e61a4fd04fbda329c9af387ca948.pdf, accessed January 7, 2024.

34. "Q & A with Hall of Famer Willie McCovey," https://baseballhall.org/discover-more/stories/baseball-history/q-and-a-willie-mccovey, accessed August 19, 2023.

EPILOGUE

1. Bobby Richardson in discussion with the author, January 29, 2024. All quotes in this epilogue are taken from that interview.

Bibliography

Aaron, Hank, with Lonnie Wheeler. *I Had a Hammer: The Hank Aaron Story*. New York: HarperTorch, 1991.

Alou, Felipe, with Peter Karasotis. *Alou: My Baseball Journey*. Lincoln: University of Nebraska Press, 2018.

Bavasi, Buzzie, with John Strege. *Off the Record*. Chicago: Contemporary Books, 1987.

Boyle, Kevin. *The Shattering: America in the 1960s*. New York: Norton, 2021.

Bryant, Howard. *The Last Hero: A Life of Henry Aaron*. New York: Anchor Books, 2010.

Burgos, Adrian. *Cuban Star: How One Negro-League Owner Changed the Face of Baseball*. New York: Hill and Wang, 2011.

Cepeda, Orlando, with Herb Fagen. *Baby Bull: From Hardball to Hard Time and Back*. Dallas: Taylor Publishing, 1998.

Garratt, Robert. *Home Team: The Turbulent History of the San Francisco Giants*. Lincoln: University of Nebraska Press, 2017.

Golenbock, Peter. *Wrigleyville: A Magical History Tour of the Chicago Cubs*. New York: St. Martin's Press, 1996.

Jenkins, Fergie, with Lew Freedman. *Fergie: My Life from the Cubs to Cooperstown*. Chicago: Triumph Books, 2009.

Jones, Cleon, with Gary Kaschak. *Coming Home: My Amazin' Life with the New York Mets*. Chicago: Triumph Books, 2022.

Kroc, Ray, with Robert Anderson. *Grinding It Out: The Making of McDonald's*. New York: St. Martin's Paperbacks, 1987.

Mandel, Mike. *SF Giants: An Oral History*. Self-published. 1979.

Mitchell, Lincoln. *San Francisco Year Zero: Political Upheaval, Punk Rock, and a Third-Place Baseball Team*. New Brunswick, NJ: Rutgers University Press, 2020.

———. *The Giants and Their City: Major League Baseball in San Francisco, 1976–1992*. Kent, OH: Kent State University Press, 2021.

Murphy, Mike, and Chris Haft. *From the Stick to the Cove: My Six Decades with the San Francisco Giants*. Chicago: Triumph Books, 2020.

Napoli, Lisa. *Ray & Joan: The Man Who Made the McDonald's Fortune and the Woman Who Gave It All Away*. New York: Dutton, 2016.

O'Neil, Buck, with Steve Wulf and David Conrads. *I Was Right on Time: My Journey from the Negro Leagues to the Majors*. New York: Fireside, 1996.

Posnanski, Joe. *The Soul of Baseball: A Road Trip through Buck O'Neil's America*. New York: William Morrow, 2007.

Rapoport, Ron. *Let's Play Two: The Life of Mr. Cub, The Life of Ernie Banks*. New York: Hachette, 2019.

Rogers, William Warren, with Robert David Ward, Leah Rawls Atkins, and Wayne Flynt. *Alabama: The History of a Deep South State* (Bicentennial ed.). Tuscaloosa: University of Alabama Press, 2018.

Rosenbaum, Art, and Bob Stevens. *The Giants of San Francisco*. New York: Coward-McCann, 1963.

Santo, Ron, with Randy Minkoff. *Ron Santo: For Love of Ivy*. Chicago: Bonus Books, 1993.

Treder, Steven. *Forty Years a Giant: The Life of Horace Stoneham*. Lincoln: University of Nebraska Press, 2021.

Tye, Larry. *Satchel: The Life and Times of an American Legend*. New York: Random House, 2009.

Williams, Billy, with Fred Mitchell. *Billy Williams: My Sweet-Swinging Lifetime with the Cubs*. Chicago: Triumph Books, 2008.

Williams, Billy, and Irv Haag. *Billy: The Classic Hitter*. Chicago: Rand McNally, 1974.

Winfield, Dave, with Tom Parker. *Winfield: A Player's Life*. New York: Norton, 1988.

Young, A. S. *The Mets from Mobile: Cleon Jones and Tommy Agee*. New York: Harcourt, Brace & World, 1970.

Index

Note: Photo insert images between pages 134 and 135 are indicated by *p1, p2, p3*, etc.

Aaron, Billye, 225
Aaron, Estella, 21
Aaron, Henry: Adair with, 19; All-Star
   game and, 21–22, 77, 91–92, 104;
   career of, 14, 54; in childhood, 11;
   death of, 223; Jones, C., and, 104,
   222–23; legacy of, 75, 89, 228;
   Mays, W., and, 97, 100; Milwaukee
   Braves and, 58–59; on racism, 195;
   records by, 77, 174; with teammates,
   108; tributes to, 223–26; Whistler
   and, 11, 21–22, 106–7, 119, 130–31,
   192
Aaron, Tommie, 22, 24, 89
Adair, Bill, 19
African Americans: on Brooklyn
   Dodgers, 9–10; community for,
   130–31; in Major League Baseball,
   197, 203–4, 206, 222–24, 229; in
   minor leagues, 18–19; MLK for,
   90–91; in Mobile, 7–8, 12–13; in
   Negro Leagues, 65; in press, 32;
   racism against, 9–10, 31, 67, 194–95;
   segregation for, 25–26; in slavery,
   222–24; in United States, 13–14,
   50–51, 57–58, 111, 194–95, 217,
   224–27

Agee, Tommy, 89, 111, 119, 222–23
Agnew, Spiro, 104
Alabama. *See* Mobile, Alabama
Aldrin, Edwin, 104–5
Alioto, Mario, 172, 204–6
All-Star game: Aaron, H., and, 21–22,
   77, 91–92, 104; Bonds, Bobby, in,
   124; Hunter in, 155; Jenkins in, 89;
   Major League Baseball and, 103–5;
   Mobile and, 91–92; for players, 49,
   75, 95–96; Terry in, 68; Whistler in,
   27, 82
Alou, Felipe: career of, 86, 232;
   Cepeda, O., and, 63; Stretch and,
   35, 72; in winter ball, 33–34, *p1*; in
   World Series, 71, 73
Alou, Jesus, 154
Alou, Matty, 34–35, 71, 72, 139, 232,
   p1
Alston, Walt, 92
Altman, George, 65
Altobelli, Joe, 175–76, 178–79
Amalfitano, Joe, 31–32, 80, 118–21
Anderson, Matt, 223
Anderson, Sparky, 110, 126, 160,
   173–74
Andrews, George, 29

Angelou, Maya, 50
Antonelli, Johnny, 46
Ardmore Cardinals, 27–30
Arizona, 26, 34, 43, 142, 154–55, 169–70
Arlin, Steve, 142–43, 148
Armstrong, Neil, 104–5
Arrieta, Jake, 211
Ashburn, Richie, 48, 53, 59
Atlanta Braves: Cepeda, O., on, 108; Chicago Cubs and, 22, 106–7; Los Angeles Dodgers and, 103–4; San Diego Padres and, 147; San Francisco Giants and, 170, 177–78
Autry, Gene, 100
Ayler, Ethel, 8

Baer, Larry, 201–3, 205–6
Bailey, Ed, 48
Baker, Dusty, 130–32, 186, 216–17, 228
Balcer, Joe, 28
Ball Four (Bouton), 225
Baltimore Orioles, 153, 158, 161–62
Bando, Sal, 155
Banks, Ernie: career of, 52–53, 92, 103, 109, 220–21; for Chicago Cubs, 81–82, 95–96; death of, 210–11; injuries of, 118; legacy of, 55, 107, 116–17, 121, 123–24, 186, 209–11; Mays, W., and, 92, 97; Santo, R., and, 65; Tappe and, 64–65; with teammates, 101, 104, 162; Whistler and, 89, 156, *p5*
Barlick, Al, 56, 232
Barr, Jim, 148
baseball. *See* Major League Baseball
Bavasi, Buzzie, 138–41
Bavasi, Peter, 139–40, 160–61, 252n10
Baxter, Vivian, 50
Bay Area Seating Services, 150
Baylor, Don, 161–62
Beckert, Glenn, 83–84, 107, 108–9, 121, 139, 143, 150–51, 221
Bejar, Estela, 218
Bell, George, 186–87

Bench, Johnny, 105, 119, 131–32
Bergman, Ron, 165
Bernstein, Bill, 51
Biebel, Don, 25–27
Billingham, Jack, 174
Billingsley, Doc, 79
Billingsley, Karen. *See* McCovey, Karen
Billy Williams Day, 97, 102–3, 195, *p6*
Birmingham Black Barons, 23
Bisher, Furman, 19–20
Blass, Steve, 126–27
Blue, Vida, 156–58, 175–78, 199
Bochy, Bruce, 205
Bonds, Barry, 124–25, 203, 216, 218
Bonds, Bobby, 92–93, 99, 124, 148
Boston Red Sox, 159, 185
Bouchee, Ed, 53
Boudreau, Lou, 59, 64
Bouton, Jim, 225
Boyer, Clete, 71
Boyle, Robert, 106
Bradley, Jim, 27–28
Branca, Ralph, 54
Brandt, Jackie, 47, 49
Brazile, Robert, Jr., 223
Bressourd, Eddie, 45
Briles, Nellie, 127
Bristol, Dave, 88, 178–79, 181–82
Brock, Lou, 84
Brock, Louis Clark, 64
Broglio, Ernie, 84
Brooklyn Dodgers, 9–10, 14, 194–95
Brooks, Ellis, 57–58
Brooks-Moon, Renel, 203–4, 218
Brown, James, 50
Brown, Ollie, 88
Buck, Jack, 87
Buckner, Bill, 185–86
Buhl, Bob, 84
Bunning, James Paul David, 87
Burdette, Lew, 10
Burlington Bees, 39
Busch, Corey, 168, 178–82, 228, 246n41
Byrd, Edward, 23

Caldwell, Mike, 138, 145, 148–49
Caldwell, Palestine, 24
California Angels, 100, 164–65
Callison, Johnny, 96
Campanis, Al, 194–95
Campbell, Carolyn, 21
Campbell, Ethel (née McCovey), 15–16, 21–22
Canada, 90
Candlestick Park. *See* San Francisco Giants
Cardenal, José, 219–20
Carey, Harry, 87
Carrithers, Don, 125
Carter, Jimmy, 135
Case, Paul, 115
Cash, Dave, 127
Castillo, Bobby, 180–81
Ceccarelli, Art, 53
Cedeño, César, 143
Cepeda, Ali, 86
Cepeda, Orlando: Alou, F., and, 63; on Atlanta Braves, 108; career of, 17–18, 55, 66–67, 85, 98, 156–57; legacy of, 207–8; Mays, W., and, 60, 246n27; psychology of, 48–49; reputation of, 43–44, 48; for St. Louis Cardinals, 86–87; San Francisco Giants and, 77; Stretch and, 66–68, 79; with teammates, 45; in World Series, 72
Chandler, Albert, 196–97
Charles, Ray, 21
Chauhan, Jaqueline, 50
Chicago American Giants, 9
Chicago Bulls, 194
Chicago Cubs: Atlanta Braves and, 22, 106–7; Banks for, 81–82, 95–96; Billy Williams Day for, 97, 102–3, 195, *p6*; Cincinnati Reds and, 124, 126, 131–32, 151; Cleveland Indians and, 211–12; fans, 96–97, 101–3, 105–6, 118–19, 129, 131–32, 151, 153, 162–63; front office of, 77–78, 150–52; history of, 51–52, 81, 90;

Holland for, 39–40, 42–43, 51, 59, 64, 84; Houston Astros and, 152; leadership of, 64–65, 183–88; Los Angeles Dodgers and, 54, 59–60, 82–83, 105–6, 211; Milwaukee Braves and, 51, 54, 77–78; Minnesota Twins and, 151; minor leagues for, 59, 184–86; Montreal Expos and, 97, 118; New York Mets and, 102–4, 211; in 1969 season, 95–97, 105–9; Oakland Athletics and, 153–54; Philadelphia Phillies and, 52–54, 96–97, 118; Pittsburgh Pirates and, 53, 119, 123, 211; in press, 59, 97, 106; reputation of, 128–31, 155–56; St. Louis Cardinals and, 102–3, 121–24, 187–88, 211; San Francisco Giants and, 53–54, 64–65, 75, 92, 95–96, 100–101, 103–4, 191, 227–29; scouting for, 84; spring training for, 89–90; stars on, 42, *p5*, *p10*; Whistler and, 24–31, 58–60, 64–65, 116–17, 119–24, 150–52, 200, 208–13; in World Series, 211–12. *See also specific topics*
Chicago White Sox, 156–59, 162
Chortkoff, Mitch, 141–42
Christopher, George, 60
Cincinnati Reds: Chicago Cubs and, 124, 126, 131–32, 151; history of, 119, 147, 168; leadership of, 110; Los Angeles Dodgers and, 176–77; New York Mets and, 88; New York Yankees and, 231–32; San Diego Padres and, 146, 159–60; San Francisco Giants and, 67, 108; in World Series, 159, 173
Clark, Jack, 170, 182–83
Clark, Jane Forbes, 209
Clark, Will, 200–201
Clemente, Roberto, 47, 126–28, 187, 192
Cleveland Indians (Guardians), 211–12
Clotilda (slave ship), 222–24
coaching, 17–18

Colbert, Nate, 125, 148
Cole, Nat King, 50
Collier, Phil, 144
Collins, Michael, 104–5
Comeback Player of the Year Award, 175
Condon, David, 97, 102
Corcoran, Larry, 107
Corkins, Mike, 143
Corte, Danny, 223
Count Basie Orchestra, 88
Cowan, Billy, 78–79
Craft, Harry, 64
Craig, Roger, 77, 189
Creamer, Robert, 76
Crosby, Ralph, 18–19
Cub Power, 107

D'Acquisto, John, 132–33
Daley, Richard, 91
Dallas Eagles, 31–33
Dandridge, Ray, 196
Daniel, Karen, 229
Danville Leafs, 31
Danzansky, Joseph, 137, 139
Dark, Alvin, 66–71, 73, 77, 155–56, 159, 161, 233–34
Davenport, Jim, 98, 169–70
Davis, C. B., 185
Dawson, Andre, *p10*
DeMott, John, 143, 253n23
Denver Bears, 59
Detroit Tigers, 173
DiMaggio, Joe, 71
Dixon, Lilly, 196
Doby, Larry, 48
Dominican Republic, 34–35, *p1*
Donovan, Jerry, 147–48
Dozer, Richard, 131–32
Drabowsky, Moe, 53
Drysdale, Don, 49–50, 61–62, 76–77, 99–100
Dudum, John, 76, 80, 113–14
Dudum, Rocky, 76, 113–14, 139, 149–50, 179–80, *p4*

Duffy, Frank, 124
Dunn, J. C., 27–30
Durocher, Leo: career of, 61, 63, 84–85, 96–97; Gehrig and, 102; as manager, 106, 108, 116–17, 123, 157; McDermott on, 132; with players, 119–20; Wrigley and, 123–24

Eaddy, Don, 42–43
Easterly, Jamie, 177–78
Eisenhower, Dwight, 37
Ellington, Duke, 50
Ellsworth, Dick, 59
Elston, Don, 64
Evans, Bobby, 206
Evans, Darrell, 170–74, 180–81, 183
Everett, Marje, 137–39

Feeney, Chub, 62, 98, 114, 168, 193
Fette, Lou, 1
Fimrite, Ron, 177
Fingers, Rollie, 184
Finley, Charlie O., 117, 152–56, 161–64, 175–76
Florida, 16–17, 22, 23
football, 13
Ford, Gerald, 158
Ford, Whitey, 68–70, 73
Foster, George, 124
Foster, William, 222
Fox, Charlie, 125, 127–28, 138, 140–41
Franco, Francisco, 135
Fuentes, Tito, 88, 116, 124, 126, 148, 172–73
Furlong, Bill, 42–43

Gallagher, Pat, 169–70, 183
Garr, Ralph, 130–32
Garratt, Rob, 258n21
Gatewood, Bill, 23
Gehrig, Lou, 102, 195–96
Geishert, Vern, 124
Georgia, 18–21
Germany, 5–6, 7
Getter, Dick, 32

Giant Food Inc., 137
Gibson, Bob, 78, 87, 89, 91, 95, 102, 119–24, 147
Gibson, Josh, 198
Giles, Warren, 102–3
Golden State Warriors, 169
Golenbock, Peter, 64
Goodman, Harold, 29
Gossage, Goose, 184
Grant, Cary, 178
Great Depression, 5
Green, Blake, 179
Grieve, Curley, 46, 62
Griffey, Ken, Sr., 131
Griffin, Ivy, 24–25
Grill, Brett, 224–26
Grimm, Charlie, 59
Grinding It Out (Kroc, R.), 145
Gross, Greg, 143
Gulf, Mobile, and Ohio Railroad, 5–6
gun violence, 28–29
Gustafson, Bert, 98, 113

Haag, Irv, 42, 119
Hadden, A. O., 20
Haddix, Harvey, 46–47
Haise, Fred, 118
Halas, George, 145
Haller, Tom, 216
Haney, Fred, 48
Hano, Arnold, 16
Hart, Jimmy Ray, 92, 99
Hartman, J. C., 40–42
Hatton, Grady, 40–41x
Hearst, Patty, 158
Hebner, Richie, 127
Henderson, Ken, 126–27
Hendley, Bob, 82–83
Hernandez, Enzo, 148
Herrnstein, John, 84
Herseth, Bud, 168–69
Hiatt, Jack, 77, 80, 87, 122
Hickman, Jim, 151
Hill, Valarie, 128–29, 198, 213
Hiller, Chuck, 69, 71, 232

Himsl, Vedie, 64
Hodges, Gil, 88
Hodges, Russ, 92–93
Hoerner, Joe, 174
Hoffman, Trevor, 185
Holland, John: for Chicago Cubs, 39–40, 42–43, 51, 59, 64, 84; negotiations with, 120, 150–51, 153
Holtzman, Ken, 84, 105–7, 109, 155–56, 159, 161–62
Hornsby, Rogers, 26–27, 39–40
Hotel Otesaga, 35, 196, 198
Houk, Ralph, 71–73, 231–32
Houston Astros: Chicago Cubs and, 152; Philadelphia Phillies and, 229; San Diego Padres and, 143; San Francisco Giants and, 138
Howard, Elston, 72
Hubbell, Carl, 17, 183
Hughes, Leo, 98
Hughes, Pat, 208
Hundley, Randy: career of, 83–85, 91, 96–97, 118, 151; friendship with, 219–20; as manager, 185, 208; Stretch and, 101; on Whistler, 122, 228
Hunter, Catfish, 115, 155–57, 159

Idelson, Jeff, 187–88, 199, 222
I Had a Hammer (Aaron, H.), 11, 19, 21–22
Irvin, Monte, 198, 207–8
Ivey, Kay, 223
Ivie, Mike, 160, 178

Jackson, Al, 87–88
Jackson, Larry, 84
Jackson, Reggie, 11, 117, 154–56, 159, 161–62
Japan, 62, 115–16
Jenkins, Fergie: in All-Star game, 89; career of, 83–84, 89–90, 101, 121, 157, 221; family of, 130; friendship with, 208–9, 219–20; Gibson and, 102; leadership of, 116–17;

Santo, R., and, 95–96; Whistler and, 211, *p10*

Johnson, Bob, 127

Johnson, Deron, 96, 154

Johnson, Earvin, 229

Johnson, James, 27–30, 242nn42–43

Johnson, Lou, 25, 91, 96–97

Jones, Cleon: Aaron, H., and, 104, 222–23; activism by, 222–23, 226; in All-Star Game, 104–5; career of, 15, 89, 111, 119, 183

Jones, Ester. *See* McCovey, Ester

Jones, Randy, 159–60

Jones, Sylvania, 3

Judge, Walter, 61

Kahn, Charlotte, 193

Kamin, Ira, 180

Kansas City Monarchs, 65

Kansas City Royals, 72, 158, 162, 164

Kawano, Yosh, 52, 188

Keeler, Jerry, 27–28

Kendall, Jerry, 59

Kennedy, Bob, 77–78, 184

Kennedy, Terry, 78

Kenney, Crane, 212, 219–21, 228

Kerlan, Robert, 98, 113–16, 250n7

Kessinger, Don: career of, 82, 84, 95–97, 107–9, 151; with teammates, 119, 122, 228

Killebrew, Harmon, 11

Kimura, Sam, 115–16, 250n7

King, Clyde, 98–99

King, Martin Luther, Jr. (MLK), 20, 37, 90–91

Kingman, Dave, 125, 141

Kirkland, Willie, 46–47, 57, 63

Knowles, Darold, 153

Koppe, Joe, 53

Koppel, Ted, 194–95

Koppett, Leonard, 202

Koufax, Sandy, 82–83, 89

Kroc, Joan, 144, 149–50

Kroc, Ray, 140, 142–45, 149–50, 253n23, 253n31

Kubek, Tony, 68, 71–72, 231–32

Kuhn, Bowie, 145, 175–76

Kuiper, Duane, 203

Labatt Brewing, 167

Landis, Kenesaw Mountain, 196

Landrith, Hobie, 93, 216

Lang, Jack, 194

Lavelle, Gary, 169–70

Law, Vern, 53

Lee, Jess, 28

legal segregation, 22–23

LeMaster, Johnnie, 181

Lersch, Barry, 96

Little Richard, 50

Locker, Bob, 153

Lockman, Whitey, 66, 71, 152

Logan, Eddie, 44, 172

Lonnett, Joe, 46, 52–53

Los Angeles Dodgers: Atlanta Braves and, 103–4; Chicago Cubs and, 54, 59–60, 82–83, 105–6, 211; Cincinnati Reds and, 176–77; history of, 194–95; Koufax for, 82–83; in playoffs, 68; San Diego Padres and, 142–43; San Francisco Giants and, 47–51, 61–62, 99–100, 125, 170, 180–82

Louisiana, 31

Lovell, Jim, 118

"Love Train," 218

Lupica, Mike, 87

Lurie, Bob, 66, 166–69, 171, 178, 180, 193, 201, 258n21

Lurie, Connie, 193

Maddon, Joe, 211

Maddox, Garry, 148

Maddux, Greg, 201, 220

Madlock, Bill, 170, 172

Magowan, Peter, 201–2, 205–6, 258n21

Mahomes, Patrick, 229

Major League Baseball: African Americans in, 197, 203–4, 206, 222–24, 229; All-Star game and,

103–5; in Arizona, 26, 43; Comeback Player of the Year Award, 175; culture of, 1; economics of, 117; fans, 133–34; in Florida, 16–17, 23; history of, 195–96; IQ, 47–48; in Japan, 62, 115–16; Major League Baseball Players Association, 98, 114, 133, 155, 248n6; Mobile and, 10–12, 89, 91–92, 155–56; National Baseball Hall of Fame, 10–11, 182–83, 187–88, 191–99, 209–10, 221–22, *p9*; in Negro Leagues, 9; in 1969 season, 103–5; pitching in, 185; in press, 46, 73, 76, 99, 119–24, 135, 144–45; racism in, 63, 65, 88, 194–95; records in, 118–19, 130–31, 173, 182–83, 185–88; rules changes in, 95; salaries, 98–99; scouting in, 16–17, 24–25; segregation in, 18–19; semipro, 12–14; in spring training, 63–64; for Stretch, 13–14; United States and, 104, 110–11, 137; Whistler after, 183–88. *See also specific topics*

Mantle, Mickey, 11, 68–69, 71, 103

Marciano, Rocky, 48

Marichal, Juan: career of, 45, 62, 76, 79; Cepeda, O., and, 86; Gibson and, 89; legacy of, 125, 183, 207–8; Mays, W., and, 88, 104, 114, 124, 132; in playoffs, 127; reputation of, 110; teammates and, 85, 93; in winter ball, 35, *p1*

Maris, Roger, 37, 68–69, 71–72, 187–88

Marshall, Jim, 52–53, 152

Martin, Fred, 65

Mathews, Eddie, 173

Mathews, Nelson, 64

Matthews, Garry, 149

May, Milt, 180–81

Mays, Marghuerite, 47

Mays, Michael, 47

Mays, Willie: Aaron, H., and, 97, 100; Banks and, 92, 97; career of, 46, 49–50, 63; Cepeda, O., and, 60, 246n27;

legacy of, 77, 119, 183; Marichal and, 88, 104, 114, 124, 132; in playoffs, 126–27; reputation of, 125; San Francisco Giants and, 76, 207; Stretch and, 47, 80, 109–10, 142, 182–83, 217–18; with teammates, 98–99, 232–33; Whistler and, 121

Mazeroski, Bill, 71–72, 231–32

McCants, Valena, 13, 193

McCarthy, Bob, 43

McCarver, Tim, 87–88

McClain, Denny, 105

McCormick, Mike, 63

McCovey, Adeline, 4

McCovey, Allison, 80–81, 124, 183, 193, 199–200, 219, 227

McCovey, Clauzell, 6, 11–12, 15–16, 192–93

McCovey, Ester (née Jones), 3–7, 18, 193, 227

McCovey, Ethel. *See* Campbell, Ethel

McCovey, Frances, 3, 6, 193

McCovey, Frank, 78

McCovey, Frank, Jr., 3–7, 13–14, 16

McCovey, Frank, Sr., 4

McCovey, Karen (née Billingsley), 78–81

McCovey, Willie (Stretch): in All-Star game, 104–5; Alou, F., and, 35, 72; birth of, 3; career of, 6–7, 89, 91–92, 98–99, 103–5; Cepeda, O., and, 66–68, 79; childhood of, 4–7, 11–12; with colleagues, 117; in debut, *p2*; debut of, 44–46; development of, 76–77, 85–88; with family, 15–16, 199–200; in final season, 176–83; Hundley, Randy and, 101; injuries for, 33–34, 113–16, 250n7; legacy of, 50, 132–33, 191–92, 215–19, 227–29, *p5*; Major League Baseball for, 13–14; Mays, W., and, 47, 80, 109–10, 142, 182–83, 217–18; in minor leagues, 31–33, 43–44, 61–62; Mobile for, 227; in National Baseball Hall of Fame, 192–93; in

1969 season, 95, 109–11; Oakland Athletics and, 135, 163–66; personal life of, 78–81; in playoffs, 126–28; press and, 19–20, 33, 37, 179–80, 202–3, 248n6, 250n7, 252n13; reputation of, 97–101, 110–11; Richardson, B., and, 231–34; in rookie season, 47–51, 55–56, *p2*; in Sandersville, 18–21; San Diego Padres and, 141–50, 159–61; San Francisco Giants and, 16–18, 55–56, 60–63, 65–68, 107–8, 124–25, 168–75, 200–208; Silen, Hal, and, 57–58; with teammates, 92–93; in trade, 137–41, *p4*; tributes to, 221–22; uniforms to, *p3*; Whistler and, 9–10, 63–64, 75, 111, 133–34, 164–65, 189, 222–25; in winter ball, 34–35, *p1*; in World Series, 68–73. *See also specific topics*
McCovey, Wyatt, 15–16
McDermott, Barry, 132
McDonald's, 140
McDowell, Sam, 86
McGee, Jim, 250n7
McGwire, Mark, 187–88
McMullen, Ken, 164–65
McNamara, John, 140, 142–43, 146–48, 160
McNamara, Robert, 37
McPhail, Andy, 208
Meaher, Timothy, 222
Menke, Denis, 144
Metro, Charlie, 65
Metzger, Roger, 143
Mieuli, Franklin, 174, 193, *p4*
Milkes, Marvin, 42
Miller, Marvin, 98–99, 133
Milwaukee Braves, 10, 48, 51, 54, 56, 58–59, 77–78
Milwaukee Brewers, 187–88
Minnesota Twins, 151
minor leagues: African Americans in, 18–19; for Chicago Cubs, 59, 184–86; Pittsburgh Pirates in, 20,

24; Santo, R., in, 103; scouting in, 26; Stretch in, 31–33, 43–44, 61–62; tryouts in, 17–19; Whistler in, 39–40, 42–43. *See also specific teams*
Miñoso, Minnie, 139
Mississippi, 15, 22
Mitchell, Fred, 195, 226
Mitchell, Lincoln, 170–71, 181
Mitchell, Paul, 161–62
Mitterwald, George, 151
MLK. *See* King, Martin Luther, Jr.
Mobile, Alabama: African Americans in, 7–8, 12–13; All-Star game and, 91–92; culture of, 3–10, 12–14, 222–27; Major League Baseball and, 10–12, 89, 91–92, 155–56; Mississippi and, 15; Mobile Hall of Fame, 24, 222–27; racism in, 88, 111. *See also specific topics*
Mobile and Ohio Railroad Company, 7
Mobile Black Bears, 9–10, 12–14, 21, 24, 174
Molkenbuhr, Edward, 47
Money, Don, 96
Montague, Ed, 86
Montreal Expos, 95, 97, 118, 161
Morales, Jerry, 150–51
Morgan, Joe, 131, 150, 171, 219, 233
Moscone, George, 167–68
Mota, Manny, 34–35, *p1*
Murphy, Dan, 64
Murphy, Jack, 142
Murphy, Mike, 44–45, 207
Murray, Jim, 119
Murray, Ray, 31
Murray, Rich, 180–81
Murtaugh, Danny, 47, 127
Musial, Stan, 60, 66, 78, 102, 173, 233–34, *p6*
Napoli, Lisa, 253n23
National Baseball Hall of Fame, 10–11, 182–83, 187–88, 191–99, 209–10, 221–22, *p9*
Negro Leagues, 9, 17, 54, 65, 196, 223–24

New York Cubans, 16–17
New York Mets: Chicago Cubs and, 102–4, 211; Cincinnati Reds and, 88; reputation of, 123; St. Louis Cardinals and, 106; San Francisco Giants and, 77; success of, 107–8; in World Series, 15, 108, 111
New York Yankees, 68–73, 102, 164, 207, 231–34
Niekro, Phil, 106
1969 season: Chicago Cubs in, 95–97, 105–9; Major League Baseball in, 103–5; San Francisco Giants in, 97–101; Stretch in, 95, 109–11
Nixon, Richard, 60, 104–5, 135
Nolan, Dick, 48
Norris, Mike, 45–46, 49, 156–57, 159, 162, 164
North, Bill: career of, 122–23, 131, 134, 154–57, 164–65; observations from, 223, 229; reputation of, 178–79

Oakland Athletics: Baltimore Orioles and, 158, 161–62; Chicago Cubs and, 153–54; Chicago White Sox and, 156–57; front office, 152, 154–55, 161–62, 164–65; Jackson, R., and, 117; Kansas City Royals and, 158, 164; San Diego Padres and, 167; San Francisco Giants and, 114, 155–56, 175–76; stars for, 104–5; Stretch and, 135, 163–66; success of, 191–92; Texas Rangers and, 157; in trades, *p8*; Whistler and, 135, 154–59, 186; in World Series, 153–54
Obama, Barack, 217
O'Dell, Billy, 68
Odom, Blue Moon, 104–5
the O'Jays, 218
Oliver, Al, 127–28
O'Malley, Peter, 178
O'Neil, Buck, 26, 41–42, 65, 185
Osteen, Claude, 92
Otis, Amos, 89, 222–23

Ott, Mel, 1, 173
Owens, Jim, 53

Pagán, José, 31, 44
Paige, Lahoma, 23–24
Paige, Satchel, 9, 22–24, 223, 225–26
Palmer, Jim, 165
Papiano, Neil, 138
Pappas, Milt, 123
Parker, Salty, 18, 31–33
Parker, Wes, 83
Pascagoula Giants, 13–14
Patterson, Ken, 186–87
Pavlick, Pete, 19
Peanuts (comic), 73
Perry, Gaylord, 86, 122, 126–27, 207–8, 216, 234
Petersen, Sue, 204–5
Peterson, Peter, 7
Philadelphia Phillies: Chicago Cubs and, 52–54, 96–97, 118; Houston Astros and, 229; Jenkins on, 157; San Diego Padres and, 146; San Francisco Giants and, 45–46, 62, 78, 173
Phillips, Adolfo, 84
physical therapy, 98
Pierce, Billy, 70
Pittsburgh Pirates: Chicago Cubs and, 53, 119, 123, 211; dominance by, 132; in minor leagues, 20, 24; San Francisco Giants and, 46–47, 61, 66, 126–28, 171, 202–3, 233; in World Series, 71–72, 231–32
Plessy v. Ferguson, 22–23
Pompez, Alex, 16–18
Ponca City Cubs, 25–30
Posnanski, Joe, 41–42
Prescott, Bobby, 31
press: African Americans in, 32; Chicago Cubs in, 59, 97, 106; controversy in, 194–95; Johnson, J., in, 242n42; Major League Baseball in, 46, 73, 76, 99, 119–24, 135, 144–45; O'Neil in, 41–42; San Diego

Padres in, 141–42; in San Francisco, 62; sports in, 43, Stretch and, 19–20, 33, 37, 179–80, 202–3, 248n6, 250n7, 252n13; transactions in, 175–76; Whistler and, 37, 118–19
Pueblo Bruins, 39
Purdy, Mark, 202

racism: against African Americans, 9–10, 31, 67, 194–95; in Major League Baseball, 63, 65, 88, 194–95; in Mobile, 88, 111; in press, 42; social dynamics of, 20; in sports, 13–14; in Texas, 40–41; in United States, 5–7, 18–19, 27–28, 32–33, 90–91, 194–97; for Whistler, 55
Radcliffe, Ted, 9–10
Rapoport, Ron, 220
Reagan, Ronald, 194
Reese, Pee Wee, 198
Richardson, Bobby, 71–73, 207, 231–34, 246n41
Richardson, Spec, 175–76, 179–80
Rickey, Branch, 196–97
Rigney, Bill, 43–44, 46–49, 55, 58, 61, 77, 161
Rivera, Mariano, 185
Rizzo, Anthony, 211
Roberts, Robin, 45–46, 156, 181, 204
Robertson, Bob, 126
Robinson, Bernice, 54
Robinson, Bill, 9, 54
Robinson, Jackie, 24, 194–96, 198, *p9*
Rodgers, Andre, 45
Roller Derby, 150
rookie season: Stretch in, 47–50, 55–56, *p2*; Whistler in, 51–55, 65
Rose, Pete, 19, 171
Rosenwald, Julius, 12–13
Rudi, Joe, 155, 163
Rupert, Jaime, 126–27
Ryan, Rosy, 44, 58

Sadecki, Ray, 86
Sadek, Mike, 169–70

St. Louis Cardinals: Cepeda, O., for, 86–87; Chicago Cubs and, 102–3, 121–24, 187–88, 211; history of, 27, 92, 95, 109; New York Mets and, 106; San Francisco Giants and, 58, 60, 87–88
Salmon, Harry, 23
Salter, Stephanie, 183
Sandberg, Ryne, 211, *p10*
Sandersville, Georgia, 18–21
San Diego Padres: Atlanta Braves and, 147; Cincinnati Reds and, 146, 159–60; fans, 142–44, 169, 253n23, 253n31; front office of, 137–40; Houston Astros and, 143; Kroc, R., and, 140, 142–45, 149–50; Los Angeles Dodgers and, 142–43; Montreal Expos and, 95, 161; Oakland Athletics and, 167; Philadelphia Phillies and, 146; in press, 141–42; reputation of, 163; San Francisco Giants and, 86, 145–46, 173, 178; Stretch and, 141–50, 159–61; in trades, *p4*
Sanford, Jack, 47, 63, 68–69
San Francisco Giants: Atlanta Braves and, 170, 177–78; Bonds, Bobby on, 92–93; Brooklyn Dodgers and, 14; Cepeda, O., and, 77; Chicago Cubs and, 53–54, 64–65, 75, 92, 95–96, 100–101, 103–4, 191, 227–29; Cincinnati Reds and, 67, 108; Dark for, 66–71, 73, 77; fans, 47, 49, 73, 87–88, 128, 140–41, 148–49, 174–83; front office of, 43–44, 85–86, 110, 137–41, 147–48, 160–61, 166; history of, 258n21; Houston Astros and, 138; Kansas City Royals and, 72; Los Angeles Dodgers and, 47–51, 61–62, 99–100, 125, 170, 180–82; Mays, W., and, 76, 207; Milwaukee Braves and, 48, 56; New York Mets and, 77; New York Yankees and, 68–73, 231–33; in 1969 season, 97–101; Oakland

Athletics and, 114, 155–56, 175–76; ownership of, 167–68; Philadelphia Phillies and, 45–46, 62, 78, 173; Pittsburgh Pirates and, 46–47, 61, 66, 126–28, 171, 202–3, 233; St. Louis Cardinals and, 58, 60, 87–88; San Diego Padres and, 86, 145–46, 173, 178; stars on, 44–45; Stoneham, H., for, 16–17, 61–63, 66, 76, 110, 115, 193, 201; Stretch and, 16–18, 55–56, 60–63, 65–68, 107–8, 124–25, 168–75, 200–208; team dynamics of, 85–86; Willie Mac Award on, 203–4, *p5*; Willie McCovey Day for, 174, 183; in World Series, 68–73, 207–8. *See also specific topics*

Santo, Ron: Banks and, 65; career of, 39–40, 42, 59, 106, 132, 157; fans of, 108–9; friendship with, 208–11; Jenkins and, 95–96; on Koufax, 82; legacy of, 97, 122–23, 221; in minor leagues, 103; Whistler and, 78

Santo, Vicki, 209–10

Santo Domingo Escogido Lions, 34–35

Sauer, Hank, 133

Savage, Fred, 110–11

Saviano, Josh, 110–11

Schelling, Bill, 52

Schoonmeir, Al, 108–9

Schulz, Charles M., 73

Schwarz, Jack, 17–18

Scott, Ed, 21

scouting, 16–18, 24–25, 26, 84

Seals Stadium. *See* San Francisco Giants

Seattle Mariners, 165

segregation: for African Americans, 25–26; legal, 22–23; in Louisiana, 31; in Major League Baseball, 18–19; in United States, 20

Selma, Dick, 106

Seltzer, Jerry, 150

Seltzer, Leo, 150

semipro baseball, 12–14

Semmes, Raphael, 224

Shannon, Mike, 87

Shaw, Bob, 86

Sheehan, Tom, 61–63

Shelton, William, 7

Short, Bob, 167–68

Silen, Hal: financial advice from, 139, 150, 252n10; negotiations with, 160–61, 201–2; support from, 51, 57–58, 76, 81, 98, 193, 217

Silen, Helen, 193

Simmons, Lon, 93, 100, 126–27, 193, *p4*

Simpson, Sandra, 129–30

Skowren, Bill, 71

slavery, 4, 7

Smith, C. Arnholdt, 137–38, 140

Smith, Coy, 27–29, 242n43

Smith, Gary, 27

Smith, Lee, 184–85, *p10*

Smith, Ozzie, 223

Smith, Willie, 96–97, 107

Snider, Duke, 49

Sosa, Elias, 148–49

Sosa, Sammy, 186–88

Spahn, Warren, 78

Speier, Chris, 124, 172–73, 183

sports. *See specific sports*

spring training, 63–64, 89–90, 115, 142, 154–55, 169–70

Stargell, Willie, 126–28, 131, 171

Stengel, Casey, 77

Stennett, Rennie, 180–81

Sterling, Barnett, 81–82

Stevens, Bob, 73, 246n41

Stimpson, Sandy, 222–25

Stock, Milt, 155–56

Stoneham, Charles, 167

Stoneham, Horace: family of, 126–27, 167; negotiations with, 114, 124, 138; reputation of, 140–41, 148; for San Francisco Giants, 16–17, 61–63, 66, 76, 110, 115, 193, 201

Stovall, Ruth, 51, 57, 76, 193

Streeter, Sam, 23

Stretch. *See* McCovey, Willie

Stretch Drive events, 205
Supreme Court, 22–23
Sutton, Don, 105–6
Swigert, John, 118

Tanner, Chuck, 161–62, 164–65
Tappe, El, 64–65
Taylor, Tony, 31, 52
Tenace, Gene, 163, 165
Terrell, Roy, 63
Terry, Ralph, 68–69, 71–73, 207,
    231–32
Texas, 31–33, 39–41, 184–85
Texas Rangers, 157–58, 207–8
Thomas, Derrel, 174–75, 181
Thomas, Frank, 59
Thomas, Jesse, 16
Thomasson, Gary, 141, 174
Thomson, Bobby, 54
Thornton, Andy, 152
Tolan, Bobby, 139
Toronto Blue Jays, 165
Torrez, Mike, 161–62
Treder, Steven, 140
Tresh, Tom, 71
Trillo, Manny, 153
Tucker, Ed, 21–22
Twombly, Wells, 252n13
Tyrone, Jim, 152

United States: African Americans in,
    13–14, 50–51, 57–58, 111, 194–95,
    217, 224–27; Canada and, 90;
    economy, 204–5; gun violence in,
    28–29; Major League Baseball
    and, 104, 110–11, 137; racism in,
    5–7, 18–19, 27–28, 32–33, 90–91,
    194–97; segregation in, 20; slavery
    in, 4, 7; sports in, 1; Supreme Court,
    22–23; in Vietnam War, 135; in
    World War II, 5–6. *See also specific
    locations*

Van Bommel, Bill, 161–62
Vascellaro, Charlie, 117

Venzon, Tony, 66
Vietnam War, 135

Wagner, Leon, 31, 47, 57
Wallace, Dave, 146
Washington, Booker T., 12–13
Washington, Claudell, 154
Washington, Dinah, 50
Watson, Bob, 143
Weir, Tom, 175
West, Mae, 135
Whistler. *See* Williams, Billy
Whistler, Alabama. *See* Mobile,
    Alabama
White, Bill, 34–35, 48, *p1*
Whitfield, Terry, 172, 217–18
Will, Bob, 59
Williams, Adolph, 8
Williams, Bernie, 138
Williams, Billy (Whistler): Aaron, H.,
    and, 11, 21–22, 106–7, 119, 130–31,
    192; in All-Star game, 27, 82;
    Banks and, 89, 156, *p5*; career of,
    89, 91–92, 98–99, 105–9, 128–31,
    162–63; Chicago Cubs and, 24–31,
    58–60, 64–65, 116–17, 119–24,
    150–52, 200, 208–13; in childhood,
    8–9; development of, 77–78, 81–85,
    118–19; education of, 12–13; family
    of, 20; for fans, 101–3; friends of,
    p10; Gibson and, 119–24; Jenkins
    and, 211, *p10*; legacy of, 131–32,
    191–92, 219–21, 227–29; after
    Major League Baseball, 183–88;
    Mays, W., and, 121; in minor
    leagues, 39–40, 42–43; in National
    Baseball Hall of Fame, 193–99;
    Oakland Athletics and, 135, 154–59,
    186; O'Neil and, 41–42; Paige,
    S., and, 22–24; personal life of,
    75, 89–90; press and, 37, 118–19;
    racism for, 55; reputation of, 95–97;
    retirement of, 165–66; Robinson,
    J., and, *p9*; in rookie season, 51–55,
    65; in semipro baseball, 12; Stretch

and, 9–10, 63–64, 75, 111, 133–34, 164–65, 189, 222–24; swing of, *p7*; with teammates, 108–9; in trade, *p8*; tributes to, 221–22. *See also specific topics*
Williams, Clyde, 8, 12
Williams, Frank (father), 8–10
Williams, Frank (friend), 54
Williams, Franklin (brother), 20, 23–25, 51–52, 154
Williams, Jessie Mary, 8–9
Williams, Joe, 88
Williams, Julia, 130, 213
Williams, Louis, 8–9
Williams, Mitch, 201
Williams, Nina, 102–3, 130, 213
Williams, Roger, 148
Williams, Sadie, 50
Williams, Shirley: death of, 212–13; marriage to, 13, 75, 102, 122–23, 130, 159, 165–66, 229; support from, 193–94, 198–99, 221
Williams, Ted, 61, 109–10, 158, 192, 195–96
Williams, Vera, 8
Willie Mac Award, 183, 203–4, *p5*
Willie McCovey Day, 174, 183

Willie McCovey Golf Classic, 204–5
Willis, Jan, 252n10
Wills, Maury, 194–95
Wilson, Pete, 139–40
Wilson, Rube, 84
Winfield, Dave, 146–47
winter ball, 33–35, *p1*
Wirth, Gustavus Adolphus, 7
Witt, John, 139–40
Wonder, Stevie, 21
The Wonder Years (TV show), 110–11
World Series: Chicago Cubs in, 211–12; Cincinnati Reds in, 159, 173; legacy of, 231–33; New York Mets in, 15, 108, 111; Oakland Athletics in, 153–54; Pittsburgh Pirates in, 71–72, 231–32; San Francisco Giants in, 68–73, 207–8; Stretch in, 68–73
World War II, 5–6
Wrigley, Phillip K., 85, 120, 123–24, 140, 151
Wrigley Field. *See* Chicago Cubs

Yastrzemski, Carl, 105
Yick, Joe, 215–16
Young, Don, 83

About the Author

Jason Cannon is a teacher and writer. His first book, *Charlie Murphy: The Iconoclastic Showman behind the Chicago Cubs*, won the 2023 Larry Ritter Award, and his articles have appeared in *NINE: A Journal of Baseball History and Culture*. He lives in Colorado.